COMPANY INVESTIGATIONS AND PUBLIC LAW

For Elisabeth

Company Investigations and Public Law

A PRACTICAL GUIDE TO GOVERNMENT INVESTIGATIONS

Andrew Lidbetter
M.A. (Oxon), B.C.L.; solicitor

HART PUBLISHING
OXFORD - PORTLAND
1999

Hart Publishing
Oxford and Portland, Oregon

Published in North America (US and Canada) by
Hart Publishing c/o
International Specialized Book Services
5804 NE Hassalo Street
Portland, Oregon
97213-3644
USA

Distributed in Netherlands, Belgium and Luxembourg by
Intersentia, Churchillaan 108
B2900 Schoten
Antwerpen
Belgium

Distributed in Australia and New Zealand by
Federation Press
John St
Leichardt
NSW 2000

Hart Publishing is a specialist legal publisher based in Oxford, England. To order further copies of this book or to request a list of other publications please write to:

Hart Publishing, 19, Whitehouse Road, Oxford, OX1 4PA
Telephone: +44 (0)1865 434459 Fax: +44 (0) 1865 794882
email: hartpub@janep.demon.co.uk

British Library Cataloguing in Publication Data
Data Available

ISBN 1 84113-074-5 (cloth)

Typeset in 11/13 pt Sabon by The Midlands Book Typesetting Company, Loughborough, Leicestershire.
Printed and bound in Great Britain by Bookcraft (Bath) Ltd, Midsomer Norton, Somerset.

CONTENTS

PREFACE

In recent years there has been a rapid growth in administrative law. Simultaneously, commercial law has become increasingly complex. Not surprisingly, greater regulation by public authorities is bringing the link between public law and commercial law more sharply into focus. This book reflects just one fragment of the link — governmental powers to investigate companies. The irony is that, in an era of complex statutory regulation, the process upon which this text focuses has its origins with the appointment of inspectors by the Board of Trade in the nineteenth century. Nonetheless, as far as I am aware, it is the first law book (other than the DTI's own handbook) devoted entirely to the subject.

My thanks go to those who first gave me an interest in law at Worcester College, Oxford; to Lucy Hutchinson at Herbert Smith and Martyn Hopper at the FSA for taking time to read a draft of the text; to other colleagues at Herbert Smith, particularly Carl Powlson, Philip Allcock and Nick Diamand for checking the text; and to Michael Fordham.

Most of all I thank my wife, Elisabeth, to whom this book is dedicated and our son, Michael, for giving up valuable family time for this project.

Andrew Lidbetter
Herbert Smith, London
July 1998

I am pleased to have the opportunity to add a brief annex (Appendix 2) in the light of the publication of the draft Financial Services and Markets Bill.

Andrew Lidbetter
Herbert Smith, London
August 1998

TABLE OF CASES

Cases

TABLE OF STATUTES

Statutes

Index to Appendix of Statutory Provisions

Chapter 1

INTRODUCTION

An investigation into the affairs of a company or an aspect of those affairs can have far reaching implications for those involved. It may necessitate devoting considerable energy to dealing with requests for oral and documentary evidence. Those involved must also be aware of the possible implications both in terms of adverse publicity and the range of actions that may be taken by the Department of Trade and Industry (DTI) and others consequent upon an investigation. These actions may include civil and criminal proceedings. Similarly, those undertaking the investigation, including individuals appointed by the DTI to act as inspectors and others from outside the DTI who assist in investigations under, for example, Companies Act 1985 s.447, must have a clear understanding of their powers and the constraints upon those powers. **1.1.1**

The purpose of this text is to place statutory investigations into their public law context. To do so, it is appropriate to consider the stages and themes that run through such investigations rather than to approach each statutory regime governing investigations in isolation. This is because in many cases the general public law principles governing a particular aspect, such as the decision to initiate an investigation[1]or public interest immunity,[2] will not particularly vary from context to context. That is not to underestimate, however, the precise words of each statutory regime. Indeed the statutory provisions lead to a different emphasis in different types of investigations. Thus investigations under Companies Act 1985 s.432 involve an examination of the affairs of a company whereas investigations under Financial Services Act 1986 s.177, which concern suspected insider dealing, will clearly involve considering an aspect of the company's affairs but the focus of attention will be on investigating whether an offence of insider dealing pursuant to Criminal Justice Act 1993 Part V has been committed. This leads to a number of significant differences in that, for example, the Secretary of State[3]may publish reports produced by inspectors appointed under Companies Act 1985 s.432 but not reports produced by inspectors appointed under **1.1.2**

1 See Ch 4.
2 See 8.8 below.
3 Note that for convenience and to follow the legislation, references in the text to the Secretary of State are in the masculine only.

Financial Services Act 1986 s.177.[4] Indeed, the starting point for investigations by the DTI (or, in the case of insurance companies, HM Treasury) or those appointed by them will be the statutory framework.

The investigations covered in the text involve the exercise of the following powers. 1.1.3

(i) To appoint inspectors to investigate the affairs of a company pursuant to Companies Act 1985 ss.431 and 432.
(ii) To appoint inspectors to investigate the ownership of a company pursuant to Companies Act 1985 s.442.
(iii) To obtain information as to those interested in shares or debentures etc. pursuant to Companies Act 1985 s.444.
(iv) To appoint inspectors to investigate dealings in a company's shares or debentures pursuant to Companies Act 1985 s.446.
(v) To require the production of documents by a company pursuant to Companies Act 1985 s.447.
(vi) To require the production and inspection of a company's books and records where an offence is suspected pursuant to Companies Act 1985 s.721.
(vii) To appoint inspectors to investigate the affairs of a unit trust, a recognised scheme or any other collective investment scheme pursuant to Financial Services Act 1986 s.94.
(viii) To investigate an investment business pursuant to Financial Services Act 1986 s.105.
(ix) To appoint inspectors to investigate suspected insider dealing pursuant to Financial Services Act 1986 s.177.
(x) To investigate the affairs of an investment company with variable capital pursuant to the Open-ended Investment Companies (Investment Companies with Variable Capital) Regulations 1996.[5]
(xi) To obtain information and require the production of documents pursuant to Insurance Companies Act 1982 s.44.[6]
(xii) To investigate following a report by a liquidator in the course of a voluntary winding up of a company pursuant to Insolvency Act 1986 s.218.
(xiii) To require information, documents or other assistance for an overseas regulatory authority pursuant to Companies Act 1989 s.83.

---

4 Compare 9.1 and 9.3 below.
5 SI 1996/2827.
6 On 5 January 1998 most insurance matters were transferred from the DTI to HM treasury — see the Transfer of Functions (Insurance) Order 1997 (SI 1997/2781).

1.1.4 Various individuals or organisations other than the DTI, or those appointed by it, may be involved in investigations into the affairs of companies. This may range from a company's auditors through to the police and the SFO. In the case of the auditor, although Companies Act 1985 s.384 provides for the statutory appointment of an auditor, the relationship between an auditor and a company is largely governed by the law of contract (usually through a letter of engagement) rather than public law. In the case of the police and the SFO, although there will be public law constraints on the exercise of their powers, e.g. a search warrant may be set aside by way of an application for judicial review, the focus of such investigations is one governed by the provisions of general criminal law procedure such as the Police and Criminal Evidence Act 1984. The investigative powers of other authorities, which may relate only to a specific aspect of a company's affairs and are governed predominantly by public law such as tax and competition authorities, are properly the subject of texts on those subjects rather than one that looks more generally at statutory investigations into the affairs of companies. This text does not deal with investigations under Banking Act 1987 (as amended) in view of the particular nature of banking institutions. The distinction, which sees the inclusion of investigations into the affairs of insurance companies and upon the voluntary winding up of a company but which excludes investigations under the Banking Act, is also reflected in the DTI's *Investigations Handbook*.[7] The text does, however, refer to cases from contexts otherwise excluded where they have general application.[8] Finally, in the case of a public company, the company itself may investigate to ascertain who is interested in the company's shares.[9] However, this text aims to put investigations in their public law context, and the case where a public company investigates to ascertain who is interested in its share capital will be governed entirely by private law.

1.1.5 The different types of investigation considered in this text occur with widely differing frequency and by far the most common are those where the Secretary of State requires the production of documents pursuant to Companies Act 1985 s.447.[10] The large scale inspections under s.432 have largely died-out currently but the principles established in caselaw concerning such inspections remain relevant for investigations generally.

---

7 See Ch 3.
8 See, e.g. the privilege against self-incrimination at 6.10 below.
9 See Companies Act 1985 ss.212 to 220.
10 See 6.2 below.

In considering an investigation into a company there will necessarily be links between different aspects. For example Chapter 5 considers the conduct of investigations generally, Chapter 6 deals with obtaining evidence and Chapter 7 deals with the preparation of the report. Questions of procedural fairness permeate all three chapters since the need to give those who may be criticised in a report the opportunity to rebut the criticisms is to be borne in mind in relation to the conduct of an investigation generally[11]and also, more particularly, in relation to the writing of the report.[12] Similarly, the divergence between English law and the principles of the European Convention on Human Rights in relation to the use that can be made of incriminating answers to questions put by inspectors appointed by the DTI raises issues concerning the privilege against self-incrimination,[13] the link between statutory investigations into companies and investigations by the police and SFO[14] and the use of incriminating answers as evidence in criminal proceedings.[15] **1.1.6**

The focus of the text is on the investigation process itself. However, it is important to provide a route-map for the possible consequences of an investigation and the text therefore gives an outline of the possible subsequent action by the Secretary of State for Trade and Industry.[16] For example, the text explains the specific principles governing proceedings seeking the disqualification of directors where those proceedings are founded on an investigation[17] but does not provide a detailed account of the law governing the disqualification of company directors generally (which is fully dealt with in other texts). **1.1.7**

Where the investigator or a person who may be required to assist in an investigation is considering whether a particular course of action is within the investigator's powers, it is important to ask the right questions. The practical application of public law principles may vary depending on the precise context in which the questions are asked. For example, the role for the principles of procedural fairness is different at **1.1.8**

---

11 See 5.6 and 6.11 below.

12 See 7.2 and 7.7 below. Since the writing of this report is the focal point of many investigations much of the material on procedural fairness is to be found in Ch 7, even though some of the material in that chapter is also applicable in relation to the gathering of evidence.

13 See 6.10 below.

14 See 11.4 below.

15 See 13.2 below.

16 See Ch 13.

17 Company Directors Disqualification Act 1986 s.8.

the stage of the decision to initiate an investigation[18] compared with at the stage of writing a report.[19] It is appropriate, however, to have a checklist of the relevant questions.

(i) Is the action within the ambit of the statutory power (illegality/ultra vires)?
(ii) Has the investigator misdirected himself in law?
(iii) Has the investigator taken an irrelevant matter or failed to take a relevant matter into consideration?
(iv) Is the investigator's action one that is so unreasonable that it would not have been done by any reasonable investigator?
(v) Has the investigator acted in bad faith?
(vi) Has the investigator acted for an improper purpose?
(vii) Has the investigator adopted an inflexible policy such that he or she is not exercising a discretionary power with an open mind?
(viii) Has the investigator improperly delegated his or her power to another?
(ix) Has the investigator acted in such a way as to amount to an abuse of power?
(x) Has the investigator acted so as to infringe a legitimate expectation?
(xi) Has the investigator acted in breach of express procedural rules?
(xii) Has the investigator breached his or her general obligations to provide a fair hearing etc.?
(xiii) Is the investigator's action tainted because of the appearance (a real danger) of bias?

The text aims to demonstrate the application of the above principles where they apply in the context of investigations into companies.[20] In this context the normal mechanism for alleging a breach of these general public law principles by investigators is judicial review. It is important to note that when examining these principles in judicial review proceedings the court will be acting as a review mechanism rather than as a substantive appeal mechanism and will, accordingly, only intervene in limited circumstances.

---

18 See 4.8 below.

19 See 7.2 to 7.7 below.

20 For a detailed exposition of the above public law principles see Wade & Forsyth *Administrative Law* 7th edn (1994); De Smith, Woolf & Jowell *Judicial Review of Administrative Action* 5th edn (1995) and Fordham *Judicial Review Handbook* 2nd edn (1997).

Finally, although the text aims to be a practical guide to investigations into companies some of the proposals for reform are set out in a concluding chapter.[21] **1.1.9**

[21] See Ch 14. For a study of lessons to be learnt from inspections see P. Boys *Raising Auditing Standards: The Impact of DTI Inspectors' Reports 1971–1995* (1997).

Chapter 2

HISTORICAL BACKGROUND

The roots of the modern company investigations regimes can be traced back to legislation in the mid-nineteenth century since when the legislative provisions have gradually evolved to the present day. Recent statistics show the trends in terms of the frequency with which the provisions governing the different types of investigations are invoked and, in particular, the increase in the number of investigations under what is now Companies Act 1985 s.447.

2.1 COMPANIES ACTS INVESTIGATIONS

The powers of the Board of Trade to appoint inspectors to examine the affairs of a company date back to Joint Stock Companies Act 1856 ss.48 to 52. The 1856 Act provided that the Board of Trade could appoint one or more inspectors to examine the affairs of a company and report thereon upon the application of one-fifth in number and value of the shareholders of any company registered under the Act.[1] This was amended by Companies Act 1862 to provide that the Board of Trade could appoint inspectors upon the application of shareholders holding one-third of the shares in a banking company or one-fifth of the shares in any other company or, in the case of any company not having a capital divided into shares, one-fifth of the members.[2] From 1862 the application had to be supported by evidence showing that the applicants had good reason for requiring the investigation to be made and that they were not actuated by malicious motives and the Board of Trade could require the applicants to give security for the costs of the inquiry before appointing inspectors.[3] Officers and agents were required to produce documents and could be examined on oath.[4] The inspectors' report was 2.1.1

1 S.48.
2 Companies Act 1862 s.56.
3 S.57.
4 Joint Stock Companies Act 1856 s.49; Companies Act 1862 s.58.

to be written or printed as the Board of Trade directed.[5] The 1856 Act provided that the costs of the inspectors' examination were to be defrayed by the members upon whose application the inspectors were appointed[6] although the 1862 Act provided that the Board of Trade could direct the costs to be paid out of the assets of the company.[7] The legislation also provided for the company to appoint inspectors to report to it.[8] A copy of the inspectors' report authenticated by the seal of the company concerned was admissible in any legal proceedings as evidence.[9] The most obvious limitation in this early legislation was the requirement that the Board of Trade could only appoint inspectors upon the application of a significant proportion of the shareholders or members of the company.[10]

The Report of the Company Law Amendment Committee (1925–1926) (the Greene Report)[11] noted that while the company was a going concern an investigation was difficult to obtain and shareholders were discouraged from applying by the fact that they were in general required to give security for costs, whereas the costs in the last resort fell either on themselves or the company in which they were interested and the company may have had no assets.[12] The Greene Report therefore recommended that the provision as to security for costs be altered so as to fix a nominal maximum sum of £100, that the Board of Trade could refer a matter arising in a report to the Director of Public Prosecutions and that the costs of an application should be defrayed by the Board of Trade where a prosecution was initiated and by the company unless the Board of Trade directed a payment by the applicants where no prosecution was initiated. Amendments were accordingly included in Companies Act 1929.[13] **2.1.2**

---

5 Joint Stock Companies Act 1956 s.50; Companies Act 1862 s.59.

6 Joint Stock Companies Act 1856 s.50.

7 Companies Act 1862 s.59.

8 Joint Stock Companies Act 1856 s.51; Companies Act 1862 s.60.

9 Joint Stock Companies Act 1856 s.52; Companies Act 1862 s.61. The 1862 Act made clear that the report was evidence of the opinion of the inspectors in relation to any matter contained in the report.

10 By the time of Companies (Consolidation) Act 1908 s.109 the proportion of shareholders required for an application in a company other than a banking company had been reduced to one-tenth.

11 Cmd. 2657/1926.

12 Para. 58.

13 See Companies Act 1929 ss.135 and 136. Note that s.136(3) provided that the maximum that applicants could be required to pay towards the costs of the inspection was £100.

The Report of the Committee on Company Law Amendment (1945) (the Cohen Report)[14] considered the powers of the Board of Trade under Companies Act 1929.[15] The Report recommended the abolition of the requirement that applicants should have to establish that they were not actuated by malicious motives and a relaxation of the requirement on the percentage of shareholders or number of members required to bring an application.[16] Importantly the Report recommended that the Board of Trade should have the power to appoint inspectors on its own initiative in certain circumstances.[17] It recommended that an inspector should have the power to apply to the court for an examination before the court on oath of anyone capable of giving information regarding the subject of his investigation, and should have the power to extend his investigation to any subsidiary of the first-mentioned company or to a holding company of which the first-mentioned company was a subsidiary and to any other subsidiary of such holding company.[18] The Report recommended that the Board of Trade should have the power to apply to the court for an order to wind up the company or, where they considered it in the public interest, to bring proceedings in the name of the company to recover money for the benefit of the company from those involved in acts prejudicial to the company.[19] The Report made recommendations in relation to the costs of an investigation and, in particular, that the Board of Trade should pay the costs of an investigation initiated by them.[20] The Report did not favour the widening of the powers conferred on inspectors appointed by the company rather than by the Board of Trade.[21] These recommendations were adopted in Companies Act 1947 ss.42 to 45. The 1947 Act also included provisions concerning the appointment and powers of inspectors to investigate the ownership of a company,[22] the power to require information as to persons interested in shares or debentures,[23] the power to impose restrictions on shares or debentures,[24] and to clarify the privilege for communications between a solicitor and his client and the position of a 2.1.3

14 Cmd. 6659/1945.
15 Paras 154–160 and recommendations.
16 Para. 156.
17 Para. 156.
18 Para. 156.
19 Para. 157.
20 Para. 158.
21 Para. 160.
22 S.46.
23 S.47.
24 S.48.

company's bankers in respect of information as to the affairs of their customers.[25] The company investigation provisions were consolidated in Companies Act 1948 ss.164 to 175.

2.1.4 The Report of the Company Law Committee (1962) (the Jenkins Report)[26] dealt with the Board of Trade's powers to appoint inspectors under the section of its report on 'Minorities'.[27] It recommended extending the scope of the statutory provisions so as to require the Board of Trade to appoint an inspector when over 200 members or the holders of one-quarter or more of the issued shares of any class or, in the case of any company not having a share capital, one-quarter or more of the members, requested such appointment, unless the Board of Trade considered that the application was vexatious or that sufficient facts were known to the applicants to enable them to assert their rights on their own behalf. Further, the Report recommended that the Board of Trade should be expressly empowered to obtain documents or information from the directors and officers of companies in respect of which applications for inspections had been made or in respect of which it otherwise appeared that there were circumstances suggesting that any of the conditions that may have triggered an investigation may have been present. It proposed that the Board of Trade should not regard themselves as bound to forward a statement of facts provided by the complainant to the company complained against.[28] The Report also made a number of supplemental recommendations, including giving the Board of Trade an additional power to appoint inspectors to investigate the affairs of a company on the ground that it was necessary for the purpose of the inspection of another company already pending; to expressly require the preservation of documents by the company's officers when an investigation was to be made and in respect of costs. Following the Jenkins Report, the Companies Act 1967 s.109 introduced the power of the Secretary of State to require the production of documents and to require an explanation of the documents that are produced, and was the forerunner of Companies Act 1985 s.447. It is the investigation power most widely used nowadays.[29] Companies Act 1967 made a number of other changes to the investigation regime[30] including

[25] S.49.
[26] Cmnd. 1749/1962.
[27] Paras 213 to 218. See R.D. Fraser *Administrative Powers of Investigation Into Companies* (1971) 34 MLR 260.
[28] Paras 215, 216, 218.
[29] Companies Act 1967 s.111 provided for the security of the information obtained.
[30] See Companies Act 1967 ss.35–42.

amending the powers of inspectors to secure the attendance of persons before them for the purposes of an investigation[31] and to extend the powers of investigation to cover bodies incorporated outside Great Britain but that carry on business in Great Britain.[32]

2.1.5 Additional changes were introduced by Companies Act 1981,[33] which made further amendment to Companies Act 1948. This included replacing the provision that the Secretary of State had to appoint inspectors if the company so resolved by special resolution, with a provision that enabled the company to apply to have its affairs investigated.[34] The maximum amount of security that could be requested from applicants was increased from £100 to £5,000 or such other sum as might, by order, be specified.[35] The 1981 Act increased the duty of directors and others to assist inspectors, and included the power to examine directors' bank accounts in certain circumstances and it no longer required a court order to compel the production of documents or the attendance of a person before the inspectors.[36] The Secretary of State was also no longer obliged to send a copy of the report to the company investigated.[37] The powers of the Secretary of State in relation to investigations into the ownership of companies, the power to require information as to persons interested in shares or debentures and the power to impose restrictions on shares or debentures were all increased.[38]

2.1.6 The present legislation is contained in Companies Act 1985 Part XIV (sections 431 to 453) as amended by Companies Act 1989 ss.55 to 71. In addition to drafting changes and various other adjustments to the regime, the 1989 Act introduced a number of substantive amendments such as the power of the Secretary of State to appoint inspectors on terms that any report they make is not for publication[39] and the power of the Secretary of State to direct the inspectors to take no further steps in the investigation in certain circumstances.[40]

2.1.7 Companies Act 1947 s.102 and subsequently Companies Act 1948 s.441 made provision for the case where there was reasonable cause to

31 S.39.
32 S.42.
33 See D Chaikin *The Companies Act 1981 (3)* (1982) 3 Co Law 115.
34 Companies Act 1981 s.86.
35 S.86.
36 S.87.
37 S.88.
38 Ss. 89 to 91.
39 Companies Act 1985 s.432(2A).
40 Companies Act 1985 s.437(1B).

believe that a person, whilst an officer of the company, had committed an offence in connection with the management of the company's affairs. It enabled an application to be made to the court seeking an order that a person be authorised to inspect the company's books or papers. This is now found in Companies Act 1985 s.721.

2.2 FINANCIAL SERVICES INVESTIGATIONS

The Prevention of Fraud (Investments) Act 1958 s.12 provided the Board of Trade with the power to appoint inspectors to investigate the administration of any unit trust. The Jenkins Report[41] recommended[42] that legislation should provide for the appointment of inspectors by the Board of Trade to investigate the affairs of a registered unit trust on their own initiative, or on application by the manager or trustee, or by holders of at least 10% of the units in issue provided the Board of Trade were satisfied that an application by the latter was not merely vexatious. The power of the Secretary of State to initiate an investigation is now contained in Financial Services Act 1986 s.94. **2.2.1**

Financial Services Act 1986 s.105 introduced powers for the Secretary of State to investigate investment businesses. S.177 introduced powers for the Secretary of State to appoint inspectors to investigate whether or not there had been any contravention of the Company Securities (Insider Dealing) Act 1985. In view of changes to the underlying criminal law statute concerning insider dealing, the power to appoint inspectors under s.177 now relates to whether or not an offence may have been committed under Part V of the Criminal Justice Act 1993. **2.2.2**

The Open-ended Investment Companies (Investment Companies with Variable Capital) Regulations 1996[43] provide a legislative framework 'in relation to measures relating to open-ended collective investment schemes which have as their purpose investment in transferable securities, with the aim of spreading investment risk, of funds raised from the public'.[44] **2.2.3**

---

41 The *Report of the Company Law Committee* (1962) Cmnd. 1749/1962.
42 At para. 322.
43 SI 1996/2827.
44 Recitals to the Regulations. The Regulations were made by the Treasury pursuant to powers conferred on them by European Communities Act 1972 s. 2(2) and other enabling powers. Regulations 21 to 24 provide for investigations by the Secretary of State and the Financial Services Authority.

2.3 INSURANCE COMPANIES

Industrial Assurance Act 1923 s.17 and subsequently Insurance Companies Act 1958 s.14 provided various powers to require the production and explanation of books and papers relating to insurance companies. The powers to investigate insurance companies are now contained in Insurance Companies Act 1982. 2.3.1

2.4 INVESTIGATIONS OF COMPANIES IN A VOLUNTARY WINDING UP

Companies Act 1929 s.277 and Companies Act 1948 s.334 provided powers for the Board of Trade to investigate companies in a voluntary winding up. Companies Act 1981 s.92 amended the regime to bring it into line with the powers of inspectors under the Companies Act regime, including that answers given by a person to a question put in exercise of the powers in Companies Act 1948 s.334 could be used in evidence against him.[45] The provisions were carried into Companies Act 1985[46] and are now found in Insolvency Act 1986 s.218. 2.4.1

2.5 POWERS EXERCISABLE TO ASSIST OVERSEAS REGULATORY AUTHORITIES

The powers exercisable to assist overseas regulatory authorities were introduced for the first time in Companies Act 1989.[47] 2.5.1

2.6 RECENT STATISTICS

The DTI produce an annual report on companies pursuant to the obligation contained in Companies Act 1985 s.729 requiring the Secretary of 2.6.1

---

45 Companies Act 1981 s.92(2).
46 Ss.632 to 633.
47 Companies Act 1989 ss.82 to 91.

State to prepare and lay before Parliament a general annual report of matters within the Companies Acts. The most recent report covers the period April 1996 to March 1997. The statistics set out below are drawn from these annual reports.[48]

Companies Act investigations (also including Companies Act 1989 s.84 and Insurance Companies Act 1982 s.44) **2.6.2**

Year	**Requests considered**	**Investigations commenced**
1986/87	495	134
1987/88	441	135
1988/89	640	151
1989/90	616	167
1990/91	739	179
1991/92	850	177
1992/93	1083	187
1993/94	1066	246
1994/95	1024	323
1995/96	1341	411
1996/97	1297	417

Investigations commenced

Year				**Companies Act 1985**			**Companies Act 1989**	**Insurance Companies Act 1982**
	s.431	s.432	s.442	s.444	s.446	s.447	s.84	s.44
1986/87	–	1	3	–	–	130	–	–
1987/88	–	2	–	–	–	133	–	–
1988/89	–	7	6	–	–	138	–	1
1989/90	–	5	4	–	1	157	–	–
1990/91	1	4	–	–	2	171	1	2
1991/92	–	4	3	–	1	155	10	4
1992/93	–	1	1	–	1	171	7	7
1993/94	–	2	–	–	–	229	5	10
1994/95	–	1	–	–	–	308	7	7
1995/96	–	–	–	1	–	389	13	8
1996/97	–	–	–	–	–	395	6	15[49]

48 Note in each case the period runs from April of one year to March of the next. For a statistical summary of investigations year by year from 1948 to 1989/1990 see *Investigations Handbook* (1990) Appendix A.

49 In 1996–97 there was also one investigation pursuant to Insurance Companies Act 1982 s.12, which concerns the authorisation of insurance companies.

It will be apparent from the above table that by far the greater proportion of investigations that are commenced are under Companies Act 1985 s.447. However, much of the literature and caselaw concerning investigations into companies centres on investigations carried out pursuant to Companies Act 1985 s.432. Reports prepared under s.432(2) and s.442 may be published.[50] The following table lists the reports published in recent years.[51]

Reports published by the Secretary of State

Date	Companies Act section	Company
17.04.91	s.432(1)	The Animal Defence Society Limited
01.05.91	s.432(2)	Sound Diffusion plc
24.07.91	s.432(2), s.442	Rotaprint plc
16.01.92	s.432(2)	The Milford Docks Company
27.02.92	s.432(2)	BOM Holdings plc
24.09.92	s.432(2)	Blue Arrow plc
14.01.93	s.432(2)	National Westminster Bank plc
21.01.93	s.442	James Neill Holdings plc and others
18.02.93	s.432(2)	Edencorp Leisure plc
11.03.93	s.432(2)	Norton Group plc
07.04.93	s.432(2)	Astra Holdings plc
23.09.93	s.432(2)	London United Investments plc/CR Driver & Co. Ltd (in liquidation)
20.01.94	s.432(2), s.442	The Bestwood plc
19.07.94	s.432(2)	Atlantic Computers plc/Atlantic Computer Systems plc
29.09.94	s.442	Consolidated Goldfields plc
06.07.95	s.432(2), s.442/s.432(2)	James Ferguson Holdings plc/Barlow Clowes Gilt Managers Ltd
27.11.97	s.432(2), s.442	Guinness plc

[50] See Ch. 9.
[51] From 1st April 1991.

2.6.3

Financial Services Act 1986 s.177 investigations

Year	Cases referred by the London Stock Exchange for consideration	Appointment of inspectors under s.177
1986/87	13	3
1987/88	29	15
1988/89	33	12
1989/90	21	12
1990/91	8	4
1991/92	11	3
1992/93	5	1
1993/94	17	5
1994/95	13	6
1995/96	28	13
1996/97	36	21

Prosecutions for contravention of Companies Securities (Insider Dealing) Act 1985[52]

Year	Convictions (following s.177 inquiry)	Acquittals (following s.177 inquiry)
1986/87	1(–)	–(–)
1987/88	3(2)	–(–)
1988/89	–(–)	1(–)
1989/90	4(3)	9(2)
1990/91	2(–)	–(–)
1991/92	3(3)	5(2)
1992/93	5**(4*)	2(2)
1993/94	2(2)	6(5)
1994/95	–(–)	–(–)
1995/96	1(1)	–(–)
1996/97	2(–)	2(2)

In the above Table the figures relate to the number of defendants and the start of a prosecution is taken to be the laying of an information before the court.

** Includes one conviction acquitted on appeal in 1993/94 and three convictions acquitted on appeal in 1994/1995.

* Includes three convictions acquitted on appeal in 1994/1995.

52 The Company Securities (Insider Dealing) Act 1985 was repealed and replaced by Criminal Justice Act 1993 Part V, which came into force on 1st March 1994.

Chapter 3

THE *INVESTIGATIONS HANDBOOK*

3.1 INTRODUCTION

The DTI produced a publication in 1980 entitled *Handbook of the Companies Inspection System* to explain inspections and other types of DTI investigations.[1] In 1990, they replaced it with a new publication entitled the *Investigations Handbook*. The *Investigations Handbook* has no statutory force and there is an issue as to whether the DTI and inspectors may be required to comply with its contents.[2] As the DTI point out in the handbook, Companies Act 1981 (consolidated in Companies Act 1985), Financial Services Act 1986 and Companies Act 1989 greatly extended the Secretary of State's powers and the Handbook was prepared 'to explain the purpose of investigations under the Companies Acts 1985 and 1989 and the Financial Services Act 1986, how they are initiated and conducted and the use to which information can be put'.[3] The Handbook also refers to investigations under Insurance Companies Act 1982 and Insolvency Act 1986 s.218. The law and departmental practice referred to in the Handbook are said to be as at 1st April 1990.[4] **3.1.1**

There are various appendices to the *Investigations Handbook*. Appendix A sets out a statistical summary of investigations under the Companies Acts and Financial Services Act 1986. Appendices B and C provide notes for the guidance of inspectors appointed under Companies Act 1985 and under Financial Services Act 1986 s.177, respectively. Appendix D lists the self-regulating organisations and recognised professional bodies under Financial Services Act 1986. Finally, Appendices E and F set out the Court of Appeal judgments in *Re Pergamon Press Ltd*[5] and *Maxwell v Department of Trade and Industry and others*,[6] cases of importance in relation to procedural issues. **3.1.2**

---

1 A second edition was published in 1986.
2 See 3.3 below.
3 *Investigations Handbook* para. 1.
4 *Investigations Handbook* para. 2.
5 [1971] Ch 388.
6 [1974] QB 523.

3.2 STATUS OF THE NOTES FOR GUIDANCE OF INSPECTORS

Appendix B explains that inspectors appointed by the Secretary of State under Companies Act 1985 are invested with statutory duties and powers and the responsibility for the conduct of the investigation is theirs alone. It also states: **3.2.1**

> The following notes have been prepared by the Department of Trade and Industry for the guidance of such inspectors. It is, however, impossible to be definitive about every situation which inspectors may encounter during the course of an investigation, accordingly inspectors are encouraged to refer to the Department for advice if at any time they are in doubt.[7]

Thus the responsibility for the investigation rests with the inspectors, but the DTI give them guidance.

Appendix C explains that notes have been prepared by the DTI for the guidance of inspectors appointed under Financial Services Act 1986, s.177. However, it adds that 'the circumstances of inspections vary and it is impossible to offer guidance about every situation which inspectors may encounter'.[8] Appendix C also states: **3.2.2**

> The Department cannot fetter the discretion of inspectors with respect to how they carry out their enquiries and these notes are not intended to give that impression. Inspectors are masters of their own procedure. The responsibility for the conduct of the investigation is theirs. However, they must act fairly and reasonably. Inspectors are encouraged to refer to the Department for advice if they are in doubt, and are particularly asked to consult the Department in the circumstances where these notes specifically recommend that they should.[9]

Therefore, again the responsibility for the investigation rests with the inspectors but the DTI give them guidance. However, Appendix C (unlike Appendix B) expressly provides that the DTI cannot fetter the inspectors' discretion as to how they carry out their enquiries and this may have implications for whether or not inspectors can be required to comply with the contents of the *Investigations Handbook*. A witness may, however, wish to seek a confirmation from inspectors that they will carry out their inspection in accordance with the relevant guidance.

7 *Investigations Handbook* App B, para. 1.
8 App C, para. 2.
9 App C, para. 3.

3.3 COMPLIANCE WITH THE CONTENTS OF THE *INVESTIGATIONS HANDBOOK*

The *Investigations Handbook* and the guidance contained therein do not have the force of statute[10] and therefore in the event of any inconsistency between the Handbook on the one hand, and statute or caselaw on the other, the DTI or inspectors would have to comply with the statute or caselaw. An obvious example of this inconsistency would be where a new statutory provision is enacted that causes a particular statement of law in the Handbook to no longer represent the law. **3.3.1**

However, where the *Investigations Handbook* lays down guidance that provides safeguards that go beyond the general law for those who are the subject of investigation, there may in some circumstances be a legitimate expectation that there will be compliance with the guidance or that there will be a fair hearing given to the person adversely affected by the decision to act in a way contrary to the guidance. **3.3.2**

The precise ambit and effect of the principle of protecting a legitimate expectation is unclear. However, it has been suggested that the approach that both best explains the current state of the law and offers a principle by which the courts may balance the countervailing propositions of the weight of the legitimacy of an expectation and the policy change that it threatens to frustrate is:[11] **3.3.3**

> [T]he Courts now expect government departments to honour their statements of policy or intention or else to treat the citizen with the fullest personal consideration ... . But those demands cannot be pressed to the point where they obstruct changes of policy, which a government should be at liberty to make within its discretionary powers.

It would appear, in the context of the *Investigations Handbook*, that if the Secretary of State or inspectors propose to depart from any of the guidance, they may face a challenge by way of an application for judicial review if they fail to provide a fair hearing to a directly affected person before doing so. It is less likely that the Secretary of State or inspectors **3.3.4**

---

[10] But note *Gillick v W Norfolk AHA* [1986] AC 112 in which the court considered a challenge to a 'memorandum of guidance'.

[11] Wade and Forsyth *Administrative Law* 7th edn (1994) pp. 419–20 cited with approval by Sedley J in *R v Ministry of Agriculture, Fisheries and Food ex p. Hamble Fisheries (Offshore) Ltd* [1995] 2 All ER 714 at p. 732.

could be prevented from departing from the guidance in respect of procedures (rather than merely being required first to give a hearing in respect of the proposed procedural change), even where to do so would adversely affect the position of a directly affected person.[12] It seems, however, that in some circumstances courts may hold that there is a legitimate expectation that a practice will continue in the absence of notice of its discontinuance.[13] Finally, in so far as it may be suggested that the Handbook introduces any substantive rights rather than only procedural safeguards, courts have given conflicting views as to the concept of a substantive legitimate expectation. One approach is to say that whether there is a legitimate expectation of a substantive right involves a similar approach to whether there is a legitimate expectation of procedural safeguards. However, another view is that a substantive legitimate expectation can always be overridden save where it would be Wednesbury unreasonable to do so (i.e. so unreasonable that no reasonable investigator would do so).[14]

A major difficulty with the proposition that there are legitimate expectations contained in the *Investigations Handbook* worthy of protection is the issue as to whether any provisions in the Handbook create expectations in any event. The principle of legitimate expectation may be seen as arising either from an express promise given on behalf of a public authority or from the existence of a regular practice that the claimant can reasonably expect to continue.[15] Any obligation on the Secretary of State or inspectors to act in accordance with the Handbook or afford a fair hearing before departing from the practice in the Handbook could be based on the premise either that the Handbook makes promises, or that it lays down a regular practice that the claimant **3.3.5**

---

12 Compare the contrasting approaches in, for example, *R v Department of Trade and Industry ex p. Blenheim Queensdale Ltd* [1992] COD 453 with *R v Panel on Takeovers and Mergers ex p. Fayed* (1993) 5 Admin LR 337.

13 See, e.g. *R v Inland Revenue Commissioners ex p. Unilever plc* [1996] STC 681.

14 Compare *R v Inland Revenue Commissioners ex p. Unilever* (above) and *R v Secretary of State for the Home Department ex p. Hargreaves* [1997] 1 All ER 397. Note Fordham *Judicial Review Handbook* 2nd edn [1997] at pp. 481–3 and Craig *Substantive Legitimate Expectations in Domestic and Community Law* [1996] CLJ 289. Consider the effect of the reasoning in *R v Secretary of State for the Home Department ex p. Pierson* [1997] 3 WLR 492 restricting the Secretary of State's power to increase the length of the penal element of a prisoner's life sentence before he was eligible to be considered for parole, which period had been fixed and communicated to a prisoner.

15 *Council of Civil Service Unions v Minister for the Civil Service* [1985] AC 374.

can reasonably expect to continue.[16] The obstacle to any challenge in the present case, however, is that the guidance has been formulated in such a way that it may well not give rise to any expectation. This is particularly so in the case of Appendix C, which makes clear that the DTI cannot fetter the inspectors' discretion with respect to how they carry out their enquiries and that the notes are 'not intended to give that impression'.[17] Thus anyone seeking to hold the DTI or inspectors to any point in the Handbook will need clearly to establish that the relevant passage creates an expectation and will probably be unable to do so.

---

[16] See, e.g. *R v Secretary of State for the Home Department ex p. Asif Mahmood Khan* [1984] 1 WLR 1337 and *R v Secretary of State for the Home Department ex p. Ruddock* [1987] 1 WLR 1482. Consider the analysis of the different effects of promises and practices by Sedley J in *R v Ministry of Agriculture, Fisheries and Food ex p. Hamble Fisheries (Offshore) Limited* [1995] 2 All ER 714 at pp. 728–9.

[17] App C, para. 3.

Chapter 4

THE INSTIGATION OF INVESTIGATIONS

The decision to investigate a company in the manner specified in the relevant legislation ultimately rests with the Secretary of State, the Treasury, the Financial Services Authority or the court.

4.1 WHERE THE COURT DECLARES THAT THE AFFAIRS OF A COMPANY OUGHT TO BE INVESTIGATED BY THE SECRETARY OF STATE

The Secretary of State shall appoint inspectors if the court by order declares that the affairs of a company ought to be investigated.[1] The legislation gives no guidance as to when it should be concluded that the affairs of a company ought to be investigated. However, it appears that the legislation is not intended to give rise to inspections where what is in issue is, for example, a dispute between two shareholders in a private company.[2] In considering analogous South African provisions in *Buckingham and Others v Combined Holdings and Industries* Ltd[3] O'Hagan J said[4] that the court is concerned only with issues of substance, not minor irregularities that may occur from time to time in any commercial organisation. If the substantial complaints appear to be well-founded, lesser grievances may tip the balance in favour of the applicant seeking an investigation, but if the chief elements in the applicant's contentions do not in any way warrant an investigation, little else calls for consideration.

1 Companies Act 1985 s.432(1).
2 See *Irvin & Johnson Ltd v Gelcer & Co (Pty) Ltd* [1958] (2) SA 59 in the context of analogous South African provisions.
3 [1961] 1 SALR 326.
4 At p. 333.

The phrase 'the affairs of a company' has been given a wide meaning. In *R v Board of Trade ex p. St Martins Preserving Co. Ltd*[5] Phillimore J was of the view that it included 'its goodwill, its profits or losses, its contracts and assets including its shareholding in and ability to control the affairs of a subsidiary, or perhaps in the latter regard a sub-subsidiary'.[6] Winn J stated that it 'comprises all its business affairs, interests or transactions, all its investment or other property interests, all its profits and losses or balance of profits or losses, and its goodwill'.[7] Winn J also stated[8] that the 'affairs of the company' applies to: **4.1.1**

> transactions brought about by a receiver and manager by the use of property or powers possessed by the company but effected by a separate legal persona which is a subsidiary company of the company in question: additionally the material consequences of any transaction of such a subsidiary company in relation to the undertaking of a sub-subsidiary company, changing the value of the parent company's indirect interest in the trading of the sub-subsidiary company are affairs of the parent company.

He added that the use by a receiver of voting power conferred by shares of a subsidiary company held by a parent company to change the constitution of the board of the subsidiary company, is part of the affairs of the parent company, even though what is thereafter done by that new board is more strictly part of the affairs of the subsidiary.[9]

An application to the court is made by originating motion.[10] The Companies Act 1985 does not specify who may make the application to the court and the category of potential applicants appears unrestricted. It has been suggested that an application may be made 'by any person interested'[11] and although the statute does not impose this limit, in principle it seems likely that a court would be less willing to order an investigation if the application were made by someone with no interest in the company. **4.1.2**

---

5 [1965] 1 QB 603.
6 At p. 613.
7 At p. 618.
8 At p. 622.
9 At pp. 622–3. See also the approach of Scott J in *Re London United Investments Plc* [1992] BCLC 91 at pp. 105–7 (appealed at [1992] Ch 578). Note also the specific power contained in Companies Act 1985 s.433(1) allowing inspectors to investigate subsidiaries and holding companies.
10 Rules of the Supreme Court, Order 102 rule 3(1)(b).
11 See Rules of the Supreme Court, note 102/3/3.

The notice of motion by which any such application is made may be issued out of the office of the companies court or any Chancery district registry.[12] The notice of motion must be served on the company. It need not be served on the DTI, but notice of the intended application should be sent to the DTI solicitor together with copies of any affidavits intended to be used at the hearing.[13] Evidence should be filed at court proving that this has been complied with[14] and the affidavit in support of the application should set out the facts relied on as justifying the appointment of an inspector.[15] **4.1.3**

The court has a discretion as to whether or not to make a costs order in respect of the application. In *Re Miles Aircraft Ltd (No.2)*[16] Roxburgh J ordered that the question of costs be reserved until the Board of Trade had furnished to the court a copy of the inspector's report. This was on the basis that, since the court had only to be satisfied that a prima facie case had arisen for investigation by the Board of Trade, it would be wrong to direct at the stage of declaring that the company's affairs ought to be investigated that anyone should pay the costs of the application. **4.1.4**

4.2 OTHER CIRCUMSTANCES WHERE THE SECRETARY OF STATE IS REQUIRED TO APPOINT INSPECTORS

The Secretary of State shall appoint inspectors if an application is made to him for an investigation into the membership of any company and otherwise to determine the identity of those persons who are or have been financially interested in the success or failure (real or apparent) of the company or able to control or materially to influence its policy.[17] Such an application requires in the case of a company having a share capital either not less than 200 members or members holding not less than one-tenth of the shares issued and, in the case of a company not **4.2.1**

---

12 Rules of the Supreme Court, Order 102 rule 3(2).
13 Practice Direction [1954] 1 WLR 563; [1954] 1 All ER 604.
14 *ibid.*
15 Rules of the Supreme Court, note 102/3/3.
16 [1948] WN 178.
17 Companies Act 1985 s.442(1).

having a share capital, on the application of not less than one-fifth in number of the persons on the company's register of members.[18] Although the starting point is that upon such application the Secretary of State shall appoint inspectors to conduct the investigation applied for,[19] there are provisos:

(i) the Secretary of State shall not appoint inspectors if he is satisfied that the application is vexatious; and where inspectors are appointed their terms of appointment shall exclude any matter in so far as the Secretary of State is satisfied that it is unreasonable for it to be investigated;[20]
(ii) the Secretary of State may, before appointing inspectors, require the applicant or applicants to give security to an amount not exceeding £5,000 for payment of the costs of the investigation;[21] and
(iii) if it appears to the Secretary of State that the powers conferred by Companies Act 1985 s.444 are sufficient for the purposes of investigating the matters that inspectors would be appointed to investigate, he may instead conduct the investigation under that section.[22]

If the Secretary of State were to refuse to appoint inspectors pursuant to the provisions at 4.2, although it may be possible to apply for a declaration under Companies Act 1985 s.431,[23] it would also be open to one with sufficient interest in his decision[24] to apply for judicial review seeking an order of mandamus to require the Secretary of State to appoint inspectors.[25] **4.2.2**

[18] Companies Act 1985 s.442(3).
[19] Companies Act 1985 s.442(3).
[20] Companies Act 1985 s.442(3A).
[21] Companies Act 1985 s.442(3B). The Secretary of State has the power by order to specify a different sum but has not done so. Such order would have to be made by statutory instrument subject to annulment in pursuance of a resolution of either House of Parliament.
[22] Companies Act 1985 s.442(3C). S.444 concerns an investigation into the ownership of a company.
[23] See 4.1 above.
[24] Rules of the Supreme Court Order 53 r.3(7).
[25] See *R v Board of Trade ex p. St Martins Preserving Co. Ltd* [1965] 1 QB 603. In so far as courts may, in recent years, have been reluctant to entertain applications for judicial review where there is an alternative remedy, applications for a mandamus to enforce an obligation under s.432 or Insolvency Act 1986 s.218(4) would not appear to be exact alternatives to an application for a declaration under s.431. See 4.9 below.

4.3 SECRETARY OF STATE'S DISCRETIONARY POWER TO APPOINT INSPECTORS TO INVESTIGATE THE AFFAIRS OF A COMPANY

Where the power to investigate a company or its affairs rests with the Secretary of State it is not an entirely unrestricted power. The statutory framework specifies the circumstances that must exist before the Secretary of State may decide to investigate a company.

The Secretary of State may appoint one or more competent inspectors to investigate the affairs of a company and to report on them in such manner as he may direct[26] on an application by the company[27] or by its members. The appointment may be made in the case of a company having a share capital, on the application either of not less than 200 members or of members holding not less than one-tenth of the shares issued;[28] in the case of a company not having a share capital, on the application of not less than one-fifth in number of the persons on the company's register of members;[29] and in any case on application of the company.[30] The application must be supported by such evidence as the Secretary of State requires for the purpose of showing that the applicant has good reason for requiring the investigation.[31] The Secretary of State may, before appointing inspectors, require the applicant to give security, to an amount not exceeding £5,000 for payment of the costs of the investigation.[32] 4.3.1

The Secretary of State may appoint one or more competent inspectors to investigate the affairs of a company and report on them in such manner as he directs if it appears to him that there are circumstances suggesting:[33] 4.3.2

[26] Companies Act 1985 s.431(1).
[27] Companies Act 1985 s.431(2)(c).
[28] Companies Act 1985 s.431(2)(a).
[29] Companies Act 1985 s.431(2)(b).
[30] Companies Act 1985 s.431(2)(c).
[31] Companies Act 1985 s.431(3).
[32] Companies Act 1985 s.431(4). As in the case of s.442(3B) the Secretary of State has the power by order to specify a different sum but has not done so.
[33] Companies Act 1985 s.432(2)(a)–(d). Note that the Secretary of State need not state at the time of appointment which of (a) to (d) has led him to make the appointment.

(i) that the company's affairs are being or have been conducted with intent to defraud its creditors or the creditors of any other person, or otherwise for a fraudulent or unlawful purpose, or in a manner that is unfairly prejudicial to some part of its members, or[34]

(ii) that any actual or proposed act or omission of the company (including an act or omission on its behalf) is or would be so prejudicial, or that the company was formed for any fraudulent or unlawful purpose, or

(iii) that persons connected with the company's formation or the management of its affairs have in connection therewith been guilty of fraud, misfeasance or other misconduct towards it or towards its members;[35]

(iv) that the company's members have not been given all the information with respect to its affairs which they might reasonably expect.[36]

These powers are without prejudice to the powers referred to at 4.3.1 and are exercisable with respect to a body corporate notwithstanding that it is in the course of being voluntarily wound up.[37]

---

[34] The phrase 'intent to defraud' imports actual dishonesty, *Re Patrick Lyon Limited* [1933] Ch 786. However, in the context of winding up a company it has been held that a company carrying on business and incurring debts, when to the knowledge of the directors there is no reasonable prospect of the debts being paid may, in general, be properly inferred to be carrying on a business with intend to defraud creditors — *Re William C Leith Brothers Limited* [1932] 2 Ch 71. See also *Hardie v Hanson* (1960) 105 CLR 451.

[35] 'Other misconduct' is to be construed ejusdem generis with 'fraud' and 'misfeasance' and does not connote 'moral turpitude' and would not extend simply to negligence without more — see *SBA Properties Ltd v Cradock* [1967] 1 WLR 716.

[36] This goes beyond information to which shareholders have a legal entitlement but an investigation would not, for example, be ordered simply to enable shareholders to obtain information in advance of a general meeting about a matter that directors had decided to submit to a shareholders meeting — see *Candice Investments (Pty) Ltd v Harmony Gold Mining Co. Ltd* [1961] 4 SA 123.

[37] Companies Act 1985 s.432(3). The reference at (a) to a company's members includes any person who is not a member but to whom shares in the company have been transferred or transmitted by operation of law — Companies Act 1985 s.432(4).

4.4 OTHER DISCRETIONARY POWERS OF THE SECRETARY OF STATE OR FINANCIAL SERVICES AUTHORITY TO APPOINT INSPECTORS

In addition to the powers to appoint inspectors to investigate the affairs of a company, in certain circumstances the Secretary of State has the power to appoint inspectors for specific purposes or in relation to specific aspects of a company or its affairs.

Where it appears to the Secretary of State that there is good reason to do so he may appoint one or more competent inspectors to investigate and report on the membership of any company, and otherwise with respect to the company for the purpose of determining the true persons who are or have been financially interested in the success or failure (real or apparent) of the company or able to control or materially to influence its policy.[38] The appointment may define the scope of the investigation (whether as respects the matter or the period to which it is to extend or otherwise) and in particular may limit the investigation to matters connected with particular shares or debentures.[39] **4.4.1**

If it appears to the Secretary of State that there are circumstances suggesting that contraventions may have occurred in relation to a company's shares or debentures, of Companies Act 1985 s.323 or s.324 (taken with Schedule 13) or of s.328(3) to (5),[40] he may appoint one or more competent inspectors to carry out such investigations as are requisite to establish whether or not such contraventions have occurred and to report the result of their investigations to him.[41] Such appointment may limit the period to which their investigation is to extend or confine it to shares or debentures of a particular class, or both.[42] **4.4.2**

The Secretary of State has the power under the Financial Services Act 1986 to appoint one or more competent inspectors to investigate and report on: **4.4.3**

38 Companies Act 1985 s.442(1).
39 Companies Act 1985 s.442(2).
40 These provisions relate to the prohibition on directors dealing in share options and the duty of directors to disclose their shareholdings in the company.
41 Companies Act 1985 s.446(1).
42 Companies Act 1985 s.446(2).

(i) the affairs of, or the manager or trustee of, any authorised unit trust scheme;
(ii) the affairs of, or of the operator or trustee of, any recognised scheme so far as relating to activities carried on in the United Kingdom; or
(iii) the affairs of, or of the operator or trustee of, any other collective investment scheme,

if it appears to the Secretary of State that it is in the interests of the participants to do so or that the matter is of public concern.[43] This power applies to any investment business whether run by a company, a partnership or an individual and is not therefore restricted to an investigation of companies or an aspect of companies unlike the powers to investigate conferred by the Companies Act 1985. The Secretary of State has delegated this power to the Securities and Investments Board, now the Financial Services Authority, which may exercise the powers concurrently with the Secretary of State.[44] Therefore, in any particular case it may be either the Secretary of State or the Financial Services Authority that could exercise the power.

The Secretary of State has the power to order an investigation into insider dealing. If it appears to the Secretary of State that there are circumstances suggesting that an offence under Part V of the Criminal Justice Act 1993 (Insider Dealing) may have been committed, he may appoint one or more competent inspectors to carry out such investigations as are requisite to establish whether or not any such offence has been committed and to report the results of their investigations to him.[45] The appointment may limit the period during which the inspector is to continue his investigation or confine it to particular matters.[46] Also, at any time during the investigation, the Secretary of State may vary the appointment by limiting or extending the period during which the inspector is to continue his investigation or by confining the investigation to particular matters.[47] The appointment of such inspectors is normally triggered by information passed to the DTI by the surveillance group of the London Stock Exchange. **4.4.4**

43 Financial Services Act 1986 s.94.
44 Financial Services Act 1986 s.114 and Financial Services Act 1986 (Delegation) Order 1987 (SI 1987/942).
45 Financial Services Act 1986 s.177(1).
46 Financial Services Act 1986 s.177(2). In practice the period is not normally limited in the appointment.
47 Financial Services Act 1986 s.177(2A).

The Secretary of State and the Financial Services Authority (formerly the Securities and Investments Board) may appoint one or more inspectors to investigate and report on the affairs of, or any director or depositary of, an investment company with variable capital if it appears to the Secretary of State or the Financial Services Authority that it is in the interests of shareholders of the company to do so or that the matter is of public concern.[48] 4.4.5

The Director of Public Prosecutions or the Lord Advocate may refer the matter to the Secretary of State for enquiry when a reference is made to them by the voluntary liquidator of a company to whom it appears that any past or present officer or member of the company has been guilty of a criminal offence in relation to the company.[49] Where a report is made, the Secretary of State shall investigate the matter and may appoint inspectors.[50] 4.4.6

4.5 INVESTIGATION POWERS EXERCISABLE BY THE SECRETARY OF STATE OR THE TREASURY OTHER THAN THE APPOINTMENT OF INSPECTORS

The provisions described at 4.1 to 4.4 require or enable the Secretary of State to appoint inspectors to investigate various matters and to require the inspectors to report to him. There are, however, various powers that enable the Secretary of State or the Treasury directly to investigate. 4.5.1

If it appears to the Secretary of State that there is good reason to investigate the ownership of any shares in or debentures of a company and that it is unnecessary to appoint inspectors for the purpose, he may require any person whom he has reasonable cause to believe to have or to be able to obtain any information as to the present and past interests in those shares or debentures and the names and addresses of the persons 4.5.2

48 Open-ended Investment Companies (Investment Companies with Variable Capital) Regulations 1996 (SI 1996/2827) reg. 22(1). Note also the further powers to investigate the affairs of the directors, depositary, trustee or operator contained in reg. 22(2) and in relation to shadow directors in reg. 22(5).

49 Insolvency Act 1986 s.218(4).

50 Insolvency Act 1986 s.218(5).

interested, and of any persons who act or have acted on their behalf in relation to the shares or debentures to give any such information to the Secretary of State.[51] For this purpose a person is deemed to have an interest in shares or debentures if he has any right to acquire or dispose of them or of any interest in them, or to vote in respect of them, or if his consent is necessary for the exercise of any of the rights of other persons interested in them, or if other persons interested in them can be required, or are accustomed, to exercise their rights in accordance with his instructions.[52]

The Secretary of State may at any time, if he thinks there is good reason to do so, give directions to a company requiring it, at such time and place as may be specified in the directions, to produce such documents as may be so specified.[53] This is the most commonly used power of investigation under Companies Act 1985[54] and may be used as a precursor to other investigations. The power may effectively be delegated in that the Secretary of State may at any time, if he thinks there is good reason to do so, authorise an officer of his or any other competent person, on producing (if so required) evidence of his authority, to require a company to produce to him (the officer or other competent person) forthwith any documents that the officer or other person may specify.[55] **4.5.3**

The Secretary of State has powers, which are exercisable where it appears to him that there is good reason to do so, to investigate the affairs, or any aspect of the affairs, of any person so far as relevant to any investment business[56] that he is or was carrying on or appears to the Secretary of State to be or to have been carrying on.[57] However, these powers are not exercisable for the purpose of investigating the affairs of any exempted person[58] unless he is an appointed representative or the investigation is in respect of investment business in respect of which he is not an exempted person. These powers are also not exercisable for the purpose of investigating the affairs of a member of a **4.5.4**

---

[51] Companies Act 1985 s.444(1).
[52] Companies Act 1985 s.444(2).
[53] Companies Act 1985 s.447(2).
[54] See 2.6.2 above.
[55] Companies Act 1985 s.447(3). Generally for the power to obtain evidence See Ch 6.
[56] Investment business is defined at Financial Services Act 1986 s.1 and Sch 1. The exclusions in Sch 1 part IV do not apply when considering 'investment business' in the context of s.105.
[57] Financial Services Act 1986 s.105(1).
[58] See Financial Services Act 1986 Ch IV.

recognised self-regulating organisation[59] or a person certified by a recognised professional body[60] in respect of investment business where he is subject to its rules unless (a) that organisation or body has requested the Secretary of State to investigate those affairs; or (b) it appears to him that the organisation or body is unable or unwilling to investigate them in a satisfactory manner.[61] The Secretary of State may authorise any officer of his or any other competent person to exercise these powers[62] but no person is bound to comply unless the person exercising the powers has, if required to do so, produced evidence of his authority.[63] These functions are exercisable concurrently by the Secretary of State and the Financial Services Authority, so that in any particular case it may be either of them exercising the power.[64] The power to investigate conferred by the Financial Services Act 1986 s.105 does not entitle the Secretary of State to investigate business transactions that took place before the material provisions of that Act, which set out his investigative powers and characterises the different types of business activity that can be investigated, came into effect, i.e. 18 December 1986.[65]

Where the prosecuting authority makes a report to the Secretary of State for further enquiry in the context of the winding up of a company[66] the Secretary of State shall investigate the matter reported to him and such other matters relating to the affairs of the company as appear to him to require investigation.[67] **4.5.5**

59 See Financial Services Act 1986 ss.7–14.
60 See Financial Services Act 1986 ss.15–21
61 For the powers contained in s.105, including the power to require the person under investigation to attend for questioning (Financial Services Act 1986 s.105(3)) and to require the provision of documents (Financial Services Act 1986 s.105(4)), see 6.6 below.
62 Financial Services Act 1986 s.106(1).
63 Financial Services Act 1986 s.106(2).
64 See Financial Services Act 1986 s.114 and the Financial Services Act 1986 (Delegation) Order 1987 (SI 1987/942).
65 *R v Secretary of State for Trade and Industry ex p. R* [1989] 1 WLR 372.
66 Insolvency Act 1986 s.218.
67 Insolvency Act 1986 s.218(5)(a). For the purpose of his investigation he may exercise any of the powers that are exerciseable by inspectors appointed under Companies Act 1985 ss.431 or 432 to investigate a company's affairs — s.218(5)(b).

INSURANCE COMPANIES 4.5.6

The Treasury and (to a lesser extent)[68] the Secretary of State have specific powers in relation to the investigation of insurance companies. These powers are exercisable in relation to any insurance company to which Part II[69] of the Insurance Companies Act 1982[70] applies and are exercisable in accordance with the provisions at 4.5.7 to 4.5.10.

The Treasury may require a company that carries on long-term business to cause its actuary to make an investigation into the company's financial condition in respect of that business, or any specified part of that business, as at a specified date.[71] The Treasury may require the company to cause an abstract of that person's report of the investigation to be made[72] and to prepare a statement of its long-term business, or of that part thereof as at that date.[73] The Treasury may provide for the acceleration of information required by the accounting provisions of Insurance Companies Act 1982.[74] The Treasury and Secretary of State also have the power to obtain information and require production of documents[75] and in certain circumstances to enter and search premises.[76] 4.5.7

The powers at 4.5.7 are exercisable on any of the following grounds: 4.5.8

(i) that the Treasury consider the exercise of the power to be desirable for protecting policy holders or potential policy holders of the company against the risk that the company may be unable to meet its liabilities or, in the case of long-term business, to fulfil the reasonable expectations of the policy holders or potential policy holders;[77]
(ii) that the company is a UK or non-EC company and it appears to the Treasury that any of the criteria of sound and prudent

[68] See the Transfer of Functions (Insurance) Order 1997 (SI 1997/2781).
[69] Part II is entitled 'The Regulation of Insurance Companies'.
[70] Insurance Companies Act 1982 s.37(1).
[71] Insurance Companies Act 1982 s.42(1)(a).
[72] Insurance Companies Act 1982 s.42(1)(b).
[73] Insurance Companies Act 1982 s.42(1)(c). See also s.42(2)–(4).
[74] Insurance Companies Act 1982 s.43. Note also s.43A concerning investigations as to whether the criteria of sound and prudent management are or would be fulfilled.
[75] Insurance Companies Act 1982 s.44. See 6.7 below.
[76] Insurance Companies Act 1982 s.44A. See 6.7 below.
[77] Insurance Companies Act 1982 s.37(2)(a).

management is not or has not been, or may not be, or may not have been fulfilled with respect to the company;[78]

(iii) that it appears to the Treasury:
- that the company has failed to satisfy an obligation to which it is or was subject by virtue of Insurance Companies Act 1982 or any enactment repealed by that Act or by Insurance Companies Act 1974;
- that a company of which it is a subsidiary has failed to satisfy an obligation to which it is or was subject by virtue of Insurance Companies Act 1982 s.29(7) or Insurance Companies Act 1974 s.24(6) or Insurance Companies Amendment Act 1973 s.8(6); or
- that a subordinate company within the meaning of Insurance Companies Act 1982 s.31 of the company has failed to satisfy an obligation to which it is or was subject by virtue of that section or s.26, or of Insurance Companies Act 1974 ss.22 or 26, or of Insurance Companies Amendment Act 1973 ss.6 or 10;[79]

(iv) that it appears to the Treasury that the company has furnished misleading or inaccurate information to them under or for the purposes of any provision of, or any enactment repealed by, Insurance Companies Acts 1982 or 1974;[80]

(v) that the Treasury are not satisfied that adequate arrangements are in force or will be made for the reinsurance of risks against which persons are insured by the company in the course of carrying on business, being risks of a class in the case of which they consider that such arrangements are required;[81]

(vi) that there exists a ground on which the Treasury would be prohibited, by Insurance Companies Act 1982 ss.5(1B) or (1C), 7, 8 or 9, from issuing an authorisation with respect to the company if it were applied for;[82]

(vii) that it appears to the Treasury that there has been a substantial departure from any proposal or forecast submitted to them by

---

78 Insurance Companies Act 1982 s.37(2)(aa).

79 Insurance Companies Act 1982 s.37(2)(b).

80 Insurance Companies Act 1982 s.37(2)(c).

81 Insurance Companies Act 1982 s.37(2)(d).

82 Insurance Companies Act 1982 s.37(2)(e). Note the requirement in s.46 for the service of a notice where the exercise of the power is proposed on the ground that the Treasury would be prohibited from issuing an authorisation to the company because of the unfitness of a person for the position held by him.

the company in accordance with Insurance Companies Act 1982 s.5;[83]

(viii) that the company has ceased to be authorised to effect contracts of insurance, or contracts of a particular description, in an EFTA State where it has its head office, or an EEA State where it has, in accordance with Insurance Companies Act 1982 s.9(2), made a deposit;[84]

(ix) that the company is a Swiss general insurance company that has ceased to be authorised to effect contracts of insurance, or contracts of a particular description in Switzerland.[85]

The power conferred on the Treasury to require the production of documents[86]is exercisable on the ground that they consider its exercise to be desirable in the general interests of persons who are or may become policy holders of insurance companies to which Insurance Companies Act 1982 Part II applies, and references to a company include references to any body (whether incorporated or not) that appears to the Treasury to be an insurance company to which Part II of the Act applies.[87] The grounds of intervention at (iii) to (viii) above are without prejudice to the power to intervene at (i) above.[88] The powers in this paragraph except at (v) to (vii) above are also exercisable by the Secretary of State where the powers in 4.5.7 are vested in him concurrently with the Treasury.[89] The powers are exercisable in respect of a UK or non-EC company to obtain information to enable the Treasury to perform their functions under Insurance Companies Act 1982.

The Treasury's powers in relation to actuarial investigations[90] and to obtain information[91] are also exercisable, whether or not any of the grounds specified in 4.5.8 exist, in relation to **4.5.9**

(i) any body in respect of which the Treasury have issued an authorisation;

(ii) any insurance company to which Insurance Companies Act 1982

[83] Insurance Companies Act 1982 s.37(2)(f).
[84] Insurance Companies Act 1982 s.37(2)(g).
[85] Insurance Companies Act 1982 s.37(2)(h).
[86] Insurance Companies Act 1982 s.44(2) to (4).
[87] Insurance Companies Act 1982 s.37(4).
[88] Insurance Companies Act 1982 s.37(8).
[89] Insurance Companies Act 1982 s.37(9).
[90] Insurance Companies Act 1982 s.42.
[91] Insurance Companies Act 1982 s.44(1).

Part II applies in the case of which a person has become a controller within the meaning of s.96C(1)(c), (d) or (e); and

(iii) any UK company in a case where a person has notified an intention to acquire a notifiable holding in accordance with s.61A(1)[92]

if that power is exercised before the expiration of the period of five years beginning with the date on which the authorisation was issued, or that person became such a controller or acquired such a holding, as the case may be; but no requirement imposed by virtue of the exercise of this power shall continue in force after the expiration of the period of 10 years beginning with that date.[93]

The Treasury and Secretary of State, when exercising any power at 4.5.7 above, are required to state the ground on which they are exercising it or, if the Treasury are exercising it by virtue of the provision at 4.5.9 above, that they are so exercising it; but this requirement does not apply where the Treasury have given notice of their proposed exercise of powers because of the unfitness of certain persons.[94] 4.5.10

4.6 INVESTIGATIONS BY THOSE OTHER THAN THE SECRETARY OF STATE OR THE TREASURY

WHERE AN OFFENCE IS SUSPECTED 4.6.1

Specific provision is made in Companies Act 1985 for a criminal investigation where an offence is suspected.[95] Inspection or production of documents may be ordered.[96] This applies if, on an application to a judge of the High Court by the Director of Public Prosecutions, the Secretary of State or a chief officer of police, or in Scotland to one of the Lords Commissioners of Judiciary by the Lord Advocate, there is shown to be reasonable cause to believe that any person has, while an officer of a company, committed an offence in connection with the

92 Insurance Companies Act 1982 s.37(4A).
93 Insurance Companies Act 1982 s.37(5). Note also s.47(2) concerning the variation of requirements.
94 Insurance Companies Act 1982 s.37(7) and s.46.
95 See also Ch 11.
96 Companies Act 1985 s.721(2) and (3).

management of the company's affairs, and that evidence of the commission of the offence is to be found in any books or papers of or under the control of the company.[97] The decision of the High Court judge or Lord Commissioner of Justiciary is specifically said not to be appealable.[98]

THE FINANCIAL SERVICES AUTHORITY 4.6.2

As appears above,[99] certain of the Secretary of State's powers to appoint inspectors and to conduct investigations may be exercised concurrently by the Financial Services Authority, formerly the Securities and Investments Board.

4.7 ASSISTANCE TO OVERSEAS REGULATORY AUTHORITIES

The Secretary of State has the power to assist an overseas regulatory authority that has requested his assistance in connection with inquiries being carried out by it or on its behalf.[100] The Secretary of State's powers include the requirement that persons attend to answer questions and produce specified documents.[101] 4.7.1

An 'overseas regulatory authority' is an authority that, outside the United Kingdom, exercises 4.7.2

(i) any function corresponding to a function under Financial Services Act 1986 of a designated agency,[102] transferee body or competent authority (within the meaning of that Act), a function of the Secretary of State under Insurance Companies Act 1982, Companies Act 1985 or Financial Services Act 1986, or a

---

[97] Companies Act 1985 s.721(1).
[98] Companies Act 1985 s.721(4). See also *Re Racal Communications Ltd* [1981] AC 374.
[99] See 4.4.3, 4.4.5 and 4.5.4. See also Ch 11.
[100] Companies Act 1989 s.82(1).
[101] Companies Act 1989 s.83(2) and see 6.8 below.
[102] The Financial Services Authority is the designated agency.

function of the Financial Services Authority under Banking Act 1987,[103] or

(ii) any function in connection with the investigation of, or the enforcement of rules (whether or not having the force of law) relating to conduct of the kind prohibited by Criminal Justice Act 1993 Part V (insider dealing),[104] or

(iii) any function prescribed for the purposes of this subsection by order of the Secretary of State, being a function that, in the opinion of the Secretary of State, relates to companies or financial services.[105]

The Secretary of State must take into account various matters before exercising his power to assist an overseas regulatory authority. He shall not exercise the powers to assist conferred by Companies Act 1989 s.83 unless he is satisfied that the assistance requested by the overseas regulatory authority is for the purposes of its regulatory functions.[106] In deciding whether to exercise his powers the Secretary of State may take into account, in particular **4.7.3**

(i) whether corresponding assistance would be given in that country or territory to an authority exercising regulatory functions in the United Kingdom;[107]

(ii) whether the inquiries relate to the possible breach of a law, or other requirement, which has no close parallel in the United Kingdom or involves the assertion of a jurisdiction not recognised by the United Kingdom;[108]

(iii) the seriousness of the matter to which the inquiries relate, the importance to the inquiries of the information sought in the United Kingdom and whether the assistance could be obtained by other means;[109] and

---

[103] Companies Act 1989 s.82(2)(a).

[104] Companies Act 1989 s.82(2)(b).

[105] Companies Act 1989 s.82(2)(c). An order under (2) above shall be made by statutory instrument, which shall be subject to annulment in pursuance of a resolution of either House of Parliament. References in 4.7.2 and 4.7.3 to financial services include, in particular, investment business, insurance and banking — Companies Act 1989 s.82(7).

[106] Companies Act 1989 s.82(3). An authority's 'regulatory functions' means any functions falling within s.82(2) and any other functions relating to companies or financial services.

[107] Companies Act 1989 s.82(4)(a).

[108] Companies Act 1989 s.82(4)(b).

[109] Companies Act 1989 s.82(4)(c).

(iv) whether it is otherwise appropriate in the public interest to give the assistance sought.[110]

Before deciding whether to exercise his powers in a case where the overseas regulatory authority is a banking supervisor, the Secretary of State must consult the Financial Services Authority.[111] The Secretary of State may decline to exercise his powers unless the overseas regulatory authority undertakes to make such contribution towards the costs of their exercise as the Secretary of State considers appropriate.[112]

The Secretary of State may authorise an officer or any other competent person to exercise on his behalf all or any of the powers in relation to an overseas company.[113] Such authority may only be granted for the purpose of investigating the affairs, or any aspects of the affairs, of a person specified in the authority or a subject-matter so specified, and these must be a person or subject-matter that are the subject of the inquiries being carried out by or on behalf of the overseas regulatory authority.[114] Where the Secretary of State authorises a person other than one of his officers, that person shall make a report to the Secretary of State in such manner as he may require on the exercise of those powers and the results of exercising them.[115] **4.7.4**

In practice the requests are initially received by HM Treasury. One particular source of requests is the EC Insider Dealing Directive requiring Member States to cooperate in the investigation of suspected insider dealing offences. Further, specific Memoranda of Understanding exist with authorities in Australia, China, Hong Kong, Italy, Japan, The Netherlands, Sweden, Switzerland and the USA. A number of requests are dealt with without the need for the DTI to use formal powers or are dealt with by other regulators including the Financial Services Authority.[116] **4.7.5**

---

110 Companies Act 1989 s.82(4)(d).
111 Companies Act 1989 s.82(5). S.82(5) also provides that a 'banking supervisor' means an overseas regulatory authority with respect to which the Financial Services Authority has notified the Secretary of State, for the purposes of this subsection, that it exercises functions corresponding to those of the Authority under Banking Act 1987.
112 Companies Act 1989 s.82(6).
113 Companies Act 1989 s.84(1).
114 Companies Act 1989 s.84(2).
115 Companies Act 1989 s.84(5).
116 The powers under ss.82–84 were used in seven cases in 1994–1995, 13 cases in 1995–1996 and six cases in 1996–1997 (in each case the year running from April to March; see the DTI's annual reports on companies).

4.8 NATURAL JUSTICE AT THE STAGE OF INSTITUTING AN INVESTIGATION

In *Norwest Holst Ltd v Secretary of State for Trade*[117] the Secretary of State had ordered an inquiry under Companies Act 1948 s.165(b)(ii), a provision allowing the Board of Trade to appoint one or more inspectors to investigate the affairs of a company if it appeared to the Board that there were circumstances suggesting that persons concerned with its formation or the management of its affairs had in connection therewith been guilty of fraud, misfeasance or other misconduct towards it or towards its members. *Norwest Holst plc* argued that the principles of natural justice required that both sides should be heard before an inspector was appointed. However, the Court of Appeal held that so long as the minister acted in good faith there was no requirement to disclose the material he had before him or the reasons for the investigation.[118] It was pointed out that this was only the preliminary stage. Reference was made to the speech of Lord Reid in *Wiseman v Borneman*[119]who stated: 4.8.1

> Every public officer who has to decide whether to prosecute or raise proceedings ought first to decide whether there is a prima facie case, but no one supposes that justice requires that he should first seek the comments of the accused or the defendant on the material before him. So there is nothing inherently unjust in reaching such a decision in the absence of the other party.[120]

After quoting that passage, Ormrod LJ added:

> To my mind that passage applies precisely to the present case. The only conceivable distinction between the present case and that passage is the use of the words 'to prosecute or raise proceedings'. Here the raising of proceedings has taken the form of ordering an investigation by the inspectors at which the persons involved will have their opportunity of stating their case. That to my mind is a distinction without a difference.

The *Norwest Holst* approach also required that the burden was 'firmly and heavily upon the company in question to make out that the minister

[117] [1978] Ch 201.
[118] See Lord Denning MR at p. 224F–G.
[119] [1971] AC 297.
[120] At pp. 226H–227A.

is not acting bona fide in accordance with his powers under that section'.[121]

The proposition that the rules of natural justice do not require the Secretary of State to give his reasons for investigating a company and to seek the comments of the company concerned before directing an inquiry is based on the principle that those concerned will have an opportunity to put their case at a later stage of the investigation and is supported by more recent cases in other contexts. For example, in *R v Panel on Take-overs and Mergers ex p. FayedI*[122] it was held that the decision of the executive of the Panel on Take-overs and Mergers to institute disciplinary proceedings on the basis of a prima facie case, did not require the giving of notice.[123] A further justification for this approach in the case of investigating companies is that the exercise of powers to investigate is a disadvantage that corresponds to the great advantages enjoyed by limited companies.[124] **4.8.2**

The current approach to the application of the rules of natural justice in the context of an investigation with various stages was set out by Lord Slynn of Hadley in *Rees v Crane*[125]who stated[126] **4.8.3**

> It is clear from the English and Commonwealth decisions which have been cited that there are many situations in which natural justice does not require that a person must be told of the complaints made against him and given a chance to answer them at the particular stage in question. Essential features leading the courts to this conclusion have included the fact that the investigation is purely preliminary, that there will be a full chance adequately to deal with the complaints later, that the making of the inquiry without observing the audi alteram partem maxim is justified by urgency or administrative necessity, that no penalty or serious damage to reputation is inflicted by proceeding to the next stage without such preliminary notice, that the statutory scheme properly construed excludes such a right to know and to reply at the earlier stage.

---

121 Geoffrey Lane LJ at p. 230D–E.
122 (1993) 5 Admin LR 337.
123 See also *Moran v Lloyd's* [1981]1 Ll R 423; *Giles v The Law Society* (1996) 8 Admin LR 105.
124 See *Norwest Holst Ltd v Secretary of State for Trade* [1978] Ch 201 per Ormrod LJ at p. 227G–H and Geoffrey Lane LJ at p. 229H. Note also *Collier Garland (Properties) Pty Ltd, v O'Hair* [1964] NSWR 775 concerning an investigation into a company.
125 [1994] 2 AC 173.
126 At p. 191G–H.

The dicta of Lord Slynn were approved in *Huntley v A-G for Jamaica*.[127] In *Huntley*, Lord Woolf cited the above passage from *Rees* but pointed out that Lord Slynn had added that[128]'there is no absolute rule to this effect' and the court in considering whether the general practice should be followed 'should not be bound by rigid rules'. However, *Rees v Crane* concerned an appeal from the Court of Appeal of Trinidad and Tobago in connection with the exclusion of a High Court judge and *Huntley* was a case concerning Jamaican legislation introduced to review capital offences and sentences. Therefore, these cases were in a somewhat different context and, given that *Norwest Holst* is a reasoned decision at Court of Appeal level and that the rules of natural justice are applicable to the subsequent stages of an investigation,[129] the principle that the company concerned need not be given an opportunity to respond at the time of an investigation being instituted appears to represent the current law.

However, the gradual development in the circumstances where public bodies may be obliged to give reasons for decisions[130] may have weakened the force of the statement in the *Investigations Handbook* that **4.8.4**

> The Secretary of State does not disclose to a company the reasons for the appointment of inspectors and the courts have decided that he is under no legal obligation to do so (see *Norwest Holst* ....).[131]

In so far as any obligation to give reasons is the consequence of the rules of natural justice, the approach towards natural justice at the stage of instituting an investigation strongly suggests that there will be no obligation to give reasons for an investigation. However, in so far as it is for a wider purpose of, for example, enabling a court on judicial review to see whether an authority has made a decision lawfully and rationally, it is arguable that reasons should be given for the investigation

127 [1995] 2 AC 1. But note the approach in *Cornall v AB* [1995] 1VR 372 in which the court held that there was no obligation to afford procedural fairness in an investigation at a preliminary or administrative stage if, looking at the procedure in its entirety, the person to be affected had a fair and complete right to put his case.

128 At p. 15F.

129 See *Re Pergamon Press* [1971] Ch 388 and *Maxwell v DTI* [1974] QB 523 and Ch 7 generally.

130 See Wade and Forsyth, *Administrative Law* 7th edn (1994) at pp. 541–5, Craig *Administrative Law* 3rd edn (1994) at pp. 310–6, De Smith, Woolf and Jowell *Judicial Review of Administrative Action* 5th edn (1995) at pp. 457–73 and Fordham, *Judicial Review Handbook* 2nd edn (1997) at pp. 639–55.

131 Appendix B, para. 2.

even if the company has no right to make representations to the Secretary of State in relation to his decision to exercise powers to investigate the company.

4.9 CHALLENGING THE DECISION TO INVESTIGATE OR THE APPOINTMENT OF INSPECTORS

Where the decision to investigate is at the discretion of the Secretary of State the case will first be considered by the Companies Investigation Branches within the Company Law and Investigations Directorate. The DTI make an initial assessment of requests for an investigation to see whether or not they appear to require formal consideration or should be refused because they clearly do not come within the criteria for an investigation. The DTI will decide whether the relevant statutory criteria for an appointment are satisfied[132] and also whether a full scale investigation under Companies Act 1985 ss.431 and 432 is justified or whether, for example, s.447 is more appropriate. Requests that are formally considered by the DTI may, in practice, be refused because the complainant has an adequate civil remedy,[133] or because another body such as the police or the Serious Fraud Office has begun or is about to start an investigation.[134] The fact of these other investigations has led to a reduction in the number of investigations commenced under Companies Act 1985 ss.431 and 432.[135] The Company Law and Investigations Directorate aim to complete the consideration of requests for company investigations within an average of 48 days.[136] One aggrieved by the decision to (or not to) investigate a company may seek to challenge that decision. The possibility of challenge to the relevant decision by the Secretary of State arises because there are limits on his **4.9.1**

---

132 *Investigations Handbook* paras 29 and 30.

133 Cf the comments of Lord Denning MR in *Wallersteiner v Moir (No.2)* [1975] 1 All ER 849 at p. 856.

134 See the DTI's annual report, *Companies in 1996–97*, p. 10. Of the cases accepted for investigation in 1996–1997 (excluding enquiries on behalf of overseas regulators) the allegations included 51 fraudulent trading, 187 theft, 43 undischarged bankrupt/disqualified director managing a company, 51 unauthorised insurance business, 26 illegal pyramid selling schemes and 53 miscellaneous, making a total of 411 — *Companies in 1996–1997*, p. 13.

135 Note the statistics concerning requests for investigations at 2.6.2.

136 *Companies in 1996–1997*, p. 11.

discretion. The Secretary of State's decision to investigate a company or to appoint inspectors may be challenged by way of judicial review.[137] It is unclear whether it is possible also to allege invalidity in relation to the decision or appointment as a defence when facing sanctions for refusing to comply with, for example, provisions relating to supplying information.[138]

The decision in *Norwest Holst Ltd v Secretary of State for Trade*[139] that so long as the minister acts in good faith it is not incumbent upon him to disclose the material he has before him, or the reasons for the inquiry[140] relates to the issue of natural justice at the initial stage of an investigation and is not authority for the proposition that actions of the Secretary of State at that stage will never be inquired into unless it is shown that he is not acting in good faith.[141] Thus, the decision could be challenged if it were ultra vires[142] or were otherwise an abuse of power or irrational.[143] However, if the Secretary of State does not disclose the reasons for his decision to investigate, it will, as a practical matter, be difficult to challenge the exercise of his powers to instigate an investigation.[144] **4.9.2**

Much of the legislation empowers the Secretary of State to order an investigation merely if he is satisfied that certain circumstances exist. There have been cases in other contexts where the courts have taken a literal approach to this type of legislation and have declined to review the exercise of a minister's discretion where the minister himself was **4.9.3**

---

137 See *R v Secretary of State for Trade ex p. Perestrello* [1981] 1 QB 19.

138 See *Re London United Investments plc* [1992] BCLC 91 at pp. 99–104, in which Scott J referred to *Wandsworth LBC v Winder* [1985] AC 461 and held that if inspectors have been invalidly appointed (which on the facts of the case was not the position) the statutory obligation to assist the inspectors with their inquiries does not apply. The Court of Appeal, however, specifically chose not to decide the point — [1992] Ch 578 at p. 594D–E. Note also the discussion at 6.12 below.

139 [1978] Ch 201.

140 See 4.8.1 above.

141 See the comment of Lord Denning MR in *Norwest Holst* at p. 225D. Also see the explanation of *Norwest Holst* given by Woolf J in *R v Secretary of State for Trade ex p. Perestrello* [1981] 1 QB 19 and Griffiths LJ in *R v Commission for Racial Equality ex p. Hillingdon LBC* [1982] 1 QB 276 at p. 300B–D.

142 See the argument in *Re London United Investments Ltd* [1992] BCLC 91.

143 See Wade and Forsyth, *Administrative Law* 7th edn (1994) at pp. 347–459.

144 Also note the analogy with *R v Panel on Takeovers and Mergers ex p. Fayed* (1993) 5 Admin LR 337 where Steyn LJ observed that in the absence of evidence of fraud, corruption and mala fides, judicial review would not be allowed to probe a decision to charge individuals in criminal proceedings.

satisfied.[145] The more frequent approach, however, is for the courts to maintain some control. For example in *Secretary of State for Education and Science v Thameside Metropolitan Borough Council*[146] the House of Lords intervened and held that the Secretary of State had misdirected himself in law and misunderstood the meaning of 'unreasonable' in legislation, which empowered him to issue directions if he was 'satisfied ... that any local authority ... have acted or are proposing to act unreasonably'.[147]

Certain statutory provisions require that it must appear to the Secretary of State that there is 'good reason' before instituting investigations.[148] The *Investigations Handbook*[149] describes the requirement: **4.9.4**

> There is no statutory definition of 'good reason', but for the purposes of considering such investigations under [Companies Act 1985] section 447 it is taken to include grounds for suspicion of fraud, misfeasance, conduct unfairly prejudicial to shareholders or of failure to supply shareholders with information they may reasonably expect. The powers under [Financial Services Act 1986] section 105 are typically used where there is cause for disquiet or there is uncertainty which needs to be resolved about the way in which an investment business is being run.

In these circumstances it may be easier to show that the Secretary of State did not exercise his discretion properly when instigating the investigation than where the legislation is not limited by the requirement of 'good reason'. However, the difference is likely to be marginal only because, as explained at 4.9.3, the courts are likely to assume some control even where the legislation is not limited by 'good reason' and the concept of 'good reason' is itself a broad one, so the difficulty in successfully challenging a decision to investigate a company should not be underestimated.[150]

In addition to a challenge from a company being investigated, a challenge in the context of the initiation of an investigation may alternatively **4.9.5**

[145] See e.g. *Robinson v Minister of Town and Country Planning* [1947] KB 702 and Wade and Forsyth at pp. 444–5.
[146] [1977] AC 1014 discussed in Wade and Forsyth at pp. 447–9.
[147] See for an example *Kelsall (Inspector of Taxes) v Stipplechoice* [1995] STC 681.
[148] Companies Act 1985 s.447; Financial Services Act 1986 s.105.
[149] At para. 31.
[150] But note the approach of the Court of Appeal in *R v Commission for Racial Equality ex p. Hillingdon London Borough Council* [1982] 1 QB 276 in questioning the Commission's determination to embark upon a formal investigation under Race Relations Act 1976 s.48.

come from someone aggrieved at a decision by the Secretary of State not to commence an investigation. The aggrieved complainant will need to establish sufficient interest to bring judicial review proceedings[151] and then would be in a position to rely on the same grounds as any applicant in the converse case.[152] In practice, the courts will be slow to allow judicial review of a discretionary decision not to commence an investigation.[153]

4.10 POLICY ON ANNOUNCEMENTS

Investigations by inspectors appointed under Companies Act 1985 ss.431, 432 or 442 or Financial Services Act 1986 s.94 lead to a report that may be published and are announced when they are set up.[154] However, inspections may also be carried out under Companies Act 1985 s.432(2A) where the report is not for publication and it is not the DTI's practice to announce the appointment of inspectors in these circumstances.[155] **4.10.1**

It has never been the practice to announce Companies Act 1985 s.447 enquiries; 'public announcement would undermine the effectiveness of the enquiries and would unduly damage the business of the companies concerned'. However, the existence of such an enquiry might be confirmed if it had already been announced by the company concerned and no further prejudicial consequence was involved in such confirmation.[156] **4.10.2**

A policy similar to that relating to Companies Act 1985 s.447 is applied to investigations under Financial Services Act 1986 s.105, **4.10.3**

---

151 Rules of the Supreme Court Order 53 rule 3(7) and Supreme Court Act 1981 s.31(3)

152 See e.g. *R v Police Complaints Board ex p. Madden* [1983] 1 WLR 447; *R v General Council of the Bar ex p. Percival* [1991] 1 QB 212.

153 See e.g. *ex p. Percival;* note also *R v Director of Public Prosecutions ex p. C* (1995) 7 Admin LR 385 and *R v Director of Public Prosecutions ex p. Camelot* (1998) 10 Admin LR 93 in the analogous context of the decision to prosecute although in this latter context there is an even more restrictive approach towards judicial review where a successful application would effectively lead to someone being branded a criminal. Note also the possibility of a complaint to the Parliamentary Commissioner — see D. Foulkes *The Supervision of Companies – The Parliamentary Commissioner's Reports* [1974] JBL 23.

154 *Investigations Handbook* para. 35.

155 DTI's annual report *Companies in 1996–1997*, p. 14.

156 *Investigations Handbook* para. 35, *Companies in 1996–1997*, p. 13.

Companies Act 1989 s.83, Insurance Companies Act 1982 s.44(2) and Insolvency Act 1986 s.218.[157]

The Financial Services Authority normally announce Financial Services Act s.105 investigations by them if it is considered to be in the public interest to do so.[158] **4.10.4**

Reports of insider dealing investigations under Financial Services Act 1986 s.177 cannot be published and investigations are not normally announced or confirmed. 'However, announcement is considered if it is in the public interest: for example if public officials are thought to be involved; or there has already been publicity for an investigation and it is judged to be less damaging to the individuals or organisations concerned and appropriate in the circumstances if the existence of the investigation were to be acknowledged'.[159] Such announcements are very rare. **4.10.5**

Policy on announcement of enquiries under Companies Act 1985 s.446 is similar to that under Financial Services Act 1986 s.177, though reports of such enquiries may be published whereas reports of s.177 investigations cannot be published.[160] **4.10.6**

[157] *Investigations Handbook* para. 35.
[158] *Investigations Handbook* para. 35.
[159] *Investigations Handbook* para. 36.
[160] *Investigations Handbook* para. 37.

Chapter 5

THE CONDUCT OF INVESTIGATIONS

The starting point is each statutory regime and relevant caselaw, but general questions of confidentiality and procedural fairness are relevant to all statutory investigations. However, in addition to statute and caselaw the *Investigations Handbook*, in particular, provides some explanation as to how investigations are conducted and includes notes for the guidance of inspectors appointed under Companies Act 1985[1] and under Financial Services Act 1986 s.177.[2]

5.1 TIMESCALE

The *Investigations Handbook* notes that the 'Secretary of State attaches great importance to investigations being completed as quickly as possible consistent with a fair and thorough enquiry'.[3] The intention is that enquiries under Companies Act 1985 s.447 are normally concluded in a few weeks.[4] The Company Law and Investigations Directorate currently aims to complete investigations under s.447 within an average of 90 days. There is also an overall target of six months for the average time taken from the receipt of a request for an investigation to the completion of the statutory investigation. There is a distinct target of seven days for the start of an investigation where the public is directly at risk.[5] **5.1.1**

Outside inspectors appointed under Companies Act 1985 and Financial Services Act 1986 are required to give their investigation top priority and as much time as it proves to require.[6] Timescales for the completion of the inquiry are agreed with the DTI at an early stage and **5.1.2**

---

1 App B. This guidance applies to inspectors appointed under Companies Act 1985 ss.431, 432, 442 and 446.
2 App C.
3 Para. 45.
4 Para. 45.
5 DTI's annual report *Companies in 1996–1997*, pp. 12–3.
6 *Investigations Handbook* para. 45, App B, para. 5 and App C, para. 8.

the *Investigations Handbook* envisages regular meetings between inspectors and DTI officials to discuss the progress of the enquiry.[7] The Handbook notes that inspectors 'are made aware of the necessity to complete their investigations as quickly and effectively as possible'.[8] The guidance for inspectors requires that the inspector providing administrative support, often an accountant, should make available the resources required for the completion of investigations as quickly as possible.[9]

The guidance for inspectors appointed under Companies Act s.432 records that the length of time between the date of appointment and submission of the inspectors' report can affect the ability to take action or the utility of subsequent actions by the DTI or others 'and it is preferable that minor issues should be ignored if they would unduly prolong the enquiries and submission of a report'.[10] Similarly, in the context of inspectors appointed under Financial Services Act 1986 s.177 it is recorded that inspectors should ensure that there is no delay in the submission of a report, together with its supporting documents and that this is particularly important where their report is likely to result in the institution of criminal proceedings or where its contents are likely to require other follow-up action.[11] **5.1.3**

5.2 THE DTI'S INVOLVEMENT WITH INSPECTORS

The DTI's *Investigations Handbook* provides guidance to inspectors appointed under Companies Act 1985 and under Financial Services Act 1986 s.177.[12] It is for the inspectors to carry out their enquiries in such manner as they see fit but the DTI seek some information from them prior to the submission of the final report and also provide some back up.

The *Investigations Handbook* envisages the DTI providing a certain amount of information to the appointed inspectors. In the context of Companies Act 1985 it is recorded that the initial direction and thrust **5.2.1**

7 Para. 45, App B, para. 5 and App C, para. 9.
8 Para. 45.
9 App B para. 5, App C para. 8.
10 App B para. 5.
11 App C para. 9.
12 See Ch 3 and *Investigations Handbook* para. 38.

of an enquiry will be indicated to the inspectors by the terms of their appointment and information passed to them by the DTI on appointment. The Handbook adds that this will include any information on the basis of which the Secretary of State made his decision to appoint inspectors and any other relevant information he has.[13] This information may include information that has been given by informants to the DTI in confidence.[14]

The DTI do not involve themselves with the day to day conduct of inspections. They will, however, assist inspectors by facilitating access to public records 'and in such other ways as the circumstances of a particular case may permit'.[15] The DTI will assist inspectors to obtain technical or professional assistance where necessary and will introduce inspectors to those officers of public bodies such as the Bank of England, the Securities and Futures Authority, the Financial Services Authority (formerly the Securities and Investments Board) and the Panel on Takeovers and Mergers in addition to officials in other government departments who may be able to assist.[16] The *Investigations Handbook*, when considering investigations under Companies Act 1985 s.432, records that if an inspection involves an enquiry into the affairs of a life assurance office, inspectors will be advised about the possible advantages of discussing with the Government Actuary's Department the position and function of the appointed actuary.[17] In the context of inspections under Financial Services Act 1986 s.177, the Handbook invites inspectors to discuss problems concerning the interpretation of the Company Securities (Insider Dealing) Act 1985 (now replaced by the Criminal Justice Act 1993) and the Financial Services Act 1986.[18] 5.2.2

The DTI wish to keep themselves informed of the progress of investigations so arrange regular discussions with inspectors including inviting brief informal progress reports in advance of such discussion.[19] Inspectors are encouraged to discuss the progress of their investigation with the DTI at any time and to raise any matters on which they feel the DTI could provide guidance or assistance.[20] In the context of investigations under Financial Services Act 1986 s.177 the *Investigations Handbook* 5.2.3

[13] App B, para. 6.
[14] See 5.5.5.
[15] *Investigations Handbook* App B, para. 31; App C, para. 12.
[16] *Investigations Handbook* App B, para. 31.
[17] *Investigations Handbook* App B, para. 33.
[18] *Investigations Handbook* App C, para. 13.
[19] *Investigations Handbook* App B, para. 32; App C, para. 11.
[20] *Investigations Handbook* App B, para. 32; App C, para. 11.

encourages inspectors to keep the DTI informed of the progress, direction and likely cost of the investigation[21] and although there is no reference to the likely cost in the context of guidance to inspectors appointed under Companies Act 1985, the likely cost is a relevant issue here also.[22]

5.3 PROVISION OF INFORMATION TO THE SECRETARY OF STATE DURING THE COURSE OF AN INVESTIGATION

Both the Companies Act 1985 and the Financial Services Act 1986 envisage that inspectors may provide or be required to provide information to the Secretary of State during the course of an investigation rather than only submitting a final report at the end of an investigation.

Any inspectors appointed under Companies Act 1985 s.431 or s.432 **5.3.1**
or under Financial Services Act 1986 s.177 may, and if so directed by the Secretary of State shall, make interim reports to the Secretary of State, and on the conclusion of their investigation shall make a final report to him.[23] Similarly, any inspectors appointed under Financial Services Act 1986 s.94 or under the Open-ended Investment Companies (Investment Companies with Variable Capital) Regulations 1996 reg. 22 may, and if directed by the Secretary of State or the Financial Services Authority shall, make interim reports and on the conclusion of their investigation shall make a final report.[24]

Any inspectors appointed under Companies Act 1985 s.431 or s.432 **5.3.2**
may at any time and, if the Secretary of State directs them to do so, shall inform him of 'any matters coming to their knowledge as a result of their investigations'.[25] No guidance is given in the statute as to what is meant by 'any matters coming to their knowledge'. However, the *Investigations Handbook* states that such matters do not include judgments, evaluations or opinions formed by the inspectors in the course

[21] App C, para. 11.

[22] See also 5.4.2 below in relation to inspectors consulting the DTI.

[23] Companies Act 1985 s.437(1); Financial Services Act 1986 s.177(5).

[24] Financial Services Act 1986 s.94(8); Open-ended Investment Companies (Investment Companies with Variable Capital) Regulations 1996, reg. 24(2).

[25] Companies Act 1985 s.437(1A).

of their investigations.[26] In the Handbook the DTI specifically ask inspectors to advise them promptly of any matter that comes to light during the course of an inspection which suggests that an offence has been committed or that consideration may need to be given to regulatory or disciplinary action or that information may need to be disclosed to other investigators or to a competent authority.[27] Inspectors should note that proceedings for an offence under Companies Act 1985, which is triable only summarily, cannot be instituted more than 3 years after it has been committed.[28]

If it appears to the Secretary of State or the Financial Services Authority in connection with an investigation under Financial Services Act 1986 s.94 or the Open-ended Investment Companies (Investment Companies with Variable Capital) Regulations 1996 reg. 22 that matters have come to light in the case of an inspector's investigation that suggest that a criminal offence has been committed, and those matters have been referred to the appropriate prosecuting authority, the Secretary of State or Financial Services Authority may direct the inspectors to take no further steps in the investigation or to take only such further steps as are specified in the direction.[29] When an investigation is the subject of such a direction the inspector shall make a final report to the Secretary of State or Financial Services Authority only where they direct him to do so.[30] **5.3.3**

5.4 SCOPE OF THE INQUIRY

Inspectors will not be permitted to investigate matters that fall outside the scope of their appointment.[31] In addition, in order to avoid unnecessary delay in the production of a report, it may be appropriate for them to ignore minor matters[32] or limit the scope of their enquiry rather than investigating everything that is technically within the terms of their **5.4.1**

---

26 *Investigations Handbook* App B, para. 43.
27 See *Investigations Handbook* App B, para. 44 and Companies Act 1985 s.449.
28 Companies Act 1985 s.731.
29 Financial Services Act 1986 s.94(8A); Open-ended Investment Companies (Investment Companies with Variable Capital) Regulations 1996, reg. 24(3).
30 Financial Services Act 1986 s.94(8B); Open-ended Investment Companies (Investment Companies with Variable Capital) Regulations 1996, reg. 24(4).
31 See *Re London United Investments Plc* [1992] BCLC 91 and [1992] Ch 578 and 4.9.1 above.
32 *Investigations Handbook* App B, para. 5.

minute of appointment.[33] Indeed, in the context of inspectors appointed under Financial Services Act 1986 s.177 the *Investigations Handbook* informs inspectors that they should concentrate their attention on the possible contraventions suggested by the documents that were the basis for their appointment and supplied to them by the DTI together with any other promising lines of enquiry that emerge from their investigations.[34]

5.4.2 The circumstances may, however, be such that the inspectors believe they need greater powers for the purposes of their investigation. In such circumstances inspectors appointed under Companies Act 1985 may also investigate the affairs of another body corporate that is or at any relevant time has been the company's subsidiary or holding company, or a subsidiary of its holding company or a holding company of its subsidiary.[35] When exercising these powers the inspectors shall report on the affairs of the other body corporate so far as they consider that the results of their investigation of its affairs are relevant to the affairs of the first company.[36] In the case of inspectors appointed under Financial Services Act 1986 s.177, the *Investigations Handbook* informs inspectors that they should consult the DTI as soon as possible if they believe the DTI should consider (i) appointing them (or others) to investigate suspected contraventions of the provisions now in Part V of the Criminal Justice Act 1993 not covered by their initial appointment, (ii) authorising enquiries under Companies Act 1985 ss.432, 442 or 447, (iii) informing the police or regulatory or enforcement authorities, whether in the UK or abroad, of matters which have come to their attention, and (iv) taking any other enforcement action.[37]

5.4.3 One particular difficulty that may face inspectors is the effective territorial limits of their jurisdiction, since there is no obligation upon anyone resident outside the United Kingdom to assist them. It may be that a witness will cooperate voluntarily and the investigators may be able to proceed accordingly, involving any overseas authority as appropriate. If, however, the witness will not cooperate voluntarily, then unless the state where the witness concerned is located has provisions analogous to Companies Act 1989 ss.83 and 84, which the DTI or inspectors can invoke to require cooperation, the inspectors will be

[33] *Investigations Handbook* App C, para. 7.
[34] *Investigations Handbook* App C, para. 7.
[35] Companies Act 1985 s.433(1).
[36] Companies Act 1985 s.433(1).
[37] *Investigations Handbook* App C, para. 10.

reliant on obtaining the evidence from another source. There is no reason why, however, provided that the appropriate rules of natural justice are followed in the preparation of the report, the report should not draw appropriate relevant inferences about the actions of anyone who has refused to cooperate. The *Investigations Handbook* suggests that if inspectors wish to obtain evidence or information from a person overseas or that it would be desirable to conduct interviews with witnesses overseas they should first consult the DTI Company Law and Investigations Directorate.[38]

5.5 CONFIDENTIALITY

There are provisions governing when inspectors and others may and may not disclose information received during the course of an investigation.[39] However, those carrying out an inquiry will not be able to assure the witnesses or those providing documents that the evidence will be kept confidential.[40] This is because the investigators may wish to be able to show documents or transcripts to other witnesses or may wish to refer to the evidence in the final report.[41] Further, the evidence may be released to certain other authorities pursuant to statutory powers.[42] Indeed, the guidance to inspectors notes that whilst inspectors may tell witnesses that they are conducting their inquiry in private, it would be wrong to lead witnesses to think that any evidence they give will remain completely confidential and inspectors should not give any witness any assurance about confidentiality without consulting the DTI.[43] **5.5.1**

Those requested to provide information, whether it be documentary or oral, should consider whether the provision of information conflicts with obligations of confidence owed to others. There are some compulsory powers contained in the legislation by which those carrying out investigations can require the production of documents or the giving of oral evidence.[44] Thus a person receiving a request to divulge **5.5.2**

38 *Investigations Handbook* App B, para. 16; App C, para. 49.
39 See Ch 8.
40 See *Investigations Handbook* App B, para. 22.
41 This reflects the approach in *R v Monopolies and Mergers Commission ex p. Elders IXL Ltd* [1987] 1 WLR 1221.
42 See Ch 8.
43 App B, para. 22.
44 See Ch 6. But note the restrictions in relation to banking secrecy at 6.1 to 6.8 and legal professional privilege at 6.9.

confidential information, e.g. an auditor with accounting records, should require the person making the request to supply evidence of his authorisation and check that the information falls within that which can be obtained pursuant to the compulsory powers. Where the information cannot be the subject of compulsory powers, for example, in the case of Companies Act 1985 because it does not technically relate to the affairs of the company, the person requested to supply the information will need to consider whether to comply with a request for assistance and, before divulging the information, will need to obtain the consent of those to whom he owes the obligation of confidence. However, the consents may not be forthcoming or, alternatively, the witness may not be in a position to seek such consents where, for example, obtaining a consent would involve the witness tipping off someone who the investigators wanted to remain unaware of the investigation at that stage. In extreme circumstances, the law recognises that the public interest in maintaining professional duties of confidence may be overridden where there is held to be a stronger public interest in disclosure.[45] However, the circumstances in a statutory investigation into a company where the public interest in voluntary disclosure outweighs the professional duty of confidence are likely to arise only very rarely. The prudent professional should therefore usually ensure that any disclosure is pursuant to the investigators' compulsory powers or that relevant consents have been obtained rather than disclosing material voluntarily and then seeking to justify the disclosure on public interest grounds. In circumstances where the conflict remains unresolved it will ultimately be for the witness to make an application to court seeking a declaration as to whether he should or should not disclose the information rather than risk having sanctions imposed by a court for non-compliance with investigators validly (as it turns out) exercising a compulsory power. In circumstances where there is a concern about disclosing the fact of an investigation to someone to whom an overriding obligation of confidence may be owed it would be appropriate, in the first instance, to make such an application on an ex parte basis.[46]

Although the legislation concerning company investigations does not specifically deal with the point, those carrying out an investigation may 5.5.3

[45] See e.g. *Tournier v National Provincial and Union Bank of England* [1924] 1 KB 461 (banker), *Price Waterhouse (a firm) v BCCI Holdings (Luxembourg) SA and Others* [1992] BCLC 583 (accountant), *Parry-Jones v Law Society* [1969] 1 Ch 1 (solicitor) and *W v Egdell* [1990] 1 Ch 359 (doctor).

[46] Note also the issue of disclosure to investigators in the face of an injunction preventing disclosure — see 6. 11.4 below and *A v B Bank* [1993] QB 311.

quite properly wish the fact of the investigation, or their approach to a particular witness or their pursuit of a particular line of enquiry to be kept confidential. They may wish, for example, to prevent one witness from tipping off another witness who has not yet been seen by the investigators and who may be tempted to change his evidence in the light of knowing what was said by the first witness. To this end the investigators might seek an undertaking of confidentiality from the person to whom they address their request for assistance. However, although investigators can require witnesses to give assistance in connection with the investigation there is no specific power to require undertakings from witnesses and, in any event, undertakings will be subject to normal public law limits, such as whether the request falls within the ambit of the purposes for which an undertaking may be required. For example, an undertaking that requires a witness not to disclose any information that is discussed at an interview would normally plainly be going too far, since on a strict reading this would cover matters such as the witness's own personal details.[47] The ambit of undertakings sought from witnesses should therefore be carefully focused on the mischief that they are quite properly designed to avoid, i.e. they should be sufficient to ensure that information is not disclosed to third parties in such a way as would inhibit or frustrate the proper and efficient conduct of the investigation. They should not be more far-reaching than is necessary. If a witness refuses to sign an undertaking there is no mechanism specifically enabling the investigators to requiere the witness to sign but this does mean the witness can avoid questions of confidentiality. Particularly in view of the sanctions for wrongful disclosure of information,[48] the witness should certainly not simply ignore the investigators' wishes in respect of confidentiality even if he believes them to be too far-reaching.[49]

One particular issue in relation to confidentiality is how it links in to the rules of natural justice in respect of someone who may be criticised in a report.[50] Those carrying out an investigation should be particularly cautious about seeking a restrictive undertaking where there is a possibility that the witness may face criticism in the report. This is because those facing criticism in a report must, in accordance with the rules of natural justice, know at least the gist of the allegations against them and have an adequate opportunity of responding. It may be that what witnesses should **5.5.4**

[47] Note, however, that there may be special circumstances where investigators asking questions in relation to certain personal details may properly wish the line of questioning to be kept confidential.

[48] See Ch 8.

[49] Note that undertakings may also be sought from a witness's professional advisers.

[50] See Ch 7.

keep confidential when they first give their evidence, may be disclosed to an extent at the stage of the witnesses responding to provisional criticism. An example is the extent to which it is appropriate to seek to prevent one employee of an organisation from discussing his evidence with another employee. The employees may need to be in a position to discuss their evidence in order to rebut criticism of themselves or of their employer. A similar concern arises in respect of a witness seeking to defend himself by adducing expert evidence. If, for example, an auditor or banker is facing criticism he may wish to be able to put forward expert evidence to show that his course of action was reasonable and should not be the subject of criticism.[51] Where the investigators are faced with such a request they should consider how to permit the witness a proper opportunity of rebutting provisional criticisms.[52]

A related concern is where informants give information to the DTI or inspectors. In such circumstances it may be necessary to conceal the source of the information during the inquiry so as to avoid any breach of confidence or to protect an informant against retaliatory action. It may be possible to obtain the same information from the books and papers of the company or another source so that other witnesses can be asked questions about the relevant matter without revealing the original source of the information.[53] The *Investigations Handbook* provides guidance for inspectors who propose to carry out an interview with an informant.[54] Inspectors are informed that they should discuss any such proposed interview with the DTI beforehand. So far as possible they should avoid identifying an informant as such in the formal transcript and it is advisable to discuss the point before the interview with the informant. To emphasise the DTI's concern in this respect, the guidance records that neither the informant's identify nor any information that might enable others to identify him should be disclosed to anyone else without prior discussion with the DTI. The concern to protect the identify of informants links in to the question of natural justice towards those who may be criticised in any report if, to rebut a criticism, witnesses wish to be able to challenge the credibility of the source of the evidence against them.[55] **5.5.5**

---

[51] See e.g. *R v Kent Police Authority ex p. Godden* [1971] 2 QB 662.

[52] Note that another reason for a witness wishing to disclose information is where he or she may feel the need to respond to issues that arise outside the investigation, e.g. press enquiries, but care needs to be taken not to breach any requirements of confidentiality.

[53] *Investigations Handbook* App B, para. 6; App C, para. 20.

[54] App B, para. 7; App C, para. 21.

[55] See Ch 7. See also the cases in Fordham *Judicial Review Handbook* 2nd edn (1997) at pp. 627–8. The identify of informants may also be subject to public interest immunity — see 8.8. below.

5.6 PROCEDURAL FAIRNESS

When carrying out a statutory investigation the investigators are obliged to act in accordance with the principles of natural justice. This emerges from the decisions of the Court of Appeal in *Re. Pergamon Press Ltd*[56] and *Maxwell v DTI*[57] and although this is most obviously relevant when the investigators come to prepare their report,[58] procedural fairness and other public law obligations may arise at other stages, e.g. the ambit of requests for evidence.[59] **5.6.1**

5.7 LEGAL REPRESENTATION

There is no general principle of administrative law that a witness to a statutory inquiry is automatically entitled to legal representation.[60] The general principles of fairness must, however, be observed.[61] In practice the *Investigations Handbook* notes (in the context of guidance for inspectors appointed under Companies Act 1985) that some witnesses attend interviews accompanied by their legal advisers.[62] The guidance records that there can be no question of a lawyer answering questions on behalf of the witness but that legal advisers 'may, on occasion, be able to assist by intervening on such matters as the clarity of a question or on the implications of non-compliance with the inspectors' requirements' and should be given an opportunity to question their clients if they wish to do so and to make representations. It is a matter for debate whether the limited nature of the rights accorded to lawyers is appropriate.[63] **5.7.1**

---

56 [1971] Ch 388.

57 [1974] QB 523.

58 See Ch 7, although certain matters discussed in relation to the preparation of a report at 7.2 to 7.7 are also relevant to the exercise of gathering evidence, e.g. the need to put points to witnesses at 7.2.7.

59 See 6.11 to 6.13.

60 See e.g. *R v Board of Visitors of HM Prison, The Maze ex p. Hone* [1988] AC 379; *R v Secretary of State for the Home Department ex p. Tarrant* [1985] 1 QB 251.

61 Note De Smith, Woolf and Jowell, *Judicial Review of Administrative Action* 5th edn (1995) at pp. 450–4; Fordham *Judicial Review Handbook* 2nd edn (1997) at pp. 628–9.

62 App B, para. 19.

63 See, e.g. the Royal Commission on Tribunals of Inquiry (Cmnd. 3121 (1966) (the Salmon Report), Sir Richard Scott *Procedures at Inquiries: the Duty to be Fair* (1995) 111 LQR 596 and Lord Howe *Procedure at the Scott Inquiry* [1996] PL 445 at pp. 449–55.

5.7.2 The *Investigations Handbook* also gives guidance to inspectors on how to deal with any possible conflict of interest where legal advisers are acting for more than one witness.[64] The guidance records that it is desirable for legal advisers to identify at the outset of an interview all the witnesses for whom they are acting and for this to be recorded on the transcript. The guidance notes that in some cases inspectors may feel that they should ask the legal advisers to consider whether their representation of different clients involves a conflict of interest and in exceptional instances inspectors may feel that the investigation would be prejudiced if the same legal adviser were to act for more than one client. It may often be convenient for the same lawyer to act for the company and all the directors and employees, save those who need independent representation, but the Handbook notes that particular care may be needed where the legal adviser acts for both a witness and his employer.[65] The Handbook suggests that in some cases the concern may be met by the adviser undertaking not to use the information in one interview when advising another witness. However, this will give the adviser a difficulty given his professional obligations to act in his client's best interests, which will involve using all relevant information. Thus, the lawyer would need to ensure that all his clients were content for such an undertaking to be given. The Handbook concludes that in other instances inspectors may feel the risk of prejudice is such that they should tell the legal adviser and his clients that one or more of the clients should seek separate legal representation. Where the inspectors have real grounds for concern that, by having the same lawyer, information will be passed between witnesses, which will prejudice the investigation, e.g. a witness will change his evidence in the light of the other witness's evidence, then it may be appropriate for the investigators effectively to insist on separate representation. However, where the concern is the broader one that a lawyer may have a conflict of interest, the investigators should be particularly cautious about intervening in cases where a witness wishes to have a lawyer, given the public importance attached to the issue of instructing an appropriate lawyer.[66]

64 App B, para. 20.

65 A difficulty could also arise if, for example, a solicitor was a director of a company under investigation but additionally sought to advise the company and employees generally in relation to the investigation.

66 E.g. *R v Legal Aid Board ex p. Donn & Co (a firm)* [1996] 3 All ER 1.

Chapter 6

OBTAINING EVIDENCE

Investigating companies have the power to compel the production of documents and to require witnesses to give oral evidence subject to certain limits and there are sanctions for non-compliance.

6.1 INSPECTORS APPOINTED UNDER COMPANIES ACT 1985

When inspectors are appointed under Companies Act 1985 ss.431 or 432 it is the duty of all officers and agents of the company, and of all officers and agents of any body corporate whose affairs are investigated under s.433(1) to produce to the inspectors all documents of or relating to the company or, as the case may be, the other body corporate that are in their custody or power.[1] The officers and agents also have a duty to attend before the inspectors when required to do so.[2] The duty further requires the officers and agents to give the inspectors all assistance in connection with the investigation which they are reasonably able to give[3] (and this duty is separate from the duties in relation to documents and to attend before the inspectors). **6.1.1**

If the inspectors consider that an officer or agent of the company or any other body corporate, or any other person, is or may be in possession of information relating to a matter that they believe to be relevant to the investigation they may require him to produce to them any documents in his custody or power relating to that matter,[4] to attend before them,[5] and separately from the inspectors' specific powers in relation to documents and requiring witnesses to attend before them, may require the officers or agents to otherwise give them all assistance in connection with the investigation that they are reasonably able to give.[6] **6.1.2**

1 Companies Act 1985 s.434(1)(a).
2 Companies Act 1985 s.434(1)(b).
3 Companies Act 1985 s.434(1)(c).
4 Companies Act 1985 s.434(2)(a).
5 Companies Act 1985 s.434(2)(b).
6 Companies Act 1985 s.434(2)(c).

The reference to officers or agents in 6.1.1 and 6.1.2 includes past as well as present officers or agents; and 'agents' includes bankers, solicitors[7] and auditors whether or not officers of the company or other body corporate.[8] 'Documents' in 6.1.1 and 6.1.2 includes information recorded in any form and, in relation to information recorded otherwise than in legible form, the power to require its production includes the power to require the production of a copy of the information in legible form.[9] **6.1.3**

An answer given by a person to a question put to him in exercise of the powers at 6.1.1 or 6.1.2 may be used in evidence against him.[10] **6.1.4**

The obligations of officers and agents of the company under investigation and of any body corporate whose affairs are investigated under s.433 are more extensive than the obligations upon others. This is because they have the proactive duty to produce all documents relating to the company or body corporate that are in their possession or power, to attend before the inspectors when required to do so, and to give the inspectors all assistance in connection with the investigation that they are reasonably able to give rather than simply responding when required to do so by the inspectors. In practice, however, the obligations upon officers and agents may not particularly differ from the obligations upon others since the performance of their duties by officers and agents will inevitably follow the requirements of the inspectors. **6.1.5**

The provisions at 6.1.1 to 6.1.4 apply to investigations conducted under Companies Act 1985 s.442 with the necessary modifications of references to the affairs of the company (or to those of any other body corporate)[11] save that the provisions apply to: **6.1.6**

(i) all persons who are or have been, or whom the inspector has reasonable cause to believe to be or have been, financially interested in the success or failure or the apparent success or failure of the company or any other body corporate whose membership is investigated with that of the company, or able to control or materially influence its policy (including persons concerned only on behalf of others); and

7 Although see the issue of legal professional privilege at 6.9 below.
8 Companies Act 1985 s.434(4).
9 Companies Act 1985 s.434(6).
10 Companies Act 1985 s.434(5).
11 Companies Act 1985 s.443(1).

(ii) any other person whom the inspector has reasonable cause to believe possesses information relevant to the investigation,

as they apply in relation to officers and agents of the company or the other body corporate.[12]

The provisions at 6.1.1. to 6.1.4 also apply to investigations of share dealings conducted under Companies Act 1985 s.446 with the substitution, for references to any other body whose affairs are investigated under s.442(1), of a reference to any other body corporate that is, or has at any relevant time been the company's subsidiary or holding company, or a subsidiary of its holding company[13] and they apply: **6.1.7**

(i) to any individual who is an authorised person within the meaning of Financial Services Act 1986;
(ii) to any individual who holds a permission granted under Financial Services Act 1986, Schedule 1;
(iii) to any officer (whether past or present) of a body corporate, who is such an authorised person or holds such a permission;
(iv) to any partner (whether past or present) in a partnership, who is such an authorised person or holds such a permission; and
(v) to any member of the governing body or officer (in either case whether past or present) of an unincorporated association, who is such an authorised person or holds such a permission;

as they apply to officers of the company or of the other body corporate.[14]

If any person fails to comply with the obligations at 6.1.1 to 6.1.7 above the inspectors may certify the fact in writing to the court.[15] The court may enquire into the case and after hearing any witnesses who may be produced against or on behalf of the alleged offender and any statement that may be offered in defence, the court may punish the offender in the like manner as if he had been guilty of contempt of court.[16] This may involve a fine and/or imprisonment. The DTI ask inspectors who are considering certifying a witness to raise the matter with them (and it is the practice of inspectors to instruct lawyers within the Treasury Solicitor's Department on their behalf).[17] In *McClelland,* **6.1.8**

---

12 Companies Act 1985 s.443(2).
13 Companies Act 1985 s.446(3).
14 Companies Act 1985 s.446(4).
15 Companies Act 1985 s.436(1).
16 Companies Act 1985 s.436(3). See 6.11 below.
17 *Investigations Handbook* App B, para. 13.

Pope & Langley Ltd v Howard[18] the House of Lords explained (in the context of the forerunner provision — Companies Act 1967 s.167(3)) that a witness may refuse to answer questions and, if he does so, the question whether he did so properly is a matter for the court, if the inspectors so refer the matter, and not for the inspectors.[19] In *Re Westminster Property Group plc*[20] Vinelott J was faced with an application where a person had initially refused to answer questions but who had sworn an affidavit providing answers prior to the hearing of the application. Vinelott J held[21] that the court's duty was to decide whether any and, if any, what punishment should be imposed. The court had no jurisdiction to investigate the ownership of shares that were the subject of the investigation in question. He held that in many, if not most, cases the court could decide what punishment, if any, should be imposed while the investigation was still pending but, in the present case, the acceptance of the witness's explanation for his failure to answer the inspectors' questions necessarily involved acceptance of his explanation of the source of the moneys used to purchase certain shares. Vinelott J therefore decided to stand over the application until after the inspectors had completed their investigation and had reported to the Secretary of State.

6.2 INFORMATION AS TO THOSE INTERESTED IN SHARES ETC. AND RESTRICTIONS ON SHARES

If the Secretary of State decides to investigate the shares in or debentures **6.2.1** of a company pursuant to Companies Act 1985 s.444[22] he may require any person whom he has reasonable cause to believe to have or to be able to obtain any information as to the present and past interests in those shares or debentures and the names and addresses of the persons interested, and of any persons who act or have acted on their behalf in relation to the shares or debentures to give any such information to the Secretary of State.[23]

---

18 (Note) [1968] 1 All ER 569.
19 See also *Investigations Handbook*, App B, para. 21.
20 (1984) 1 BCC 241.
21 At p. 247.
22 See 4.5 above.
23 Companies Act 1985 s.444(1).

6.2.2 A person who fails to give information required of him under 6.2.1,[24] or who in giving such information makes any statement that he knows to be false in a material particular, or recklessly makes any statement that is false in a material particular, is liable to imprisonment or a fine or both.[25]

6.2.3 If in connection with an investigation under Companies Act 1985 ss.442 or 444 it appears to the Secretary of State that there is difficulty in finding out the relevant facts about any shares or debentures (whether issued or to be issued), he may, by order, direct that the shares or debentures shall until further order be subject to the restrictions at 6.2.4 to 6.2.9 below.[26] If the Secretary of State is satisfied that such an order may unfairly affect the rights of third parties in respect of shares (but not debentures) then the Secretary of State, for the purpose of protecting such rights and subject to such terms as he thinks fit, may direct that such acts by such persons or such descriptions of persons and for such purposes as may be set out in the order, shall not constitute a breach of the restrictions at 6.2.4 to 6.2.9.[27] As appears from *Re FH Lloyd Holdings plc*[28] orders may be imposed on foreigners.

6.2.4 Companies Act 1985, Part XV[29] sets out the statutory regime for orders imposing restrictions on shares.[30] So long as shares are directed to be subject to various restrictions the following provisions apply.

(i) Any transfer of those shares or, in the case of unissued shares,

24 And see 4.5 above.

25 Companies Act 1985 s.444(3).

26 Companies Act 1985 s.445(1). When considering Companies Act 1985 s.212 and s.216 which may also trigger restrictions on shares, Vinelott J in *Re Lonrho plc* [1988] BCLC 53 held that the wording of the statute had the effect that if there was sufficient ground for suspecting that a person had failed to give information about certain shares an order could be made in respect of other shares in relation to which his interest had already been disclosed. It is unclear whether s.445 would be interpreted in the same way.

27 Companies Act 1985 s.445(1A). Companies Act 1989 s.135 provides that the Secretary of State may by regulations made by statutory instrument make such amendments to the provisions of the Act relating to orders imposing restrictions on shares as appear to him necessary or expedient for enabling orders to be made in a form protecting the rights of third parties; with respect to the circumstances in which restrictions may be relaxed or removed; and with respect to the making of interim orders by a court. The current wording in s.445(1A) and in certain parts of Part XV was consequent upon amendments made by Companies (Disclosure of Interests in Shares) (Orders imposing restrictions on shares) Regulations 1991 (SI 1991/1646).

28 (1985) 1 BCC 99, 402.

29 Ss 454–9.

30 The same regime applies to restrictions imposed under Companies Act 1985 s.210 and s.216 concerning a failure to disclose interests in shares in addition to restrictions under s.445. (For the principles governing the exercise of the court's discretion to make an order under s.212 and to discharge it see, e.g. *Re Ricardo Group plc* [1989] BCLC 566, (*No.2*) [1989] BCLC 766 and (*No.3*) [1989] BCLC 771.)

any transfer of the right to be issued with them, and any issue of them, is void.[31] Any agreement to transfer the shares, or in the case of unissued shares, the right to be issued with them is void except such agreement or right as may be exercised under the terms of directions made by the Secretary of State under 6.2.3 or by the court under the provisions relating specifically to the rights of third parties at 6.2.6.[32]

(ii) No voting rights are exercisable in respect of the shares.[33]

(iii) No further shares shall be issued in right of them or in pursuance of any offer made to their holder.[34]

(iv) Except in a liquidation, no payment shall be made of any sums due from the company on the shares, whether in respect of capital or otherwise.[35]

Where shares are subject to the restrictions at (iii) or (iv), an agreement to transfer any right to be issued with other shares in right of those shares, or to receive any payment on them (otherwise than in a liquidation) is void except such agreement or right as may be made or exercised under the terms of directions made by the Secretary of State under 6.2.3, or the court under the provisions relating specifically to the rights of third parties at 6.2.6, or an agreement to transfer any such right on the transfer of the shares on the making of an order under 6.2.6(ii).[36]

An attempted evasion of the restrictions may be punished by a fine. Subject to the terms of any directions made under 6.2.3 or 6.2.6 a person is liable if he: **6.2.5**

(i) exercises or purports to exercise any right to dispose of any shares, which, to his knowledge, are for the time being subject to the restrictions, or of any right to be issued with any such shares;[37] or

[31] Companies Act 1985 s.454(1)(a).
[32] Companies Act 1985 s.454(2).
[33] Companies Act 1985 s.454(1)(b).
[34] Companies Act 1985 s.454(1)(c).
[35] Companies Act 1985 s.454(1)(d).
[36] Companies Act 1985 s.454(3).
[37] Companies Act 1985 s.455(1)(a).

(ii) votes in respect of any such shares (whether as holder or proxy), or appoints a proxy to vote in respect of them;[38] or

(iii) being the holder of any such shares, fails to notify of their being subject to those restrictions any person whom he does not know to be aware of that fact but does know to be entitled (apart from the restrictions) to vote in respect of those shares whether as holder or as proxy;[39] or

(iv) being the holder of any such shares, or being entitled to any right to be issued with other shares in right of them, or to receive any payment on them (otherwise than in a liquidation), enters into any agreement that is void under 6.2.4.[40]

Subject to the terms of any directions made at 6.2.3 or 6.2.6, if shares in a company are issued in contravention of the restrictions, the company and every officer of it who is in default is liable to a fine.[41]

Where shares in a company are, by order, subject to restrictions an application may be made to the court for an order that the restrictions be removed.[42] An application to court must be made by originating motion.[43] In addition, where the order imposing the restrictions unfairly affects the rights of third parties in respect of those shares then the court, for the purpose of protecting such rights and subject to such terms as it thinks fit, may direct that such acts by such persons or descriptions of persons and for such purposes, as may be set out in the order, shall not constitute a breach of the restrictions.[44] The application to court may be made by any person aggrieved.[45] Save where the order is made because the restrictions unfairly affect the rights of third parties, an order of the court or the Secretary of State lifting the restrictions may only be made if: **6.2.6**

(i) the court or (as the case may be) the Secretary of State is satisfied that the relevant facts about the shares have been disclosed

[38] Companies Act 1985 s.455(1)(b).

[39] Companies Act 1985 s.455(1)(c).

[40] Companies Act 1985 s.455(1)(d).

[41] Companies Act 1985 s.455(2). A prosecution in England may only be brought by or with the consent of the Secretary of State — s.455(3) and s.732.

[42] Companies Act 1985 s.456(1). For example in *House of Fraser plc v Midland Bank (Overseas) Nominees Ltd* (1985) 1 BCC 99, 526 the court found that there was no good reason to prevent the registration of transfers by purchasers where the purchasers concerned had acquired an interest before the restriction was imposed.

[43] Rules of the Supreme Court, Order 102 r.3.

[44] Companies Act 1985 s.456(1A).

[45] Companies Act 1985 s.456(2).

to the company and no unfair advantage has occurred to any person as a result of the earlier failure to make that disclosure,[46] or

(ii) the shares are to be transferred for valuable consideration and the court or (as the case may be) the Secretary of State approves the transfer.[47]

In *Re Geers Gross plc*[48] the Court of Appeal, when rejecting an application for restrictions to be lifted to allow a sale of shares, noted that the company would be less able to determine the beneficial ownership of shares and whether there had been a breach of an agreement not to acquire more than 20% of the company's share capital. The Court of Appeal held that the applicants' failure to disclose the identity of the owners of the shares was sufficient reason for the court to refuse to give approval to the sale of the shares, notwithstanding that innocent purchasers of the shares might be deprived of the benefit of ownership for an indefinite period. *Re Geers Gross plc* was a case where an order had been obtained under Companies Act 1985 s.216 rather than under s.445 and was decided before Companies Act 1985 Part XV was amended to take greater account of the rights of innocent third parties, but it appears that a transfer might be refused if the court believes that to permit the transfer will make it more likely that information as to share ownership will not be forthcoming.

Where shares are subject to restrictions the court may, on an application by the Secretary of State or the company, order the shares to be sold, subject to the court's approval as to the sale, and may also direct that the shares cease to be subject to the restrictions.[49] Where such an order has been made, an application may be made to the court by the Secretary of State, the company, the person appointed by or in pursuance of the order to effect the sale or any person interested in the shares, **6.2.7**

---

46 Companies Act 1985 s.456(3)(a).

47 Companies Act 1985 s.456(3)(b) was amended by Companies Act 1989 to allow an order to be made where there is a share exchange, thereby reversing the result of *Re Westminster Property Group plc* [1985] 2 All ER 426 in which the Court of Appeal had held that an order could not be made because the then current legislation (Companies Act 1948 s.174(3A)) required the shares 'to be sold'.

48 [1988] 1 All ER 224.

49 Companies Act 1985 s.456(4). As appears from *Re Westminster Property Group plc* above, at p. 431j–2c the word 'sold' denotes an exchange of property for cash and not for any other form of property.

for such further order relating to the sale or transfer as the court thinks fit.[50]

An order (whether of the Secretary of State or the court) directing that shares shall cease to be subject to restrictions, if it is expressed to be made with a view to permitting a transfer of the shares, or made under 6.2.7, may continue the restrictions at 6.2.4(iii) and (iv) in whole or in part so far as they relate to any right acquired or offer made before the transfer.[51] In *Re Ashbourne Investments Ltd*[52] the Secretary of State had appointed inspectors to investigate the affairs of a company. The investigation disclosed that a number of shares were registered in the names of agents who were acting for a Swiss bank that had purchased the shares on behalf of a customer. The bank, acting under Swiss law, declined to give the customer's name without his consent and this consent was withheld. The Secretary of State therefore ordered that the shares were to be subject to restrictions. Templeman J held that the court was entitled to make a partial release so as to permit the shares to be transferred on a takeover and that the purchase price would be paid by the transferee to the company but then frozen such that the company would not pay the sum due from it to the transferor. The limitations on the power to lift restrictions at 6.2.6(i) and (ii) do not apply to an order directing that shares shall cease to be subject to any restrictions that have been continued in force in relation to those shares under this provision.[53] **6.2.8**

Where shares are sold pursuant to a court order under 6.2.7 the proceeds of sale, less the costs of the sale, are to be paid into court for the benefit of the persons who are beneficially interested in the shares, and any such person may apply to the court for the whole or part of those proceeds to be paid to him.[54] On such application the court will, subject to what follows concerning the applicant's costs, order the payment to the applicant of the whole of the proceeds of sale together with any interest thereon or, if any other person had a beneficial interest in the shares at the time of their sale, such proportion of those proceeds and interest as is equal to the proportion which the value of the applicant's interest in the shares bears to the total value of the shares.[55] **6.2.9**

50 Companies Act 1985 s.456(5).
51 Companies Act 1985 s.456(6).
52 [1978] 2 All ER 418.
53 Companies Act 1985 s.456(7).
54 Companies Act 1985 s.457(1).
55 Companies Act 1985 s.457(2).

On granting an order under 6.2.7 the court may order the applicant's costs to be paid out of the proceeds of sale; and if that order is made, the applicant is entitled to payment of his costs out of those proceeds before any person interested in the shares in question receives any part of those proceeds.[56]

6.3 REQUISITION AND SEIZURE OF BOOKS AND PAPERS

The Secretary of State may at any time, if he thinks there is good reason to do so: **6.3.1**

(i) give directions to a company requiring it, at such time and place as may be specified, to produce such documents as may be specified;[57] and

(ii) authorise an officer of his or any other competent person (on producing (if so required) evidence of his authority), to require a company to produce to him, the officer or other person forthwith any documents that he, the officer or other person, may specify.[58]

There is a like power to require production of documents from any person who appears to the Secretary of State or an officer or other authorised person to be in possession of them but where any such person claims a lien on documents produced by him, the production is without prejudice to the lien.[59] This power to require the production of documents includes the power to take copies of them or extracts from them, and to require the person who produces them or any other person who is a present or past officer of, or is or was at any time employed by the company in question to provide an explanation of any of them.[60] If the documents are not produced there is power to require the person who was required to produce them to state, to the best of his knowledge and belief, where they are.[61] 'Documents' in this paragraph bears the same meaning as at 6.1.3.

[56] Companies Act 1985 s.457(3).
[57] Companies Act 1985 s.447(2).
[58] Companies Act 1985 s.447(3).
[59] Companies Act 1985 s.447(4).
[60] Companies Act 1985 s.447(5)(a).
[61] Companies Act 1985 s.447(5)(b).

If there is failure to comply with an obligation at 6.3.1 the company or other person on whom the requirement was imposed is guilty of an offence and is liable to a fine.[62] Where a person is charged with an offence in respect of a requirement to produce any documents it is a defence to prove that they were not in his possession or under his control and that it was not reasonably practicable for him to comply with the requirement.[63] However, a statement made by a person in compliance with such a requirement may be used in evidence against him.[64] A person who, in purported compliance with a requirement to provide an explanation or make a statement, provides or makes an explanation or statement that he knows to be false in a material particular, or recklessly provides or makes a false explanation or statement, is guilty of an offence and liable to imprisonment or a fine, or both.[65] **6.3.2**

The Secretary of State shall not under the provision at 6.3.1 require or authorise an officer or other person to require the production by a person carrying on the business of banking of a document relating to the affairs of his customer unless either it appears to the Secretary of State that it is necessary to investigate the affairs of the first-mentioned person, or the customer is a person on whom a requirement has been imposed under the provision at 6.3.1 or under Insurance Companies Act 1982 s.44(2) to (4). **6.3.3**

There is a statutory power to enter premises to seize documents. A justice of the peace may issue a warrant if satisfied on information on oath given by or on behalf of the Secretary of State, or by a person appointed or authorised to exercise powers under Companies Act 1985 Part XIV: **6.3.4**

(i) that there are reasonable grounds for believing that there are on any premises documents whose production has been required under Part XIV and that have not been produced in compliance with this requirement;[66] or

---

62 Companies Act 1985 s.447(6). Note the provisions of Companies Act 1985 ss.730–4 which apply to the offence and Schedule 24, which specifies that on summary prosecution the maximum fine is the statutory maximum, i.e. £5,000, and on indictment there is no limit.

63 Companies Act 1985 s.447(7).

64 Companies Act 1985 s.447(8).

65 Companies Act 1985 s.451. The provisions of Companies Act 1985 ss.730–4 apply to this offence. By virtue of Sch 24 on summary prosecution the maximum sentence is six months imprisonment and/or the statutory maximum fine, i.e. £5,000, and on indictment the maximum is two years imprisonment and/or an unlimited fine.

66 Companies Act 1985 s.448(1).

(ii) that there are reasonable grounds for believing that an offence has been committed for which the penalty on conviction on indictment is imprisonment for a term of not less than two years, and that there are on any premises documents relating to whether the offence has been committed; that the Secretary of State, or the person so appointed or authorised, has power to require the production of the documents under Part XIV; and that there are reasonable grounds for believing that if production was so required the documents would not be produced but would be removed from the premises, hidden, tampered with or destroyed.[67]

'Document' in this context includes information recorded in any form.

A warrant under 6.3.4 authorises police constables together with any other person named in the warrant to enter the premises specified in the information, using such force as is reasonably necessary for the purpose:[68] **6.3.5**

(i) to search the premises and take possession of any documents appearing to be such documents as are mentioned in 6.3.2 or to take, in relation to any such documents, any other steps that may appear to be necessary for preserving them or preventing interference with them;[69]
(ii) to take copies of any such documents;[70] and
(iii) to require any person named in the warrant to provide an explanation of them or to state where they may be found.[71]

If in the case of a warrant under (ii) at 6.3.4 above the justice of the peace is satisfied on information on oath that there are reasonable grounds for believing that there are also on the premises other documents relevant to this investigation, these foregoing actions may also be taken in relation to those documents.[72]

A warrant under 6.3.4 continues in force until the end of the period of one month beginning with the day on which it is issued.[73] Documents of which possession is taken may be retained for three months, **6.3.6**

67 Companies Act 1985 s.448(2).
68 Companies Act 1985 s.448(3)(a).
69 Companies Act 1985 s.448(3)(b).
70 Companies Act 1985 s.448(3)(c).
71 Companies Act 1985 s.448(3)(d).
72 Companies Act 1985 s.448(4).
73 Companies Act 1985 s.448(5).

and if within three months proceedings to which the documents are relevant are commenced against any person for any criminal offence they may be kept until the conclusion of those proceedings.[74]

Anyone who intentionally obstructs the exercise of any rights conferred by such a warrant or fails, if named in the warrant, without reasonable excuse to provide an explanation of the documents or state where they may be found, is guilty of an offence and liable to a fine.[75] 6.3.7

6.4 DESTRUCTION, MUTILATION OR FALSIFICATION OF DOCUMENTS

In addition to the above general provisions concerning the obstruction of or a failure to comply with requirements imposed by investigators, there is an additional provision affecting officers of companies. An officer of a company or an insurance company to which Part II of the Insurance Companies Act 1982 applies who 6.4.1

(i) destroys, mutilates or falsifies, or is privy to the destruction, mutilation or falsification of a document affecting or relating to the company's property or affairs, or
(ii) makes, or is privy to the making of a false entry in such a document,

is guilty of an offence, unless he proves he had no intention to conceal the state of affairs of the company or to defeat the law.[76] Such a person who fraudulently either parts with, alters or makes an omission in any such document or is privy to fraudulent parting with, fraudulent altering or fraudulent making of an omission in any such document, is guilty of an offence[77] and is liable to imprisonment or a fine or both.[78]

---

74 Companies Act 1985 s.448(6).
75 Companies Act 1985 s.448(7). The provisions of Companies Act 1985 ss.730–4 apply to this offence and note Sch 24, which specifies that on summary prosecution the maximum fine is the statutory maximum, i.e. £5,000, and on indictment there is no limit.
76 Companies Act 1985 s.450(1).
77 Companies Act 1985 s.450(2).
78 Companies Act 1985 s.450(3) and (4). The provisions of Companies Act 1985 ss. 730–4 apply. Pursuant to Sch 24 on summary prosecution the maximum sentence is six months imprisonment and/or the statutory maximum fine, i.e. currently £5,000, whilst on indictment the maximum sentence is seven years' imprisonment and/or an unlimited fine.

6.5 INSPECTORS APPOINTED UNDER THE FINANCIAL SERVICES LEGISLATION

The provisions at 6.1.1 to 6.1.4 above apply to investigations concerning collective investment schemes carried out under Financial Services Act s.94[79] save that for any reference to a company there is substituted a reference to the scheme under investigation by virtue of s.94, and any reference to an officer of the company includes a reference to any director or the manager, trustee or operator of the scheme. Where a person claims a lien on a document, its production under s.94 is without prejudice to the lien.[80] **6.5.1**

A person cannot be required under Financial Services Act s.94 to disclose any information or produce any document in respect of which he owes an obligation of confidence by carrying on a banking business, unless the person to whom the obligation of confidence is owed consents or the requirement was authorised by the Secretary of State.[81] However, this restriction does not apply where the person owing the obligation of confidence or the person to whom it is owed is either (i) the manager, operator or trustee of the scheme under investigation, or (ii) a manager, operator or trustee whose own affairs are under investigation.[82] **6.5.2**

Turning to investigations into alleged insider dealing, if inspectors appointed under Financial Services Act 1986 consider that any person is or may be able to give information concerning an offence under Part V of the Criminal Justice Act 1993 they may require that person to produce to them any documents in his possession or under his control, which appear to them to be relevant to the investigation,[83] to attend before them[84] and to otherwise give them all assistance in connection with the investigation that he is reasonably able to give[85] and it shall be the duty of that person to comply with that requirement.[86] Where a person claims a lien on a document its production under Financial **6.5.3**

[79] Financial Services Act 1986 s.94(3).
[80] Financial Services Act 1986 s.94(6).
[81] Financial Services Act 1986 s.94(7).
[82] Financial Services Act 1986 s.94(7A).
[83] Financial Services Act 1986 s.177(3)(a).
[84] Financial Services Act 1986 s.177(3)(b).
[85] Financial Services Act 1986 s.177(3)(c).
[86] Financial Services Act 1986 s.177(3).

Services Act 1986 s.177 is without prejudice to his lien. For the purpose of 6.5.3 and 6.5.4 below 'document' includes information recorded in any form; and in relation to information recorded otherwise than in legible form the power to require its production includes power to require the production of a copy of the information in legible form.[87]

An inspector may examine on oath any person who he considers is or may be able to give information concerning any offence under Part V of the Criminal Justice Act 1993.[88] A statement made by a person in compliance with a requirement imposed on him by virtue of the provisions at 6.5.1 to 6.5.4 may be used in evidence against him.[89] **6.5.4**

A person shall not under s.177 be required to disclose any information or produce any document in respect of which he owes an obligation of confidence by virtue of carrying on a banking business unless the person to whom the obligation of confidence is owed consents, or the requirement was authorised by the Secretary of State.[90] The DTI *Investigations Handbook* states that any request to the Secretary of State for such authorisation should be made in a letter signed by both inspectors, and if the Secretary of State agrees to such a request the inspectors will be sent a letter granting authorisation that may be produced to the bank in support of the requirement from the inspectors.[91] **6.5.5**

If any person refuses to comply with a request under s.177(3) the inspectors may certify that fact in writing to the court and the court may inquire into the case.[92] If after hearing any witness, who may be produced against or on behalf of the alleged offender and any statement that may be offered in defence, the court is satisfied that he did without reasonable excuse refuse to comply with such a request, the court may (i) punish him in like manner as if he had been guilty of contempt of court, or (ii) direct that the Secretary of State may exercise his powers under Financial Services Act 1986 s.178 in respect of him, and the court may give a direction notwithstanding that the offender is not within the jurisdiction of the court if the court is satisfied that he **6.5.6**

87 Financial Services Act 1986 s.177(10).
88 Financial Services Act 1986 s.177(4).
89 Financial Services Act 1986 s.177(6).
90 Financial Services Act 1986 s.177(8).
91 *Investigations Handbook*, App C, para. 37.
92 Financial Services Act 1986 s.178(1).

was notified of his right to appear before the court and of the powers available under s.177.[93]

Where the court gives a direction under 6.5.6 in respect of an authorised person[94] the Secretary of State may serve a notice on him: 6.5.7

(i) cancelling any authorisation of his to carry on investment business after the expiry of a specified period after the service of the notice;[95]
(ii) disqualifying him from becoming authorised to carry on investment business after the expiry of a specified period;[96]
(iii) restricting any authorisation of his in respect of investment business during a specified period to the performance of contracts entered into before the notice comes into force;[97]
(iv) prohibiting him from entering into transactions of a specified kind or entering into them except in specified circumstances or to a specified extent;[98]
(v) prohibiting him from soliciting business from persons of a specified kind or otherwise than from such persons;[99] or
(vi) prohibiting him from carrying on business in a specified manner or otherwise than in a specified manner.[100]

The specified period in 6.5.7 (i) and (iii) above is such as appears to the Secretary of State reasonable to enable the person on whom the notice is served to complete the performance of any contracts entered into before the notice comes into force, and to terminate such of them as are of a continuing nature.[101]

A notice served on a person under 6.5.7 may be revoked at any time by the Secretary of State by serving a revocation notice on him; and the Secretary of State shall revoke such a notice if it appears to him that he has agreed to comply with the relevant request or answer the relevant question.[102] The revocation of such a notice as is mentioned in 6.5.7 (i) 6.5.8

[93] Financial Services Act 1986 s.178(2). Note *Re An Inquiry under the Company Securities (Insider Dealing) Act 1985* [1988] AC 660. See 6.11.
[94] See Financial Services Act 1986 s.3 and Ch III.
[95] Financial Services Act 1986 s.178(3)(a).
[96] Financial Services Act 1986 s.178(3)(b).
[97] Financial Services Act 1986 s.178(3)(c).
[98] Financial Services Act 1986 s.178(3)(d).
[99] Financial Services Act 1986 s.178(3)(e).
[100] Financial Services Act 1986 s.178(3)(f).
[101] Financial Services Act 1986 s.178(4).
[102] Financial Services Act 1986 s.178(7).

above shall not have the effect of reviving the authorisation cancelled by the notice except where the person would (apart from the notice) at the time of the revocation be an authorised person by virtue of his membership of a recognised self-regulating organisation or certification by a recognised professional body; but nothing in this provision shall prevent any person who has been subject to such a notice from again becoming authorised after the revocation of the notice.[103]

If it appears to the Secretary of State: **6.5.9**

(i) that a person on whom he serves a notice under 6.5.7 above is an authorised person by virtue of an authorisation granted by a designated agency or by virtue of membership of a recognised self-regulating organisation or certification by a recognised professional body;[104] or
(ii) that a person on whom he serves a revocation notice under 6.5.8 above was such an authorised person at the time that the notice, which is being revoked, was served,[105]

he must serve a copy of the notice on that agency, organisation or body.[106]

Where the court gives a direction under 6.5.6 above in the case of an unauthorised person the Secretary of State may direct that any authorised person who knowingly transacts investment business of a specified kind, or in specified circumstances or to a specified extent, with or on behalf of that unauthorised person shall be treated as having contravened rules made under Financial Services Act 1986 Part I Chapter V or, in the case of a person who is an authorised person by virtue of his membership of a recognised self-regulating organisation or certification by a recognised professional body, the rules of that organisation or body.[107] **6.5.10**

A person shall not be treated for the purposes of 6.5.6 as having a reasonable excuse for refusing to comply with a request or answer a question in a case where the offence or suspected offence being investigated relates to dealings by him on the instructions or for the account of another person, by reason that at the time of the refusal: **6.5.11**

103 Financial Services Act 1986 s.178(8).
104 Financial Services Act 1986 s.178(9)(a).
105 Financial Services Act 1986 s.178(9)(b).
106 Financial Services Act 1986 s.178(9)(b).
107 Financial Services Act 1986 s.178(5).

(i) he did not know the identity of that other person;[108] or
(ii) he was subject to the law of a country or territory outside the United Kingdom that prohibited him from disclosing information relating to the dealing without the consent of that other person, if he might have obtained that consent or obtained exemption from that law.[109]

The functions of the Secretary of State under 6.5.6 to 6.5.10 may be exercised concurrently by the Secretary of State and the Financial Services Authority subject in the latter case to such conditions as the Secretary of State may from time to time impose.[110] **6.5.12**

A justice of the peace may issue a warrant if satisfied on information on oath given by or on behalf of the Secretary of State, or by a person appointed or authorised to exercise powers under Financial Services Act ss.94, 106 or 177, that there are reasonable grounds for believing that there are on any premises documents (a term defined to include information in any form[111]) whose production has been required under ss.94, 105 or 177 and that have not been produced in compliance with the requirement.[112] A warrant authorises a constable, together with any other person named in it and any other constables **6.5.13**

(i) to enter the premises specified in the information, using such force as is reasonably necessary for the purpose;
(ii) to search the premises and take possession of any documents appearing to be such documents as are mentioned above or to take, in relation to any such documents, any other steps that may appear to be necessary for preserving them or preventing interference with them;
(iii) to take copies of any such documents; and
(iv) to require any person named in the warrant to provide an explanation of them or to state where they may be found.[113]

Such a warrant shall continue in force until the end of the period of one month beginning with the day on which it is issued.[114] Any documents

[108] Financial Services Act 1986 s.178(6)(a).
[109] Financial Services Act 1986 s.178(6)(b).
[110] See Financial Services Act 1986 s.178(10) and the Financial Services Act 1986 (Delegation) Order 1987 (SI 1987/942). Note also Banking Coordination (Second Council Directive) Regulations 1992 (SI 1992/3218) reg. 55 and Sch 9 para. 39.
[111] Financial Services Act 1986 s.199(9).
[112] Financial Services Act 1986 s.199(2).
[113] Financial Services Act 1986 s.199(3).
[114] Financial Services Act 1986 s.199(4).

of which possession is taken under this provision may be retained for a period of three months; or if within that period proceedings to which the documents are relevant are commenced against any person for any criminal offence, until the conclusion of those proceedings.[115] The functions under this provision may be transferred to the Financial Services Authority (previously the Securities and Investments Board) but the transfer may be subject to a reservation that the functions are exercisable concurrently by the Secretary of State.[116]

Any person who intentionally obstructs the exercise of any rights conferred by a warrant issued under 6.5.13 or fails without reasonable excuse to comply with any requirement imposed in accordance with 6.5.13 (iv) above shall be guilty of an offence and liable on conviction on indictment, to a fine and on summary conviction, to a fine not exceeding the statutory maximum.[117] Proceedings in England and Wales may not be instituted except by or with the consent of the Secretary of State or the Director of Public Prosecutions.[118] The function of instituting proceedings may be transferred to the Financial Services Authority but the transfer may be subject to a reservation that the function is exercisable concurrently by the Secretary of State.[119] **6.5.14**

Where an offence committed by a body corporate is proved to have been committed with the consent or connivance of, or to be attributable to, any neglect on the part of, any director, manager, secretary or other similar officer of the body corporate, or any person who was purporting to act in any such capacity, or a controller of the body corporate, he, as well as the body corporate, shall be guilty of that offence and liable to be proceeded against and punished accordingly.[120] Where the affairs of a body corporate are managed by the members this provision shall apply in relation to the acts and defaults of a member in connection with his functions of management as if he were a director of the body corporate.[121] Where a partnership is guilty of an offence every **6.5.15**

[115] Financial Services Act 1986 s.199(5).
[116] Financial Services Act 1986 s.199(7).
[117] Financial Services Act 1986 s.199(6). The statutory maximum is currently £5,000. (Note also Financial Services Act 1986 s.200(1) concerning the provision of false or misleading information.)
[118] Financial Services Act 1986 s.201(1).
[119] Financial Services Act 1986 s.201(4).
[120] Financial Services Act 1986 s.202(1).
[121] Financial Services Act 1986 s.202(2).

partner, other than a partner who is proved to have been ignorant of or to have attempted to prevent the commission of the offence, shall also be guilty of that offence and be liable to be proceeded against and punished accordingly.[122] Where an unincorporated association (other than a partnership) is guilty of an offence every officer of the association who is bound to fulfil any duty of which the breach is the offence, or if there is no such officer, every member of the governing body other than a member who is proved to have been ignorant of or to have attempted to prevent the commission of the offence, shall also be guilty of the offence and be liable to be proceeded against and punished accordingly.[123]

Summary proceedings for an offence may, without prejudice to any jurisdiction exercisable apart from this provision, be taken against any body corporate or unincorporated association at any place at which it has a place of business and against an individual at any place where he is for the time being.[124] Proceedings for an offence alleged to have been committed by an unincorporated association shall be brought in the name of the association (and not in that of any of its members) and for the purposes of any such proceedings any rules of court relating to the service of documents shall have effect as if the association were a corporation.[125] Criminal Justice Act 1925 s.33 and Magistrates' Courts Act 1980 schedule 3 (procedure on charge of offence against a corporation) apply in a case in which an unincorporated association is charged in England and Wales with an offence in like manner as they apply in the case of a corporation.[126] A fine imposed on an unincorporated association on its conviction of an offence under Financial Services Act 1986 must be paid out of the funds of the association.[127] **6.5.16**

The powers at 6.1.1 to 6.1.4 apply to investigations carried out under the Open-ended Investment Companies (Investment Companies with Variable Capital) Regulations 1996[128] reg. 22(3) but with the following modifications. For any reference to a company there is substituted a **6.5.17**

[122] Financial Services Act 1986 s.202(3).
[123] Financial Services Act 1986 s.202(4).
[124] Financial Services Act 1986 s.203(1).
[125] Financial Services Act 1986 s.203(2).
[126] Financial Services Act 1986 s.203(3). Note Financial Services Act 1986 s.203(4) and (5) for provisions relating to the prosecution of unincorporated associations in Scotland and Northern Ireland.
[127] Financial Services Act 1986 s.203(6).
[128] SI 1996/2827.

reference to the company, director or depositary under investigation.[129] Any reference to an officer of the company includes any director of the company or depositary under investigation or where the director under investigation is a body corporate, any director of that body.[130] For any reference to any other body corporate whose affairs are investigated under Companies Act 1985 s.433(1) there is substituted a reference to any other investment company with variable capital or collective investment scheme under investigation.[131] Any reference to an officer of such a body corporate includes the depositary and directors of an investment company with variable capital or the trustee and operator of a collective investment scheme.[132] The same powers also apply in relation to a shadow director of an investment company with a variable capital as they do in relation to a director of such a company.[133]

A person cannot be required to disclose any information or produce any document in respect of which he owes an obligation of confidence by virtue of carrying on the business of banking unless the person to whom the obligation of confidence is owed consents to the disclosure or production, or the making of the requirement was authorised by the Secretary of State or Financial Services Authority.[134] However, this restriction does not apply where the person owing the obligation of confidence or to whom it is owed is either (i) an investment company with variable capital, director or shadow director,[135] or depositary under investigation,[136] or (ii) an investment company with variable capital or any other person under investigation.[137] Where a person claims a lien on a document its production is without prejudice to the lien.[138] **6.5.18**

6.6 OTHER INVESTIGATIONS UNDER FINANCIAL SERVICES ACT 1986

Where the Secretary of State or the Financial Services Authority conduct an investigation under Financial Services Act 1986 s.105 they may **6.6.1**

[129] As defined in reg. 22(1); reg. 22(4)(a).
[130] Reg. 22(4)(b).
[131] As defined in reg. 22(2); reg. 22(4)(c).
[132] Reg. 22(4)(d).
[133] Reg. 22(5).
[134] Reg. 23(2).
[135] Reg. 22(5).
[136] Reg. 22(1).
[137] Reg. 22(2); reg. 23(3).
[138] Reg. 24(1).

require the person whose affairs are to be investigated ('the person under investigation') or any connected person to attend before them at a specified time and place and answer questions or otherwise furnish information with respect to any matter relevant to the investigation.[139] They may require the person under investigation or any other person to produce at a specified time and place any specified documents that appear to the Secretary of State or the Financial Services Authority to relate to any matter relevant to the investigation, and

(i) if any such documents are produced copies or extracts may be taken from them and the person producing them or any connected person[140] may be required to produce an explanation of any of them; and
(ii) if any such documents are not produced, the person who was required to produce them may be required to state to the best of his knowledge and belief where they are.[141]

A statement by a person in compliance with a requirement imposed by virtue of this provision may be used in evidence against him.[142] Any person who without reasonable excuse fails to comply with a requirement imposed on him under this provision is guilty of an offence and liable on summary conviction to imprisonment for a term not exceeding six months or to a fine not exceeding the fifth level on the standard scale or both.[143]

For the purpose of the provision at 6.6.1, 'documents' includes information recorded in any form and, in relation to information recorded otherwise than in legible form, the power to require its production includes the power to require the production of a copy of the information in legible form.[144] 'Connected person' in relation to any other person in 6.6.1 means: **6.6.2**

(i) any person who is or was that other person's partner, employee, agent, appointed representative, banker, auditor or solicitor; and
(ii) where the other person is a body corporate, any person who is or was a director, secretary or controller of that body corporate

[139] Financial Services Act 1986 s.105(3).
[140] See 6.6.2 below.
[141] Financial Services Act 1986 s.105(4).
[142] Financial Services Act 1986 s.105(5).
[143] Financial Services Act 1986 s.105(10). Level 5 on the standard scale is currently £5,000.
[144] Financial Services Act 1986 s.105(9).

or of another body corporate of which it is or was a subsidiary; and

(iii) where the other person is an unincorporated association, any person who is or was a member of the governing body or an officer or controller of the association; and

(iv) where the other person is an appointed representative, any person who is or was his principal; and

(v) where the other person is the person under investigation (being a body corporate), any related company of that body corporate and any person who is a connected person in relation to that company.[145]

'Related company' in relation to a person under investigation (being a body corporate), means any other body corporate, which is or at any material time was:

(i) a holding company or subsidiary of the person under investigation;

(ii) a subsidiary of a holding company of that person; or

(iii) a holding company of a subsidiary of that person, and whose affairs it is in the Secretary of State's opinion necessary to investigate. [146]

Where the Secretary of State authorises an officer of his or any other competent person to exercise on his behalf the powers conferred by s.105[147] a person shall not by virtue of such an authority be required to disclose any information or produce any documents in respect of which he owes an obligation of confidence by virtue of carrying on a banking business unless (i) he is the person under investigation or a related company,[148] (ii) the person to whom the obligation of confidence is owed is the person under investigation or a related company, (iii) the person to whom the obligation of confidence is owed consents to the disclosure or production, or (iv) the imposing on him of a requirement with respect to such information or documents has been specifically authorised by the Secretary of State.[149] The provisions at 6.5.13 and 6.5.14 above 6.6.3

145 Financial Services Act 1986 s.105(9).
146 Financial Services Act 1986 s.105(9).
147 Financial Services Act 1986 s.106(1).
148 'Documents' and 'related company' have the same meaning as 6.6.2 above.
149 Financial Services Act 1986 s.106(2A).

apply to the exercise of powers under s.106 and the provisions at 6.5.13 are exercisable by the Financial Services Authority.[150]

6.7 INSURANCE COMPANIES

The Treasury or Secretary of State may require a company to furnish them, at specified times or intervals, with information about specified matters being, if they so require, information verified in a specified manner.[151] The Treasury or Secretary of State may require a company to produce at such time and place as they may specify such documents as they may specify, or authorise any person on producing (if required to do so) evidence of his authority, to require a company to produce to him forthwith any documents which that person may specify.[152] The Treasury, Secretary of State or authorised person have the like power to require the production of those documents from any person who appears to them to be in possession of such documents, but where any person from whom such production is required claims a lien on documents produced by him, the production shall be without prejudice to the lien.[153] This power to require a company or other person to produce documents includes power **6.7.1**

(i) if documents are produced to take copies of them or extracts from them and to require that person or any other person who is a present or past director, controller or auditor of, or is or was at any time employed by the company in question, to provide an explanation of any of them,[154] and
(ii) if the documents are not produced to require the person who was required to produce them to state, to the best of his knowledge and belief, where they are.[155]

Any person authorised by the Treasury or the Secretary of State may, upon producing (if required) evidence of his authority, enter any premises

[150] Financial Services Act 1986 s.199(7) and Financial Services Act 1986 (Delegation) Order 1987 (SI 1987/942).
[151] Insurance Companies Act 1982 s.44(1).
[152] Insurance Companies Act 1982 s.44(2). The reference to a company in this provision includes a controller, officer, agent or employee of a UK or non-EC company and specified related undertakings — see Insurance Companies Act 1982 s.44(2A).
[153] Insurance Companies Act 1982 s.44(3).
[154] Insurance Companies Act 1982 s.44(4)(a).
[155] Insurance Companies Act 1982 s.44(4)(b). For the purpose of this provision 'documents' bears the same meaning as in 6.6.2 above — Insurance Companies Act 1982 s.44(6).

occupied by a company or undertaking upon which or a person upon whom a requirement has been imposed for the purpose of obtaining the information or documents required to be furnished or produced and exercising the powers under this provision.[156] A statement made by a person in compliance with a requirement imposed by virtue of this provision may be used in evidence against him.[157]

A justice of the peace may issue a warrant if satisfied on information on oath given by or on behalf of the Treasury or Secretary of State, or by a person authorised to exercise powers under 6.7.1: **6.7.2**

(i) that there are reasonable grounds for believing that there are on any premises documents whose production has been required under 6.7.1 and that have not been produced in compliance with the requirement;[158]
(ii) that there are reasonable grounds for believing that an offence has been committed for which the penalty on conviction on indictment is imprisonment for a term of not less than two years and that there are on any premises documents relating to whether the offence has been committed;[159]
(iii) that the Treasury or Secretary of State or, as the case may be, the authorised person have power to require the production of the documents under 6.7.1;[160] and
(iv) that there are reasonable grounds for believing that if production was so required the documents would not be produced but would be removed from the premises, hidden, tampered with or destroyed.[161]

A warrant under the provision at 6.7.2 authorises a constable, together with any other person named in it and any other constables: **6.7.3**

(i) to enter the premises specified in the information, using such force as is reasonably necessary for the purpose;[162]
(ii) to search the premises and take possession of any documents appearing to be such documents as are mentioned in 6.7.2, or to take, in relation to any such documents, any other steps that

[156] Insurance Companies Act 1982 s.44(4A).
[157] Insurance Companies Act 1982 s.44(5). Note that the Treasury or Secretary of State may rescind a requirement imposed under this provision if it appears to them that it is no longer necessary for the requirement to continue in force and they may also vary any such requirement — Insurance Companies Act 1982 s.47(1) and (1A).
[158] Insurance Companies Act 1982 s.44A(1).
[159] Insurance Companies Act 1982 s.44A(2)(a).
[160] Insurance Companies Act 1982 s.44A(2)(b).
[161] Insurance Companies Act 1982 s.44A(2)(c).
[162] Insurance Companies Act 1982 s.44A(3)(a).

may appear to be necessary for preserving them or preventing interference with them;[163]

(iii) to take copies of any such documents;[164] and

(iv) to require any person named in the warrant to provide an explanation of them or to state where they may be found.[165]

If in the case of a warrant under 6.7.2 (ii) to (iv) the justice of the peace is satisfied on information on oath that there are reasonable grounds for believing that there are also on the premises other documents relevant to the investigation, the warrant shall also authorise the actions at (i) to (iv) to be taken in relation to such documents.[166]

6.7.4 A warrant under 6.7.2 and 6.7.3 continues in force until the end of the period of one month beginning with the day on which it is issued.[167] Any documents of which possession is taken may be retained:

(i) for a period of three months;[168] or

(ii) if within that period proceedings to which the documents are relevant are commenced against any person for any criminal offence, until the conclusion of those proceedings.

In 6.7.2 to 6.7.4 'document' includes information recorded in any form.[169]

6.7.5 The Treasury or Secretary of State may require a UK or non-EC company to provide at a specified time a report by a specified person, being an actuary, accountant or person with other relevant professional skills, on any matter about which the Treasury or Secretary of State could require the company to provide information under 6.7.1 above.[170]

6.8 POWERS EXERCISABLE TO ASSIST OVERSEAS REGULATORY AUTHORITIES

6.8.1 To assist an overseas regulatory authority in accordance with Companies Act 1989 s.82, if the Secretary of State considers there is good reason,

---

163 Insurance Companies Act 1982 s.44A(3)(b) .
164 Insurance Companies Act 1982 s.44A(3)(c).
165 Insurance Companies Act 1982 s.44A(3)(d)
166 Insurance Companies Act 1982 s.44A(4).
167 Insurance Companies Act 1982 s.44A(5).
168 Insurance Companies Act 1982 s.44A(6)(a).
169 Insurance Companies Act 1982 s.44A(8).
170 Insurance Companies Act 1982 s.44(2B).

he may require any person to attend before him at a specified time and place and answer questions or otherwise furnish information with respect to any matter relevant to the inquiries[171] (and may examine a person on oath). [172] He may also require such a person to produce at a specified time and place any specified documents that appear to the Secretary of State to relate to any matter relevant to the inquiries[173] and otherwise to give him such assistance in connection with the inquiries as he is reasonably able to give.[174] A statement made by a person under this provision may be used in evidence against him.[175] Where documents are produced, the Secretary of State may take copies or extracts from them.[176] Where a person claims a lien on a document, its production is without prejudice to his lien.[177]

Where the Secretary of State authorises an officer of his or any other competent person to exercise on his behalf all or any of the powers conferred by s.83 a person shall not be required to disclose any information or produce any documents in respect of which he owes an obligation of confidence by virtue of carrying on the business of banking, unless the imposing on him of a requirement with respect to such information or documents has been specifically authorised by the Secretary of State or the person to whom the obligation of confidence is owed consents to the disclosure or production.[178] **6.8.2**

A person who without reasonable excuse fails to comply with a requirement imposed on him under 6.8.1 above commits an offence and is liable on summary conviction to imprisonment for a term not exceeding six months or to a fine not exceeding level 5 on the standard scale[179] or to both.[180] A person who in purported compliance with any such requirement furnishes information that he knows to be false or misleading in a material particular, or recklessly furnishes information that is false or misleading in a material particular, commits an offence and is liable on conviction on indictment, to imprisonment for a term **6.8.3**

---

[171] Companies Act 1989 s.83(2)(a).
[172] Companies Act 1989 s.83(3).
[173] Companies Act 1989 s.83(2)(b).
[174] Companies Act 1989 s.83(2)(c).
[175] Companies Act 1989 s.83(6).
[176] Companies Act 1989 s.83(4).
[177] For the purpose of this provision 'documents' bears the same meaning as at 6.6.2 above — Companies Act 1989 s.83(8).
[178] Companies Act 1989 s.84(4). 'Documents' bears the same meaning as at 6.6.2 above.
[179] Level 5 is currently £5,000.
[180] Companies Act 1989 s.85(1).

not exceeding two years or to a fine, or both; and on summary conviction to imprisonment for a term not exceeding six months or to a fine not exceeding the statutory maximum[181] or both.[182]

Criminal proceedings for an offence under 6.8.3 will not be instituted without the consent of the Secretary of State or the Director of Public Prosecutions.[183] Where an offence at 6.8.3 is proved to have been committed with the consent or connivance of, or to be attributable to any neglect on the part of, a director, manager, secretary or other similar officer of the body, or a person purporting to act in any such capacity, he as well as the body corporate is guilty of the offence and liable to be proceeded against and punished accordingly. Where the affairs of a body corporate are managed by its members this liability applies in relation to the acts and defaults of a member in connection with his functions of management as to a director of a body corporate.[184] Similarly, where an offence at 6.8.3 above that is committed by a partnership is proved to have been committed with the consent or connivance of, or to be attributable to any neglect on the part of, a partner, he as well as the partnership is guilty of the offence and liable to be proceeded against and punished accordingly.[185] Finally, where an offence at 6.8.3 above that is committed by an unincorporated association (other than a partnership) is proved to have been committed with the consent or connivance of, or to be attributable to any neglect on the part of, any officer of the association or any member of its governing body, he as well as the association is guilty of the offence and liable to be proceeded against and punished accordingly.[186] Summary proceedings for an offence at 6.8.3 may, without prejudice to any other jurisdiction, be taken against a body corporate or unincorporated association at any place at which it has a place of business, and against an individual at any place where he is for the time being.[187] **6.8.4**

Proceedings against an unincorporated association must be brought in the name of the association (and not in that of any of its members), and in any such proceedings any rules of court relating to the service of **6.8.5**

[181] Currently £5,000.
[182] Companies Act 1989 s.85(2).
[183] Companies Act 1989 s.89.
[184] Companies Act 1989 s.90(2).
[185] Companies Act 1989 s.90(3).
[186] Companies Act 1989 s.90(4).
[187] Companies Act 1989 s.91(1).

documents apply as in relation to a body corporate.[188] The following provisions apply when an unincorporated association is charged with an offence under 6.8.3 as they do to a corporation:

(i) in England s.33 of the Criminal Justice Act 1925 and schedule 3 to the Magistrates' Courts Act 1980 (procedure on charge of offence against a corporation).[189]
(ii) in relation to proceedings on indictment in Scotland, s.74 of the Criminal Procedure (Scotland) Act 1975 (proceedings on indictment against bodies corporate).[190]
(iii) in Northern Ireland s.18 of the Criminal Justice Act (Northern Ireland) 1945 and sch 4 to the Magistrates' Court (Northern Ireland) Order 1981 (procedure on charge of offence against a corporation).[191]
(iv) A fine imposed on an unincorporated association on its conviction of such an offence is to be paid out of the funds of the association.[192]

6.9 LEGAL PROFESSIONAL PRIVILEGE

A person is not required to disclose to inspectors appointed under Companies Act 1985 ss.431 to 446, Financial Services Act s.94 or the Open-ended Investment Companies (Investment Companies with Variable Capital) Regulations 1996[193] reg. 22 information that he would in an action in the High Court or the Court of Session be entitled to refuse to disclose on the grounds of legal professional privilege except, if he is a lawyer, the name and address of his client.[194] The same provision applies to the requirement to provide information to the Secretary of State under Financial Services Act 1986 s.105[195] and Companies Act 1989 s.83.[196] 6.9.1

---

[188] Companies Act 1989 s.91(2).
[189] Companies Act 1989 s.91(3).
[190] Companies Act 1989 s.91(4).
[191] Companies Act 1989 s.91(5).
[192] Companies Act 1989 s.91(6).
[193] SI 1996/2827.
[194] Companies Act 1985 s.452(1)(a), Financial Services Act 1986 s.94(5) and Open-ended Investment Companies (Investment Companies with Variable Capital) Regulations 1996 reg. 23(1).
[195] Financial Services Act 1986 s.105(6).
[196] Companies Act 1989 s.83(5).

The approach towards legal professional privilege at 6.9.1 also applies to the production of documents or taking possession of them pursuant to Companies Act 1985 ss.447 to 451,[197] the provision of information to the Secretary of State pursuant to Insurance Companies Act 1982 s.44[198] and the provision of information to inspectors appointed under Financial Services Act 1986 s.177,[199] but in each case without the limitation that requires a lawyer to disclose the name and address of his client. **6.9.2**

Thus, the witness and his legal advisers will need to bear in mind the usual rules of legal professional privilege. For example, the privilege may only be waived by the client and not by the lawyer, not every communication passing between a lawyer and his client will necessarily be privileged and documents that are in themselves part of a criminal or fraudulent purpose will not be privileged.[200] **6.9.3**

6.10 SELF-INCRIMINATION

The legislation concerning statutory investigations into companies typically provides for the inspectors or investigators to be able to require a witness to attend to give evidence. The relevant legislation[201] is, however, silent in relation to whether a witness can be compelled to answer questions where the witness's answers would tend to incriminate the witness. In certain statutory contexts this privilege against self-incrimination is expressly excluded.[202] However, caselaw has interpreted legislative silence to exclude the privilege in other contexts, including the relation to statutory investigations into companies.[203] **6.10.1**

In *Bank of England v Riley*[204] the question arose in the context of Banking Act 1987, s.42 which provided that: **6.10.2**

[197] Companies Act 1985 s.452(2).
[198] Insurance Companies Act 1982 s.47B.
[199] Financial Services Act 1986 s.177(7).
[200] See Style and Hollander *Documentary Evidence* 6th edn (1997) at pp. 203–7.
[201] E.g. Companies Act 1985 s.434(1) and (2).
[202] E.g. Theft Act 1968 s.31(1) 'A person shall not be excused, by reason that to do so may incriminate that person ... of an offence under this Act ... from answering any question ... in proceedings for the recovery or administration of any property [etc.] ... but no statement or admission made by a person in answering a question put ... shall ... be admissible in evidence against that person ...'.
[203] See also Ch 13.
[204] [1992] 1 All ER 769.

> (1) Where the Bank has reasonable grounds for suspecting that a person is guilty of contravening section 3 or 35 above the Bank or any duly authorised officer, servant or agent of the Bank may ... require that or any other person — (a) to provide ... such information as the Bank may reasonably require for the purpose of investigating the suspected contravention; (b) to produce, ... such documents, or documents of such description, as may be specified, being documents the production of which may be reasonably required by the Bank for that purpose; (c) to attend at such place and time as may be specified ... and answer questions relevant for determining whether such a contravention has occurred.
>
> (4) Any person who without reasonable excuse fails to comply with a requirement imposed on him under this section or intentionally obstructs a person in the exercise of the rights conferred by subsection (3) above shall be guilty of an offence and liable on summary conviction to imprisonment for a term not exceeding six months or to a fine not exceeding the fifth level on the standard scale or to both.
>
> (5) A statement made by a person in compliance with a requirement imposed by virtue of this section may be used in evidence against him.[205]

The defendant refused to answer certain interrogatories, relying on the privilege against self-incrimination. However, Ralph Gibson LJ, giving the judgment of the Court of Appeal stated that[206]

> the language of s.42(1) does by necessary implication provide that a person, suspected of contravening s.3 or s.35 of the 1987 Act, when required to provide information pursuant to the power there given, is under a duty to provide that information and is not excused from so doing because the information would tend to show that he has indeed contravened that provision of the Act or any other provision of the criminal law.

In reaching this conclusion Ralph Gibson LJ relied on *Customs and Excise Commissioners v Harz*[207] concerning s.24(6) of the Purchase Tax Act 1963 where the privilege against self-incrimination was held to have been abrogated by the words 'shall furnish ... such information to the Commissioners as they may specify'.[208]

---

[205] s.3 provides that (subject to s.4, which deals with exempted persons), no person shall in the United Kingdom accept a deposit in the course of carrying on a deposit-taking business unless that person is an institution authorised by the Bank under the Act. s.35 provides that it is an offence fraudulently to induce the making of a deposit.

[206] At p. 776f–h.

[207] [1967] 1 AC 760.

[208] A similar result was reached in *R v Hertfordshire County Council ex p. Green*

In *Re. London United Investments plc*[209] the question whether the privilege against self-incrimination applied arose in the context of Companies Act 1985 s.434. An individual refused to answer questions that were sent to him and oral questions put to him at an interview. After considering earlier cases and *Bank of England v Riley*, Dillon LJ giving the judgment of the Court of the Appeal stated[210] **6.10.3**

> I reach without hesitation the conclusion that as (i) inspectors will in very many cases have been appointed where there are circumstances suggesting that there has been fraud in the conduct or management of a company's affairs, and (ii) persons questioned are bound to answer the inspectors' questions and (iii) the inspectors' report may lead the Secretary of State to petition for the winding up of the company or to bring civil proceedings in the company's name in the public interest, the privilege against self-incrimination is impliedly excluded and is not available to the person being questioned by the inspectors.

Thus, the privilege against self-incrimination has impliedly been excluded in the case of investigations under Companies Act 1985 where witnesses can be compelled to answer questions. The same approach has been taken in relation to investigations under Financial Services Act 1986 s.177. In *Styr v HM Advocate*[211] the Lord Justice Clerk (Ross) stated[212]

> In our judgment the provisions of s.177 clearly override the common law privilege of a witness not to incriminate himself. Section 177(6) expressly provides that a statement made by a person in compliance with a requirement imposed by s.177 may be used in evidence against him. A statement could hardly be used in evidence against a person unless it was of an incriminating nature, and it seems clear that Parliament must have intended to override the normal privilege which a witness has against incriminating himself.

He referred, in particular, to *R v Director of the Serious Fraud Office ex p. Smith*[213] when concluding that the immunity should be overridden(although in the context of the SFO Criminal Justice Act 1987 s.2(8)

Environmental Industries Ltd [1997] *The Times*, 9 October, where the Court of Appeal considered Environmental Protection Act 1990 s.71, which enabled a waste regulation authority to obtain information that it reasonably considered it needed and it was held that the mere fact that the provision of the information might assist the authority to establish a criminal offence against the provider of the information could not have been intended to provide a reasonable excuse for not providing the information.

209 [1992] Ch 578.
210 At p. 598C–E.
211 [1994] SLT 5.
212 At p. 11B–C.
213 [1993] AC 1.

provides protection as to the use that can be made of incriminating answers unlike Financial Services Act 1986 s. 177).[214]

A similar approach towards the privilege was adopted by Vinelott J in *Re Jeffrey S Levitt Ltd (in Administrative Receivership)*[215] and by the Court of Appeal in *Bishopsgate Investment Management Ltd v Maxwell*[216] both in the context of the compulsory powers in Insolvency Act 1986 ss.235 and 236[217] and in *AT & T Istel Ltd v Tully*[218] concerning a mareva order. Further, it appears that since investigators are not persons charged to investigate offences or charge offenders within Police and Criminal Evidence Act 1984 s.67(9) there is no need for them to administer a caution before asking questions where the witness may give a self-incriminating answer.[219] Thus, although the privilege remains part of the common law,[220] the statutory provisions that enable an investigator to obtain information pursuant to compulsory power can override the privilege not to incriminate oneself. Thus the witness will not be able to rely on the privilege against self-incrimination save in so far as it is relevant to the limitations on investigators' powers based on oppression[221] and restrictions that may apply to the use of information obtained by investigators.[222] **6.10.4**

6.11 REQUESTS FOR EVIDENCE, PUBLIC LAW PRINCIPLES AND OPPRESSION

A number of the regimes have mechanisms whereby the courts can relieve witnesses of obligations imposed upon them by investigators. Further, general public law principles constrain the exercise of statutory powers. For example, requests should not be so extreme as to amount to an

214 See 13.2.4 below.
215 [1992] Ch 457.
216 [1992] 2 All ER 856.
217 Note the criticism by A Tomkins and B Bix *The Sounds of Silence: A Duty to Incriminate Oneself* [1992] PL 364.
218 [1993] AC 45.
219 See *R v Seelig* [1992] 1 WLR 148 and note 13.2 below.
220 See, e.g. *United Norwest Cooperatives Ltd v Johnstone* [1994] *The Times*, 24 February.
221 See 6.11.9 below.
222 See Ch 13.

abuse of power[223] and if the exercise of the power requires the investigator to have a particular state of mind, such as 'reasonable cause to believe' that the documents he intends to seize will be destroyed if he serves a notice before entering premises, the investigator must have the requisite state of mind.[224] One particular restriction is that the request for evidence should not amount to oppression. This may be seen in public law terms, but it may also be seen as a free-standing restriction given its origins in connection with the examination of witnesses in other contexts, particularly insolvency.[225]

REASONABLE EXCUSE

Where a witness fails to comply with certain requirements imposed by inspectors appointed under Financial Services Act 1986 s.177 and the inspectors certify the matter to the court, if the court is satisfied that he refused to comply 'without reasonable excuse', it may punish him or direct that the Secretary of State exercise certain powers.[226] In *Re an Inquiry under the Company Securities (Insider Dealing) Act 1985*[227] the House of Lords considered the application of the defence of reasonable excuse. A journalist, in writing two newspaper articles concerning inquiries into two take-over bids, appeared to have used information leaked to him or given to him by a source close to the leak. Inspectors who had been appointed to investigate leaks from government departments of price-sensitive information about takeover bids requested the journalist to reveal the source of his information. When he refused to do so (arguing that to reveal the sources would destroy the trust on which such journalistic work is based) the inspectors certified the matter pursuant to Financial Services Act 1986 s.178(1).[228] Hoffman J decided that the journalist had a reasonable excuse for refusing to answer questions about his source.[229] The Court of Appeal, however, allowed an appeal by the Inspectors[230] and this was also the result in the House of Lords. The House of Lords approached the matter by reference to the 6.11.1

[223] See 6.11.6 to 6.11.8 below.
[224] See *Nakkuda Ali v Jayaratne* [1951] AC 66 and *R v Inland Revenue Commissioners ex p Rossminster* [1980] AC 952.
[225] See 6.11.9 and 6.11.10 below.
[226] See 6.5.6 above.
[227] [1988] AC 660.
[228] See 6.5.6.
[229] [1987] BCLC 506.
[230] [1988] BCLC 76.

provisions of the Contempt of Court Act 1981. The House of Lords considered whether on the material before it the court should have been satisfied that disclosure of the journalist's sources was 'necessary ... for the prevention of ... crime' within Contempt of Court Act 1981 s.10 and held that disclosure was necessary in this case.

As a general point the House of Lords referred to Contempt of Court Act 1981 s.10 because the parties agreed to interpret 'reasonable excuse' for Financial Services Act s.178(2) by reference to that provision. However, notwithstanding that s.178(2)(a) itself refers to contempt of the court,[231] the Lords held that the Contempt of Court Act was not directly applicable but that it was an applicable analogy.[232] As a point of principle, courts will be required to consider the evidence placed before them before taking steps under s.178(2). Thus Lord Griffiths stated:[233] **6.11.2**

> The inspectors obviously consider that [the journalist] ... has no reasonable excuse for not revealing his source otherwise they would not have reported the matter to the High Court. It is, however, the duty of the High Court to satisfy itself on evidence placed before it of the necessity that the source should not be revealed, and it must not act as a rubber stamp to support the view of the inspectors.

Similarly, Lord Oliver stated[234]

> Obviously the court will pay a proper regard to the views of those constituting the inquiry body, who, in the nature of things, know better than anyone else the stage which their inquiries have reached and what is needful for their successful prosecution. But ... [t]he court must, in my judgment, be presented at least with sufficient material to enable it to exercise an independent judgment on the extent of the need.

Although this case was in the specific context of a journalist and his sources the principle of the need for the court to 'exercise an independent judgment' and not act as 'a rubber stamp' appears to be of general application.

Following the decision of the House of Lords the matter was remitted back to the Chancery Division where Sir Nicolas Browne-Wilkinson VC imposed a fine of £20,000.[235] The judge declined to impose a custodial sentence because he took into account that the newspaper articles were **6.11.3**

---

[231] The court may 'punish him in like manner as if he had been guilty of contempt of the court'.

[232] See Lord Griffiths [1988] AC 660 at p. 703 (a)–(e) and Lord Oliver at p. 708 (f) – (g).

[233] At p. 706 (h)–7(a).

[234] At p. 709(g)–10(a).

[235] [1988] *The Times*, 27 January.

published before the Financial Services Act 1986 came into force, so at the time of publication the journalist had no reason to expect that as a result of publication he could be brought into conflict with the law; that the journalist had a genuinely-held ethical objection to revelation of the facts; and that a custodial sentence in this case would be more likely to lead to the creation of a martyr than the bringing home to those who defy the law of the wrongness in so doing.[236]

The 'without reasonable excuse' formulation was considered briefly in *Bank of England v Riley*[237] in the context of an argument that the use of those words in Banking Act 1987 s.42(4) retained the privilege against self-incrimination but the Court of Appeal rejected this argument, Ralph Gibson LJ commenting[238]that **6.11.4**

> The concept of reasonable excuse ... was clearly necessary to cover such matters as physical inability to comply with a requirement for information or documents arising from illness or accidental destruction of papers etc.

A further example from the Banking Act context is provided by *A v B Bank*.[239] An injunction had been obtained preventing a bank from disclosing documents. The bank then received a notice from the Bank of England requiring it to produce the documents pursuant to Banking Act 1987 s.39(3)(a). Hirst J held that the existence of the injunction did not constitute a reasonable excuse under s.39(11) for failing to comply with the notice. However, in addition to considering the 'reasonable excuse' defence it is also necessary to consider the more general principle that compulsory powers should not be exercised oppressively.

---

236 The House of Commons Trade and Industry Committee, Third Report, Company Investigations (1990) HC 36 said the experience of this case showed there was little to be gained by inspectors pursuing disinterested journalists. Extreme cases may arise where either a current threat to investors or to the financial markets justifies pressing a journalist to reveal his sources and a journalist with a direct financial interest in a case should not be allowed to hide behind this protection. The Committee concluded that the DTI guidance to inspectors should caution them against pursuing journalists for their sources other than in exceptional cases and when it is essential for a prosecution – see paragraph 29 of the Report. Generally, in the context of journalists' sources see *Goodwin v United Kingdom* (1996) 22 EHRR 123 and *Camelot v Centaur Communications Ltd* [1997] *The Times*, 30 October concerning Article 10 of the European Convention on Human Rights (freedom of expression).

237 [1992] 1 All ER 769.

238 At p. 774(c). See also *R v Hertfordshire County Council ex p. Green Environmental Industries Limited* [1997] *The Times*, 9 October.

239 [1993] QB 311.

The relevant wording in relation to Financial Services Act 1986 s.105 differs from s.177 in that there is no reference to the court punishing as if there had been a contempt of the court and there are no specific powers for the Secretary of State where a witness fails to comply with an obligation. However, an offence is committed by one who fails to comply with a requirement 'without reasonable excuse' and this will allow the court to consider the nature of the requirement in the particular case.[240] A different approach is, however, required by the courts considering legislation, which does not contain the 'without reasonable excuse' formulation. 6.11.5

PUBLIC LAW PRINCIPLES

Where the legislation permits those carrying out an investigation to require the provision of evidence, the investigators will have wide powers to serve notices requiring evidence relating to the matter under investigation. Such powers are not, however, untrammelled since they are subject to public law principles.[241] The powers are initially restricted by the wording of the legislation. For example, where legislation permits inspectors to require the provision of evidence where 'they consider that ... [a] person, is or may be in possession of information relating to a matter which they believe to be relevant to the investigation'[242] any request must be based on the relevant belief being held by the inspectors.[243] By analogy, in *R v O'Kane ex p. Northern Bank Ltd*[244] a wide ranging notice served by Inland Revenue officers pursuant to Income and Corporation Taxes Act 1988 s.20(3) was struck down for a failure to comply with the wording of the particular legislation since the notices purported to require the production of conjectural, as distinct from actual, documents. However, the Court of Appeal in *R v Commissioners of Inland Revenue ex p. Ulster Bank Ltd*[245] considered *ex p. Northern Bank* and found that the wording in s.20(8D), which referred to documents 'specified or described' was, by virtue of the word 'described', appropriate to cover classes or categories of documents. The 6.11.6

[240] See also Companies Act 1989 s.85(1).

[241] Note that certain of the matters discussed in relation to the preparation of a report at 7.2 to 7.7 are also relevant to the exercise of gathering evidence, e.g. the need to put points to witnesses at 7.2.7.

[242] Companies Act 1985 s.434(2).

[243] See, e.g. *R v Inland Revenue Commissioners ex p. Rossminster* [1980] AC 952.

[244] [1996] STC 1249.

[245] [1997] STC 832.

particular tax legislation did not require the description permissible in a notice to exclude classes or categories of documents that were not known to exist or to be in the possession or power of the recipient of the notice, and which were to that extent conjectural.[246]

The principles of abuse of power are also relevant in the context of a far reaching request for evidence. In *R v Secretary of State for Trade and Others ex p. Perestrello*,[247] authorised officers served a notice pursuant to Companies Act 1967 s.109 that required an individual to produce, at the DTI's offices, various categories of documents including 'all accounting records of the company such as to disclose the financial position of the company' and 'all files of correspondence relating to the affairs of the company, including ... '. In the circumstances, which had included prior cooperation by the person concerned, Woolf J took the view that the notices were 'unreasonable and excessive in the circumstances'.[248] The particular points noted by Woolf J were **6.11.7**

(i) if the notice was meant to refer only to documents in the individual's possession, then bearing in mind the nature of the documents, it should have said so; and it should not be a notice which is drawn in a manner that relies upon the individual ascertaining his rights under the legislation, and then reading the notice as being subject to the legislation in order to understand what the notice requires;
(ii) in the circumstances, if the notice was only intended to refer to documents in the United Kingdom it should have said so;
(iii) the notice went too far bearing in mind that the documents had to be taken to the DTI's premises; that the applicants would therefore be without the documents for a time; and it was not a situation where the individual who had been cooperating until that time, was merely being required to deal with a general request in circumstances where the documents would be produced but remain at his own business premises so that the business could be conducted in the meantime.[249]

---

[246] Note also *R v Secretary of State for the Home Department ex p. Fininvest SpA* [1997] 1 All ER 942 in the context of a request by the Italian prosecuting authorities to the Secretary of State under the European Convention on Mutual Assistance in Criminal Matters 1959 requesting assistance in obtaining documents held by a company and *R. Thames Magistrates' Court ex p. Hormoz* [1998] COD 370 in the context of Customs and Excise Management Act 1979 s.118D.

[247] [1981] 1 QB 19.

[248] At p. 31A–B.

[249] At p. 31B–G.

Woolf J concluded that what he had said applied to the facts of the case and that there may be other circumstances where different considerations apply.

The concerns about the ambit of the notice in *ex p. Perestrello* were used by the applicants to support an application that DTI officers should act fairly and without bias. Woolf J rejected the case of bias and held that in the context of Companies Act 1967 s.109 (which involved the appointment of officers where the Secretary of State believed there were matters to be investigated and where the officers' function was to see whether the suspicions are justified), even if the case of bias had been made out it would not have been critical in this situation. However, Woolf J summarised the limits on the discretion given by s.109 (although he did not intend the summary to be exhaustive).[250] **6.11.8**

> First of all, the persons exercising the power must not exceed or abuse the discretion which is granted to them by the section; and not acting bona fide and not acting honestly are examples of that.
>
> Secondly, the person concerned must not use the discretion for some ulterior purpose. If the person concerned is so prejudiced against someone that he is using the section, not for the purposes for which the power was given, but, for example, to punish someone, then that is using it for an ulterior purpose which would be outside the statute. It appears to me that it is a requirement of this power that it should be exercised fairly in the sense that the statutory discretion which it gives should not be abused.

This approach to the exercise of a discretion to compel the production of documents was adopted in *R v O'Kane ex p. Northern Bank*[251] where Ferris J regarded the service of the notice on a bank as being so wide-reaching as to be unfair and oppressive given the considerable effort and hence expense that the bank would have incurred in producing all its records relating to a particular taxpayer.[252] Public law principles may

---

[250] At p. 35E G.

[251] Supra.

[252] In *R v Commissioners of Inland Revenue ex p. Ulster Bank Ltd* [1997] STC 832 the Court of Appeal considered the approach of Ferris J in *ex p. Northern Bank* but did not express a view on whether the particular request before them was irrational because according to the tax legislation the notice served by the Inland Revenue required the consent of a Special Commissioner and the bank also had the right to apply to the Special Commissioner to cancel or vary the notice on the ground that it was too onerous, so it was premature for the Court to make an order in judicial review proceedings before the consent of the Special Commissioners had been sought and obtained. See also *Royal Bank of Canada v IRC* [1972] Ch 665 and *Rv Thames Magistrates' Court ex p. Hormoz* [1998] COD 370.

also be relied upon to restrict the ambit of questioning or to argue that notice of a line of questioning should be given. For example in *R v Serious Fraud Office ex p. Asil Nadir*[253] the Divisional Court granted leave to apply for judicial review of a refusal of the SFO to provide particulars of the suspected offences that were the subject of an investigation. Leave was granted because having regard to the terms of Criminal Justice Act 1987 s.1(3) and s.2, which involve a power to question a suspect and oblige him to answer, it was arguable that there was a duty that particulars should be given.[254]

OPPRESSION

There is a long-established general principle that where a private examination of a witness is taking place under compulsory statutory powers the procedure is not to be exercised in a manner oppressive to the person to be examined.[255] The principle was also applied in relation to public examinations in bankruptcy.[256] Thus a similar issue arises in relation to, for example, the powers of company administrators under Insolvency Act 1986 ss.235 and 236[257] and of the Serious Fraud Office.[258] In *Re London United Investments plc*[259] the Court of Appeal considered the argument that it was unfair to require a particular witness to answer certain incriminating questions by reference to the line of authorities concerning the oppression defence. After concluding that the privilege against self-incrimination did not apply,[260] Dillon LJ found **6.11.9**

[253] 1 November 1990, unrep.

[254] Transcript p. 31 but note the limited content of the obligation of fairness in Ch 7. Note also *R v Securities and Investments Board ex p. Interdata (UK) Ltd* 13 September 1996, unrep. in which SIB failed in an appeal to the Court of Appeal following the grant of leave to apply for judicial review and the granting of a stay of the operation of certain requests by SIB to Interdata in the meanwhile. A request on 10 September 1996, had required the production of documents, including in relation to the design of software, by 4.30 p.m. on 12 September 1996, in circumstances where the designer of the software was in Hong Kong and was expected to remain there until 23 September 1996.

[255] See, e.g. *Heiron's case; In re Metropolitan Bank* (1880) 15 Ch D 139; *Registrar of Restrictive Trading Agreements v W. H. Smith & Son Ltd* [1969] 1 WLR 1460.

[256] *Re Atherton* [1912] 2 KB 251.

[257] See *Cloverbay Ltd (Joint Administrators) v Bank of Credit and Commerce International S.A.* [1991] Ch 90.

[258] See *R v Director of the Serious Fraud Office ex p. Maxwell* [1992] *The Times*, 9 October, *Morris and Others v Director of the Serious Fraud Office* [1993] Ch 372 and *R v Director of the Serious Fraud Office ex p. Smith* [1993] AC 1.

[259] [1992] Ch 578.

[260] See 6.10.3.

that the witness should answer the questions, and on the question of fairness said it was highly relevant that the witness's position in the three companies made it likely that he knew the answers to the questions that the inspectors wanted to ask him and, also, that because of his position he owed a fiduciary duty to the companies.[261] Generally, it appears that a far reaching request addressed to an officer of the company is less likely to be regarded as oppressive than a request addressed to a third party because officers owe a fiduciary duty to the company and are in certain instances under a duty to assist the investigators, whereas the same duty does not extend to third parties.[262] Also, an order for examination is more likely to be oppressive than an order for the production of documents. Finally, if someone is suspected of wrongdoing and, in particular, fraud, it is oppressive to require him effectively to prove the case against himself on oath before any proceedings are brought.[263] Generally, the analytical distinction between seeing oppression as an aspect of public law abuse of power, or seeing it as a free-standing defence based on the same principles as in the insolvency context, will be relevant to how the defence may be raised.[264]

One particular complication is where there is a risk that the person who is believed to hold documents may destroy them. This particular point was considered by Lord Denning MR in *Norwest Holst Ltd v Secretary of State for Trade*[265] who stated that in the context of Companies Act 1967 s.109, when DTI officers are appointed to examine the books 'there is no need for the rules of natural justice to be applied'. He based this on the grounds that 'if the company was forewarned and told that the officers were coming, what is to happen to the books? In a wicked world, it is not unknown for books or papers to be destroyed or lost'.[266] However, Lord Denning MR's comments were made in the context of the principles governing the decision to instigate an investigation[267] rather than an on-going investigation. The correct approach **6.11.10**

261 At p. 601C. Note also the analysis of Scott J [1992] BCLC 91 at p. 115.
262 *Cf.* Companies Act 1985 s.434(1).
263 See in the context of Insolvency Act 1986 ss.235 and 236 *Cloverbay Ltd (Joint Administrator) v Bank of Credit and Commerce International S.A.* [1991] Ch 90 at pp. 102–3, *British & Commonwealth Holdings plc (Joint Administrator) v Spicer and Oppenheim* [1992] Ch 342 and [1993] AC 426 and *Re Bank of Credit and Commerce International SA (in liquidation) (No. 11)* [1997] *The Times*, 10 February.
264 See 6.12.
265 [1978] Ch 201.
266 At p. 224C.
267 See 4.8 and 4.9 above.

towards someone who it is feared may destroy papers is for the inspectors or authorised officers to serve an appropriate notice, which may be in wide terms if they have concerns, and at the same time to secure the documents and then to give an opportunity to the person concerned to make representations at the first opportunity thereafter as to why the notice is defective or is unfair or oppressive.[268]

6.12 OPPOSITION TO REQUESTS FOR EVIDENCE

One particular issue is how a witness who opposes a request for evidence may raise the point. The issue arises because of the procedural exclusivity divide between public law matters where judicial review is the appropriate procedure, on the one hand, and private law matters where judicial review is inappropriate, on the other.[269] This distinction is of relevance given, for example, the strict time limits in judicial review proceedings.[270] Thus, in *A v B Bank*[271] there was an argument that proceedings challenging a notice under Banking Act 1987 s.39 should have been brought by way of judicial review proceedings rather than by way of an application for directions in the context of an injunction in civil proceedings that restrained a bank from disclosing information. Hirst J observed[272] **6.12.1**

> I have no doubt that judicial review is a proper and perhaps in the ordinary run of cases (where no injunction exists) the proper mode of challenge. However, where ... there is an injunction in force ... it is open to the court to consider the issue of validity, since, if the notice were indeed invalid, it could not override the injunction or give grounds for a variation.

In so far as oppression may constitute a reasonable excuse for failing to comply with a requirement of an investigator it may be raised as a defence upon a certification by an inspector under Financial Services Act 1986 s.178(1), or in criminal proceedings under Financial Services **6.12.2**

268 See in other contexts *R v Birmingham City Council ex p. Ferrero Ltd* [1993] 1 All ER 530 and *R v LAUTRO ex p. Ross* [1993] QB 17.

269 See *O'Reilly v Mackman* [1983] 2 AC 237, *Roy v Kensington & Chelsea & Westminster Family Practitioner Committee* [1992] 1 AC 624 and *Trustees of the Dennis Rye Pension Fund v Sheffield City Council* [1998] 1 WLR 840.

270 See Rules of the Supreme Court Order 53 rule 4(1) and Supreme Court Act 1981 s.31(6).

271 [1993] QB 311 and see 6.11.4.

272 At p. 326A.

Act 1986 s.105 as an alternative to a challenge by way of judicial review. Where the failure to comply leads to certification under s.436(1) and a consequent court enquiry under s.436(3), it appears that oppression may be raised either by way of judicial review, or as a reason for non-compliance such that there should be no punishment or direction by the court pursuant to s.436(3).[273] This is not free from doubt, however, in so far as it is a public law defence that is being raised.[274] However, even if the particular statutory approach in Companies Act 1985 s.436[275] allows a defence of oppression or unfairness to be raised to an application under s.436(3), there is not the same statutory approach in, for example, Companies Act 1985 s.447, which merely provides that a failure to comply with a requirement constitutes a criminal offence.[276] The principles governing when a public law defence can be raised in criminal proceedings are unclear. Notwithstanding, the recent liberalisation of the procedural exclusivity rule[277]and the principle that public law defences can be raised by way of collateral challenge to the underlying decisions in some instances[278]there is considerable uncertainty as to when public law defences can be raised. For example, in *Vasquez v R*[279] the Privy Council allowed appeals against conviction, because in placing the onus of proving provocation on the accused, the Belize Criminal Code was inconsistent with the Belize Constitution. Conversely, in *R v Ettrick Trout Co Ltd*[280] the Court of Appeal held that a defendant could not challenge the validity of a condition attached to a licence in criminal proceedings for breach of a licence condition. The Court of Appeal held that the challenge to the licence condition should have been by way of judicial review or statutory appeal. Similarly in *R v Wicks*[281] the owner of a building commenced work without planning permission. The local authority served an enforcement notice under the planning legislation. The landowner appealed against the enforcement notice but the appeal was dismissed. In subsequent criminal proceedings he wished to raise a ground of invalidity not provided for

---

[273] See 6.1.8 and the approach in *Re London United Investments Plc*, above.
[274] See the issue in relation to challenging the validity of the appointment of inspectors at 4.9.1 above.
[275] And see also Financial Services Act 1986 s.94.
[276] See 6.3.2 above and also Companies Act 1985 s.444.
[277] See *Roy v Kensington & Chelsea & Westminster Family Practitioner Committee* [1992] 1 AC 624 and *Trustees of the Dennis Rye Pension Fund v Sheffield City Council* [1998] 1 WLR 840.
[278] See *Wandsworth London Borough Council v Winder* [1985] AC 461.
[279] [1994] 3 All ER 674.
[280] [1995] COD 53.
[281] [1997] 2 WLR 876.

in the statutory grounds of appeal. However, the House of Lords took a restrictive approach as to when a public law defence could be run in criminal proceedings. Although it would depend on a construction of each particular statutory regime as to whether a public law defence could be raised in criminal proceedings, a person who was prosecuted for failing to comply with an enforcement notice could not raise, by way of defence, the argument that the decision to issue the notice was tainted by bias or because an immaterial consideration was taken into account.[282]

Thus one who objects to a requirement imposed by investigators has a tactical choice: he may either challenge the requirement to which he has an objection at the outset by way of prompt judicial review proceedings, or, alternatively, in the hope that no action will be taken for a failure to comply, make no court application and see whether a court will allow him to raise a public law defence in the court proceedings. In this connection it seems, perhaps surprisingly, that a court may be more likely to allow a public law defence to be raised in proceedings where the statutory regime permits non-compliance where there is reasonable excuse[283] under Companies Act 1985 s.436(3) with its particular wording than in the criminal proceedings contemplated by certain other of the legislative provisions.[284] **6.12.3**

6.13 CROSS-EXAMINATION OF WITNESSES

The guidance in the *Investigations Handbook* records that witnesses or their advisers have no right to cross-examine other witnesses who have given evidence, or to see transcripts of evidence of other witnesses.[285] Although the position is set out in the context of guidance to inspectors appointed under Companies Act 1985 the principles seem equally applicable to all statutory investigations into companies. Investigators may have a duty to consider exercising their discretion to allow one witness to cross-examine another in any particular case,[286] but it would **6.13.1**

282 See *Boddington v British Transport Police* [1998] 2 All ER 203 in relation to raising the invalidity of byelaws as a defence to criminal proceedings.
283 E.g. Financial Services Act 1986 s.178.
284 See by analogy *Waverley Borough Council v Marney* (1995) 93 LGR 86.
285 App B, para. 19. This principle was established in *Re Pergamon Press Limited* [1971] Ch 388. See 7. 2 below.
286 See, e.g. *Bushell v Secretary of State for the Environment* [1981] AC 75, *R v Criminal Injuries Compensation Board ex p. Cobb* [1995] COD 126.

be surprising if a court held in the context of a statutory investigation into a company that fairness required that one witness's representatives had the right to cross-examine another witness except in an extreme case.[287] Further, investigators probably do not have the statutory power to compel anyone to attend for cross-examination by another witness's representatives[288] so it may well be that any such cross-examination would only take place in the unlikely event of a witness agreeing to be cross-examined.[289] However, since inspectors will be able to call witnesses for interview, there will be an obligation upon them, as a matter of fairness, to take account of a request by one witness that the investigators should ask particular questions of another witness, but there will be a wide discretion afforded to the inspectors in deciding which witnesses to call and what questions to ask.[290]

6.14 SOME PRACTICAL POINTS FOR THOSE PROVIDING EVIDENCE

There are a number of practical matters that should be borne in mind by witnesses in relation to assisting the inspectors or those carrying out an investigation by providing documents and in assisting by giving written evidence or oral evidence at an interview.

When asked to provide documents it may be helpful to the holder of the documents and to the investigation generally if the person concerned keeps a record of what items are inspected by those carrying out the investigation. Similarly, if originals or copies are supplied to the investigators it may be helpful to keep a separate copy set or at least a record of what items are supplied. This is of particular relevance if the person concerned is subsequently called to give oral evidence since, if he refreshes his mind before attending an interview, he will know which of his own documents he may be asked about. **6.14.1**

[287] See, e.g. *R v Commission for Racial Equality ex p. Cottrell & Rothon (a firm)* [1980] 3 All ER 265, *R v London Borough of Camden ex p. Paddock* [1995] COD 130 and 31 October 1995, unrep.

[288] See *Re Pergamon Press Ltd* [1971] Ch 388, Buckley LJ at p. 407E.

[289] Generally, see De Smith, Woolf and Jowell *Judicial Review of Administrative Action* 5th edn (1995) at pp. 454–7.

[290] See *R v Panel on Take-overs and Mergers ex p. Guinness plc* [1990] 1 QB 146.

The *Investigations Handbook* gives guidance to inspectors on the oral examination of witnesses.[291] A witness should always be given reasonable notice that he is required for an interview and it is suggested in the Handbook that this might vary between a day and two weeks. The guidance also records that inspectors might find their enquiries will be facilitated if a witness is given advance notice in general terms of the matters on which he is to be examined, together with particulars of any documents that the inspectors require him to produce or propose to refer to while examining him.[292] Clearly, when a witness is expected to prepare in advance for an interview on certain matters, particularly where the events may have taken place some years ago, he will require time to prepare and, in these circumstances, two weeks may be inadequate notice. Further, if there is a risk that the witness concerned may face criticism in the report because there is evidence that is adverse to him he should be told the substance of the allegations or evidence and have an adequate opportunity to prepare for the interview accordingly.[293] This may, however, in the first instance, need to be modified, where to allow him this opportunity may lead to the inquiry being prejudiced. The same issue arises in relation to the Handbook's further suggestion that in some cases it may be worthwhile to ask witnesses for a brief written statement about the matters on which they are to be questioned.[294] The guidance records that where there is more than one inspector both should, if possible, be present when any witness is examined[295] (and in the context of inspectors appointed under Financial Services Act 1986 s.177 notes that inspectors have found that it is normally preferable not to conduct such interviews on the witness's own premises)[296] and that normally there should be a short break for refreshment at intervals of about two hours.[297] **6.14.2**

The obligation of a witness giving oral evidence varies slightly depending on the particular type of statutory investigation.[298] However, a witness answering questions should approach the giving of evidence with the same degree of seriousness as in a court of law, and should, for **6.14.3**

291 *Investigations Handbook* App B, paras 17–26; App C paras 23–35.
292 App B, para. 17; App C, para. 25.
293 See Ch 7. Also note Report of the Royal Commission on Tribunals of Inquiry (Cmnd. 3121 (1966)) (The Salmon Report) (principle (ii)) and Sir Richard Scott *Procedures at Inquiries — The Duty to be Fair* [1995] 111 LQR 596 at pp. 602–3.
294 App B, para. 17; App C, para. 25.
295 App B, para. 23; App C, para. 27.
296 App C, para. 27.
297 App B, para. 23; App C, para. 26.
298 See 6.1 to 6.8 above.

example, say if he cannot recall the answer to a particular question. Those carrying out an investigation may well arrange for a shorthand writer to produce a transcript of the interview, which the witness may be asked to check and sign.[299] If during such a process or at any other time the witness believes he has left the investigators with an inaccurate impression of the events he should contact the investigators and seek to correct the position either in writing or possibly, if appropriate, by requesting a further interview. Indeed the witness may wish to ascertain in advance that he will be given a copy of the transcript and be allowed to correct anything that is inaccurate or expand upon his evidence.[300]

---

[299] See the *Investigations Handbook* App B, paras 23–6.

[300] Note that there will usually be a limit on the number of copies of a transcript that the witness may have or make, and there will also be confidentiality requirements.

Chapter 7

PREPARATION OF REPORTS AND PROCEDURAL FAIRNESS

The investigations regimes will usually lead to the writing of a report, whether that be by inspectors appointed by the Secretary of State or by investigators looking at a particular aspect of a company.[1] Certain reports may be published[2] and may, depending on their contents, adversely affect the reputations of those individuals referred to in the reports. All reports may form the basis of a decision to take further action, e.g. winding up proceedings, criminal proceedings, etc.[3] However, in each case the report itself is not determinative of any individual rights. Further, in certain regimes, the writing of a report is clearly central to the purpose of the investigation[4] whereas in other cases the report (if any) is more incidental to the exercise of the power.[5]

7.1 GENERAL

The reports will be set in the context of their particular statutory framework. However, in each case, the starting point is that the investigators' 'function is in essence to conduct an investigation designed to discover whether there are facts which may result in others taking action: it is no part of their function to take a decision as to whether action be taken'[6] and their role is essentially a 'statutory fact finding' one.[7] **7.1.1**

---

1 E.g. Companies Act 1985 s.447.
2 See Ch 9.
3 See Ch 11 and Ch 12.
4 E.g. Companies Act 1985 s.432 and Financial Services Act 1986 s.177.
5 E.g. Companies Act 1985 s.447 and Financial Services Act 1986 s.105.
6 Sachs LJ in *Re Pergamon Press Ltd* [1971] 1 Ch 388 at p. 401.
7 See *Re Travel & Holiday Clubs Ltd* [1967] 1 WLR 711, *Re SBA Properties Ltd* [1967] 1 WLR 799. Note also *Re Grosvenor and West-End Railway Terminus Hotel Co. Ltd* [1897] 76 LT 337 and R. Instone *Inspectors, Investigations and Their Aftermath* [1978] JBL 121.

This approach is followed by the DTI in the *Investigations Handbook* which records that:[8]

> The immediate purpose of most investigations is to find out what has happened or is happening when there are grounds to suggest some irregularity in the conduct of a company, business or individual in order to provide the Secretary of State with the information needed to decide what is to be done.

When writing a report the investigators will need to bear a number of general points in mind: **7.1.2**

(i) those reading the report may have little or no prior knowledge of the company or the matters under investigation;
(ii) it may be of assistance to provide a general guide to the group structure if the company is or has subsidiaries;[9]
(iii) it may be of assistance to include a dramatis personae and a chronology;
(iv) whether issues should be ignored as being irrelevant;
(v) the level of detail to include in the report;[10]
(vi) whether to include a summary;[11] and
(vii) whether to make any interim reports.[12]

Lord Denning MR explained in *Re Pergamon Press Ltd*[13] that inspectors 'should make their report with courage and frankness, keeping nothing back' and in *Maxwell v DTI*[14] **7.1.3**

> They should state their findings on the evidence and their opinions on the matters referred to them. If their report is to be of value, they should make it with courage and frankness, keeping nothing back. The public interest demands it. It may on occasion be necessary for them to condemn or criticise a man.

However, the DTI's approach is that inspectors 'should exercise restraint in the manner and the extent of their criticisms ... and should make criticisms only to the extent necessary for a proper appreciation of their report'.[15] Further, inspectors are advised that they 'should avoid

8 Para. 9.
9 See *Investigations Handbook* App B, para. 48.
10 App B, para. 49.
11 App B, para. 50.
12 App B, para. 51–2.
13 [1971] Ch 388 at p. 400.
14 [1974] 1 QB 523 at p. 533.
15 *Investigations Handbook* App B, para. 34.

superfluous epithets and the eye catching phrase which is likely to lead to unbalanced comments, and to limit remarks about conduct to conduct in the company's affairs'.[16]

When preparing their report it appears that investigators acting pursuant to statutory appointment may well be covered by absolute privilege[17] rather than only qualified privilege[18] although the point is not free from doubt,[19] whereas witnesses will probably only be covered by qualified privilege[20] if allegations of defamation are raised. **7.1.4**

Those writing a report will need to base their findings on evidence that has some probative value otherwise it may be subject to attack in judicial review proceedings. This was explained by Lord Diplock in *Mahon v Air New Zealand*[21] **7.1.5**

> The technical rules of evidence applicable to civil or criminal litigation form no part of the rules of natural justice. What is required ... is that the decision to make the finding must be based upon some material that tends logically to show the existence of facts consistent with the finding and that the reasoning supportive of the finding, if it be disclosed, is not logically self-contradictory.

Although Lord Diplock regarded the requirement that a finding must be based on probative evidence as an aspect of natural justice this may also be seen as a free standing requirement[22] or an element of irrationality. The requirement that findings be based on probative evidence stresses the need for the investigators to evaluate evidence placed before them and to be particularly cautious about evidence based on recollections of events that took place many years earlier or where the evidence may lead to a finding suggesting impropriety.

In addition to the requirement that a finding must be based on probative evidence, the contents of a report may be attacked if the investigator **7.1.6**

---

16 App B, para. 35. See also App C, para. 55. Note 7.2 below.

17 See *Re Pergamon Press Ltd* [1971] Ch 388 at p. 400G.

18 Where qualified privilege attaches, the person suing for defamation would need to show that the investigators or the Secretary of State were actuated by malice, i.e. a desire to injure as the dominant motive for the defamatory publication — see *Horrocks v Lowe* [1975] AC 135.

19 Compare *Trapp v Mackie* [1979] 1 WLR 377 with the earlier *O'Connor v Waldron* [1935] AC 76. Generally see *Gatley on Libel and Slander* 9th edn (1998) at pp. 282–301.

20 *Re Pergamon Press Ltd* [1971] Ch 388 at p. 400C.

21 [1984] 1 AC 808 at p. 821A–B and see 7.4.3 below.

22 See the approach in *Edwards v Bairstow* [1956] AC 14.

strays outside the terms of his appointment or, for example, fails to take account of a relevant consideration or takes into account an irrelevant consideration.[23] However, a mistake of fact on the part of the person writing a report will not be a ground for judicial review except where the existence of the fact is a condition precedent to the exercise of the investigator's jurisdiction, or the fact provided the only evidential basis for the decision, or the mistake of fact was as to a matter which expressly or impliedly was required to be taken into account.[24]

Against the background of the consequences of a report being produced it is necessary to consider the extent to which the rules of procedural fairness constrain the conduct of investigations in circumstances where the primary legislation is silent in relation to the procedures to be adopted.[25] This is because a failure to comply with any applicable principles of procedural fairness could lead to the report being attacked in judicial review proceedings. **7.1.7**

7.2 *RE PERGAMON PRESS LTD* AND *MAXWELL V DEPARTMENT OF TRADE AND INDUSTRY*

The questions of whether an obligation of fairness rests on DTI inspectors and the content of that obligation were considered in the important and linked cases of *Re Pergamon Press Ltd*[26] and *Maxwell v Department of Trade and Industry*.[27] The content of the obligation of fairness has been considered briefly in more recent cases and has also since been considered in analogous contexts. **7.2.1**

---

23 See *Secretary of State for Education and Science v Thameside MBC* [1977] AC 1014 at pp. 1020, 1047.

24 See *R v London Residuary Body ex p. Inner London Education Authority* [1987] *The Times*, 24 July; *R v Teeside Development Corporation ex p. William Morrison Supermarket plc* unrep, 16 May 1997 (NLP).

25 Generally see the discussion in De Smith, Woolf and Jowell *Judicial Review of Administrative Action* 5th edn (1995) at pp. 491–8 and M. Beloff in Supperstone and Goudie *Judicial Review* 2nd edn (1997) at pp. 8.34–8.37 and for a comparative Australian view see Aronson and Dyer *Judicial Review of Administrative Action* (1996) at pp. 468–76.

26 [1971] Ch 388.

27 [1974] 1 QB 523. See R. Pennington *Investigations under the Companies Acts and the Pergamon Affair* (1974) 118 Sol. Jo. 507.

The role for the rules of natural justice in relation to reports prepared pursuant to Companies Act 1948 s.165 (now Companies Act 1985 s.432) was considered in *Re Pergamon Press Ltd.*[28] Certain past and present directors of the company (including Mr Robert Maxwell) were concerned about foreign proceedings relating to the sale of the company's shares and the possibility of the inspectors making an interim report that would reach the plaintiff in the US litigation and be used against them. The directors refused to answer the inspectors' questions without certain assurances. Lord Denning MR explained[29] 7.2.2

> In short, the directors claimed that the inspectors should conduct the inquiry much as if it were a judicial inquiry in a Court of law in which Mr Maxwell and his colleagues were being charged with an offence.

The judges in the Court of Appeal noted that the inspectors determined nothing and that they only investigate and report. However, against this they also noted that the inspectors' report may have wide repercussions in that it may ruin reputations or careers and may expose persons to criminal prosecutions or civil proceedings.

All three judges were of the view that inspectors must act fairly but went on to consider the content of this obligation in the context of investigations under Companies Act 1948 s.165. Lord Denning MR stated[30] 7.2.3

> The inspectors can obtain information in any way they think best, but before they condemn or criticise a man, they must give him a fair opportunity for correcting or contradicting what is said against him. They need not quote chapter and verse. An outline of the charge will usually suffice.

Lord Denning MR took the view that there was no right for the directors to see the transcripts of the witnesses who spoke adversely of them, to see any documents which may be used against them and to cross-examine the witnesses. However, he held that the inspectors 'must not use the evidence of a witness so as to make it the basis of an adverse finding unless they give the party affected sufficient information to enable him to deal with it'.[31] Thus, if the evidence of a witness is so confidential that it cannot be put to those affected by it, the evidence must be

[28] [1971] Ch 388.
[29] At p. 399B.
[30] At p. 399H–400A.
[31] At p. 400E.

disregarded so far as that person is concerned.[32] Lord Denning MR also found that there was no obligation on inspectors, before deciding a conflict of evidence or making adverse criticisms of someone, to draft the proposed passage of their report and put it before the party for his comments before including it.[33] He concluded that this should be left to the discretion of the inspectors who, subject to being fair, 'must be masters of their own procedure'.[34]

Sachs LJ stated that it should be assumed at the outset that inspectors will provide 'fair play in action' and that[35] it was appropriate **7.2.4**

> to give at the appropriate later stage to anyone in danger of being criticised notice of the potential criticism in general terms sufficient to enable him to know what the allegation was and to enable him to give such explanation as he might wish. The precise form and manner of attaining this objective may vary greatly according to the circumstances and is a matter for the discretion of the inspectors.

Buckley LJ took a similar line, linking the obligation of fairness to the possibility of the report leading to criminal or civil proceedings.[36] **7.2.5**

> If inspectors are disposed to report on the conduct of anyone in such a way that he may in consequence be proceeded against, either in criminal or civil proceedings, the inspectors should give him, if he has not already had it, such information of the complaint or criticism which they may make of him in their report and of their reasons for doing so, including such information as to the nature and effect of the evidence which disposes them so to report, as is necessary to give the person concerned a fair opportunity of dealing with the matter, and they should give him such an opportunity.

Buckley LJ's view was that the disclosure necessary would depend on the facts of the particular case. It would not in the ordinary case involve disclosing the identity of witnesses or the disclosure of transcripts. Buckley LJ added that[37] it certainly would not normally involve offering an opportunity to cross-examine any other witnesses, and, indeed it

---

32 *ibid.*

33 In practice this is how inspectors usually proceed, a procedure commonly referred to as 'Maxwellisation' — see, e.g. *Soden v Burns* [1996] 3 All ER 967 at p. 989f–g. This raises the question whether, notwithstanding *Re Pergamon Press Ltd*, a legitimate expectation has been created that this procedure will be followed in any given case. See also 3.3 above and 7.5.1 below.

34 At p. 400F–G.

35 At p. 405G–H.

36 At p. 407C–D.

37 At p. 407E–F.

seems that inspectors could not compel a witness to submit to cross-examination. Whether it would involve confronting the director or officer concerned with any documentary evidence would depend on the circumstances of the case.[38]

Thus, all three judges held that there was an obligation of fairness but gave that obligation only a limited content and emphasised that fairness should be looked at in the particular circumstances of any given case and at the time the relevant issue arose for consideration in that specific case.

Following the decision in *Re Pergamon Press Ltd* the inspectors proceeded to produce two interim reports and a final report that were very critical of Mr Maxwell and which led to proceedings, *Maxwell v Department of Trade and Industry*.[39] Forbes J refused an injunction but was of the view that the inspectors had not formulated their tentative criticisms and given Mr Maxwell an opportunity of dealing with them. At the subsequent trial, however, Wien J found that the inspectors had behaved fairly. The difference in approach between Forbes J and Wien J was summarised and considered by the Court of Appeal.[40] Forbes J thought that, at the inquiry before inspectors, there were three stages: **7.2.6**

> First, the hearing of evidence (including Mr Maxwell's) and the study of documents; secondly, the inspectors coming to a conclusion (necessarily tentative in the circumstances); and thirdly, putting the substance of that conclusion to the witness.

Wien J held that natural justice did not require those three stages. In particular, it did not require the third stage. All that was required was that the inspectors should give Mr Maxwell 'a fair opportunity of correcting what is said against him. An outline of the case is enough'.

Lord Denning MR explained that a DTI inquiry is a very special kind of inquiry and must not be confused with other inquiries:[41] **7.2.7**

> It is not a trial of anyone, nor anything like it. There is no accused person … . It is not like a disciplinary proceeding before a professional body. Nor is it like an application to expel a man from a trade union or a club

38 In relation to cross-examination see also 5.7.2 above.
39 [1974] 1 QB 523. Note the criticism of the Court of Appeal's judgements by L Sealy in *Companies — Inquisition, Twentieth-Century Style* [1974] CLJ 225.
40 At p. 533B–C.
41 At p. 533D–H.

> … . It is not even like a committee which considers whether there is a prima facie case against a person. It is simply an investigation without anyone being accused.

He noted that there is no one to present a case to the inspectors who have to do the investigative work themselves, the investigation is in private and the inspectors have to make their report. Lord Denning MR concluded by preferring the approach of Wien J:[42]

> It is sufficient for the inspectors to put the points to the witnesses as and when they come in the first place. After hearing the evidence, the inspectors have to come to their conclusions. These need not be tentative in the least. They can be final and definite, ready for their report.

Orr LJ agreed with the approach of Lord Denning MR. He referred to passages from the judgments of Sachs LJ and Buckley LJ in *Re Pergamon Press Ltd*[43] upon which Forbes J had based his conclusion and said that the passage from Buckley LJ **7.2.8**

> seems to me to imply that it is sufficient if he has been given the relevant information as it emerged from the evidence of witnesses or the study of documents before the inspectors formed their tentative conclusion, and the same qualification may well, as it appears to me, be implied in the corresponding passage from the judgment of Sachs LJ.

Further, Orr LJ felt there was nothing to indicate that Sachs LJ or Buckley LJ disagreed with Lord Denning MR who had held it was going too far to say that whenever the inspectors thought of making adverse criticisms of someone they should draft the proposed passage and put it before the party for his comments.[44] Orr LJ distinguished between an inquiry based on a charge or accusation and an investigation in which the inspectors are required in the public interest to find out what has happened, and in the course of so doing form certain views or conclusions.[45]

Similarly Lawton LJ noted[46] that the inspectors were not instructed to investigate any charge against any officer of the companies; their duty was to find out what had happened and to report their opinion. He explained that this was a very different task from that which is sometimes imposed on those holding inquiries when they are asked to decide **7.2.9**

---

42 At p. 534D.
43 [1971] Ch 388 at p. 405G and 407C and see 7.2.4 and 7.2.5 above.
44 *Maxwell v Department of Trade and Industry* [1974] QB 523 at pp. 537F–8A.
45 At p. 538D–E.
46 At p. 540C–D.

whether allegations of specific misconduct have been made out. He added[47]

> That which fairness calls for in one kind of inquiry may not be called for in another. Those conducting an inquiry are in the best position to decide what fairness calls for.

Lawton LJ continued in relation to the content of the obligation of fairness[48]

> Those who conduct inquiries have to base their decisions, findings, conclusions or opinions (whichever is the appropriate word to describe what they have a duty to do) on the evidence. In my judgment they are no more bound to tell a witness likely to be criticised in their report what they have in mind to say about him than has a judge sitting alone who has to decide which of two conflicting witnesses is telling the truth. The judge must ensure that the witness whose credibility is suspected has a fair opportunity of correcting or contradicting the substance of what other witnesses have said or are expected to say which is in conflict with his testimony. Inspectors should do the same but I can see no reason why they should do any more.[49]

Lord Denning MR appeared to go further in restricting the obligation to act fairly by adding[50] **7.2.10**

> They must do what is fair to the best of their ability. They will, of course, put to a witness the points of substance which occur to them — so as to give him the chance to explain or correct any relevant statement which is prejudicial to him. They may even recall him to do so. But they are not to be criticised because they may on occasion overlook something or other.

Lord Denning MR appears to be introducing an element of subjectivity on the part of the inspectors, which goes beyond according them a discretion in respect of the procedure by excusing them from mistakes. This approach is justified by reference to the difficulty that would be faced in finding anyone of standing to fulfil the role of inspector if 'he were liable to be pilloried'. However, the discretion given to inspectors by the restricted content of the obligation of fairness gives them some latitude in any event and one purpose of judicial review is to correct the mistakes that may be made by even the most conscientious of public

---

47 At p. 540D.
48 At p. 541B–C.
49 This extract (other than the first sentence) is quoted in the *Investigations Handbook* App B, para. 39.
50 At p. 536B–C.

authorities and public servants. It is therefore unlikely that a court would allow material oversights to stand, although one matter which courts will consider in judicial review proceedings is whether to grant relief, and a court may well, for example, decline to quash a decision to publish a report where the matter complained of is of little or no significance in relation to the report as a whole.[51]

7.3 FURTHER CASES CONCERNING COMPANY INVESTIGATIONS

The decisions in *Re Pergamon Press Ltd* and *Maxwell v DTI* were considered in *Norwest Holst Ltd v Secretary of State for Trade*[52] in which the Court of Appeal was primarily concerned with whether the rules of natural justice applied to the initial decision to investigate a company.[53] Geoffrey Lane LJ drew a distinction between the administrative phase, the judicial phase and the executive phase 'when the orders of the Court or tribunal are, if necessary, executed or promulgated'.[54] He explained that[55] **7.3.1**

> the suspect shall be given a chance of putting his side of the case before the judicial inquiry is over. That scarcely needs illustration, but if it does it is to be found in the *Pergamon* case [1971] Ch 388. But on the other side — and the other side are entitled to fairness just as the suspect is — fairness to the inquirer demands that during the administrative period he should be able to investigate without having at every stage to inquire from the suspect what his side of the matter may be.

Geoffrey Lane LJ then observed that an investigation under Companies Act 1967 s.109, the forerunner of Companies Act 1985 s.447, was administrative and he thus appeared to suggest that the rules of natural justice did not apply. However, as was pointed out by Woolf J in *R v Secretary of State for Trade ex p. Perestrello*,[56] *Norwest Holst* was concerned with the appointment of inspectors; it was not primarily

[51] See T. Bingham *Should Public Law Remedies Be Discretionary?* [1991] PL 64 at pp. 68–9. Note the approach of Lawton LJ who used the analogy of criminal appeals under Criminal Appeal Act 1968 where the court looks at the proceedings as a whole and asks whether the verdict was unsafe or unsatisfactory.

[52] [1978] Ch 201.

[53] See 4.8 above.

[54] At p. 228G.

[55] At pp. 228H–9A.

[56] [1981] 1 QB 19.

concerned with the activities of inspectors once they had been appointed.[57]

Woolf J in *ex p. Perestrello* did not dissent from what Geoffrey Lane LJ had said in *Norwest Holst* but said that it did not apply to the matters he was considering, i.e. the ambit of a notice served by inspectors appointed under s.109 (the forerunner of Companies Act 1985 s.447) and did not therefore limit his approach. The approach adopted by Woolf J in *ex p. Perestrello* is instructive because the wording of s.109 did not envisage the publication of a report unlike Companies Act 1948 s.165 (and now Companies Act 1985 s.432). Woolf J's approach was based on the particular statutory power[58] **7.3.2**

> I regard it as essential in an area such as this to first of all look at the statutory power. It is only by looking at the statutory power that it is possible to come to a conclusion as to whether the rules of natural justice apply, and if so, the extent to which those rules apply. In the case of section 109, to talk of the rules of natural justice is not really helpful. It is much better to consider the matter as indicated by Lord Parker LJ in .... [*Re HK (an infant)*],[59] and ask oneself whether in the situation, what is required by the Act requires a degree of fairness. In this particular section, the opening words make it clear that the Board of Trade, before they exercise their powers, must think there is good reason so to do. Although this is not specifically stated in the section in relation to their officers, the same must apply and the officers must also think there is good reason so to do. But although they must think there is good reason so to do, this does not seem to me to be a situation where it would be appropriate to read into the Act the requirement of lack of bias ... .

Thus Woolf J drew a distinction between the rules of natural justice and a duty to act fairly — a distinction drawn in the earlier case of *Re HK*.[60] In *Re HK* Lord Parker CJ had said that an immigration officer must give the immigrant an opportunity of satisfying him and for that purpose let the immigrant know the officer's immediate impression so that he could disabuse the officer. This was because of the obligation to act fairly. However, he added that[61]

> to the limited extent that the circumstances of any particular case allow, and within the legislative framework under which the administrator is

57 At p. 35H and p. 36C–D.
58 At pp. 34F–35A.
59 [1967] 2 QB 617
60 See Lord Parker CJ [1967] 2 QB 617 at p. 630.
61 At p. 630.

> working, only to that limited extent do the so called rules of natural justice apply, which in a case such as this is merely a duty to act fairly.

Thus, in *ex p. Perestrello*, having said that the then test for bias did not apply, Woolf J said that the power under s.109 should be exercised fairly in the sense that the statutory discretion which it gives should not be abused.[62] Therefore, it appears that the content of the obligation of fairness will vary depending on the precise legislative framework.[63]

7.4 GUIDANCE FROM OTHER CONTEXTS

It is difficult to draw principles from other contexts and apply them to statutory investigations into companies because the content of the obligation of fairness varies depending on the precise nature of the investigation or proceedings.[64] One distinguishing feature of company investigation reports is that their production may lead to action being taken against those criticised, and reports may attract publicity,[65] but the investigation and report do not directly determine rights unlike, for example, the decision of a tribunal in disciplinary proceedings. A further limitation is that in many contexts where the investigation is a preliminary act rather than being determinative of rights, the courts have held that procedural fairness does not apply at all.[66] However, with these caveats in mind and consequently considering only those other contexts that are close in procedural terms to statutory company investigations, some assistance may be gained from other cases, 7.4.1

62 At p. 35F–G. See 6.11.7 and 6.11.8. It is arguable that this approach raises issues of substantive fairness in addition to procedural fairness.

63 Note the Australian cases where investigators were not held to be subject to an obligation to act fairly — *R v Coppel; ex p. Viney Industries Pty Ltd* [1962] VR 630, *Testro Bros. Pty Ltd v Tait* [1963] 109 CLR 353 and *Re Stanhill Development Finance Ltd* [1965] VR 415 — because the proceedings were not of a judicial nature. *Testro* has been the subject of criticism — see G. Nash *The Judicial Function and Inspectors Appointed Under the Companies Act, 1961* (1964) 38 ALJ 111; G. Nash *Administrative Law, Criminal Law and Inspection under the Companies Act* (1967) 8 UWALR 143; and J.S. Lockhart *The Lawyer as an Investigator* (1971) 45 ALJ 504. Note also the restrictive approach towards fairness in *St John v Fraser* [1935] SCR 441 and *Re Imperial Tobacco Co.* [1939] O.R. 627.

64 E.g. *Lloyd v McMahon* [1987] AC 625 at p. 702H, *R v Secretary of State for the Home Department ex p. Doody* [1994] 1 AC 531.

65 But see 7.6 below.

66 See 4.8 above.

particularly those concerning statutory-based investigations leading to the publication of a report. A particular reason for examining cases from other contexts is because of the dynamic nature of public law, which necessitates a consideration of whether general principles, first set out in cases decided in 1970 and 1974,[67] remain valid. A useful starting point, however, is the more generalised approach of Lord Denning MR in *R v Race Relations Board ex p. Selvarajan*.[68]

7.4.2 In *Selvarajan* the Court of Appeal considered the content of the obligation of fairness imposed on the Race Relations Board, a body that had the power under the Race Relations Act 1968 to carry out an investigation into allegations of unlawful discrimination and to produce a report. Lord Denning MR, stated[69]

> In recent years we have had to consider the procedure of many bodies who are required to make an investigation and form an opinion. Notably, the Gaming Board, who have to inquire whether an applicant is fit to run a gaming club, see *Reg. v Gaming Board for Great Britain, ex p. Benaim and Khaida* [1970] 2 QB 417; inspectors under the Companies Act 1948 who have to investigate the affairs of a company and make a report: see *In re Pergamon Press Ltd* [1971] Ch 388; and Commissioners of Inland Revenue who have to determine whether there is a prima facie case: see *Wiseman v Borneman* [1971] AC 297. In all these cases it has been held that the investigating body is under a duty to act fairly: but that which fairness requires depends upon the nature of the investigation and the consequences which it may have on persons affected by it. The fundamental rule is that, if a person may be subjected to pains or penalties, or be exposed to prosecution or proceedings, or deprived of remedies or redress, or in some such way adversely afflicted by the investigation and report, then he should be told the case made against him and be afforded a fair opportunity of answering it. The investigating body is, however, the master of its own procedure. It need not hold a hearing. It can do everything in writing. It need not allow lawyers. It need not put every detail of the case against a man. Suffice it if the broad grounds are given. It need not name its informants. It can give the substance only. Moreover, it need not do everything itself. It can employ secretaries and assistants to do all the preliminary work and leave much to them. But, in the end, the investigating body itself must come to its own decision and make its own report.

Thus, Lord Denning MR derived some general principles from the caselaw concerning procedural fairness in a number of contexts. The

---

67 *Perestrello*, which analyses *Pergamon* and *Maxwell*, was decided in 1979.
68 [1975] 1 WLR 1686.
69 At pp. 1693H–4D.

approach of Lord Denning MR in *Selvarajan* demonstrates the restricted nature of the content of the obligation of fairness in cases where investigators have to form an opinion that is not of itself determinative of an individual's rights. The Gaming Board is an interesting example because the Gaming Board's opinion may determine rights since the Board itself decides whether to award a licence rather than merely making a preliminary decision such as a recommendation to another body or Minister. That Lord Denning MR took the Gaming Board as an example of an investigative procedure strengthens the conclusion that the content of the obligation of procedural fairness is restricted in the case of investigations that are not directly determinative of rights.[70]

In *Mahon v Air New Zealand Ltd*[71] the Privy Council considered the requirements of procedural fairness in the context of a report prepared by a Royal Commissioner into the cause and circumstances of an airline crash. The Royal Commissioner, a High Court judge, had blamed the airline for the crash (and exonerated the captain and crew). He said that he had listened 'to an orchestrated litany of lies' and made an order under section 11 of the Commissions of Inquiry Act 1908 that the airline should pay $150,000 towards the costs of the Royal Commission. The airline applied for judicial review of certain findings and the costs order. The Privy Council held that the rules of natural justice require that a person who might be adversely affected by a finding should know of the risk of such a finding being made, and should be given the opportunity to adduce additional material that might deter the making of that finding. After holding that a finding must be based on probative evidence Lord Diplock stated[72] **7.4.3**

---

70 Note the limited approach in *R v Commission for Racial Equality ex p. Cottrell & Rothon (a firm)* [1980] 3 All ER 265 concerning a challenge to the Commission for Racial Equality. The Court took account of the fact that the Commission could serve a non-discrimination notice under Race Relations Act 1976 but there were no penalties of fines or imprisonment or the like that could be imposed. See also *R v Commission for Racial Equality ex p. Westminster City Council* [1985] ICR 827. Note *Syndicat des employés de production du Québec et de l'Acadie v Canadian Human Rights Commission* (1989) 62 DLR (4th) 385 and *Re Federation of Women's Teachers' Association of Ontario and Ontario Human Rights Commission* (1989) 67 QR (2d) 492 where the parties (the complainant and the person who was the subject of the complaint) were entitled to know the substance of the investigator's report and given an opportunity to respond before the Commissions decided whether or not to proceed. See also *Fayed v United Kingdom* (1994) 18 EHRR 393 at 7.7 below.

71 [1984] AC 808

72 At p. 820G–H.

> The second rule is that he must listen fairly to any relevant evidence conflicting with the finding and any rational argument against the finding that a person represented at the inquiry, whose interests (including in that term career or reputation) may be adversely affected by it, may wish to place before him or would have so wished if he had been aware of the risk of the finding being made.

He continued[73]

> The second rule requires that any person represented at the inquiry who will be adversely affected by the decision to make the finding should not be left in the dark as to the risk of the finding being made and thus deprived of any opportunity to adduce additional material of probative value which, had it been placed before the decision-maker, might have deterred him from making the finding even though it cannot be predicted that it would inevitably have had that result.

In *Mahon*, unlike *Pergamon* or *Maxwell* there was a substantive determination of rights, i.e. a costs order, but this additional element did not appear to be the basis of Lord Diplock's brief explanation of what is required by the obligation of fairness. The formulation in *Mahon* is similar to that in *Pergamon*, which was decided 13 years earlier and the importance of *Mahon* primarily lies in the clear requirement that a finding should be based on probative evidence.[74] In the event, the Privy Council found that the judge had failed to base certain findings on probative evidence and that there had also been a failure to put allegations to witnesses and the witnesses had therefore been treated unfairly.

One particular commercial context analogous to reports pursuant to statutory investigations into companies is reports by the Monopolies and Mergers Commission (MMC). Although the MMC are under some constraints in relation to the procedures they may adopt,[75] they are otherwise free to determine their own procedure.[76] In *R v Monopolies and Mergers Commission ex p. Elders IXL Ltd*[77] Mann J issued the caveat that there is 'no set of rules of fairness which is applicable to all investigative procedures' and added 'there is no general rule that one party to an investigation should be given all of the material submitted by another'.[78] The MMC's procedures were also considered in *R v* **7.4.4**

73 At p. 821B–C.
74 See 7.1.5 above.
75 Note Fair Trading Act 1973 s.81(1).
76 S.81(2).
77 [1987] 1 WLR 1221.
78 At p. 1233C–D.

Monopolies and Mergers Commission ex p. Matthew Brown plc.[79] Again the judge, Macpherson J, emphasised that fairness depended on the particular process and particular situation.[80] Part of Macpherson J's judgment may be taken to mean that the test of unfairness may be equated with Wednesbury unreasonableness, i.e. whether the MMC have adopted a procedure so unfair that no commission would have adopted it.[81] However, in *R v Monopolies and Mergers Commission ex p. Stagecoach Holdings plc*[82] Collins J disagreed with this approach. He found that a court would give great weight to the tribunal's own view as to what was fair so that, in the vast majority of cases, in practice the adoption of a Wednesbury test would make little difference. However, he added that it was not what the MMC believed to have been fair that should prevail but what was in fact fair. Therefore, although Collins J drew back from the view of Macpherson J in so far as the MMC analogy is relevant (and one limiting factor in this respect is that courts are wary of intervening in specialist complex economic issues such as those dealt with by the MMC) it is clear that there is still considerable latitude for the MMC in respect of its procedures.[83]

The brief analysis of cases in contexts other than statutory investigations into companies supports the general theme of *Pergamon* and *Maxwell*. It is clear that there is no weakening of the general principle that the inspectors will be masters of their own procedure. However, it is also emphasised that the obligation of procedural fairness requires that those who may face criticism in reports should be told of the case against them and given an adequate opportunity of adducing evidence that might rebut what is said against them.[84] If asked to do so in particular cases, courts will consider whether inspectors have adopted fair procedures and, whilst they will give weight to the inspectors' views, the courts will consider the requirements of fairness for themselves. Further, when doing so, the courts will not look at the matter on the basis of the less strict Wednesbury test. One final point is that although the general principles have not particularly changed, given the dynamic **7.4.5**

[79] [1987] 1 WLR 1235.
[80] At p. 1241D–E.
[81] At p. 1242D–E.
[82] [1996] *The Times*, 23 July.
[83] Note also *Dyason v Secretary of State for the Environment* [1998] *The Times*, 9 February in the context of a hearing before an inspector pursuant to Town and Country Planning Act 1990 s.78 upon the refusal of an application for planning permission.
[84] See also *Scott-Malden and others v Auriol Housing Foundation Ltd and others* 7 July 1980, unrep. *Cf Herring v Templeman* [1973] 3 All ER 569.

nature of public law, specific aspects of procedural fairness may evolve over the course of time.

7.5 THE *INVESTIGATIONS HANDBOOK*

The approach advocated by the DTI for inspectors appointed under Companies Act 1985, s.432 in the light of, in particular, *Pergamon* and *Maxwell* is set out in the *Investigations Handbook*.[85] The DTI's approach is that 7.5.1

> The inspectors will discharge their duty to treat a witness fairly if they give him notice of the evidence on which their intended criticisms are based in terms which are sufficient to enable him to know what is being said against him and to enable him to give such explanations as he may wish. Inspectors are not bound to put to a witness all the statements which have been made by other witnesses which may be prejudicial to him. Nor are they bound to name such witnesses, identify sources of information or provide the witness with transcripts of evidence adverse to him. Their duty is to put to him points of substance so as to give him a chance to explain the relevant evidence which is prejudicial to him.

This approach is a valid one, subject to the point that in some cases the only way in which a witness may be able to explain the relevant evidence which is prejudicial to him is if he is informed as to who provided the contrary evidence and the gist of that evidence.[86] It is of interest to note that the Handbook also discourages inspectors from sending extracts of draft reports to witnesses[87] since inspectors will often take this very course of action (commonly referred to as Maxwellisation) to head off any allegation that they have not treated a witness fairly. The sending of very limited extracts of criticism will not itself, however, be sufficient to discharge the obligation of acting fairly if the only way in which the witness can have an adequate opportunity of rebutting criticism is by being able to place the precise criticism in context. For example, if a criticism of witness A is based on inspectors accepting one piece of evidence given by witness B whose evidence was in many other respects discredited, it may be that witness A ought, in fairness, to be told at

---

85 App B, paras 35–41.
86 See 5.5.5 above.
87 App B, para. 40.

least in general terms that there are reservations about witness B's evidence.[88]

7.5.2 In so far as there is any possible conflict between what is said in caselaw on the one hand and publications, e.g. the *Investigations Handbook* on the other, the inspectors will be obliged to follow caselaw, although if the publications provide greater procedural safeguards, this may create a legitimate expectation that the procedures set out in such publications will be followed.[89]

7.6 WHERE REPORTS WILL NOT BE PUBLISHED

7.6.1 One particular issue for consideration is the extent to which the content of the obligation of fairness that arises in the context of investigations where the reports may be published[90] is the same in contexts where the reports may not be published.[91] This has not been specifically addressed in the caselaw and depends on how one interprets what was said in *Re Pergamon Press Ltd* and *Maxwell v DTI* and, in so far as applicable, caselaw from other relevant contexts. In so far as the judges in *Pergamon* and *Maxwell* imposed a requirement of fairness on inspectors because of a concern that the final reports may be published and have an impact on the reputations of those criticised in them, the reasoning would not require a similar degree of procedural protection towards those who may face criticism in a report that may not be published, whereas in so far as the obligation of fairness arises because of the use that may be made of the reports, then similar procedural protection may be called for. In fact in *Re Pergamon Press Ltd* the two lines of reasoning were intertwined. Thus Lord Denning MR stated[92]

> They have to make a report which may have wide repercussions. They may, if they think fit, make findings of fact which are very damaging to those whom they name. They may accuse some; they may condemn others; they may ruin reputations or careers. Their report may lead to judicial proceedings. It may expose persons to criminal prosecutions or to civil

88 Note the approach towards witnesses set out in the *Investigations Handbook* App B, para. 41.
89 See 3.3 above.
90 E.g. Companies Act 1985 s.432.
91 E.g. Financial Services Act s.177.
92 At p. 399F–G.

actions. It may bring about the winding up of the company, and be used itself as material for the winding up: see *In re. SBA Properties Ltd* [1967] 1 WLR 799. Even before the inspectors make their report, they may inform the Board of Trade of facts which tend to show that an offence has been committed: see section 41 of the Act of 1967. When they do make their report, the Board are bound to send a copy of it to the company; and the board may, in their discretion, publish it, if they think fit, to the public at large.

Sachs LJ, when concluding that the inspectors had to use fair procedures noted[93]

> it is the characteristics of the procedure that matter, not the precise compartment or compartments into which it falls — and one of the principal characteristics of the proceedings under consideration is to be found in the inspectors' duty, in their statutory fact-finding capacity, to produce a report which may be made public and may thus cause severe injury to an individual by its findings.

Sachs LJ's decision that procedural fairness was required was based on the possible publication of the report and damage to reputation rather than the decisions that may be based on the report. Buckley LJ, on the other hand stated[94]

> ... having regard to the circumstances which may lead to the appointment of an inspector under section 165, paragraph (b), which is the paragraph with which we are concerned in the present case, and to the fact that under the Act a copy of the report must be furnished to the company, a need for due regard to fair treatment may arise if inspectors propose to report adversely on the conduct of any director or officer. If it is found that a director or officer has made some default or acted improperly in relation to the conduct of the company's affairs, this may well prompt others to institute proceedings against him. In those proceedings the person proceeded against would have the full protection of a judicial process, but, particularly since the company is entitled to a copy of the report, he should not be exposed to the risk of such proceedings without being given a fair opportunity by the inspectors to forestall an adverse report. If inspectors are disposed to report on the conduct of anyone in such a way that he may in consequence be proceeded against, either in criminal or civil proceedings, the inspectors should give him, if he has not already had it, such information of the complaint or criticism which they may make of him in their report and of their reasons for doing

93 At p. 402H–3A.
94 At p. 407A–D.

so, including such information as to the nature and effect of the evidence which disposes them so to report, as is necessary to give the person concerned a fair opportunity of dealing with the matter, and they should give him such an opportunity.

Given that two of the three judges in *Re Pergamon Press Ltd* appeared to base their decision at least in part on the basis that the report could lead to proceedings being commenced against individuals, it appears that the obligation of fairness will apply in those contexts where reports may not be published in addition to those contexts where publication is a possibility. Further support for this is provided by Lord Denning MR who, when speaking of investigations more generally in *R v Race Relations Board ex p. Selvarajan*,[95] referred to a person being exposed to prosecution or proceedings as leading to the obligation that he should be told the case against him and given an opportunity of answering it. The above principles[96] will therefore determine the content of the obligation of fairness where reports will not be published subject to the qualification that it may vary depending on the precise statutory framework. Thus, the DTI's *Investigations Handbook*, when considering investigations under Financial Services Act 1986 s.177 with the section's specific reference to the Criminal Justice Act 1993 (Insider Dealing) notes that if inspectors are 'minded to conclude that a person has contravened the Act then they should put to him the substance of the evidence against him and give him an opportunity to respond, either at an interview (or further interview) or in writing if he so wishes'[97] and where 'criticism of individuals is contemplated it is suggested that inspectors inform the individual of the criticism intended and the evidence for it with a fixed period of, for example, 21 days for response'.[98] This same purposive approach is appropriate in other contexts where reports may not be published.

[95] [1975] 1 WLR 1686 at pp. 1693–4 — see 7.4.2 above.

[96] At 7.2 to 7.5.

[97] *Investigations Handbook* App C, para. 42 Note also App B, para. 42.

[98] App C, para. 55. Whether 21 days is a sufficient period will depend on what is a reasonable period of time in which to respond to the intended criticism.

7.7 PREPARATION OF REPORTS AND THE EUROPEAN CONVENTION ON HUMAN RIGHTS

In *Fayed v United Kingdom*[99] the applicants argued that in violation of Article 6(1) of the European Convention the inspectors' report on House of Fraser Holdings plc had determined their civil right to honour and reputation and denied them effective access to a court in determination of this civil right. The European Court of Human Rights agreed with the applicants that neither judicial review against the Secretary of State or the inspectors nor libel actions against a third party provided a remedy against the responsible authorities for determination of the truth of damaging statements about the applicants in the inspectors' report. The Court then considered the two aspects of the applicants' claims based on Article 6(1). The material part of Article 6(1) provides **7.7.1**

> In the determination of his civil rights and obligations, ... everyone is entitled to a fair and public hearing ... by an independent and impartial tribunal established by law ... .

The applicants' first argument was that Article 6(1) was applicable to the investigation by the inspectors. The Court, however, found that although the inspectors' published report damaged the applicants' reputations, the functions performed by the inspectors were, in practice as well as in theory, essentially investigative.[100] The main judgment explained[101] **7.7.2**

> The inspectors did not adjudicate, either in form or in substance ... . They did not make a legal determination as to criminal or civil liability concerning the Fayed brothers, and in particular concerning the latter's civil right to honour and reputation. The purpose of their inquiry was to ascertain and record facts which might subsequently be used as the basis for action by other competent authorities — prosecuting, regulatory, disciplinary or even legislative.

Thus, Article 6(1) was not applicable to the investigation. The Court added that the applicants' argument would entail that a body carrying

[99] (1994) 18 EHRR 393.
[100] Judgment, para. 61. The leading judgment referred to the analysis by the US Supreme Court of the function of the Federal Civil Rights Commission in *Hannah v Larche* 363 US 420 (1960).
[101] Para. 61.

out preparatory investigations for regulatory or other authorities should always be subject to the guarantees in Article 6(1), and that such an interpretation would 'unduly hamper the effective regulation in the public interest of complex financial and commercial activities'.[102]

The applicants' second argument was that English law denied them an entitlement under Article 6(1) to access to a court to have determined whether there was any justification for this attack on their reputations. The court did not need to rule upon the Government's proposition that the law of defamation and the defence of privilege set out the limits of the content of the applicants' right to a good reputation.[103] The Court considered the relevant principles[104] **7.7.3**

> (a) The right of access to the courts secured by Article 6(1) is not absolute, but may be subject to limitations; these are permitted by implication since the right of access by its very nature calls for regulation by the State, regulation which may vary in time and in place according to the needs and resources of the community and of individuals.
>
> (b) In laying down such regulation, the Contracting States enjoy a certain margin of appreciation, but the final decision as to observance of the Convention's requirements rests with the Court. It must be satisfied that the limitations applied do not restrict or reduce the access left to the individual in such a way or to such an extent that the very essence of the right is impaired.
>
> (c) Furthermore, a limitation will not be compatible with Article 6(1) if it does not pursue a legitimate aim and if there is not a reasonable relationship of proportionality between the means employed and the aim sought to be achieved.

The Court found that the underlying aim of the system of investigation and reporting under Companies Act 1985 was the furtherance of the public interest in the proper conduct of the affairs of public companies whose owners benefit from limited liability and that the system contributes to safeguarding the interests of the various parties concerned in the affairs of public companies. The Court concluded that the investigation and publication of the resultant report in themselves

[102] Para. 62. It is not clear that the applicants' argument would in fact entail such a necessary consequence. Further, it is not clear what this paragraph of the judgment adds to the main point which the Court found, i.e. that Article 6(1) was inapplicable since there was no determination of civil rights in the investigation.

[103] Paras 66–8.

[104] Para. 65.

pursued legitimate aims[105] and that the underlying objective in according inspectors freedom to report ('with courage and frankness' — per Lord Denning in *Re Pergamon Press Ltd*) was likewise legitimate.[106] Finally, the applicants argued that proportionality required a system that satisfied the aim pursued in a manner less harmful to their human rights, e.g. full judicial scrutiny of the report prior to publication.[107] The Court made a number of significant points.

(i) Limitations on access to a court may be more extensive when regulation of activities in the public sphere is at stake than in relation to litigation over the conduct of persons in their private capacity. As to enforcement of the right to a good reputation under domestic law, the limits of acceptable criticism are wider with regard to businessmen actively involved in the affairs of large public companies than with regard to private individuals.[108]

(ii) The findings in the inspectors' report in this case to which the applicants took exception related to matters that the applicants themselves had made great efforts to bring into the public domain.[109]

(iii) Judicial review would not have provided a remedy enabling the applicants to argue before a court that the inspectors' findings of fact were simply erroneous. It would, however, provide safeguards intended to ensure a fair procedure and the reliability of findings of fact.[110]

(iv) The applicants were made aware by the inspectors of the information required of them and were given every opportunity to respond to the allegations against them, etc.[111]

(v) The inspectors' report was published with the benefit of protection from liability in defamation, even though the authorities decided that there was no cause for instituting either criminal or civil proceedings. The applicants submitted evidence showing that there is a body of informed opinion in the United Kingdom

[105] Para. 69.
[106] Para. 70.
[107] Para. 72.
[108] Para. 75.
[109] Para. 76.
[110] Para. 78.
[111] Para. 79.

that believes that these consequences of the Companies Act 1985 system are not desirable.[112]

(vi) It is not for the Court to substitute its own view for that of the national legislature as to what would be the most appropriate policy. An entitlement not to have the report published until after a judicial hearing 'repeating, doubtless over a longer time-scale, the same fact-finding exercise as that already carried out by the Inspectors ... could effectively destroy the utility of informing the public of the results' of investigations under Companies Act 1985 s.432.[113]

(vii) The Court therefore concluded that the national authorities had not exceeded their margin of appreciation to limit access to the courts under Article 6(1), either as regards the state of the applicable law or as regards the effects of the application of that law. The Court added that having regard to the safeguards that existed, there was a reasonable relationship of proportionality between the freedom of reporting accorded to the inspectors and the legitimate aim pursued in the public interest.[114]

The applicants in *Fayed v United Kingdom* had also made a separate argument that, contrary to Article 13 of the Convention, no effective remedy was available under English law in respect of their complaint of a violation of Article 6(1) but the Commission concluded in their report that no separate issue arose under Article 13 and the Court's judgment records that this aspect was not pursued.[115] **7.7.4**

Fayed v United Kingdom shows that the European Convention on Human Rights Articles 6 and 13 have no direct role to play in the context of investigations under Companies Act 1985 s.432. It is hard to see how those articles would have any role in relation to investigations into companies under other statutory provisions, although there is a role for the European Convention in relation to the use that can be made of evidence obtained during investigations, and this may influence the way in which powers are exercised, particularly where a question may lead a witness to give evidence that would tend to incriminate himself.[116] Prior to the Human Rights Bill receiving Royal Assent and coming into force the Convention has not been incorporated into English law, **7.7.5**

---

[112] Para. 80.
[113] Para. 81.
[114] Para. 82.
[115] Paras 86–8.
[116] See 11.4 and 13.2 below.

although its jurisprudence influences English public law where domestic law is ambiguous or unclear.[117] Thus a number of points of relevance emerge from *Fayed*. First, the Court regarded the investigation process under Companies Act 1985 s.432 as not determining any civil rights. This is supportive of domestic law affording only limited procedural safeguards to witnesses. Secondly, the Court regarded judicial review as providing safeguards intended to ensure a fair procedure and the reliability of findings of fact. For this to be the case, the role for judicial review should not be unduly emasculated. Finally, the Court provided some guidance on proportionality in the context of investigations into companies and this may be of assistance for the future, whether one sees proportionality in English law as merely one aspect of irrationality[118] or as an emerging free-standing ground for judicial review.[119]

[117] See, e.g. *R v Secretary of State for the Home Department ex p. McQuillan* [1995] 4 All ER 400, *R v Mid Glamorgan Family Health Services ex p. Martin* [1995] 1 WLR 110. See also 7.2 above.

[118] See *R v Secretary of State for the Home Department ex p. Brind* [1991] 1 AC 696.

[119] See *R v Ministry of Defence ex p. Smith* [1996] QB 517

Chapter 8

DISCLOSURE OF INFORMATION RECEIVED DURING THE COURSE OF INVESTIGATIONS

8.1 INTRODUCTION

There are restrictions on the circumstances when information obtained by regulators pursuant to compulsory powers may be disclosed by those regulators. Similarly there are restrictions on disclosure of information obtained by others during the course of an investigation, such as witnesses.[1] The common law starting point is that a public authority that obtains documents or other information by compulsory powers may use them only for the purposes for which the compulsory powers were given.[2] The issue of disclosure of information arose in the context of investigations into companies in a case concerning an inspector appointed by the Industrial Assurance Commissioner pursuant to Industrial Assurance Act 1923 s.17(1). A question arose as to whether the inspector was entitled to conduct the examination in public. In *Hearts of Oak Assurance Company v Attorney General*[3] the House of Lords held that the examination ought not to be conducted in public. Lord Thankerton explained[4] **8.1.1**

> Except in so far as the statutory provisions otherwise direct, it seems to me that the affairs either of a collecting society or of an industrial assurance company are their own domestic matter, and that, therefore, in the absence of any statutory provision providing otherwise, the examination under s.17 of the Act of 1923 ought not to be conducted in public. The

1 See in particular 8.7.8 and 8.7.9 below in addition to the statutory provisions.
2 See *Marcel v Commissioner of Police of the Metropolis* [1992] Ch 225 and note *Taylor v Serious Fraud Office* [1997] *The Times*, 27 August in the context of documents created during criminal investigations. See also 8.9 below.
3 [1932] AC 392.
4 At p. 397.

> Commissioner cannot properly deal with the situation disclosed by the examination until the latter is completed, and it would seem to be of importance that the credit of the society or company and the confidence of its policy-holders should not be open to any risk before the Commissioner has decided on what steps, if any, it is expedient for him to take. If the examination were to be held in public, it might well be that unfavourable opinions as to the financial position of the society or company might be prematurely and wrongly formed in the minds of the public or the policy-holders either through reports in the press or as the results of attendance at the examination of some of the persons to be examined on oath.

He regarded the closest analogy as being inspectors appointed by the Board of Trade to investigate the affairs of a company and said that[5] 'the reasons against publicity in such an investigation would be equally strong in my opinion'.[6] However, the House of Lords declared that although the inspector was not entitled to conduct his inspection in public this should not prevent him from admitting from time to time any persons the presence of whom is reasonably necessary to enable him properly to carry out his duty under the statute. In *Re Gaumont British Picture Corporation Limited*[7] Crossman J held that the presence of a shorthand writer was reasonably necessary to enable an inspector appointed by the Board of Trade properly to carry out his duty under Companies Act 1929.

A number of the statutory regimes governing the investigation of companies now have specific provisions setting out the circumstances in which information may be disclosed.[8] The purpose of statutory provisions restricting disclosure was explained by Donaldson LJ in *R v Director General of Fair Trading ex p. FH Taylor & Co. Ltd*[9] who said of certain analogous provisions in the Fair Trading Act 1973 that they 'seem to me to constitute a clear warning and direction to the Director General and the Office of Fair Trading that, so far as practicable, they are to avoid disclosing matters that would seriously and prejudicially affect the interests of named or identifiable individuals'.[10] Further, such **8.1.2**

5 At p. 398.
6 Note the dissenting judgment of Viscount Dunedin at pp. 405–6 who said that the statute did not say whether the inquiry should be in public or in private and he could not see how a court could 'have power to say that it must be in private simply because it thinks that conditions of expediency all point that way'.
7 [1940] 1 Ch 506.
8 8.2 to 8.6 below.
9 [1981] ICR 292.
10 At p. 297.

provisions are to be 'strictly construed'.[11] In addition to the specific provisions set out below it is implicit that information obtained by regulators pursuant to compulsory powers may be disclosed for criminal proceedings in so far as the regulator may rely on the general principle that there is no confidence in an iniquity,[12] or the broader principle that disclosure of confidential information will not be restrained when there is just cause for disclosing it.[13]

8.2 INVESTIGATIONS UNDER COMPANIES ACT 1985

Information obtained under 6.1.1 to 6.1.8[14]may be disclosed by the Secretary of State if he thinks fit or he may authorise or require an inspector appointed under Companies Act 1985 to disclose such information but (subject to 8.1.2 and 8.2.5 below), whether disclosure be by the Secretary of State or inspectors it may only be in one of the following circumstances:[15] **8.2.1**

(i) with the consent in writing of the company where the information or document relates to the company;[16]
(ii) where disclosure is to a competent authority[17] or to any officer or servant of the competent authority;[18]
(iii) with a view to the institution of or otherwise for the purposes of criminal proceedings;[19]
(iv) with a view to the institution of, or otherwise for the purposes

---

11 See also *Murtagh v Newspaper Publishing Plc* [1990] CCLR 64 concerning Consumer Credit Act 1974 s.174. Note the approach in *Melton Medes Ltd v Securities and Investments Board* [1995] Ch 137 concerning Financial Services Act 1986 s.179 and see 8.3.6 below.
12 *Gartside v Outram* [1856] 26 LJ Ch 113.
13 *Fraser v Evans* [1969] 1 QB 349 at p. 361; *Lion Laboratories v Evans* [1985] QB 526; *Initial Services Ltd v Putterill* [1968] 1 QB 396. The DTI *Investigations Handbook* at para. 52 takes the view that where there are no specific statutory provisions information may be disclosed for criminal proceedings. See 8.5 below.
14 Companies Act 1985 ss.434 to 446.
15 Companies Act 1985 s.451A(2) and s.449.
16 Companies Act 1985 s.449.
17 Companies Act 1985 s.449 and see 8.2.2 below.
18 Companies Act 1985 s.449(3A).
19 Companies Act 1985 s.449(1)(a).

of, any proceedings on an application under Company Directors Disqualification Act 1986 ss.6, 7 or 8;[20]

(v) for the purposes of enabling or assisting any inspector appointed under Companies Act 1985 Part XIV, or under Financial Services Act 1986 ss.94 or 177, to discharge his functions;[21]

(vi) for the purpose of enabling or assisting any person authorised to exercise powers under Insurance Companies Act 1982 s.44, Companies Act 1985 s.447, Financial Services Act 1986 s.106 or Companies Act 1989 s.84 to discharge his functions;[22]

(vii) for the purpose of enabling or assisting the Secretary of State or the Treasury to exercise any of their functions under Companies Act 1985, the insider dealing legislation, Prevention of Fraud (Investments) Act 1958, Insurance Companies Act 1982, Insolvency Act 1986, Company Directors Disqualification Act 1986, Financial Services Act 1986 or Companies Act 1989 Part II, III or VII;[23]

(viii) for the purpose of enabling or assisting the Department of Economic Development for Northern Ireland to exercise any powers conferred on it by the enactments relating to companies or insolvency, or for the purpose of enabling or assisting any inspector appointed by it under the enactments relating to companies to discharge his functions;[24]

(ix) for the purpose of enabling or assisting the Chief Registrar of friendly societies or the Assistant Registrar of friendly societies for Scotland to discharge his functions under the enactments relating to friendly societies;[25]

(x) for the purpose of enabling or assisting the Friendly Societies Commission to discharge its functions under Financial Services Act 1986;[26]

(xi) for the purpose of enabling or assisting the Occupational Pensions Regulatory Authority to discharge their functions under Pension Schemes Act 1993 or Pensions Act 1995, or

---

20 Companies Act 1985 s.449(1)(ba).
21 Companies Act 1985 s.449(1)(c).
22 Companies Act 1985 s.449(1)(cc).
23 Companies Act 1985 s.449(1)(d).
24 Companies Act 1985 s.449(1)(dd).
25 Companies Act 1985 s.449(1)(de).
26 Companies Act 1985 s.449(1)(df).

any enactment in force in Northern Ireland corresponding to either of them;[27]

(xii) for the purpose of enabling or assisting the Bank of England to discharge its functions;[28]

(xiii) for the purpose of enabling or assisting the Financial Services Authority to discharge any functions under Financial Services Act 1986, other than as a designated agency within the meaning of that Act, its functions under Banking Act 1987, or its functions under Companies Act 1989 s.171;[29]

(xiv) for the purpose of enabling or assisting the Deposit Protection Board to discharge its functions under that Act;[30]

(xv) for any purpose mentioned in Financial Services Act 1986 s.180(1)(b), (e), (h), or (n);[31]

(xvi) for the purpose of enabling or assisting a body established by order under Companies Act 1989 s.46 to discharge its functions under Part II of that Act, or of enabling or assisting a recognised supervisory or qualifying body within the meaning of that Part to discharge its functions as such;[32]

(xvii) for the purpose of enabling or assisting the Industrial Assurance Commissioner or the Industrial Assurance Commissioner for Northern Ireland to discharge his functions under the enactments relating to industrial assurance;[33]

(xviii) for the purpose of enabling or assisting the Insurance Brokers Registration Council to discharge its functions under Insurance Brokers (Registration) Act 1977;[34]

(xix) for the purpose of enabling or assisting an official receiver to discharge his functions under the enactments relating to insolvency or for the purpose of enabling or assisting a body that is for the time being a recognised professional body for the purposes of Insolvency Act 1986 s.391 to discharge its functions as such;[35]

(xx) with a view to the institution of, or otherwise for the purposes of, any disciplinary proceedings relating to the exercise by a

---

27 Companies Act 1985 s.449(1)(dg).
28 Companies Act 1985 s.449(1)(f).
29 Companies Act 1985 s.449(1)(fa).
30 Companies Act 1985 s.449(1)(g).
31 Companies Act 1985 s.449(1)(h).
32 Companies Act 1985 s.449(1)(hh).
33 Companies Act 1985 s.449(1)(i).
34 Companies Act 1985 s.449(1)(j).
35 Companies Act 1985 s.449(1)(k).

solicitor, auditor, accountant, valuer or actuary of his professional duties;[36]

(u) with a view to the institution of, or otherwise for the purposes of, any disciplinary proceedings relating to the discharge by a public servant of his duties.[37] Public servant means an officer or servant of the Crown or of any public or other authority for the time being designated for the purposes of that paragraph by the Secretary of State by order made by statutory instrument;[38]

(v) for the purpose of enabling or assisting an overseas regulatory authority to exercise its regulatory functions.[39] Overseas regulatory authority and regulatory functions have the same meaning as in Companies Act 1989 s.82;[40]

(w) for the purpose of enabling or assisting any public or other authority for the time being designated for the purposes of this subsection by the Secretary of State by an order in a statutory instrument to discharge any functions that are specified in the order;[41]

(x) where the information is mentioned in Financial Services Act 1986 s.180(5) and the disclosure is made by any person who by virtue of that section is not precluded by s.179 from disclosing it.[42]

For the purpose of 8.2.1(ii) above each of the following is a competent authority: **8.2.2**

(i) the Secretary of State;[43]

(ii) an inspector appointed under Companies Act 1985 Part XIV or under Financial Services Act 1986 ss.94 or 177;[44]

(iii) any person authorised to exercise powers under Insurance Companies Act 1982 s.44, Companies Act 1985 s.447, Financial Services Act 1986 s.106 or Companies Act 1989 s.84;[45]

---

36 Companies Act 1985 s.449(1)(l).
37 Companies Act 1985 s.449(1)(ll).
38 Companies Act 1985 s.449(1A)(a).
39 Companies Act 1985 s.449(1)(m).
40 Companies Act 1985 s.449(1A)(b). See 4.7.2 above.
41 Companies Act 1985 s.449(1B). See 8.2.3 below.
42 Companies Act 1985 s.449(1D).
43 Companies Act 1985 s.449(3)(a).
44 Companies Act 1985 s.449(3)(b).
45 Companies Act 1985 s.449(3)(c).

(iv) the Department of Economic Development in Northern Ireland;[46]
(v) the Treasury;[47]
(vi) the Bank of England;[48]
(vii) the Lord Advocate;[49]
(viii) the Director of Public Prosecutions, and the Director of Public Prosecutions for Northern Ireland;[50]
(ix) the Financial Services Authority, other than in its capacity as a designated agency within the meaning of Financial Services Act 1986;[51]
(x) any designated agency or transferee body within the meaning of Financial Services Act 1986, and any body administering a scheme under s.54 of or Schedule 11, para. 8 to that Act (schemes for compensation of investors);[52]
(xi) the Chief Registrar of friendly societies;[53]
(xii) the Friendly Societies Commission;[54]
(xiii) the Industrial Assurance Commissioner;[55]
(xiv) any constable;[56]
(xv) any procurator fiscal.[57]

An order under 8.2.1(xxiii) above may impose conditions subject to which the publication or disclosure of any information or document is permitted and otherwise restrict the circumstances in which publication or disclosure is permitted.[58] Orders currently relate to the following authorities: **8.2.3**

(i) recognised associations of dealers and recognised stock exchanges in relation to their functions as such;[59]

46 Companies Act 1985 s.449(3)(d).
47 Companies Act 1985 s.449(3)(e).
48 Companies Act 1985 s.449(3)(f).
49 Companies Act 1985 s.449(3)(g).
50 Companies Act 1985 s.449(3)(h).
51 Companies Act 1985 s.449(3)(ha).
52 Companies Act 1985 s.449(3)(i).
53 Companies Act 1985 s.449(3)(j).
54 Companies Act 1985 s.449(3)(jj).
55 Companies Act 1985 s.449(3)(k).
56 Companies Act 1985 s.449(3)(l).
57 Companies Act 1985 s.449(3)(m).
58 Companies Act 1985 s.449(1C).
59 Financial Services (Disclosure of Information) (Designated Authorities) Order 1986 (SI 1986/2046).

(ii) the Insolvency Practitioners Tribunal in relation to its function under Insolvency Act 1986;[60]
(iii) the Occupational Pensions Board in relation to its functions under Social Security Act 1973 and Social Security Acts 1975 to 1986;[61]
(iv) the Panel on Takeovers and Mergers in relation to all its functions;[62]
(v) organs of the Society of Lloyd's constituted by or under the Lloyd's Act 1982 in relation to their functions under the Lloyd's Acts 1871–1982 and the byelaws made thereunder of the Society of Lloyd's;[63]
(vi) the tribunal established under Prevention of Fraud (Investments) Act 1958 in relation to its function under that Act;[64]
(vii) the person appointed by the Secretary of State to investigate and report on certain aspects relating to various Barlow Clowes entities;[65]
(viii) the Director General of Fair Trading in relation to his functions under Fair Trading Act 1973 (other than Part II of that Act), Restrictive Trade Practices Act 1976, Competition Act 1980, Consumer Credit Act 1974, Estate Agents Act 1979 and the Control of Misleading Advertisements Regulations 1988;[66]
(ix) the Monopolies and Mergers Commission in relation to its functions under Fair Trading Act 1973 and Competition Act 1980;[67]
(x) the Charity Commissioners in relation to their functions under Charities Act 1960;[68]

---

[60] Financial Services (Disclosure of Information) (Designated Authorities) (No. 2) Order 1987 (S1 1987/859).
[61] Financial Services (Disclosure of Information) (Designated Authorities) (No. 2) Order 1987 (S1 1987/859).
[62] Financial Services (Disclosure of Information) (Designated Authorities) (No. 2) Order 1987 (S1 1987/859).
[63] Financial Services (Disclosure of Information) (Designated Authorities) (No. 3) Order 1987 (SI 1987/1141).
[64] Financial Services (Disclosure of Information) (Designated Authorities) (No. 3) Order 1987 (SI 1987/1141).
[65] Financial Services (Disclosure of Information) (Designated Authorities) (No. 4) Order 1988 (SI 1988/1058).
[66] Companies (Disclosure of Information) (Designated Authorities) Order 1988 (SI 1988/1334) and Financial Services (Disclosure of Information) (Designated Authorities) (No. 6) Order 1989 (SI 1989/2009).
[67] Companies (Disclosure of Information) (Designated Authorities) Order 1988 (SI 1988/1334).
[68] Financial Services (Disclosure of Information) (Designated Authorities) (No. 5) Order 1989 (SI 1989/940).

(xi) the Attorney General in relation to his functions in connection with charities;[69]

(xii) a person authorised by the Secretary of State under Companies Act 1985 s.245C in relation to that person's functions relating to the securing of compliance by companies with the accounting requirements of Companies Act 1985;[70]

(xiii) the Director General of the National Lottery in relation to his functions under ss.5 to 10 and 15 of National Lottery, etc. Act 1993.[71]

A statutory instrument containing an order under 8.2.1(xxi) and 8.2.1(xxiii) is subject to amendment in pursuance of a resolution of either House of Parliament.[72]

Information obtained under 6.1.1 to 6.1.8 may also be disclosed by an inspector appointed under Companies Act 1985 Part XIV to **8.2.4**

(i) another inspector appointed under Companies Act 1985 Part XIV or an inspector appointed under Financial Services Act 1986 ss.94 or 177;[73] or

(ii) a person authorised to exercise powers or appointed under Insurance Companies Act 1982 ss.43A or 44, Companies Act 1985 s.447, Financial Services Act 1986 s.106 or Companies Act 1989 s.84.[74]

Companies Act 1985 s.451(4) provides that any information, which may by virtue of s.451(3) be disclosed to 'any person', may be disclosed to any officer or servant of that person. It is clear that this allows disclosure to any officer or servant of the person authorised at (ii) above. It also seems likely that a true construction of 'any person' in s.451(4) allows disclosure to any officer or servant of an inspector.

The Secretary of State may, if he thinks fit, disclose any information obtained under Companies Act 1985 s.444 to **8.2.5**

69 Financial Services (Disclosure of Information) (Designated Authorities) (No. 5) Order 1989 (SI 1989/940).

70 Financial Services (Disclosure of Information) (Designated Authorities) (No. 7) Order 1993 (SI 1993/1826).

71 Financial Services (Disclosure of Information) (Designated Authorities) (No. 8) Order 1994 (SI 1994/340).

72 Companies Act 1985 s.449(4).

73 Companies Act 1985 s.451A(3)(a).

74 Companies Act 1985 s.451A(3)(b).

(i) the company whose ownership was the subject of the investigation;
(ii) any member of the company;
(iii) any person whose conduct was investigated in the course of the investigation;
(iv) the auditors of the company; or
(v) any person whose financial interests appear to the Secretary of State to be affected by matters covered by the investigation [75]

No information or document relating to a company, which has been obtained under the provisions of Companies Act 1985 s.447,[76] shall be published or disclosed except in accordance with the provisions at 8.2.1 to 8.2.3 above.[77] **8.2.6**

A person who publishes or discloses any information or document in contravention of 8.2.6 is guilty of an offence and liable to imprisonment or a fine, or both.[78] This sanction, which is contained in Companies Act 1985 s.449, applies to one disclosing information obtained under s.447 in breach of s.449. However, the drafting in s.451A has the effect that although information obtained under ss.434 to 446 may be disclosed for limited purposes only and some of those purposes are permitted by cross-reference to s.449, the criminal sanctions do not apply. Thus it appears that one disclosing information obtained pursuant to s.447 in unauthorised circumstances commits a criminal offence whereas one disclosing information obtained pursuant to Companies Act 1985 ss.434 to 446 in unauthorised circumstances does not. **8.2.7**

8.3 INVESTIGATIONS UNDER THE FINANCIAL SERVICES LEGISLATION

Subject to 8.3.2, 8.3.3 and 8.3.7 below, information obtained by the 'primary recipient' for the purposes of, or in the discharge of his functions under Financial Services Act 1986 or any rules or regulations made under that Act (whether or not by virtue of any requirement to supply **8.3.1**

---

75 Companies Act 1985 s.451A(5).
76 See 6.3 above.
77 Companies Act 1985 s.449.
78 Companies Act 1985 ss.732 (restriction on prosecutions), 733 (liability of individuals for corporate default) and 734 (criminal proceedings against unincorporated bodies) apply to this offence.

it made under those provisions) ('restricted information')[79] and which relates to the business or other affairs of any person shall not be disclosed without the consent of the person from whom the information was obtained by the primary recipient and, if different, the person to whom the information relates.[80]

Those who constitute the primary recipient are

(i) the Treasury;[81]
(ii) the Secretary of State;[82]
(iii) any designated agency, transferee body or body administering a scheme under Financial Services Act 1986 s.54;[83]
(iv) the Director General of Fair Trading;[84]
(v) the Chief Registrar of friendly societies;[85]
(vi) the Friendly Societies Commission;[86]
(vii) any member of the Financial Services Tribunal;[87]
(viii) any person appointed or authorised to exercise any powers under Financial Services Act 1986 ss.94, 106 or 177;[88]
(ix) any officer or servant of any such person as is mentioned in (i) to (viii) above;[89]
(x) any constable or other person named in a warrant issued under Financial Services Act 1986.[90]

Information is not treated as restricted information if it has been made available to the public by virtue of being disclosed in any circumstances in which or for any purpose for which disclosure is not precluded by this provision.[91]

8.3.1 above shall not preclude the disclosure of information in the following circumstances: **8.3.2**

79 Financial Services Act 1986 s.179(2).
80 Financial Services Act 1986 s.179(1)–(3).
81 Financial Services Act 1986 s.179(3)(aa).
82 Financial Services Act 1986 s.179(3)(a).
83 Financial Services Act 1986 s.179(3)(b).
84 Financial Services Act 1986 s.179(3)(c).
85 Financial Services Act 1986 s.179(3)(d).
86 Financial Services Act 1986 s.179(3)(e).
87 Financial Services Act 1986 s.179(3)(g).
88 Financial Services Act 1986 s.179(3)(h).
89 Financial Services Act 1986 s.179(3)(i).
90 Financial Services Act 1986 s.179(3)(j).
91 Financial Services Act 1986 s.179(4).

(i) with a view to the institution of or otherwise for the purposes of criminal proceedings;[92]

(ii) with a view to the institution of or otherwise for the purposes of any civil proceedings arising under or by virtue of Financial Services Act 1986 or proceedings before the Financial Services Tribunal;[93]

(iii) for the purpose of enabling or assisting the Treasury to exercise any of their powers under the enactments relating to insurance companies, Financial Services Act 1986 or Companies Act 1989 Part III or VII;[94]

(iv) for the purpose of enabling or assisting the Secretary of State to exercise any powers conferred on him by Financial Services Act 1986, or by the enactments relating to companies, insurance companies or insolvency or by Companies Act 1989 Part II, III or VII, or for the purpose of enabling or assisting any inspector appointed by him under the enactments relating to companies to discharge his functions;[95]

(v) for the purpose of enabling or assisting the Department of Economic Development for Northern Ireland to exercise any powers conferred on it by the enactments relating to companies or insolvency or for the purpose of enabling or assisting any inspector appointed by it under the enactments relating to companies to discharge his functions;[96]

(vi) for the purpose
  (a) of enabling or assisting a designated agency to discharge its functions under Financial Services Act 1986 or Companies Act 1989 Part VII,
  (b) of enabling or assisting a transferee body or the competent authority to discharge its functions under Financial Services Act 1986, or
  (c) of enabling or assisting the body administering a scheme under Financial Services Act 1986 s.54 to discharge its functions under the scheme;[97]

(vii) for the purpose of enabling or assisting the Bank of England

---

92 Financial Services Act 1986 s.180(1)(a).
93 Financial Services Act 1986 s.180(1)(b).
94 Financial Services Act 1986 s.180(1)(bb).
95 Financial Services Act 1986 s.180(1)(c).
96 Financial Services Act 1986 s.180(1)(d).
97 Financial Services Act 1986 s.180(1)(e).

to discharge its functions under Banking Act 1987 or any other functions;[98]

(viii) for the purpose of enabling or assisting the Deposit Protection Board to discharge its functions under that Act;[99]

(ix) for the purpose of enabling or assisting the Friendly Societies Commission to discharge its functions under Financial Services Act 1986, the enactments relating to friendly societies or the enactments relating to industrial assurance;[100]

(x) for the purpose of enabling or assisting a body established by order under Companies Act 1989 s.46 to discharge its functions under Part II of that Act, or of enabling or assisting a recognised supervisory or qualifying body within the meaning of that Part to discharge its functions as such;[101]

(xi) for the purpose of enabling or assisting the Industrial Assurance Commissioner or the Industrial Assurance Commissioner for Northern Ireland to discharge his functions under the enactments relating to industrial assurance;[102]

(xii) for the purpose of enabling or assisting the Insurance Brokers Registration Council to discharge its functions under Insurance Brokers (Registration) Act 1977;[103]

(xiii) for the purpose of enabling or assisting an official receiver to discharge his functions under the enactments relating to insolvency or for the purpose of enabling or assisting a body, which is for the time being a recognised professional body for the purposes of Insolvency Act 1986 s.391, to discharge its functions as such;[104]

(xiv) for the purpose of enabling or assisting the Building Societies Commission to discharge its functions under Building Societies Act 1986;[105]

(xv) for the purpose of enabling or assisting the Director General of Fair Trading to discharge his functions under this Act;[106]

(xvi) for the purpose of enabling or assisting the Occupational

98 Financial Services Act 1986 s.180(1)(f).
99 Financial Services Act 1986 s.180(1)(g).
100 Financial Services Act 1986 s.180(1)(h).
101 Financial Services Act 1986 s.180(1)(hh).
102 Financial Services Act 1986 s.180(1)(i).
103 Financial Services Act 1986 s.180(1)(j).
104 Financial Services Act 1986 s.180(1)(k).
105 Financial Services Act 1986 s.180(1)(l).
106 Financial Services Act 1986 s.180(1)(m).

Pensions Regulatory Authority or the Pensions Compensation Board to discharge their functions under Pensions Schemes Act 1993 or Pensions Act 1995, or any enactment in force in Northern Ireland corresponding to either of them;[107]

(xvii) for the purpose of enabling or assisting a recognised self-regulating organisation, recognised investment exchange, recognised professional body, or recognised clearing house to discharge its functions as such;[108]

(xviii) to an Operator approved under the Uncertified Securities Regulations 1995, if the information is necessary to ensure the proper functioning of a relevant system within the meaning of those Regulations in relation to defaults and potential defaults by market participants;[109]

(xix) with a view to the institution of, or otherwise for the purposes of, any disciplinary proceedings relating to the exercise by a solicitor, auditor, accountant, valuer or actuary of his professional duties;[110]

(xx) with a view to the institution of, or otherwise for the purposes of, any disciplinary proceedings relating to the discharge by a public servant of his duties.[111] Public servant means an officer or servant of the Crown, or of any public or other authority for the time being designated for this purpose by order of the Secretary of State;[112]

(xxi) for the purpose of enabling or assisting any person appointed or authorised to exercise any powers under Insurance Companies Act 1982 ss.43A or 44, Companies Act 1985 s.447, Financial Services Act 1986 ss.94, 106 or 177 or Companies Act 1989 s.84 to discharge his functions;[113]

(xxii) for the purpose of enabling or assisting an auditor of an authorised person or a person approved under Financial Services Act 1986 s.108 to discharge his functions;[114]

(xxiii) for the purpose of enabling or assisting an overseas regulatory authority to exercise its regulatory functions.[115] Overseas

---

107 Financial Services Act 1986 s.180(1)(mm).

108 Financial Services Act 1986 s.180(1)(n).

109 Financial Services Act 1986 s.180(1)(nn).

110 Financial Services Act 1986 s.180(1)(o).

111 Financial Services Act 1986 s.180(1)(oo).

112 Financial Services Act 1986 s.180(1A)(a).

113 Financial Services Act 1986 s.180(1)(p).

114 Financial Services Act 1986 s.180(1)(q).

115 Financial Services Act 1986 s.180(1)(qq).

regulatory authority and regulatory functions have the same meaning as in Companies Act 1989 s.82;[116]

(xxiv) if the information is or has been available to the public from other sources;[117]

(xxv) in a summary or collection of information framed in such a way as not to enable the identity of any person to whom the information relates to be ascertained; or[118]

(xxvi) in pursuance of any European Community obligation;[119]

(xxvii) for the purpose of enabling or assisting any public or other authority for the time being designated by an order made by the Secretary of State to discharge any functions, which are specified in the order.[120] Such an order may impose conditions subject to which the disclosure of information is permitted and otherwise restrict the circumstances in which disclosure is permitted.[121] Orders currently relate to the authorities listed at 8.2.3 above.

The Secretary of State may by order modify the application of any provision of (i) to (xxvi) above so as to prevent the disclosure by virtue of that provision, or to restrict the extent to which disclosure is permitted by virtue of that provision, of information received by a person specified in the order pursuant to a Community obligation from a person exercising functions in relation to a collective investment scheme who is also so specified .[122] An order is subject to annulment in pursuance of a resolution of either House of Parliament.[123]

Further, 8.3.1 does not preclude the disclosure of information **8.3.3**

(i) to the Secretary of State or the Treasury if the disclosure is made in the interests of investors or in the public interest;[124]

(ii) contained in an unpublished report of the Financial Services Tribunal, which has been made available to any person under Financial Services Act 1986 by the person to whom it was made

[116] Financial Services Act 1986 s 180(1A)(b). See 4.7.2 above.
[117] Financial Services Act 1986 s.180(1)(r).
[118] Financial Services Act 1986 s.180(1)(s).
[119] Financial Services Act 1986 s.180(1)(t).
[120] Financial Services Act 1986 s.180(3).
[121] Financial Services Act 1986 s.180(4).
[122] Financial Services Act 1986 s.180(8).
[123] Financial Services Act 1986 s.180(9).
[124] Financial Services Act 1986 s.180(2).

available or by any person obtaining the information directly or indirectly from him;[125]

(iii) contained in any notice or copy of a notice served under Financial Services Act 1986, notice of the contents of which has not been given to the public, by the person on whom it was served or any person obtaining the information directly or indirectly from him;[126]

(iv) contained in the register kept under Financial Services Act 1986 s.102 by virtue of s.102(1)(e) by a person who has inspected the register under s.103(2) or (3), or any person obtaining the information directly or indirectly from him;[127]

(v) by the Director-General of Fair Trading or any officer or servant of his or any person obtaining the information directly or indirectly from the Director or any such officer or servant if the information was obtained by the Director or any such officer or servant for the purposes of or in the discharge of his function under Financial Services Act 1986 (whether or not he was the primary recipient of the information within the meaning of s.179) and the disclosure is made

(a) for the purpose of enabling or assisting the Director, the Secretary of State or any other Minister, the Monopolies and Mergers Commission or any Northern Ireland department to discharge any function conferred on him or them by Fair Trading Act 1973 (other than Part II or III of that Act), Restrictive Trade Practices Act 1976 or Competition Act 1980; or

(b) for the purposes of any civil proceedings under any of those provisions;

and information shall not be treated as restricted information for the purposes of 8.3.1 if it has been made available to the public by virtue of 8.3.3(v).[128]

If it appears to the Secretary of State to be in the public interest to do so he may give a direction prohibiting the disclosure of information obtained by any person appointed or authorised to exercise any powers under Financial Services Act 1986 ss.94, 106 or 177 (or any officer or servant of any such person) to any person in any country or territory **8.3.4**

[125] Financial Services Act 1986 s.180(5)(a).
[126] Financial Services Act 1986 s.180(5)(b).
[127] Financial Services Act 1986 s.180(5)(c).
[128] Financial Services Act 1986 s.180(7).

outside the United Kingdom that is specified in the direction, or to such persons in such a country or territory as may be so specified, of such information as may be so specified.[129] A direction may prohibit disclosure by all persons or only by such persons or classes of persons as may be specified in it; and may prohibit such disclosure absolutely or in such cases or subject to such conditions as to consent or otherwise as may be specified in it.[130]

Any person who contravenes the provision at 8.3.1 (save where disclosure is permitted pursuant to the provisions at 8.3.2 and 8.3.3) is guilty of an offence and liable on conviction on indictment to imprisonment for a term not exceeding two years or to a fine or to both, and on summary conviction to imprisonment for a term not exceeding three months or to a fine not exceeding the statutory maximum[131] or to both.[132] **8.3.5**

In *Melton Medes Ltd v Securities and Investments Board*[133] the plaintiffs brought proceedings against the SIB claiming damages alleging that there had been an unauthorised disclosure in contravention of Financial Services Act s.179. Lightman J held that there was no cause of action for breach of statutory duty in respect of s.179.[134] He also considered that there had been no unauthorised disclosure. Lightman J explained that to establish a disclosure in contravention of s.179 it is necessary that[135] **8.3.6**

> (1) information obtained by the SIB for the purposes of or in discharge of the functions of the SIB under the 1986 Act (2) relating to the business or other affairs of the plaintiffs (3) has been disclosed (4) without the plaintiffs' consent; and no relevant exception from the restriction allowed by s.180 must have been shown to be applicable.

The plaintiffs alleged two unauthorised disclosures. The first plaintiff was the parent company of the second plaintiff, which was the trustee

---

129 Financial Services Act 1986 s.181(1) and (3).
130 Financial Services Act 1986 s.181(2). A direction prohibiting disclosure must be published by the Secretary of State in such manner as appears to him to be appropriate.
131 Currently £5,000. See Criminal Justice Act 1991 and SI 1992/333.
132 Financial Services Act 1986 s.179(6).
133 [1995] Ch 137.
134 See 8.9 below. Lightman J took a narrow view of 'bad faith' in Financial Services Act s.187(3), finding that lack of good faith connotes either (a) malice in the sense of personal spite or a desire to injure for improper reasons, or (b) knowledge of absence of power to make the decision in question [1995] Ch 137 at pp. 147B–E.
135 At p. 148G–H.

of pension funds. Beneficiaries of the pension funds initiated proceedings against the plaintiffs seeking orders that they compensate the funds for losses allegedly incurred as a result of the making of a £5m loan from the funds to the first plaintiff and its subsequent repayment. The SIB investigated the trustee's management of the funds and obtained information from the funds' auditors and (as permitted by Financial Services Act 1986 s.180(1)(q)) disclosed information to the auditors. The first allegedly wrongful disclosure concerned 'accounts information'. The auditors had expressed concern about their earlier audit reports to the SIB, and the SIB telephoned the beneficiaries' solicitors and asked 'Have you asked the auditors whether they are happy for your clients to continue to rely upon the auditors' earlier certificate?'. Lightman J found[136] that the statements made by the auditors to the SIB did not amount to restricted information. He said that it

> might be deduced from the statements that [the auditors] ... might take the view of their accounts suggested or might carry out a review, but disclosure of what is a mere possible deduction from information is not ..., at least in this context, disclosure of the information itself.

Further, the statement by the SIB did not amount to disclosure of the accounts information. The second alleged unauthorised disclosure concerned the SIB forwarding to the beneficiaries' solicitors an earlier letter, which it had sent to the auditors indicating that it had reason to disbelieve explanations given by the plaintiffs' directors in relation to the loan. The relevant paragraph of the letter of which complaint had been made was for practical purposes identical to a paragraph of an earlier letter from the auditors that had been read out in open court during an application in the proceedings brought by the beneficiaries against the plaintiffs. The SIB argued that the information was information that was or had been available to the public from other sources[137] so was within an exemption from disclosure. Lightman J found that other sources means 'sources other than a primary or secondary recipient' and held that the exemption applied in this case because it was sufficient that the information was disclosed in open court and that any member of the public present was free to make use of it. Further, Lightman J upheld the SIB's case that the communication that was the subject of challenge was merely an expression of opinion, not a disclosure of information. He stated[138]

---

[136] At p. 149E.
[137] See Financial Services Act 1986 s.180(1)(r).
[138] At p. 151B–E.

> I entirely agree ... that mere expressions of opinion are outside s.179, but the question arises whether the paragraph in the letter also communicated restricted information. The paragraph reveals that (a) the directors supplied a history as to the making and repayment of the loan; (b) the SIB obtained other information relating to the loan elsewhere; (c) the accounts were in the opinion of the SIB inconsistent; and (d) the SIB was minded to disbelieve the directors' account. Accordingly, whilst accepting that (c) and (d) are mere matters of opinion, (a) and (b) are statements of fact. The question is whether these statements constitute information that is protected by s.179. In my view the answer is in the negative. Section 179 protects only information relating to the business or other affairs of a person. The fact that that person or anyone else has supplied information to the SIB relating to a particular topic is information relating to the investigation or inquiries carried out by or on behalf of the SIB; but it is not information relating to that person's business or affairs. It can readily be seen that any other conclusion could seriously and unnecessarily interfere with the conduct of an investigation or inquiry by the SIB or any other primary recipient.

Thus, the approach of Lightman J draws an important distinction between expressions of opinion, on the one hand, and restricted information, on the other. It appears that opinions may be disclosed even though those opinions are based on restricted information which itself may not be disclosed. However, it may not always be easy to draw a distinction between the two, or to show that the expression of opinion was made without disclosing any underlying restricted information that had led to that particular opinion being formed. One is left with the impression that the court in *Melton Medes* did not wish to hinder the regulator's attempts to assist the beneficiaries of the funds administered by a regulated firm given the SIB's overall role in relation to investor protection.[139]

Where information is obtained by the Financial Services Authority in its capacity as an EC Investment Services Directive competent authority, and the Financial Services Authority is acting in the course of discharging its functions in relation to any investment firm (whether authorised or not) having its head or registered office in an EEA state, the provisions at 8.3.1 to 8.3.6 above are excluded.[140] In such cases disclosure is **8.3.7**

[139] Note the discussion of *Melton Medes* in *Bank of Credit and Commerce International (Overseas) Ltd (in liquidation) v Price Waterhouse (No.2)* [1997] 3 WLR 849 at pp. 858C–9E.

[140] Investment Services Regulations 1995 SI 1995/3275 reg. 48 implementing Investment Services Directive (No. 93/22/EEC) Article 25.

governed by a disclosure regime that broadly follows Investment Services Directive Article 25.[141]

There are no specific provisions governing the disclosure of information obtained during the course of an investigation under the Open-ended Investment Companies (Investment Companies with Variable Capital) Regulations 1996.[142] **8.3.8**

8.4 INSURANCE COMPANIES

The disclosure of information obtained under or by virtue of Insurance Companies Act 1982 is prohibited subject to certain exceptions.[143] Subject to 8.4.2, in the case of information relating to UK, EC and non-EC companies, restricted information, which relates to the business or other affairs of a relevant person, shall not be disclosed without the consent of the person from whom the information was obtained and, if different, the person to whom it relates.[144] Information is restricted information if it was obtained by the Treasury or Secretary of State for the purposes of, or in the discharge of, functions under Insurance Companies Act 1982 or any rules or regulations made thereunder (whether or not by virtue of any requirement to supply it under those provisions);[145] but it is not restricted information if it has been made available to the public from other sources, or it is information in the form of a summary or is so framed as not to enable information relating to any particular person to be ascertained from it.[146] Relevant persons are any UK, EC or non-EC company or any member of Lloyd's and any controller, manager, chief executive, general representative, agent or employee of such a company.[147] **8.4.1**

8.4.1 does not preclude the disclosure of information in the following circumstances: **8.4.2**

(i) in any case in which disclosure is for the purpose of enabling or

---

[141] See reg. 48 and Article 25 generally.
[142] Reference should therefore be made to the general provisions at 8.1.
[143] Insurance Companies Act 1982 s.47A and Sch 2B. Note the amendments in the Transfer of Functions (Insurance) Order 1997 SI 1997/2781.
[144] Insurance Companies Act 1982 Sch 2B para. 1(1).
[145] Insurance Companies Act 1982 Sch 2B para. 1(2).
[146] Insurance Companies Act 1982 Sch 2B para. 1(3).
[147] Insurance Companies Act 1982 Sch 2B para. 1(4).

assisting the Treasury or Secretary of State to discharge functions under Insurance Companies Act 1982 or any rules or regulations made under that Act (whether or not by virtue of any requirement to supply it made under those provisions);[148]

(ii) by the Treasury or Secretary of State to any person specified in the first column of the following table if the Treasury, or as the case may be the Secretary of State, consider that the disclosure would enable or assist that person to discharge the functions specified in relation to him in the second column of that table.

	Person	Functions
1	The Secretary of State.	Functions under Companies Act 1985, Company Securities (Insider Dealing) Act 1985, Insolvency Act 1986, Company Directors Disqualification Act 1986, Financial Services Act 1986, or Companies Act 1989 Part II, III or VII.
2	The Financial Services Authority.	Functions under Financial Services Act 1986 (other than as a designated agency within the meaning of that Act), Banking Act 1987 or Companies Act 1989 s.171.
3	The Treasury.	Functions under Financial Services Act 1986 or under Companies Act 1989 Part III or VII.
4	An inspector appointed under Companies Act 1985 Part XIV or Financial Services Act 1986 ss.94 or 177.	Functions under that Part or that section.
5	A person authorised to exercise powers under Insurance Companies Act 1982 ss.43A or 44, Companies Act 1985 s.447, Financial Services Act 1986 s.106 or Companies Act 1989 s.84.	Functions under that section.

[148] Insurance Companies Act 1982 Sch 2B para. 2.

6	The Friendly Societies Commission, the Registrar of Friendly Societies for Northern Ireland and the Assistant Registrar of Friendly Societies for Scotland.	Functions under the enactments relating to friendly societies or under Financial Services Act 1986.
7	The Industrial Assurance Commissioner or the Industrial Assurance Commissioner for Northern Ireland.	Functions under the enactments relating to industrial assurance.
8	The Building Societies Commission.	Functions under Building Societies Act 1986 and protecting the interests of the shareholders and depositors of building societies.
9	The Occupational Pensions Regulatory Authority	Functions under the Pension Schemes Act 1993 or the Pensions Act 1995, or any enactment in force in Northern Ireland corresponding to either of them.
10	The Director General of Fair Trading.	Functions under Fair Trading Act 1973 except Part II, Consumer Credit Act 1974, Restrictive Trade Practices Act 1976, Estate Agents Act 1979, Competition Act 1980 or the Control of Misleading Advertisements Regulations 1988.
11	A designated agency (within the meaning of Financial Services Act 1986).	Functions under the Act or Companies Act 1989 Part VII.
12	A transferee body (within the meaning of Financial Services Act 1986) or the competent authority (within the meaning of that Act).	Functions under that Act.
13	Any of the following (within the meaning of Financial Services Act 1986), namely, a recognised self-regulating organisation, a recognised investment exchange, a recognised professional body and a recognised clearing house.	Functions in its capacity as a recognised self-regulating organisation, recognised investment exchange, recognised professional body or a recognised clearing house.

14	The Department of Economic Development in Northern Ireland.	Functions under enactments relating to companies or insolvency.
15	An inspector appointed by the Department of Economic Development in Northern Ireland under enactments relating to companies or insolvency.	Functions under those enactments.
16	A person authorised to exercise powers under Companies (Northern Ireland) Order 1986 Article 440.	Functions under that Article.
17	An official receiver.	Functions under enactments relating to insolvency.
18	The Panel on Take-overs and Mergers.	All functions.
19	The Bank of England.	All functions.
20	A body administering a scheme under Financial Services Act 1986 s.54.	Functions under the scheme.
21	A body established by order under Companies Act 1989 s.46.	Functions under Part II of that Act.
22	A supervisory body (as defined in Companies Act 1989 s.30) or a qualifying body (as defined in s.32).	Functions under that Act.
23	The Council of Lloyd's, the Committee of Lloyd's or the Disciplinary Committee or Appeal Tribunal established under the Lloyd's Act 1982.	Functions under the Lloyd's Acts 1871 to 1982 and functions under bye-laws made under those Acts.
24	The Tribunal under Prevention of Fraud (Investments) Act 1958.	Functions under that Act.
25	The Monopolies and Mergers Commission.	Functions under Fair Trading Act 1973 and Competition Act 1980.

26	An auditor appointed under Insurance Companies Act 1982 s.21, Companies Act 1985 s.384 or Financial Services Act 1986 s.107 or a person approved under Financial Services Act 1986 s.108.	All functions.
27	A recognised supervisory body (within the meaning of Companies Act 1989 Part II or Companies (Northern Ireland) Order 1990 Part III).	Functions in its capacity as such a body under that Part, or functions in relation to disciplinary proceedings against auditors.
28	A recognised professional body (within the meaning of Insolvency Act 1986 s.391 or Insolvency (Northern Ireland) Order 1989 Article 350).	Functions in its capacity as such a body under that Act or that Order, or functions in relation to disciplinary proceedings against insolvency practitioners (within the meaning of that Act or that Order).
29	An actuary exercising functions under Insurance Companies Act 1982.	Those functions.
30	The Institute of Actuaries or the Faculty of Actuaries.	Supervisory functions in relation to an actuary exercising functions under this Act.[149]

(iii) by any person specified in the Table at (ii) above of information obtained by him by virtue of that subparagraph if he makes the disclosure:
(a) with the consent of the Treasury or the Secretary of State; and
(b) for the purpose of enabling or assisting him to discharge any functions specified in relation to him in the second column of that table;
and before deciding whether to give consent to such a disclosure by any person the Treasury or, as the case may be the Secretary of State, shall take account of any representations made by that person as to the desirability of or the necessity for the disclosure;[150]

(iv) (a) to the Treasury; or
(b) to the Secretary of State for purposes other than those specified in relation to him in (i) above,

[149] Insurance Companies Act 1982 Sch 2B para. 3(1).
[150] Insurance Companies Act 1982 Sch 2B para. 3(2).

if (in either case) disclosure is in accordance with Article 16(6) of the third general insurance Directive, or Article 15(6) of the third long-term insurance Directive.[151]

(v) for the purpose of enabling or assisting any public or other authority not specified in the first column of the Table in (ii) above to discharge any functions if disclosure is in accordance with Article 16 of the third general insurance Directive, or Article 15 of the third long-term insurance Directive.[152]

(vi) for the purpose of enabling or assisting an authority in a country or territory outside the United Kingdom to exercise functions corresponding to those of
  (a) the Bank of England;
  (b) the Treasury under Insurance Companies Act 1982 or, by virtue of Transfer of Functions (Insurance) Order 1997 article 2, under Financial Services Act 1986;
  (c) the Secretary of State under Insurance Companies Act 1982 or Financial Services 1986;
  (d) the designated agency under that Act or rules or regulations made under that Act;
  (e) the competent authority under Part IV of that Act; or
  (f) the Financial Services Authority under that Act (other than in its capacity as a designated agency) or the Banking Act 1987.[153]

  This does not apply in relation to disclosure to an authority that is not an authority in another member State unless the Treasury or the Secretary of State are satisfied that the authority is subject to restrictions on further disclosures at least equivalent to those imposed by the provisions of 8.4.1 to 8.4.2;[154]

(vii) for the purpose of enabling or assisting the Deposit Protection Board to discharge its functions under Banking Act 1987;[155]

(viii) with a view to the institution of, or otherwise for the purposes of, any criminal proceedings, whether under Insurance Companies Act 1982 or otherwise;[156]

(ix) for the purpose of enabling or assisting the Council of the Stock

---

151 Insurance Companies Act 1982 Sch 2B para. 3(3).
152 Insurance Companies Act 1982 Sch 2B para. 3(4).
153 Insurance Companies Act 1982 Sch 2B para. 3(5).
154 Insurance Companies Act 1982 Sch 2B para. 3(6).
155 Insurance Companies Act 1982 Sch 2B para. 4(1)(a).
156 Insurance Companies Act 1982 Sch 2B para. 4(1)(b).

Exchange to discharge its functions in relation to insurance companies;[157]

(x) with a view to the institution of, or otherwise for the purposes of, proceedings under Company Directors Disqualification Act 1986 ss.6, 7 or 8 in respect of a director or former director of an insurance company;[158]

(xi) with a view to the institution of, or otherwise for the purposes of, any civil proceedings arising under or by virtue of Financial Services Act 1986 or proceedings before the Financial Services Tribunal, if those proceedings relate to an insurance company;[159]

(xii) with a view to the institution of, or otherwise for the purposes of, any disciplinary proceedings relating to the exercise by an auditor or actuary of his professional duties;[160]

(xiii) in pursuance of a Community obligation;[161]

(xiv) by the Secretary of State or the Treasury to the Director of Public Prosecutions, the Director of Public Prosecutions for Northern Ireland, the Lord Advocate, a procurator fiscal or a constable of:

(a) information obtained by virtue of Insurance Companies Act 1982 ss.43A, 44 or 44A; or

(b) information in the possession of the Secretary of State or the Treasury as to any suspected contravention in relation to which the powers conferred by those sections are exerciseable.[162]

Information that is disclosed to a person in pursuance of (ii) or (iii) **8.4.3**
above shall not be used otherwise than for the purpose mentioned in that provision.[163] Any person who uses information in contravention of the prohibition in (ii) or (iii) above shall be liable on summary conviction to imprisonment for a term not exceeding three months or to a fine not exceeding level 5 on the standard scale, or to both.[164] Subject to certain exceptions[165] any reference in (ii) to (vi) to enabling or assisting any person to discharge or exercise any functions is a reference to

157 Insurance Companies Act 1982 Sch 2B para. 4(1)(c).
158 Insurance Companies Act 1982 Sch 2B para. 4(1)(d).
159 Insurance Companies Act 1982 Sch 2B para. 4(1)(e).
160 Insurance Companies Act 1982 Sch 2B para. 4(1)(f).
161 Insurance Companies Act 1982 Sch 2B para. 4(1)(g).
162 Insurance Companies Act 1982 Sch 2B para. 4(2).
163 Insurance Companies Act 1982 Sch 2B para. 3(7).
164 Insurance Companies Act 1982 Sch 2B para. 3(8).
165 Set out in Insurance Companies Act 1982 Sch 2B para. 3(10).

enabling or assisting that person to discharge or exercise those functions in relation to

(i) a financial market;
(ii) persons carrying on the business of banking, insurance, Consumer Credit Act businesses or the business of providing other financial services (and 'Consumer Credit Act business' has the same meaning as in the Banking Coordination (Second Council Directive) Regulations 1992); or
(iii) persons involved in the operation of occupational pension schemes (within the meaning of Pension Schemes Act 1993 or, in Northern Ireland, Pension Schemes (Northern Ireland) Act 1993).[166]

Any person who discloses information in contravention of 8.4.1 (subject to 8.4.2) shall be guilty of an offence and liable on conviction on indictment, to imprisonment for a term not exceeding two years or to a fine, or to both, and on summary conviction, to imprisonment for a term not exceeding three months or to a fine not exceeding the statutory maximum,[167] or to both.[168] **8.4.4**

8.4.1 above applies also to information that **8.4.5**

(i) has been supplied to the Treasury or the Secretary of State for the purposes of any relevant functions by a supervisory authority in a member State other than the United Kingdom; or
(ii) has been obtained for those purposes by the Treasury or the Secretary of State, or by a person acting on their behalf, in another member State.[169]

Information supplied or obtained as mentioned in (i) and (ii) shall not be disclosed except as provided by 8.4.1 or in the following circumstances:

(a) for the purpose of enabling or assisting the Treasury or the Secretary of State to discharge any relevant functions;[170] or
(b) with a view to the institution of, or otherwise for the purposes of, criminal proceedings, whether under Insurance Companies Act 1982 or otherwise.[171]

---

[166] Insurance Companies Act 1982 Sch 2B para. 3(9).
[167] Currently £5,000. See Criminal Justice Act 1982 s.37(2).
[168] Insurance Companies Act 1982 Sch 2B para. 1(5).
[169] Insurance Companies Act 1982 Sch 2B para. 5(1).
[170] Insurance Companies Act 1982 Sch 2B para. 5(2)(a).
[171] Insurance Companies Act 1982 Sch 2B para. 5(2)(b).

Information supplied as mentioned in (i) and (ii) above may be disclosed

(a) to a relevant recipient, if (in the case of (i)) the supervisory authority which supplied the information or (in the case of (ii)) the supervisory authority in the member state concerned consents to its disclosure, and the case is one in which information to which 8.4.1 applies could be so disclosed by virtue of 8.4.2(iv); or

(b) to the Treasury or the Secretary of State, if that authority consents to its disclosure and the case is one in which information to which 8.4.1 above applies could be so disclosed by virtue of 8.4.2(iv) above.[172] Before the Treasury or the Secretary of State disclose information to any person under this provision they must notify the supervising authority that supplied the information of the name and responsibilities of that person.[173]

In this paragraph 'relevant functions', in relation to the Treasury, means their functions under this Act, and in relation to the Secretary of State, means his functions under this Act; and 'relevant recipient' means a person specified in any of entries 1 to 8, 14, 15 and 19 in the Table in 8.4.2(ii) above.[174]

Subject to 8.4.7 no information that has been obtained under Insurance Companies Act 1982 ss.44(2) to (4) or 44A and relates to the business or other affairs of a person who is not a relevant person for the purposes of 8.4.1 shall be disclosed without the consent of the person from whom the information was obtained and, if different, the person to whom it relates.[175] A person who discloses any information in contravention of this provision shall be guilty of an offence under Companies Act 1985 s.449 or Companies (Northern Ireland) Order 1986 Article 442.[176] **8.4.6**

8.4.6 does not preclude the following **8.4.7**

(i) the disclosure of information to any person who is a competent authority for the purposes of Companies Act 1985 s.449 or

[172] Insurance Companies Act 1982 Sch 2B para. 5(3) and (4).
[173] Insurance Companies Act 1982 Sch 2B para. 5(4A).
[174] Insurance Companies Act 1982 Sch 2B para. 5(5).
[175] Insurance Companies Act 1982 Sch 2B para. 6(1).
[176] Insurance Companies Act 1982 Sch 2B para. 6(2) and see 8.2.7.

Companies (Northern Ireland) Order 1986 Article 442(1)(a) to (e);[177]

(ii) the disclosure of information as mentioned in any of the paragraphs except (m) of Financial Services Act 1986 s.180(1) or in s.180(3) or (4) or as mentioned in Companies Act 1985 s.449(1) or Companies (Northern Ireland) Order 1986, Article 442,[178] and

(iii) the disclosure of any such information as is mentioned in Financial Services Act 1986 s.180(5) by any person who by virtue of that section is not precluded by s.179 of that Act from disclosing it.[179]

8.5 INVESTIGATIONS OF COMPANIES IN A VOLUNTARY WINDING UP

There are no statutory restrictions on the disclosure of information obtained under Insolvency Act 1986, s.218 and similarly there are no circumstances in which disclosure is expressly permitted. The DTI *Investigations Handbook* takes the view that it is implicit that information may be disclosed for the purposes of criminal proceedings.[180]

8.6 POWERS EXERCISEABLE TO ASSIST OVERSEAS REGULATORY AUTHORITIES

Information relating to the business or other affairs of a person that is supplied by an overseas regulatory authority in connection with a request for assistance or is obtained by virtue of the powers conferred by Companies Act 1989 s.83, whether or not any requirement to supply it is made under that section, shall not be disclosed for any purpose save as provided in 8.6.2 by **8.6.1**

(i) the primary recipient; or

[177] Insurance Companies Act 1982 Sch 2B para. 7(1).
[178] Insurance Companies Act 1982 Sch 2B para. 7(2).
[179] Insurance Companies Act 1982 Sch 2B para. 7(3).
[180] *Investigations Handbook* para. 52. See 8.1 above.

(ii) any person obtaining the information directly or indirectly from him,

without the consent of the person from whom the primary recipient obtained the information and, if different, the person to whom it relates.[181] The primary recipient means the Secretary of State, any person authorised under Companies Act 1989 s.84 to exercise powers on his behalf and any officer or servant of any such person.[182] Information is not treated as information to which this provision applies if it has been made available to the public by virtue of being disclosed in any circumstances in which, or for any purpose for which, disclosure is not precluded by this provision.[183]

Information to which 8.6.1 applies may be disclosed in the following circumstances: **8.6.2**

(i) to any person with a view to the institution of, or otherwise for the purposes of any criminal proceedings, civil proceedings arising under or by virtue of Financial Services Act 1986 and proceedings before the Financial Services Tribunal and disciplinary proceedings relating to the exercise by a solicitor, auditor, accountant, valuer or actuary of his professional duties, or the discharge by a public servant of his duties.[184] ('Public servant' means an officer or servant of the Crown or of any public or other authority for the time being designated for the purpose of that provision by order of the Secretary of State.[185])
(ii) for the purpose of enabling or assisting a relevant authority to discharge any relevant function (including functions in relation to proceedings) as follows[186]:

	Relevant authority	Relevant functions
1	The Secretary of State	Functions under the enactments relating to companies, insurance companies or insolvency, or under Financial Services Act 1986 or Companies Act 1989 Parts II, III or VII.

[181] Companies Act 1989 s.86(1) and (2).
[182] Companies Act 1989 s.86(3).
[183] Companies Act 1989 s.86(4).
[184] Companies Act 1989 s.87(1)(a) and (2).
[185] Companies Act 1989 s.87(3).
[186] Companies Act 1989 s.87(4).

2	The Treasury	Functions under the enactments relating to insurance companies, under Financial Services Act 1986 or under Companies Act 1989 Parts III or VII.
3	An inspector appointed under Companies Act 1985 Part XIV or Financial Services Act 1986 ss.94 or 177.	Functions under that Part or that section.
4	A person authorised to exercise powers or appointed under Insurance Companies Act 1982 ss.43A or 44, Companies Act 1985 s.447, Financial Services Act 1986 s.106 or Companies Act 1989 s.84.	Functions under that section.
5	An overseas regulatory authority	Its regulatory functions (within the meaning of Companies Act 1989).
6	The Department of Economic Development in Northern Ireland or a person appointed or authorised by that Department	Functions conferred on it or him by the enactments relating to companies or insolvency.
7	A designated agency within the meaning of Financial Services Act 1986.	Functions under that Act or Companies Act 1989 Part VII.
8	A transferee body or the competent authority within the meaning of Financial Services Act 1986.	Functions under that Act.
9	The body administering a scheme under Financial Services Act 1986 s.54.	Functions under the scheme.
10	A recognised self-regulating organisation, recognised professional body, recognised investment exchange, recognised clearing house or recognised self-regulating organisation for friendly societies (within the meaning of the Financial Services Act 1986)	Functions in its capacity as an organisation, body, exchange or clearing house recognised under that Act.

11	The Chief Registrar of friendly societies, the Registrar of Friendly Societies for Northern Ireland and the Assistant Registrar of Friendly Societies for Scotland.	Functions under Financial Services Act 1986 or the enactments relating to friendly societies or building societies.
12	The Friendly Societies Commission	Functions under the enactments relating to friendly societies or under Financial Services Act 1986.
13	The Bank of England	Any of its functions.
14	The Financial Services Authority	Functions under Financial Services Act 1986 (other than as a designated agency within the meaning of that Act), Banking Act 1987 or Companies Act 1989 s.171.
15	The Deposit Protection Board	Functions under Banking Act 1987.
16	A body established by order under Companies Act 1989 s.46.	Functions under Companies Act 1989 Part II.
17	A recognised supervisory or qualifying body within the meaning of Companies Act 1989 Part II.	Functions as such a body.
18	The Industrial Assurance Commissioner and the Industrial Assurance Commissioner for Northern Ireland.	Functions under the enactments relating to industrial assurance.
19	The Insurance Brokers Registration Council.	Functions under Insurance Brokers (Registration) Act 1977.
20	The Official Receiver or, in Northern Ireland, the Official Assignee for company liquidations or for bankruptcy.	Functions under the enactments relating to insolvency.
21	A recognised professional body (within the meaning of Insolvency Act 1986 s.391).	Functions in its capacity as such a body under Insolvency Act 1986.
22	The Building Societies Commission.	Functions under Building Societies Act 1986.

23	The Occupational Pensions Regulatory Authority	Functions under Pension Schemes Act 1993 or Pensions Act 1995 or any enactment in force in Northern Ireland corresponding to either of them.
24	The Director General of Fair Trading	Functions under Financial Services Act 1986.
25	A person authorised by the Secretary of State under Companies Act 1985 s. 245C.	Functions relating to the securing of compliance by companies with the accounting requirements of that Act.
26	The Director General of the National Lottery	Functions under National Lottery etc. Act 1993 ss.5 to 10 and 15.[187]

The Secretary of State may by order amend the above list by adding or removing any authority and/or functions and the order may impose conditions subject to which, or otherwise restrict the circumstances in which, disclosure is permitted.[188]

(iii) to the Treasury, if the disclosure is made in the interests of investors or in the public interest;[189]

(iv) if the information is or has been available to the public from other sources;[190]

(v) in a summary or collection of information framed in such a way as not to enable the identity of any person to whom the information relates to be ascertained;[191] or

(vi) in pursuance of any Community obligation.[192]

A person who contravenes 8.6.1 commits an offence and is liable on conviction on indictment, to imprisonment for a term not exceeding two years or to a fine, or both, and on summary conviction, to imprisonment for a term not exceeding three months or to a fine not exceeding 8.6.3

[187] Companies Act 1989 s.87(1)(b) and (4).

[188] Companies Act 1989 s.87(5). Such an order shall be made by statutory instrument which shall be subject to annulment in pursuance of a resolution of either House of Parliament – Companies Act 1989 s.87(6).

[189] Companies Act 1989 s.87(1)(c).

[190] Companies Act 1989 s.87(1)(d).

[191] Companies Act 1989 s.87(1)(e).

[192] Companies Act 1989 s.87(1)(f).

the statutory maximum[193] or both.[194] The provisions at 6.7.3 to 6.7.4 relating to prosecutions apply to proceedings for an offence under this provision.[195]

8.7 PROCEDURE ON DISCLOSING DOCUMENTS OR TRANSCRIPTS ETC. AND THIRD PARTY RIGHTS

An investigator must not disclose information received in the exercise of compulsory powers except in accordance with the gateways at 8.2 to 8.6 above.[196] Once within the gateways the court may order the investigator to disclose information for the purpose of court proceedings subject to a consideration of third party rights and public interest immunity.[197] The starting point is that a court will not order the Secretary of State or an investigator to disclose any material that is inadmissible and irrelevant. In *Re Astra Holdings plc; Secretary of State for Trade and Industry v Anderson and others*[198] disqualification proceedings were commenced following a Companies Act 1985 s.432 inspection. A respondent sought discovery of material, such as the inspectors' internal communications, internal notes and drafts of the report. Cresswell J noted that the documents before the inspectors and transcripts of evidence had already been disclosed to the respondents and he held that the inspectors' own notes, drafts, internal materials etc. were neither admissible nor discoverable.[199] However, in a letter from the Secretary to the Inspectors to the Deputy Inspector of Companies and which was dated the same date as the report, the inspectors had expressed their views on disqualification. Cresswell J referred to the inspectors' report being admissible in legal proceedings as evidence of the inspectors' opinion and, in proceedings on an application under **8.7.1**

193 Currently £5,000.
194 Companies Act 1989 s.86(5).
195 See Companies Act 1989 ss.89 to 91. Companies Act 1989 s.91(1) applies only to offences under s.85, not s.86.
196 See, for example, *Bank of Credit and Commerce International (Overseas) Ltd (in liquidation) v Price Waterhouse (No.2)* [1997] 3 WLR 849 at pp. 865B–7D and *Re Galileo Group Limited* [1998] 2 WLR 364 at pp. 372H–3A.
197 See 8.8 below.
198 [1998] *The Times*, 13 January.
199 Note the provisions of Rules of the Supreme Court, Order 24 and *Wallace Smith Trust Co. Ltd (in liquidation) v Deloitte Haskins & Sells (a firm)* [1997] 1 WLR 257.

Company Directors (Disqualification) Act 1986, as evidence of any fact stated in the report.[200] He added that the proceedings had in many respects much more in common with criminal proceedings than with civil litigation about private rights.[201] Cresswell J concluded that the side letter should be disclosed as necessary to the fair conduct of the proceedings against certain of the respondent directors and that production of it was necessary for disposing fairly of the cause or matter or for saving costs.

Where a party to litigation seeks access to a report it is unlikely that the Secretary of State or investigator will be able to withhold it on grounds of legal professional privilege. In *Re Barings plc (in Administration); Secretary of State for Trade and Industry v Baker*[202] the Secretary of State had objected to the production of a statutory report prepared by the administrators of Barings plc under Company Directors Disqualification Act 1986 s.7 to a respondent to disqualification proceedings. However, Sir Richard Scott V-C rejected a claim that the statutory report was covered by legal professional privilege and said that the question depended instead on whether there was a public interest requiring protection from disclosure that was sufficient to override the interests of the administration of justice reflected in the discovery rights given to litigants and, in the absence of a claim of public interest immunity, there was not. **8.7.2**

Where an investigator is requested to disclose documents or transcripts of evidence he should consider the position of the third parties to whom the documents or transcripts relate. Thus in *Marcel v Commissioner of Police of the Metropolis*[203] the Court of Appeal found that where a subpoena duces tecum is served on the police seeking seized documents the police should inform the owner of the documents about the subpoena in order to give him an opportunity to make any objection. A similar approach was adopted in *Morris v Director of the Serious Fraud Office*[204] concerning an application by liquidators under Insolvency Act 1986 s.236 for an order that the SFO produce various documents where Sir Donald Nicholls V-C held that those from whom the documents **8.7.3**

---

200 Companies Act 1985 s.441. See Ch 13.

201 He referred to *Re Barings plc (in administration); Secretary of State for Trade and Industry v Baker* [1998] 2 WLR 667. *Cf. R v Secretary of State for Trade and Industry ex p. McCormick* [1998] COD 160.

202 [1998] 2 WLR 667.

203 [1992] Ch 225.

204 [1993] Ch 372.

had been seized or their true owners were in general entitled to an opportunity to advance any proper objections to the making of an order. This general approach was approved in *Soden v Burns*[205] concerning the disclosure by the Secretary of State to the joint administrators of Atlantic Computers plc of transcripts of evidence given to inspectors appointed under Companies Act 1986 s.432 in relation to the company.[206]

There may, however, be circumstances where it is inappropriate to give advance notice to a person to whom documents or transcripts relate. In *Morris v Director of the Serious Fraud Office* Sir Donald Nicholls V-C stated[207] **8.7.4**

> There will be exceptional cases. For instance, there may be cases where notice to a third party of the office-holder's application might seriously prejudice the object the office-holder is seeking to achieve in existing or proposed proceedings; or the third party may not be traceable; or the documents may be needed as a matter of dire emergency. This is not intended to be a comprehensive list. There may be cases where for other reasons it is not appropriate or practicable to follow the ordinary route. In such exceptional cases, if it is just to do so the court may make an order under section 236 in the exercise of its discretion even though the third party has not been notified.

This course of action was taken in *Re Murjani (a bankrupt)*,[208] where a trustee in bankruptcy applied to obtain documents from solicitors and was not required to join the solicitors' clients to the application for an order under Insolvency Act 1986, s.366.[209]

The duty owed to third parties is, however, only a qualified one and it may be overridden in appropriate circumstances. Thus, in *Hamilton v Naviede*[210] in the context of the disclosure of transcripts of examinations by the liquidators of a company and disclosure to the SFO, Lord **8.7.5**

---

205 [1996] 3 All ER 967.

206 The administrators were conducting litigation against British and Commonwealth Holdings plc, which had taken over Atlantic and which was also in administration. Note also *Hamilton v Naviede* [1995] 2 AC 75 concerning the disclosure to the SFO of transcripts of evidence given to liquidators of a company.

207 [1993] Ch 372 at p. 385C–D.

208 [1996] 1 All ER 65.

209 See pp. 77h 8d. Note also *Re Kingscroft Insurance Co Ltd etc.* 14 July 1993, unrep. (the KWELM case) in which Harman J ordered disclosure of transcripts of evidence before inspectors appointed by the DTI to office-holders appointed under Insolvency Act 1986 s.236, but only to a strictly limited class and only on undertakings not to use the transcripts or information contained in them for certain purposes including for litigation, without a further court hearing.

210 [1995] 2 AC 75 on appeal from *Re Arrows (No. 4)*.

Browne-Wilkinson stated[211]

> The fundamental question is the extent of the duty of confidentiality owed by liquidators to persons who are examined under section 236 ....
>
> Although the primary purpose of a section 236 examination is to assist the beneficial winding up of the company, it is not its only purpose. In my view, where information has been obtained under statutory powers the duty of confidence owed on the *Marcel* principle cannot operate so as to prevent the person obtaining the information from disclosing it to those persons to whom the statutory provisions either require or authorise him to make disclosure.
>
> The Act of 1986 contains a series of provisions which envisage that information and documents in the hands of liquidators is to be disclosed to others, including disclosure for the purposes of criminal proceedings....

In *Soden v Burns*[212] concerning Atlantic Computers plc, Robert Walker J referred to this passage from *Hamilton* and noted[213] that in relation to insolvent companies, the functions of the SFO and the functions of company inspectors are performed exclusively in the public interest, whereas office holders' concern with possible criminal proceedings and directors' disqualification is secondary to their primary function of getting in assets for the benefit of creditors.[214] Robert Walker J added[215]

> It is to be expected, therefore, that in assessing what is in the public interest the court should be more ready to countenance disclosure of documents and information by office-holders to official investigating and prosecuting authorities than disclosure by those authorities to office-holders for the purposes of civil litigation.

He concluded, therefore,[216] that

> there is a qualified (not an absolute) duty of confidence attaching to information obtained under compulsory powers and that although there are many gateways (in s.451A of the Companies Act 1985) through which that information can be disclosed for other public purposes, the court must take account of that duty, qualified though it is, before requiring transcripts to be disclosed for use in continuing civil litigation.

---

211 At p. 102E–H.
212 [1996] 3 All ER 967.
213 At p. 978j.
214 See also *Bishopsgate Investment Management Ltd v Maxwell* [1993] Ch 1.
215 At p. 978(j)–9(a).
216 At p. 979j.

Robert Walker J in *Soden v Burns* envisaged a balancing exercise. He accepted the evidence given by the respondent, a deputy inspector of companies in the investigations department at the DTI, as to obtaining evidence and concerns about confidentiality. However, he added that although considerations about confidentiality were important, they were not the only factor in the balancing exercise. Robert Walker J referred[217] to the possible oppression to individual witnesses who gave evidence to the inspectors, where those witnesses were involved in the civil litigation, in the administrators obtaining at an earlier stage of the litigation transcripts that might not otherwise come to them until a later stage, or at all.

It remains open as to when information (be it documents or transcripts of interviews) that could be disclosed pursuant to one of 8.2 to 8.6 need not be disclosed by the Secretary of State. However, some guidance emerges from *Soden v Burns* where Robert Walker J set out the points relevant to the balancing exercise which he had to carry out.[218] **8.7.6**

> (1) This is a matter of real public interest and concern, involving as it does the collapse into administration, with huge estimated deficiencies, of two major companies, one listed at the time and the other listed until its acquisition.
> (2) Protracted and expensive litigation involving two insolvent companies cannot be in the interests of the creditors of either company or in the interests of the other parties to the litigation or in the public interest. Disclosure of information may assist a settlement sooner rather than later ... .
> (3) Atlantic is primarily a defendant in both sets of proceedings ... . but is also, secondarily, in the position of claimant under contribution notices and third or fourth party notices.
> (4) The application under s.236 was not made at an early stage of the administration, but over five years into it. That (and the sequence of intermediate events) have various consequences which pull both ways. The inspectors' report has been completed and published. Numerous transcripts have been disclosed, against undertakings, in the disqualification proceedings. Disclosure of transcripts cannot now have any effect on the inspectors' investigations ... . On the other hand, Atlantic's administrators have the benefit of the inspectors' very thorough and clear report.
> (5) The administrators' evidence indicates that they have already interviewed or attempted to interview a number of potential witnesses

[217] At p. 983c–d.
[218] At pp. 984f–5g.

> but have encountered many difficulties ... . The inspectors took their evidence four or five years ago, when witnesses' recollections were much fresher.
> (6) Because of these difficulties, the administrators assert that they have a reasonable requirement for the transcripts and their views are entitled to careful consideration. But so are the views of the Department ... . These factors tend to cancel each other out: I see force both in [the] ... submission that the administrators have not been very specific about what they require the transcripts for, and hope to get out of them, and in [the] ... riposte that it is precisely because of their relative ignorance, even after five years, that the administrators require to study the transcripts.
> (7) The court has often recognised that it is less stressful, and therefore less oppressive, for a person who may have material information to give written answers to written questions, rather than undergoing oral examination (with or without a topics list). Similarly, the disclosure of a transcript of oral evidence already given must normally be less stressful and therefore less oppressive than undergoing a second oral examination. The disclosure of a transcript followed by an application for a further oral examination under s.236 might well be oppressive, though I note what Hoffman J said (about the possibly small significance of inconsistencies in evidence) in *Re Bishopsgate Investment Management Ltd v Maxwell (No. 2)* [1994] BCC 732 at 738. However, that possibility is some way into the future'.[219]

Robert Walker J ordered disclosure of the transcripts of evidence subject to notification to each of the witnesses whose evidence was covered by the order. Robert Walker J then followed the approach in *London and County Securities v Nicholson*[220] (i.e. giving the witnesses concerned an opportunity to object) but ordered that the period of notice should be 21 rather than 14 days.[221] In a subsequent application[222] Robert Walker J considered summonses by witnesses applying to set aside the order concerning disclosure of some transcripts. Robert Walker J held that the relatively advanced stage that the litigation had reached, especially as regards discovery, made it inappropriate to make a special order

---

[219] Note also Robert Walker J's comments at p. 986f–j concerning the factor whether or not an office holder had made a firm decision to commence litigation and that the factors identified in earlier cases, especially oppression to any party already facing serious allegations and a disinclination to give any party special advantages in ordinary civil litigation, must remain relevant as factors in the balancing exercise.

[220] [1980] 1 WLR 948.

[221] Note the practicalities dealt with in *Soden v Burns* [1996] 3 All ER 967 at pp. 987–92.

[222] *Re Atlantic Computers plc; British and Commonwealth Holdings plc (in administration) v Barclays de Zoete Wedd Ltd;* 26 March 1997, NLP; [1997] *The Times*, 25 April.

outside the normal processes of discovery in respect of an application by administrators of Atlantic for transcripts of evidence given to DTI inspectors by a number of witnesses of companies involved in litigation with the administrators. However, he ordered access to the transcripts of interviews of a witness who had been a director of Atlantic on the basis that even though he was a co-litigant, Atlantic was entitled to obtain 'what may be very important evidence as to what its chief executive and directing mind was saying on its behalf during the acquisition period'.

8.7.7 It may be that the person seeking disclosure of transcripts has a specific procedure available to seek the disclosure from the DTI or investigator. For example, in *Soden v Burns* the administrator was able to make an application under Insolvency Act s.236, Robert Walker J having held that Insolvency Act s.236 bound the Crown. Where criminal or civil proceedings have been commenced, a witness summons or subpoena duces tecum may be the appropriate procedure to seek disclosure provided that the relevant legislation governing the investigation permits disclosure to the person seeking access to the information. An alternative mechanism is to request the Secretary of State to disclose information and, if the request is refused or conditions are attached, the person seeking disclosure may seek judicial review of the refusal or the conditions. *Soden v Burns* was linked to *R v Secretary of State for Trade and Industry ex p. Soden*.[223] In the event, Robert Walker J held[224] that since Insolvency Act s.236 bound the Crown, the issue of judicial review did not arise. However, he added that for reasons given in relation to the s.236 application the DTI was right not to disclose transcripts of evidence without notifying the witnesses of the intention to do so and giving the witnesses an opportunity to object. The DTI's decision not to release transcripts without prior notification was not irrational or unlawful and thus the judicial review proceedings failed.

8.7.8 A related issue is the extent to which information in the hands of one who has assisted an investigation (rather than in the hands of the investigator) may or must be disclosed by that person. Clearly, new information that a person has been given by the investigators during the course of the investigation will be embargoed and cannot be disclosed. In *Bank of Credit and Commerce International (Overseas)*

[223] The s.236 application and the application for judicial review were heard together and the judgment of Robert Walker J at [1996] 3 All ER 967 covers both applications.

[224] At p. 987b–d.

Ltd (in liquidation) v Price Waterhouse (No. 2)[225] Laddie J considered the effect on discovery in civil proceedings of those provisions in Banking Act 1987 s.82, which are similar to the provisions at 8.2 to 8.6 above. He found that to be liable for a criminal offence, a recipient of information had to be aware at the time of receipt that he had received it 'under or for the purposes of' the Act. Further, he held that[226] where at the time of receipt the recipient anticipates that the information would be relevant to and used for non-Banking Act purposes and he receives it with that use in mind, it will not contravene s.82 to disclose that information even if, at the same time, the recipient also anticipates that it is relevant to and to be used for Banking Act purposes. Also, if information was initially received for a Banking Act purpose but was then received again for a non-Banking Act purpose, then upon that subsequent receipt the information could be disclosed.[227]

As to information such as those parts of transcripts of evidence not containing information to which the restrictions on disclosure at 8.2 to 8.6 above apply the position was considered in *Re Galileo Group Ltd.*[228] Lightman J held that on an application by a liquidator pursuant to Insolvency Act 1986 s.236 the court was not, in principle, precluded from ordering disclosure by persons not within Banking Act 1987 s.82(1)(a) of the relevant contents of a report produced pursuant to s.39, provided that any material embargoed by s.82[229] had first been removed. However, the jurisdiction was to be exercised 'with the greatest caution'.[230] The factors to take into account included **8.7.9**

(i) the making of such an order may be seen as undermining the protection afforded by s.82; the possibility of the exercise being required or undertaken may prejudice the free flow of information to the Bank of England;
(ii) the difficulty of the exercise, which could only be undertaken by a person with lawful access to the embargoed information;
(iii) the risk that an erroneous omission to edit out a passage might constitute a criminal offence;
(iv) the danger that the redacted document (by reason of the excisions) may prove misleading; and

225 [1997] 3 WLR 849.
226 At p. 862D–E.
227 See pp. 863F–4A.
228 [1998] 2 WLR 364.
229 A provision imposing analogous restrictions to 8.2 to 8.6 above.
230 At p. 376E.

(v) the problems that may be created by such disclosure, e.g. for a witness at trial or on an examination by the liquidator faced with a truncated document and required to answer questions on it, yet barred from explaining his answers by reference to the passages omitted.

In the present case, Lightman J was not satisfied that the liquidator reasonably required the exercise to be undertaken and held that any need was more than counterbalanced by the considerations weighing against it. A similar analysis should apply where someone seeks access to reports or transcripts of evidence obtained during the course of an investigation into a company.

8.8 PUBLIC INTEREST IMMUNITY

One issue to be considered in relation to the disclosure of documents or transcripts of interviews by those investigating companies is the extent to which the Secretary of State may refuse disclosure as a result of public interest immunity.[231] A claim to immunity by the Secretary of State may cover documents in the possession of the DTI or investigators and can extend to items in the possession of third parties (e.g. witnesses) if that extension is necessary to prevent the basis of the immunity from being undermined.[232] The approach adopted by the courts is that when a claim to withhold evidence for reasons of public interest immunity is duly made, the court must carry out an exercise to determine where, in the circumstances of a particular case, the balance should be struck between the possible prejudice to the interest of government, on the one hand, and the prejudice to the administration of justice, on the other.[233] In some cases, the court may inspect documents before deciding whether or not to order production.[234] The starting point in the balancing exercise will in civil proceedings, however, be whether or not the information concerned is relevant to the issues in the action and whether disclosure is needed.[235] The role of public interest immunity in criminal proceedings is more limited **8.8.1**

[231] Generally see De Smith, Woolf and Jowell *Judicial Review of Administrative Action* 5th edn (1995) at pp. 70–92.

[232] See *Kaufmann v Credit Lyonnais Bank* (1995) 7 Admin LR 669. *Cf. Lonrho Plc v Fayed (No. 4)* [1994] 2 WLR 209.

[233] See *Conway v Rimmer* [1968] AC 910.

[234] See *Air Canada v Secretary of State for Trade (No. 2)* [1983] 2 AC 394.

[235] See *R v Chief Constable of West Midlands ex p. Wiley* [1995] AC 274 at p. 288D–H. Note the provisions relating to discovery at Rules of the Supreme Court, Order 24 rule 13 and relating to subpoenas at Rules of the Supreme Court, Order 38.

and a claim should not be made in such a way that a defendant is deprived of a relevant defence. The strict legal position is that a claim to public interest immunity may be made in respect of either the contents of documents or classes of documents.[236] The House of Lords in *R v Chief Constable of West Midlands ex p. Wiley*[237] emphasised the need for compelling evidence to withhold documents from production on the basis of a class-based immunity. However, there has been a policy shift against a distinction between class and contents-based claims. The then Government stated its position in relation to public interest immunity in December 1996[238]:

> Under the new approach, Ministers will focus directly on the damage that disclosure would cause. The former division into class and contents claims will no longer be applied. Ministers will claim public interest immunity only when it is believed that disclosure of a document would cause real damage or harm to the public interest.
>
> That new approach constitutes a change in the practice to be adopted by Ministers, but fully respects existing legal principles, as developed by the courts, and is subject to the supervision of the courts. It also accords with the views expressed by the present Lord Chief Justice that 'public interest immunity should only be claimed for the bare minimum of documents for which the claim of serious harm can be seen to be clearly justified'.
>
> The Government intend that the test shall be vigorously applied before any public interest immunity claim is made for any Government documents. It is impossible in advance to describe such damage exhaustively. The damage may relate to the safety of an individual, such as an informant, or to a regulatory process; or it may be damage to international relations caused by the disclosure of confidential diplomatic communications.
>
> Normally it will be in the form of direct and immediate harm to, for example, the nation's economic interests or our relations with a foreign state. In some cases, it may be indirect or longer-term damage to which the disclosure of the material would contribute, as in the case of damage to a regulatory process. In any event, the nature of the harm will be clearly explained.

---

[236] For the strict legal test in respect of class claims see *Burmah Oil v Bank of England* [1979] 1 WLR 473 per Bridge LJ at p. 491.

[237] [1995] AC 274.

[238] HC Deb vol 287 col 949, 18 December 1996; HL Deb col 576, col 1507, 18 December 1996.

The effect of *ex p Wiley* and the Government statement is therefore to restrict the ambit of public interest immunity.[239]

Claims for public interest immunity have historically been raised in respect of transcripts of evidence given to those carrying out statutory investigations into companies. In *R v Cheltenham JJ ex p. Secretary of State for Trade*[240] the Secretary of State sought to quash a witness summons that had been issued by a Cheltenham justice and which required an officer of the DTI to attend to give evidence in criminal proceedings and to produce an inspectors' report, evidence taken on oath before the inspectors and other documents. Lord Widgery CJ giving the judgment of the Divisional Court quashed the witness summons. He held that the witnesses' statements would not be evidence in the criminal case (albeit that if a witness made a contrary statement at the criminal trial he could have his attention drawn to a previous statement). However, he added that if it were necessary to balance the injury to the public which may result if information of this kind were to be made public with a possible drying up of the source afterwards, and on the other hand, the prejudice to the litigant which may be suffered if the disclosure were not allowed, the public interest in maintaining the sources of information in this kind of inquiry would outweigh the private disadvantage.[241] However, the *Cheltenham JJ* case was distinguished in *London v County Securities Ltd v Nicholson*[242] and developments in the law of public interest immunity generally (particularly the recent restrictive approach to public interest immunity in criminal proceedings) make it an unreliable case. **8.8.2**

In *London & County Securities Ltd v Nicholson* the plaintiffs sought to have admitted in evidence transcripts of oral evidence given to inspectors and correspondence passing between the inspectors and the defendants' solicitors. The transcripts and correspondence amplifying the oral **8.8.3**

[239] The Government statement followed debate after publication of the Report of the Inquiry into the Export of Defence Equipment and Dual Use Goods to Iraq and Related Prosecutions (15th February 1996) (H.C.115) See also C. Forsyth *Public Interest Immunity: Recent and Future Developments* (1997) 56 CLJ 51 and G. Ganz *Volte-Face on Public Interest Immunity* (1997) 60 MLR 552.

[240] [1977] 1 WLR 95.

[241] See p. 100C–D. See also *Lonrho Ltd v Shell Petroleum Co Ltd* [1980] 1 WLR 627 where a claim to public interest immunity was upheld in relation to transcripts of evidence given to a private inquiry set up by the Foreign Secretary. But note that the inquiry in question, unlike statutory company investigations, did not have compulsory powers.

[242] [1980] 1 WLR 948.

evidence were provided by the DTI to the liquidator of the first plaintiff who wished to use them in civil proceedings against the auditors of the two plaintiff companies.[243] The defendants argued that the evidence was given to the inspectors in confidence of a kind that the public interest required to be protected. Browne-Wilkinson J pointed out, however,[244] that the confidence was not complete since the witness's evidence and identity could be disclosed by his evidence being put by the inspectors to other witnesses, by it being incorporated in a report that was distributed to the company or published, and in criminal or civil proceedings against him. He also rejected an argument based on Companies Act 1967 s.50 that the only proceedings for which such evidence was available were those commenced in the public interest. The judge could see no reason why Parliament should not have intended the fruits of the investigation to be available for use by the company in redressing the wrongs that the investigation had disclosed. When conducting a balancing exercise, Browne-Wilkinson J's starting point was a presumption that the public interest in all relevant evidence being available to the court ought to prevail.[245] The competing interest was the loss of confidence that potential witnesses would feel if they knew that their evidence could be used in proceedings brought against them by the company or its liquidator, and not only in proceedings brought by the DTI in the name of the company. Browne-Wilkinson J found that the impairment to the public interest in the evidence being disclosed did not outweigh the other public interest.[246] He noted that there was no evidence from any minister or public servant that the public interest would be harmed and commented on the DTI releasing the evidence to the liquidator without protest. Browne-Wilkinson J added[247]

> I cannot see that any potential witness who knows that his evidence may be used against him in proceedings brought in the name of the company ... is going to be appreciably further deterred from giving full and frank evidence to the inspectors by knowing that such proceedings might be brought by the company itself without the assistance of the department ... . [It] is not the identity of the bringer of the subsequent proceedings but the fact that his evidence may be used against him in any proceedings which will deter the potential witness.

---

243 On the issue of admissibility of statements to investigators and reports see Ch 13 below.
244 At p. 954C–D.
245 At p. 956. See *D v National Society for the Prevention of Cruelty to Children* [1978] AC 171.
246 At p. 956G.
247 At pp. 956G–7A.

Browne-Wilkinson J in *London & County Securities* referred to *R v Cheltenham Justices ex p. Secretary of State for Trade* and noted[248] that in that case there had been evidence of the public interest since the DTI were themselves asserting it with the support of a certificate from the minister. He added that the court there was having to weigh the public interest in maintaining confidentiality against depriving a litigant not of relevant admissible evidence but of material for cross-examination and he could see that the balance in such a case might produce a different result from the one he had reached.[249]

The issue of public interest immunity was more recently raised in *Soden v Burns*[250] in which Robert Walker J referred, in particular, to *Hamilton v Naviede*[251] where the House of Lords was faced with an argument that public interest immunity attached to the transcripts of examinations by a liquidator under Insolvency Act 1986 s.236 such that the court had a discretion as to whether to order disclosure of the transcripts to the SFO (rather than having no power to prevent the SFO gaining access to them).[252] It was argued in *Hamilton* that a purpose public interest immunity attached to the transcripts which limited their use because, first, even though the witness's own private law right to the confidentiality of information extracted from him under statutory powers was overridden by Criminal Justice Act 1987, there was a wider public interest in ensuring that information so extracted is only used for the purposes for which the statutory power was conferred and, secondly, there is a public interest in ensuring that those from whom liquidators and other office-holders seek essential information as to the company's affairs can be assured that what they say will not be communicated to others.[253] However, Lord Browne-Wilkinson pointed out[254] that where information has been obtained under statutory powers the duty of confidence owed on the principle in *Marcel v Commissioner of Police of the Metropolis*[255] cannot operate so as to prevent the person obtaining 8.8.4

[248] At p. 957D–F.
[249] See also *Continental Reinsurance Corporation (UK) Ltd v Pine Top Insurance Ltd* [1986] Ll R 8 and *Multi Guarantee Co Ltd v Cavalier Insurance Co Ltd (No. 1)* 17 June 1986, unrep.
[250] [1996] 3 All ER 967 at pp. 977–80 and 987.
[251] [1995] 2 AC 75.
[252] See also *Re Barlow Clowes Gilt Managers Ltd* [1992] Ch 208 concerning an attempt by a defendant in criminal proceedings to obtain access to transcripts of examinations by a liquidator.
[253] [1995] 2 AC 75 at p. 99.
[254] At p. 102G.
[255] [1992] Ch 225.

the information from disclosing it to those persons to whom the statutory provisions either require or authorise him to make disclosure. He added that[256]

> The statutory framework thus imposes a wide range of duties on liquidators to report, directly or indirectly, to the DTI and prosecuting authorities cases of suspected criminal and dishonest conduct and to furnish them with all documents and information they may require. Such documents include transcripts of evidence given on a section 236 examination which transcripts are admissible in evidence. The liquidator cannot be under any duty of confidence which will prevent the performance of any of these statutory duties. Therefore liquidators cannot in any event give any assurance to a person examined under section 236 that his answers will not be disclosed to prosecuting authorities. In the absence of such assurance there cannot be any maintainable claim that such answers enjoy public interest immunity on the grounds either of the public interest in preserving confidentiality or the public interest in giving an assurance to witnesses that their information will be confidential.[257]

Lord Browne-Wilkinson had made it clear that he was considering only s.236 and not s.235. He had explained that insolvency practitioners attach much greater importance to the confidentiality of information obtained informally backed by s.235 than they do to information obtained under a formal examination under s.236, and that liquidators do not normally have recourse to the more formal procedures under s.236 unless a witness has proved uncooperative.[258] Robert Walker J in *Soden* followed the approach in *Hamilton*. He noted that[259] in assessing what is in the public interest the court should be more ready to countenance disclosure of documents and information by office-holders to official investigating and prosecuting authorities than disclosure by those authorities to office-holders for the purposes of civil litigation. Also, following the approach in *Hamilton* he held[260] that the court should defer decisions on disclosure and the admission of evidence to interlocutory stages in, or the trial of, the civil proceedings in order that decisions on these questions are made on the fullest available information, and as the applications before Robert Walker J were not

---

256 At p. 103F–G.

257 Note also the comments concerning Insolvency Act s.236 by Millett J in the earlier case of *Re Barlow Clowes Gilt Managers Ltd* [1992] Ch 208 at pp. 220–3.

258 At pp. 101C–2B.

259 [1996] 3 All ER 976 at pp. 978–9.

260 At p. 979h–j.

made in the trial of the civil proceedings there was no direct question of purpose public interest immunity.

8.8.5 In the subsequent application *Re Atlantic Computers plc; British and Commonwealth Holdings plc (in administration) v Barclays de Zoete Wedd Ltd*[261] Robert Walker J felt that he was unable to decide anything definitely in relation to public interest immunity since it would be premature to do so but be expressed provisional views. He referred to the limited scope of public interest immunity in the light of the Government's statement[262] and the issue of purpose public interest immunity or compulsion, and noted that the 'narrower the scope of PII properly so called, the more frequent and the more difficult will be cases where the compulsion principle, rather than PII properly so called, may be relied on as a ground for resisting production of documents on discovery'.[263] He noted that there was clear authority that confidentiality by itself, as distinct from public interest immunity, could never be a ground for resisting discovery but felt that 'green shoots of the compulsion principle will continue appearing'.[264] Robert Walker J concluded that his provisional view was that a claim for public interest immunity in respect of material relating to the provisional criticism of witnesses[265] was compelling, whether the matter is viewed from the perspective of the inspectors or the witnesses, but he was not attracted by the argument that non-disclosure of the provisional criticism material would be likely to make the rest of the transcripts misleading.

8.8.6 In conclusion it is unclear whether public interest immunity may be raised in respect of transcripts of evidence or other documents generated during an investigation into a company, but it is clear that the issue links into the duty of confidence owed to witnesses who provide information pursuant to compulsory statutory powers and the reasons for which the statutory duties and powers may be exercised. It appears, however, that where the evidence is obtained as the result of the exercise of formal compulsory powers, the effect of *Hamilton v Naviede* may be that a

---

[261] 26th March 1997, NLP, [1997] *The Times*, 25 April.

[262] See 8.8.1.

[263] See *Science Research Council v Nasse* [1980] AC 1028 and *Wallace Smith v Deloitte Haskins & Sells* [1997] 1 WLR 257.

[264] Note *McDonald v Horn* 20 February 1995, unrep in which Vinelott J was concerned that if a witness had to disclose in civil proceedings a transcript of an interview that had been conducted under compulsory powers in a Financial Services Act 1986 s.105 investigation, the disclosure would subvert the provisions of s.179 restricting the disclosure of information.

[265] See Ch 7.

possible claim to public interest immunity[266] is more limited than where the information is obtained by the investigators on an informal basis.[267] However, in any event, where a claim to public interest immunity is raised it will normally be a matter for the judge at the trial to conduct the appropriate balancing exercise.

8.9 CIVIL LIABILITY FOR UNAUTHORISED DISCLOSURE

Where an investigator discloses confidential information for a purpose outside the purposes for which the statutory powers to investigate companies were enacted the investigator may face an action for breach of confidence. This is modified in the case of investigations pursuant to the Financial Services Act 1986 where s.187 provides an exemption from liability in damages for anything done in the discharge or purported discharge of the Financial Services Authority's functions.[268] **8.9.1**

Where there are express statutory provisions governing disclosure these often provide that unauthorised disclosure constitutes a criminal offence.[269] It does not appear, however, that there is a separate cause of action for breach of statutory duty in cases where authorisation is not permitted by a particular statutory regime. In *Melton Medes v Securities and Investments Board* concerning Financial Services Act 1986 s.179[270] Lightman J explained[271] **8.9.2**

> S.179 does not create any private law right … . The 1986 Act creates an elaborate scheme of duties backed by a mix of enforcement mechanisms but in each case the mechanism is earmarked to the duty in question …. Against this background, the specific and only sanction for breach of s.179 set out in s.179(6) of criminal prosecution is of the highest significance

[266] See also *Kaufmann v Credit Lyonnais Bank* (1995) 7 Admin LR 669 where a claim for public interest immunity in respect of communications to the SFA was rejected where the SFA's rules provided that the information could be shared with other regulators in accordance with Financial Services Act 1986 s.180.

[267] But *cf.* the comments of Vinelott J in *McDonald v Horn* 20 February 1995, unrep.

[268] See *Melton Medes v Securities and Investments Board* [1995] Ch 137 above and 8.3.6.

[269] E.g. Companies Act 1985 s.449 concerning disclosure of information obtained pursuant to s.447.

[270] [1995] Ch 137.

[271] At p. 146C–H.

> and precludes any inference of any further or other private law right or remedy.
>
> Two further factors reinforce this view. The first is that the role of the SIB is of a senior regulator in the public interest and specifically in the interest and for the protection of investors. Section 179 (and in particular its protection of the subject as well as the source, of information) is apt to control in the public interest the use and dissemination of information acquired rather than to subject the SIB in this respect to private law actions. The special interest of informants and the persons to whom information relates is safeguarded by affording them the necessary locus standi in judicial review proceedings to enforce this public duty. The second is that to recognise the creation of a statutory private right would be to recognise a new category of non-confidential information in respect of which a private right to non-disclosure exists, for information protected by s.179 need not be confidential (consider *R v Monopolies and Mergers Commission. ex p. Elders IXL Ltd* [1987] 1 All ER 451 at 462, [1987] 1 WLR 1221 at 1233). I cannot believe that Parliament intended any such thing. Ample protection already exists under the law of confidence for information (whether restricted or not) requiring private law protection, which includes information compulsorily extracted from the citizen by an authority by means of exercise of its statutory powers (see *Marcel v Commissioner of Police of the Metropolis* [1992] 1 All ER 72, [1992] Ch 225).

This reasoning would appear to apply equally to those other statutory regimes which provide that an unauthorised disclosure constitutes a criminal offence. The position is less clear in relation to those regimes that do not,[272] but even in these cases Lightman J's 'two further factors' apply such that there is probably no cause of action for breach of statutory duty.

An unauthorised disclosure may constitute misfeasance in a public office but a plaintiff would need to show that the investigator's disclosure was an abuse of power and he either intended to injure, or knew (actual knowledge or recklessness) that the disclosure was unauthorised and would probably injure the plaintiff (or those in the plaintiff's class). A plaintiff would also need to show he had suffered loss. The test to establish the tort is thus a difficult one to fulfil and it would be a rare case in the context of a statutory investigation into a company where a plaintiff could succeed.[273] 8.9.3

[272] E.g. 8.2.1 to 8.2.5 (Companies Act 1985 ss.434 to 446).

[273] E.g. Wade & Forsyth *Administrative Law* 7 edn at pp. 789–96 and see *Racz v Home Office* [1994] 2 AC 45, *Three Rivers District Council v Bank of England (No. 3)* [1996] 3 All ER 558 and *Bennett v Commissioner of Police for the Metropolis* (1998) 10 Admin LR 245.

Chapter 9

THE PUBLICATION OF REPORTS

9.1 REPORTS OF INVESTIGATIONS UNDER COMPANIES ACT 1985

Where inspectors are appointed under Companies Act 1985 ss.431, 432, 442 or 446 and make reports (including any interim reports) any report shall be written or printed as the Secretary of State directs.[1] In any such case, except where the appointment of inspectors is made on terms that any report they may make is not for publication,[2] the Secretary of State may **9.1.1**

(i) forward a copy of any report made by the inspectors to the company's registered office;[3]

(ii) furnish a copy on request and on payment of the prescribed fee[4] to

  (a) any member of the company or other body corporate which is the subject of the report,

  (b) any person whose conduct is referred to in the report,

  (c) the auditors of that company or body corporate,

  (d) the applicants for the investigation,

  (e) any other person whose financial interests appear to the Secretary of State to be affected by the matters dealt with in the report, whether as a creditor of the company or body corporate, or otherwise;[5] and

(iii) cause any such report to be printed and published.[6]

---

1 Companies Act s.437(1). S.443(1) extends the relevant provisions of s.437 to investigations pursuant to s.442, and s.446(3) does likewise for investigations pursuant to s.446.

2 Companies Act 1985 s.432(2A).

3 Companies Act 1985 s.437(3)(a).

4 See Companies (Inspectors' Reports) (Fees) Regulations 1981 (SI 1981/1686).

5 Companies Act 1985 s.437(3)(b).

6 Companies Act 1985 s.437(3)(c).

If the inspectors were appointed under s.432 in pursuance of a court order the Secretary of State must furnish a copy of any inspectors' report to the court.[7] It is not clear what steps (if any) the court may then take.

If the Secretary of State is of opinion that there is good reason for not divulging any part of a report made by virtue of s.442 and s.443 (provisions applicable on investigation under s.442), he may under 9.1.1 above disclose the report with the omission of that part; and he may cause to be kept by the registrar of companies a copy of the report with that part omitted or, in the case of any other such report, a copy of the whole report.[8] These provisions concerning publication of part only of a report and concerning the registrar of companies do not apply to investigations under s.431, s.432 or s.446.[9] **9.1.2**

There is no mechanism for publishing reports of any investigations carried out pursuant to s.444. **9.1.3**

No report of any investigation carried out pursuant to s.447 may be published generally. There are, however, limited circumstances in which such reports or parts of them may effectively come into the public domain.[10] In particular a report may be published where the prior consent in writing of the company concerned has been obtained[11] or where publication may be required for certain limited purposes such as for the purpose of criminal proceedings, which may result in any report being read out in open court (subject to, for example, the hearsay rule).[12] **9.1.4**

This is also an alternative way in which information obtained under ss.434 to 446, which is put in a report form, may effectively be published.[13] This is where the information is obtained under the powers in ss.434 to 436 by inspectors appointed on the basis that their report will not be published[14] and it appears that a distinction must be drawn between the report itself, which may not be published, and the underlying **9.1.5**

---

7 Companies Act 1985 s.437(2).

8 Companies Act 1985 s.443(3).

9 This frustrated the recommendation of the House of Commons Trade and Industry Committee, Third Report on *Company Investigations* that normally only the appendix recommending criminal proceedings or disciplinary action should not be published — paragraph 87 and recommendation 17 — and see the Government's Response Cm. 1149/1990 pp. 12–3.

10 Companies Act 1985 s.449.

11 Companies Act 1985 s.449(1).

12 Companies Act 1985 s.449(1)(a). Note also the other circumstances where disclosure or publication may be required — see 8.2 above.

13 Companies Act 1985 s.451(A) and see 8.2 above.

14 Companies Act 1985 s.432(2A)

information, which may, in limited circumstances, come into the public domain.

9.2 EXERCISE OF THE DISCRETION TO PUBLISH

The DTI's normal practice is to publish reports of investigations carried out pursuant to ss.431, 432[15] and 442 relating to the affairs of public companies where it is in the public interest.[16] In the light of this, the DTI invite inspectors appointed under s.432, who have prepared a draft of their interim or final report, to submit it to the DTI to facilitate discussion of whether the report is in a form suitable for publication and whether it contains material that might inhibit publication.[17] 9.2.1

The Secretary of State will consider whether there is any reason why the publication of a report should be delayed. One particular consideration is whether publication should be deferred until criminal proceedings are completed or a final decision is taken that no proceedings are to be brought and this will depend on whether publication will prejudice any such proceedings.[18] The House of Commons Trade and Industry Committee, Third Report on 'Company Investigations' (1989–1990 session) recommended that publication should be delayed only in cases where a criminal investigation has begun before completion of the report and where it would be hindered by publication,[19] but the Government did not accept this recommendation and took the view that whether to publish at a particular time had to be considered on the facts of the individual case having regard to the risk of prejudice to possible criminal proceedings.[20] 9.2.2

R v Secretary of State for Trade and Industry ex p. Lonrho plc[21] concerned the decision of the Secretary of State to delay the publication 9.2.3

15 But note s.432(2A).

16 DTI's annual report *Companies in 1996–1997* p. 14. The *Investigations Handbook* (para. 48) explains that reports by inspectors relating to private companies are not normally published unless they raise issues of general public interest.

17 *Investigations Handbook* App B, para. 54.

18 *Investigations Handbook* para. 49.

19 Para. 88 and recommendation 18.

20 Government's Response (Cm. 1149/1990) p. 13.

21 [1989] 1 WLR 525.

of the report into House of Fraser plc (which owned a number of department stores including Harrods) pending consideration of the report by the Serious Fraud Office and Director General of Fair Trading. The Director General subsequently decided not to refer the merger of AIT plc (subsequently House of Fraser Holdings plc) and House of Fraser plc to the Monopolies and Mergers Commission and the Secretary of State maintained his position that he intended to publish the report but would not publish it while the prosecuting authorities were conducting their inquiries. The Secretary of State's decision to delay publication was challenged by judicial review by Lonrho plc, which had for several years been attempting to obtain a controlling interest in Harrods and had made a number of submissions to the inspectors during the course of their investigation. In the House of Lords it was not disputed that[22]

> the discretion of the Secretary of State whether, and when, to publish the report, must be exercised by him (and not at the dictation of another Minister or body) by reference to relevant and not irrelevant considerations and in a manner which is not unreasonable in the Wednesbury sense (*Associated Provincial Picture Houses Ltd v Wednesbury Corporation* [1948] 1 KB 223).

The House of Lords noted that the decision to publish or withhold publication was exercisable in the public interest. The House found that factually the Secretary of State had not delegated his decision to the SFO and nor had he been influenced by incorrect advice. The House also rejected the submission that the decision of the Secretary of State to withhold early publication was 'perverse' and 'irrational' and was a decision that no reasonable Secretary of State properly advised as to facts and the law could have reached. The director of the SFO had sworn an affidavit in which he advised that to publish the report would be likely to prejudice the investigation and would run the risk of preventing a fair trial and he gave reasons for this view. Lord Keith, however, giving the leading judgment said that even without the evidence of the director (and the Director of Public Prosecutions) the Secretary of State was entitled to take the view that early publication might be prejudicial to the SFO and to a fair trial.[23]

The general importance of the House of Lords' approach in *ex p. Lonrho* (in so far as the publication aspect is concerned) is the latitude 9.2.4

22 Per Lord Keith of Kinkel at p. 533D.
23 At p. 534H.

given to the Secretary of State. The Divisional Court[24] had held in favour of Lonrho (having been confident, for example, of the ability of a jury on the instructions of a judge to forget everything they had read and seen before the trial). Against that background, Lord Keith warned against judges wrongly though unconsciously substituting their own views for the views of the decision-maker and pointed out that the question is not whether the Secretary of State came to a correct solution but whether the discretion was properly exercised.[25] Lord Keith added that there was no justification for meetings (with the DTI) at which Lonrho had argued that early publication would have no adverse effect and there were overwhelming public interest reasons in favour of early publication, and that these arguments were and could be fully set out in written submissions to which oral representations added nothing.[26] The SFO subsequently decided not to bring any criminal proceedings and the inspectors' report was then published.[27]

9.3 REPORTS OF INVESTIGATIONS UNDER THE FINANCIAL SERVICES LEGISLATION

Where inspectors are appointed under Financial Services Act 1986 s.94 **9.3.1**
and make reports (including interim reports) any report shall be written or printed as the Secretary of State or Financial Services Authority may direct[28] and they may, if they think fit

(i) furnish a copy, on request and on payment of the prescribed fee, to the manager, trustee or operator or any participant in a scheme under investigation or any other person whose conduct is referred to in the report[29]; and
(ii) cause the report to be published.[30]

24 [1989] BCC 266.
25 [1989] 1 WLR 525 p. 535B–C.
26 At p. 535F–H.
27 The House of Lords also upheld the Secretary of State's exercise of discretion not to make a reference to the Monopolies and Mergers Commission.
28 Financial Services Act 1986 s.94(9).
29 Financial Services Act 1986 s.94(9)(a). Note also Financial Services Act 1986 s.205 provides for regulations to be made prescribing fees.
30 Financial Services Act 1986 s.94(9)(b).

Similarly, where inspectors are appointed under the Open-ended Investment Companies (Investment Companies with Variable Capital) Regulations 1996 the final report shall be written or printed as the Secretary of State or Financial Services Authority may direct and the Secretary of State or Financial Services Authority may, if they think fit

(i) furnish a copy, on request and on payment of the prescribed fee (a) to any director, shadow director or shareholder, or to the depositary of a company under investigation, (b) where a director or shadow director under investigation is a body corporate, to any director of that body, (c) to any director of a depositary under investigation, or (d) to any other person whose conduct is referred to in the report[31]; and
(ii) cause the report to be published.[32]

The legal principles governing the exercise of the Secretary of State's discretion whether and when to publish any report will be the same as in relation to reports produced as a result of investigations pursuant to Companies Act 1985.[33]

There are no provisions permitting disclosure of reports produced as a result of investigations pursuant to s.105 and s.177. The information contained in the reports of such investigations (and also those pursuant to s.94) may, however, in limited circumstances come into the public domain, for example, where the requisite consents are obtained or where it is disclosed for specified regulatory proceedings that may publicise its proceedings.[34] **9.3.2**

9.4 INSURANCE COMPANIES

There is no power to publish reports of any investigations carried out pursuant to Insurance Companies Act 1982 s.44. Certain information **9.4.1**

[31] Open-ended Investment Companies (Investment Companies with Variable Capital) Regulations 1996 reg. 24(5)(a). Note also reg. 24(8) provides for regulations to be made in respect of fees.
[32] Reg. 24(5)(b).
[33] See 9.2 above.
[34] See 8.3. Note also the analogous position in respect of investigations under Companies Act 1985 where reports may not be published — 9.1.4 and 9.1.5.

may however, come into the public domain in specified limited circumstances.[35]

9.5 INVESTIGATIONS OF COMPANIES IN A VOLUNTARY WINDING UP

There is no mechanism permitting publication of any report prepared by the Secretary of State when exercising powers under Insolvency Act 1986 s.218 notwithstanding the similarity of his powers with those of inspectors appointed under Companies Act 1985 ss.431 and 432,[36] although it may be that information contained therein comes into the public domain in the course of any criminal proceedings.[37] **9.5.1**

9.6 POWERS EXERCISABLE TO ASSIST OVERSEAS REGULATORY AUTHORITIES

There is no power to publish any report prepared by any person appointed under Companies Act 1989 s.83 to assist overseas regulatory authorities. However, certain information may come into the public domain in specified limited circumstances.[38] **9.6.1**

---

35 See 8.4. Note also the analogous position at 9.1.4 and 9.1.5.
36 See Insolvency Act 1986 s.219.
37 S.219(2).
38 See 8.6. Note also the analogous position at 9.1.4 and 9.1.5.

Chapter 10

THE EXPENSES OF INVESTIGATIONS

The powers of the DTI to recover any of the costs of an investigation into a company depend on the particular statutory regime governing any particular investigation.

10.1 INVESTIGATIONS UNDER COMPANIES ACT 1985

Where an investigation is carried out under Companies Act 1985 Part XIV[1] the starting point is that the expenses are to be defrayed in the first instance by the Secretary of State.[2] These expenses may include such reasonable sums as he may determine in respect of general staff costs and overheads. The Secretary of State may recover expenses in accordance with 10.1.2 to 10.1.5 below.[3] In so far as expenses to be defrayed by the Secretary of State are not recovered in accordance with 10.1.2 to 10.1.5 they will be paid out of money provided by Parliament.[4] **10.1.1**

The Secretary of State may recover expenses from a person who is convicted on a prosecution instituted as a result of the investigation and is ordered to pay the expenses of the investigation.[5] No guidance is given as to how a court should exercise its discretion in this respect. **10.1.2**

Where proceedings are commenced under s.438 a person who is ordered to pay the whole or part of the costs of such proceedings may be ordered to pay the expenses of the investigation.[6] Again there is no guidance as to how a court should exercise its discretion. A body corporate in whose name proceedings are brought under s.438 is liable **10.1.3**

---

1 Companies Act 1985 ss.431, 432, 442, 444, 446 and 447.
2 Companies Act 1985 s.439(1).
3 Companies Act 1985 s.439(1).
4 Companies Act 1985 s.439(10).
5 Companies Act 1985 s.439(2).
6 Companies Act 1985 s.439(2). For a discussion of proceedings under s.438 see 12.1 below.

to the amount or value of any sums or property recovered by it as a result of the proceedings; and any such amount for which a body corporate is liable is a first charge on the sums or property recovered.[7] Any liability to repay the Secretary of State arising from an order in criminal proceedings or an order in s.438 proceedings to pay the expenses of an investigation is also a liability to indemnify a body corporate, which is liable to the amount or value of sums or property recovered by it in s.438 proceedings.[8] Any costs or expenses incurred by the Secretary of State in or in connection with s.438 proceedings are treated as expenses of the investigation giving rise to the proceedings.[9]

A body corporate dealt with by an inspectors' report, where the inspectors were appointed otherwise than of the Secretary of State's own motion, is liable for costs except where it was the applicant for the investigation, and except so far as the Secretary of State otherwise directs.[10] Where inspectors are appointed under s.431 or s.442(3) the applicants for the investigation are liable to such extent (if any) as the Secretary of State directs.[11] For the purposes of this provision the inspectors' report may, if they think fit, and shall if the Secretary of State so directs, include a recommendation as to the directions (if any) that they think are appropriate, in the light of the investigation.[12] **10.1.4**

Any liability to repay the Secretary of State imposed by 10.1.2 or 10.1.3 is (subject to satisfaction of his right to repayment) a liability also to indemnify all persons against liability under 10.1.4.[13] A person liable under any particular part of 10.1.2 to 10.1.4 is entitled to contribution from any other person liable under the same part, according to the amount of their respective liabilities under it.[14] **10.1.5**

---

7 Companies Act 1985 s.439(3).
8 Companies Act 1985 s.439(8).
9 Companies Act 1985 s.439(7).
10 Companies Act 1985 s.439(4).
11 Companies Act 1985 s.439(5).
12 Companies Act 1985 s.439(6).
13 Companies Act 1985 s.439(8).
14 Companies Act 1985 s.439(9) and note generally the structure of the section. For the order of priority under earlier legislation, Companies Act 1948 s.170, see *Selangor United Rubber Estates Ltd v Cradock (No. 4)* [1969] 1 WLR 1773.

10.2 INVESTIGATIONS UNDER THE FINANCIAL SERVICES LEGISLATION

A person who is convicted on a prosecution instituted as a result of an investigation commenced under any of Financial Services Act ss.94, 105 or 177 or the Open-ended Investment Companies (Investment Companies with Variable Capital) Regulations 1996 reg. 22 may in the same proceedings be ordered to pay the expenses of the investigation to such extent as may be specified in the order. These expenses include such reasonable sums as the Secretary of State may determine in respect of general staff costs and overheads.[15] **10.2.1**

10.3 RECOVERY OF COSTS OF INVESTIGATIONS UNDER COMPANIES ACT 1985 AND THE FINANCIAL SERVICES LEGISLATION IN PRACTICE

In practice the powers to recover the costs of investigations under Companies Act 1985 and the financial services legislation are used sparingly. The House of Commons Trade and Industry Committee, Third Report on 'Company Investigations' (1989–1990 session)[16] considered the level of expenditure on investigations[17] and recommended that greater steps be taken to recover the costs of investigations from the companies and individuals concerned, unless the inspectors find no evidence of wrongdoing.[18] The Government's Response[19] was to point out that the cost of the company investigations system is already largely met by the corporate sector through the fees charged by Companies House. The Response added that the Secretary of State would actively seek to recover costs in criminal and civil proceedings (the powers in this respect having been increased by Companies Act 1989, which **10.3.1**

---

15 Financial Services Act 1986 s.94(10), s.105(11) and s.177(11); Open-ended Investment Companies (Investment Companies with Variable Capital) Regulations 1996 reg. 22(6) and (7).

16 HC 36 1989–1990.

17 Paras 182–7.

18 Para. 187; recommendation 33.

19 Cm. 1149.

amended Companies Act 1985 and Financial Services Act 1986).[20] In practice, however, there have been relatively few court proceedings resulting from investigations. The Government Response also pointed out that there were other reasons against a more general power to recover costs, e.g. the company may be the victim, not the perpetrator of the fraud and a fear of having to pay the costs of an enquiry might discourage a company from reporting fraud.[21]

10.4 INSURANCE COMPANIES

There are no provisions for the recovery of the expenses of investigations carried out pursuant to Insurance Companies Act 1982 s.44. 10.4.1

10.5 INVESTIGATIONS OF COMPANIES IN A VOLUNTARY WINDING UP

There are no specific provisions for the recovery of the expenses of investigations carried out by the Secretary of State under Insolvency Act 1986 s.218.[22] 10.5.1

10.6 POWERS EXERCISEABLE TO ASSIST OVERSEAS REGULATORY AUTHORITIES

The Secretary of State may decline to exercise the powers exerciseable to assist overseas regulatory authorities contained in Companies Act 1989 s.83 unless the overseas regulatory authority undertakes to make such contribution towards the costs of their exercise as the Secretary of State considers appropriate.[23] 10.6.1

---

20 P.18.

21 P.18.

22 The Court may, however, impose a costs order on a person who fails to give assistance in criminal proceedings in the manner required under s.219(3) — see s.219(4).

23 Companies Act 1989 s.82(6).

Chapter 11

THE LINK WITH OTHER INVESTIGATIONS

11.1 GENERAL

Investigations into companies carried out by or on behalf of the DTI are not to be seen in isolation but must be seen in the context of investigations by other regulatory authorities, such as the Financial Services Authority, self-regulating organisations and recognised professional bodies; the Stock Exchange; the Serious Fraud Office and the Crown Prosecution Service. Indeed the circumstances in which information may be disclosed by inspectors and the Secretary of State demonstrate that it is envisaged that other regulators will also take appropriate action.[1] This may lead to a person or organisation having its authorisation to carry on business in a certain sector, such as securities, withdrawn. Further, where reports are published[2] this may lead to professional bodies taking disciplinary proceedings.[3] **11.1.1**

11.2 THE DUTY OF INSPECTORS TO PASS INFORMATION TO THE SECRETARY OF STATE

The legislation imposes a duty on inspectors and others to pass information to the Secretary of State. Inspectors appointed under Companies Act 1985 ss.431, 442 or 446 or Financial Services Act 1986 ss.94 or **11.2.1**

---

1 See 8.2 to 8.6 above.

2 See Ch.9.

3 See DTI *Investigations Handbook*, para. 57. Note that in *Re Barings plc; Secretary of State for Trade and Industry v Baker* [1998] *The Times*, 6 July, the Court of Appeal refused to stay proceedings brought under Company Directors Disqualification Act 1986 s.6 where the respondent had argued that to prosecute those proceedings would infringe the principle of double jeopardy since he had already successfully resisted proceedings brought by the Securities and Futures Authority in which the same, or substantially the same, charges had been made against him.

177 may at any time and, if the Secretary of State directs them to do so, shall inform him of any matters coming to their knowledge as a result of their investigations.[4] If it appears to the Secretary of State that matters have come to light in the course of the inspectors' investigation under Companies Act 1985 ss.431, 432 or 446 or Financial Services Act 1986 s.94, which suggest that a criminal offence has been committed, and those matters have been referred to the appropriate prosecuting authority, he may direct the inspectors to take no further steps in the investigation or to take only such further steps as are specified in the direction.[5] Where an investigation is the subject of such a direction, the inspectors shall make a final report to the Secretary of State only where they were appointed in pursuance of an order of the court[6] or the Secretary of State directs them to do so.[7] If the Secretary of State thinks fit he may direct an inspector appointed under Financial Services Act 1986 s.177 to take no further steps in the investigation or to take only such further steps as are specified in the direction; and where an investigation is the subject of such a direction, the inspectors shall make a final report to the Secretary of State only where the Secretary of State directs them to do so.[8]

11.2.2 The DTI's *Investigations Handbook* gives guidance to inspectors appointed under Companies Act 1985 s.431 and s.432 in relation to the exercise of the power to pass information to the Secretary of State.[9] In particular inspectors are asked to use their power to advise the DTI promptly of any matter that comes to light during the course of an inspection, which suggests that an offence has been committed or that consideration may need to be given to regulatory or disciplinary action, or that information may need to be disclosed to other investigators or a competent authority.[10]

---

4 Companies Act 1985 s.437(1A), s.443(1), s.446(3), Financial Services Act 1986 s.94(8), s.177(5).
5 Companies Act 1985 s.437(1B), Financial Services Act 1986 s.94(8A).
6 Companies Act 1985 s.432(1).
7 Companies Act 1985 s.437(1C), Financial Services Act 1986 s.94(8B).
8 Financial Services Act s.177(5A). The House of Commons Trade and Industry Committee in its Third report *Company Investigations* (1990) HC 36 did not believe that the powers to call off an inquiry should be used to forestall the investigation of wider issues involved in a case once a prosecution has been launched on some specific aspect of it — para. 60 of the Report.
9 App B, paras 43–7.
10 See 8.2 above; App B, para. 44.

11.3 THE LINK WITH INVESTIGATIONS BY THE FINANCIAL SERVICES AUTHORITY

11.3.1 Investigations carried out by inspectors or others on behalf of the Secretary of State have a particular link with investigations undertaken by or on behalf of the Financial Services Authority. The provisions allowing disclosure by the DTI or Secretary of State generally include a gateway permitting disclosure to the Financial Services Authority.[11] However, various powers in the Financial Services Act 1986 are exerciseable concurrently by the Secretary of State and the Financial Services Authority. Thus, the power under Financial Services Act 1986 s.94 to appoint inspectors to investigate authorised unit trust schemes, recognised schemes and collective investment schemes, and the power under s.105 to investigate the affairs of a person so far as relevant to an investment business, may be exercised by either or both of the Secretary of State and the Financial Services Authority.[12] In practice, the power under s.105 tends to be exercised by the Financial Services Authority rather than the Secretary of State.[13] Further, the powers to investigate open-ended investment companies in the Open-ended Investment Companies (Investment Companies with Variable Capital) Regulations 1996 are exerciseable concurrently by the Secretary of State and the Financial Services Authority.[14]

11.4 THE LINK WITH INVESTIGATIONS BY THE POLICE AND SERIOUS FRAUD OFFICE

11.4.1 In a fraud case there will be three possible mechanisms for questioning those suspected of wrongdoing (in addition to any regulator governing a particular industry or profession) — the police, the SFO and inspectors or others appointed by the DTI. As pointed out by Lord Taylor CJ

[11] See 8.2 to 8.6.
[12] See Financial Services Act 1986 (Delegation) Order 1987 (SI 1987/942) in respect of s.105 and the Financial Services Act 1986 (Delegation) (No 2) Order 1988 (SI 1988/738) in respect of s.94.
[13] The power under s.94 is not generally exercised.
[14] Reg. 21.

in *R v Saunders (No. 2)*[15] only the third course permits both questioning without the safeguards of the Police and Criminal Evidence Act 1984 and the admission of incriminating answers at a criminal trial. The Police and Criminal Evidence Act 1984 with, for example, the requirement in s.67 to comply with codes on questioning does not apply to inspectors whose duty is to investigate,[16] and the privilege enabling a witness to avoid answering questions that might incriminate himself does not apply.[17] Conversely the police and Serious Fraud Office will be bound by the requirements of the Police and Criminal Evidence Act and the Criminal Procedure and Investigations Act 1996.[18] Further, the suspect has a right of silence when answering questions put by police officers (although the court may now draw inferences from a refusal to answer questions) and whilst the SFO can compel answers to questions pursuant to Criminal Justice Act 1987 s.2(2), the witness is given a protection against the use of incriminating answers by virtue of s.2(8).[19]

The relationship between the investigation regimes was considered by the Court of Appeal in *R v Saunders (No. 2)*.[20] The Court of Appeal stated[21] **11.4.2**

> Clearly it would be wrong ... for the inspectors to be briefed by the D.P.P. or for questions the D.P.P. or CPS might have wanted answered to be put to and put by the inspectors. It would be wrong, in short, for the inspectors to be used as officers or agents of the prosecuting authority. But, although acting independently, inspectors under section 432(2) have a duty to investigate the possibility of fraud, to get to the bottom of the facts with that in mind, and to disclose any evidence of fraud which they expose to the Secretary of State via the DTI and to the prosecuting authorities. For their part, the D.P.P., the CPS and the police have the duty of investigating and prosecuting fraud. It is a matter for the discretion of the prosecuting authority at what stage and on what material to launch first a police operation and ultimately a prosecution. In a complex affair,

---

15 [1996] 1 Cr App R 463.
16 See *R v Seelig, R v Spens* [1992] 1 WLR 148, 13.2 below.
17 See *Re London United Investments Limited* [1992] Ch 579, 6.10 above.
18 Note, in particular, the code of practice on the recording and retention of evidence pursuant to s.23.
19 Note the point made by Lord Browne-Wilkinson in *Hamilton v Naviede* [1995] 2 AC 75 at pp. 107H–8A that at the time the Criminal Justice Act 1987 was enacted it was thought that the privilege against self-incrimination was applicable to such investigations and that only since then has it been established that the privilege against self-incrimination is not applicable in such inquisitorial proceedings, and see 13.2 below.
20 [1996] 1 Cr App R 463, 13.2.4 below.
21 At p.483B–E.

> such as this major company takeover, there clearly needs to be some cooperation between the inspectors and the prosecuting authorities to evaluate the material the inspectors have unearthed and as to the timing of further investigations. Parliament has provided for inspectors in the field of company fraud to conduct their inquiries under the regime of the 1985 Act and for the answers they elicit to be admissible in criminal proceedings. Parliament having put that regime in place, we do not consider it improper for the prosecuting authorities to permit it to take its course up to the point when, in their discretion, they consider a police investigation focused on specific allegations should sensibly be started.

Thus, the effect of the Court of Appeal's judgment is that the only constraints on the inspectors are that they should conduct their inquiries and interviews independently without instruction, briefing or prompting by the prosecuting authority and that the interviews must be conducted fairly and unobjectionably. What emerges from the Court of Appeal's judgment is that there is no other restriction as far as domestic law is concerned on the questions that may be put to witnesses by inspectors, and there is certainly no principle that where it appears that there may be a criminal prosecution the DTI should stop any investigations that it or inspectors appointed by it are carrying out. Similarly, there is no principle that evidence obtained by inspectors or the DTI should not be passed to and used by the prosecuting authority. There will be some limits on what the criminal trial judge will admit in evidence but the mere fact that any self-incriminating answers were obtained pursuant to compulsory powers will not, of itself, have the effect that the transcript of the answers is inadmissible under Police and Criminal Evidence Act 1984 ss.76, 78 or 82.[22]

One difficulty for those investigating possible fraud is the difference between English law and the European Convention on Human Rights. **11.4.3**
Notwithstanding, the position set out in *R v Seelig, R v Spens*[23] and *R v Saunders (No. 2)*,[24] the European Court of Human Rights in *Saunders v United Kingdom*[25] found that the use at a criminal trial of transcripts of the accused's answers, which were of an incriminating nature, resulted in an infringement of Article 6(1) of the European Convention on Human Rights concerning a fair hearing.[26] The difficulty

22 See 13.2 below.
23 [1992] 1 WLR 148.
24 See 13.2.1 to 13.2.4 below.
25 [1997] BCC 872.
26 See 13.2.5 to 13.2.7.

was identified in *R v Morrisey, R v Staines*[27] concerning the use of transcripts of answers given to inspectors appointed under Financial Services Act 1986 s.177 in which the Court of Appeal agreed that the present situation was 'very unsatisfactory' in that domestic law was as in *R v Saunders* but the appellants might have grounds for complaining to the European Court of Human Rights if the penalty were enforced. To deal with this unsatisfactory position the Attorney General has restricted the circumstances in which evidence from inspectors will be used in practice in criminal proceedings.[28]

[27] [1997] *The Times*, 1 May; transcript.

[28] See 13.2.9 below. Note that in 1990, before the European caselaw, the House of Commons Trade and Industry Committee had considered whether when the matters being investigated by inspectors were likely to lead to a criminal prosecution there should be a single process. On balance, however, the Committee concurred with the opinion that the roles of inspectors and the Serious Fraud Office should be kept separate until a report, interim or final, has been delivered — see paragraphs 59–60 of the Third Report (1990) HC 36.

Chapter 12

SUBSEQUENT ACTION BY THE SECRETARY OF STATE

In addition to passing information to other regulatory authorities the Secretary of State may himself take action following an investigation. This includes civil proceedings in the name of the company,[1] winding-up petitions,[2] unfair prejudice petitions,[3] company director disqualification proceedings[4] and criminal prosecutions.[5]

12.1 CIVIL PROCEEDINGS IN THE NAME OF THE COMPANY

If from any report made or information obtained under Companies Act 1985 Part XIV[6] it appears to the Secretary of State that any civil proceedings ought in the public interest to be brought by any body corporate he may himself bring such proceedings in the name and on behalf of the body corporate.[7] The Secretary of State must indemnify the body corporate against any costs or expenses incurred by it or in connection with such proceedings.[8] In *Selangor United Rubber Estates Ltd v Cradock*[9] proceedings were brought in the name of the company[10] and Goff J held[11] that 'any costs or expenses incurred by it or in connection with any proceedings brought'[12] covered costs ordered to be paid by the company to other parties in addition to the company's own costs. Further Goff J considered what should happen to sums paid by the Board 12.1.1

1 See 12.1.
2 See 12.2.
3 See 12.3.
4 See 12.4.
5 See 12.5.
6 Ss. 431–53.
7 Companies Act 1985 s.438(1).
8 Companies Act 1985 s.438(2).
9 [1967] 1 WLR 1168.
10 The proceedings were commenced under earlier legislation — Companies Act 1948 s.169.
11 At p. 1173E.
12 Companies Act 1948 s.169(5).

of Trade to a company in order to satisfy cost orders against the company where the proceedings had been brought by the Secretary of State in the company's name. Goff J held[13] that such sums paid to a company were to be paid to the parties to the litigation in whose favour cost orders were made rather than such sums forming part of the company's assets available for its creditors generally.

Any costs or expenses incurred by the Secretary of State in connection with the proceedings at 12.1.1 are treated as expenses of the investigation giving rise to the proceedings.[14] There are provisions for the Secretary of State to recover these expenses.[15] **12.1.2**

The Treasury and Secretary of State may also exercise the powers at 12.1.1 in respect of insurance companies.[16] **12.1.3**

There are no statutory provisions that specifically provide for the Secretary of State to commence proceedings following an investigation into a company under Financial Services Act 1986, the exercise of powers to assist regulatory authorities under Companies Act 1989 or Insolvency Act 1986 s.217. **12.1.4**

12.2 WINDING UP PETITIONS

Where it appears to the Secretary of State from any report made or information obtained following investigations into companies under Companies Act 1985 Part XIV, financial services investigations[17] or investigations carried out to assist overseas regulatory authorities[18] that it is expedient in the public interest that the company investigated should be wound up, the Secretary of State may present a petition to the court that it be wound up if the court thinks it just and equitable to do so.[19] It appears that it is not a pre-requisite to the exercise of this power to **12.2.1**

---

13 *ibid.*

14 Companies Act s.439(7). See also *Selangor United Rubber Estates Ltd v Cradock (No. 4)* [1969] 1 WLR 1773 at pp. 1785–6.

15 Companies Act 1985 s.439 and see 10.1 above.

16 Insurance Companies Act 1982 s.48.

17 This includes investigations pursuant to the Open-ended Investment Companies (Investment Companies with Variable Capital) Regulations 1996 (SI 1996/2827) — see reg. 25.

18 Companies Act 1989 s.83.

19 Insolvency Act 1986 s.124A(1). This power may also be exercised by the Secretary of State from information obtained under Criminal Justice Act 1987 s.2. In certain circumstances the Secretary of State may apply to wind up an authorised person or appointed representative (as defined in the Financial Services Act) — Financial Services Act 1986 s.72.

present a petition by the Secretary of State that the company must be acting unlawfully (because its business or its business methods are unlawful) but that instead it is for the Secretary of State to form a view as to what is expedient in the public interest and the court must then decide on the material before it whether the justice and equity of the case dictate that the company concerned should be wound up.[20] The power may not be exercised by the Secretary of State if the company is already being wound up by the Court[21] but this appears to leave open the possibility of the Secretary of State presenting a petition where the company is in voluntary liquidation.[22] The power of the Secretary of State to present a petition applies to companies incorporated in Great Britain or elsewhere.[23] The Secretary of State may also apply for a provisional liquidator to be appointed.

In *Re Lubin, Rosen and Associates Ltd*[24] the Secretary of State exercised powers under Companies Act 1967 and, following the investigation, it appeared to him that it was expedient in the public interest that the company should be wound up. Shortly after the petition was filed, the company passed a resolution for its voluntary winding up. A large number of creditors opposed the Secretary of State's petition. Megarry J was of the view[25] that the existence of a voluntary winding up is one of the factors to be considered in deciding whether or not it is just and equitable to make a compulsory winding up order. However, Megarry J stated **12.2.2**

> In this case, the investigation by the Secretary of State preceded the resolution for a voluntary winding up. Where the results of that investigation lead the Secretary of State to the conclusion that it is expedient in the public interest that the company should be wound up, and he accordingly presents a petition for a compulsory order, I do not think that the passing of a resolution for a voluntary winding up shortly before the Secretary of State presents his petition, and the subsequent confirmation of that resolution, ought to be allowed to put the voluntary winding up into an entrenched position, as it were, which can be demolished only if

---

20 See *Re Senator Hanseatische Verwaltungs GmbH and Others* [1997] 1 WLR 515 per Saville LJ at pp. 522H–523A and Millett LJ at p. 526 B–E and note also *Re Vanilla Services BV and others* 13 February 1998, unrep.
21 S.124A(2).
22 E.g. the approach in *Re Lubin, Rosen and Associates Ltd* [1975] 1 WLR 122.
23 See *Re Normandy Marketing Ltd* [1993] BCC 879.
24 [1975] 1 WLR 122.
25 At p. 128E–F.

the Secretary of State can demonstrate that the process of voluntary winding up will be markedly inferior to a compulsory winding up. The Secretary of State may, of course, reach the conclusion that a voluntary winding up will suffice, and so not proceed with his petition; but if he does proceed, then in my judgment the question is essentially whether, in all the circumstances of the case (including, of course, the existence of a voluntary winding up and the views of the creditors), it is just and equitable for the company to be wound up compulsorily. In addition to the suspicion of offences, the presence of foreign complications such as exist in this case, and the differences between the interests of the disappointed purchasers and those of any other creditors, seem to me to make it both just and equitable that this winding up should be conducted with the full authority and resources of the court.

Thus a petition by the Secretary of State will be treated with special consideration where there is a competing voluntary winding up. As Megarry J noted, creditors and contributories petition in their own interests whereas the Secretary of State is necessarily acting not in his own interests but in the interests of the public at large[26] and the court, without abdicating any of its judicial and discretionary powers, ought to give special weight to his views.[27]

The approach adopted to a petition presented by the Secretary of State will not, however, involve the court abdicating to the Secretary of State its role in considering whether or not it would be just and equitable to wind up a company. In *Re Walter L Jacob & Co. Ltd*[28] Nicholls LJ giving the leading judgment in the Court of Appeal stated[29] **12.2.3**

In respect of all such petitions, whoever may be the petitioner, the court has to weigh the factors which point to the conclusion that it would be just and equitable to wind up the company against those which point to the opposite conclusion. It is to the court that Parliament has entrusted this task, in all cases. Thus, where the reasons put forward by the petitioner are founded on considerations of public interest, the court, if it is to discharge its obligation to carry out the balancing exercise, must itself evaluate those reasons to the extent necessary for it to form a view on whether they do afford sufficient reason for making a winding up order in the particular case.

In the case of 'public interest' petitions, the court will, of course, carry out that evaluation with the assistance of evidence and submissions from

26 At p. 129A.
27 At p. 129C.
28 [1989] BCLC 345.
29 At p. 353(b)–(g).

> the Secretary of State and from other parties. When doing so the court will take note that the source of the submissions that the company should be wound up is a government department charged by Parliament with wide-ranging responsibilities in relation to the affairs of companies. The department has considerable expertise in these matters and can be expected to act with a proper sense of responsibility when seeking a winding up order. But the cogency of the submissions made on behalf of the Secretary of State will fall to be considered and tested in the same way as any other submissions. His submissions are not ipso facto endowed with such weight that those resisting a winding up petition presented by him will find the scales loaded against them. At the end of the day the court must be able to identify for itself the aspect or aspects of the public interest which, in the view of the court, would be promoted by making a winding up order in the particular case. In many, perhaps most, cases that will be a simple exercise in which the answer will be self-evident. In other cases the answer may not be so obvious.

Nicholls LJ went on to consider what was said by Megarry J in *Re Lubin Rosen & Associates Ltd* and was of the view[30] that Megarry J had not said anything different from what Nicholls LJ had sought to say, but that if Megarry J had been saying anything different Nicholls LJ disagreed with him. In the event in *Re Walter Jacob & Co. Ltd* the Court of Appeal granted the winding up order upon the Secretary of State's petition. In *Re a Company (No. 007816 of 1994) and others*[31] Jonathan Parker J referred to *Re Walter L Jacob & Co. Ltd* and the principles set out by Nicholls LJ. In the context of offshore insurance companies and UK companies that operated as brokers and intermediaries Jonathan Parker J was not persuaded that the UK companies were conducting unauthorised insurance business contrary to Insurance Companies Act 1982 s.2(1). He held that the case that the offshore companies had insufficient assets to write insurance was not made out and he found that, in the light of the facts found or admitted, it was neither just nor equitable for winding up orders to be made in respect of any of the six companies concerned.

A further aspect where the court will use its own discretion is when exercising its power to restrain the advertisement of a petition for the compulsory winding up of a company under Insolvency Rules 1986,[32] rule 4.11(1). In *Re Companies (Nos 007923 and 007924 of 1994)*[33] **12.2.4**

30 At p. 354(b).
31 [1995] *The Times*, 13 October.
32 SI 1986/1925.
33 [1995] 1 BCLC 440.

Nourse LJ in the Court of Appeal stated that the test for determining whether the court should restrain the advertisement of a petition was not the same as that regulating the court's discretion to restrain the presentation of a winding up petition. He explained[34] that the primary purpose of advertisement was to give notice of the petition to those who are entitled to be heard on it, namely the creditors and contributories of the company, and the secondary purpose must be to give notice to those who might trade with the company during the period between the presentation of the petition and its final determination. He explained that unless companies can show that advertisement may cause serious damage to their reputation and financial stability there must be advertisement of the petition. In the present case, which concerned insurance companies, and where there was evidence including that the placing of business depended on the confidence one individual has in the reputation of another, Nourse LJ explained[35]

> Although it has been well observed that the harmful effects of advertisement are liable to be exaggerated, as they may have been here, the companies' evidence is in my view sufficient to establish that it could cause serious damage to their reputation and financial stability. Adding that consideration, first, to the likelihood that if there is no advertisement in the short term no significant disadvantage will be caused to those whose interests must also be considered and, secondly, to the likely imminence of the hearing of the application for a provisional liquidator, I have come to the view that we ought to direct that the petitions should not be advertised over that hearing.

Therefore, although there is a stiff test to overcome before advertisement of a petition will be restrained, in appropriate circumstances a court may be willing to make such an order.[36]

The special position of a winding up by the Secretary of State when acting in the public interest rather than in the Crown's proprietary interest is demonstrated by *Re Highfield Commodities Ltd*[37] in which Sir Robert Megarry V-C held that the Secretary of State will be exempt from being required to offer an undertaking in damages as the price of obtaining the appointment of a provisional liquidator, save where the **12.2.5**

[34] At p. 446.
[35] At p. 447b–d.
[36] But note also *Re Golden Chemical Products Ltd* [1976] Ch 300 at pp. 309–10 and *Re a Company (No. 007946 of 1993)* [1994] Ch 198.
[37] [1985] 1 WLR 149.

company can establish special circumstances that justify such a requirement being made.[38]

Where the Secretary of State believes it appropriate to present a winding up petition he will not be obliged, as an alternative, to accept undertakings designed to secure that a company's future activities would be free from objection. If a company could oppose a petition on this basis the DTI would end up with a mass of delinquent companies on probation.[39] The Secretary of State may also seek an injunction to prevent a company from continuing to operate an activity pending the hearing of a winding up petition.[40] **12.2.6**

12.3 UNFAIR PREJUDICE PETITIONS

If the Secretary of State has received a report under Companies Act 1985 s.437 or exercised his powers under ss.447 or 448, or Insurance Companies Act 1982 ss.43A or 44(2) to (6), and it appears to him that the affairs of a body corporate that is liable to be wound up are being or have been conducted in a manner that is unfairly prejudicial to the interests of its members, or that any actual or proposed act or omission of the company (including an act or omission on its behalf) is or would be so prejudicial, he may apply to the court.[41] The Secretary of State may present such a petition in addition to or instead of presenting a petition for the winding up of the company.[42] **12.3.1**

The relief that a court may give when the Secretary of State presents a petition is the same as where the petition is presented by a member of the company.[43] **12.3.2**

---

[38] Sir Robert Megarry V-C in *Re Highfield Commodities Ltd* used the reasoning in *F Hoffman-La Roche & Co. A.G. v Secretary of State for Trade and Industry* [1975] AC 295 whereby the court may in its discretion decide that the Crown is not required to provide a cross-undertaking where it is seeking to enforce the law. See also *Kirklees Metropolitan Borough Council v Wickes Building Supplies Ltd* [1993] AC 227.

[39] *Re Bamford Publishers Ltd* [1977] *The Times*, 4 June; Brightman J.

[40] See, e.g. *Re Senator Hanseatische Verwaltungs GmbH and Others* [1997] 1WLR 515 and note the comments of Millett L.J. at pp. 526H–7A setting out the advantages of appointing a provisional liquidator as against granting temporary injunctions.

[41] Companies Act 1985 s.460. See in relation to an earlier provision, Companies Act 1948 s.210, R Instone *Inspectors, Investigations and Their Aftermath* [1978] JBL 121.

[42] Companies Act 1985 s.460(1).

[43] See Companies Act 1985 ss.459 and 461.

12.4 COMPANY DIRECTOR DISQUALIFICATION PROCEEDINGS[44]

Company Directors Disqualification Act 1986 s.8 makes particular provision for the Secretary of State to apply for a director's disqualification following an investigation into a company. The Secretary of State may make an application to the High Court or Court of Session for a director's disqualification where, from a report made by inspectors under Companies Act 1985 s.437 or Financial Services Act 1986 ss.94 or 177, or from information or documents obtained under Companies Act 1985 ss.447 or 448 or Financial Services Act 1986 s.105 or Companies Act 1989 s.83, the Secretary of State concludes that it is expedient in the public interest that a disqualification order should be made against a person who is or has been a director or shadow director of a company.[45] Upon such an application the court may make a disqualification order where it is satisfied that his conduct in relation to the company makes him unfit to be concerned in the management of a company.[46] The maximum period of disqualification is 15 years.[47] 12.4.1

Company Directors Disqualification Act 1986 s.9 and Schedule 1 set out the matters to which the court should have particular regard when it considers whether a person's conduct as a director or shadow director of any particular company makes him unfit to be concerned in the management of a company, and include matters such as misfeasance and breach of duty and responsibility for the causes of insolvency.[48] In *Re Samuel Sherman plc*[49] Judge Paul Baker QC referred to the guidance contained in *Re Sevenoaks Stationers (Retail) Ltd*[50] on the divisions of 12.4.2

---

44 Generally for the law relating to the disqualification of directors see A. Mithani and S. Wheeler *The Disqualification of Company Directors* (1996) and S. Griffin *Personal Liability and Disqualification of Company Directors* (1999) (forthcoming).

45 Company Directors Disqualification Act 1986 s.8(1). An application may also be made by the Secretary of State from information or documents obtained under Criminal Justice Act 1987 s.2.

46 S.8(2).

47 S.8(4). For the differences between the court's powers on an application under s.6 (disqualification of unfit directors of insolvent companies) and an application under s.8 see A. Mithani and S. Wheeler, supra at p. 181. The procedure for applications is governed by the Insolvent Companies (Disqualification of Unfit Directors) Proceedings Rules 1987 (SI 1987/2023).

48 For the principles generally see A. Mithani and S. Wheeler, supra at Ch 2.

49 [1991] 1 WLR 1070.

50 [1991] Ch 164. See also the approach in *Secretary of State for Trade and Industry v Griffiths* [1998] *The Times*, 13 January.

the potential 15-year disqualification period under s.6[51]:

> (i) The top bracket of disqualification for periods over 10 years should be reserved for particularly serious cases. These may include cases where a director who has already had one period of disqualification imposed upon him falls to be disqualified yet again. (ii) The minimum bracket of two to five years' disqualification should be applied where, though disqualification is mandatory, the case is, relatively, not very serious. (iii) The middle bracket of disqualification for from six to 10 years should apply for serious cases which do not merit the top bracket.

Although there is no minimum period for a disqualification under s.8 unlike under s.6, Judge Paul Baker QC in *Re Samuel Sherman plc* and Arden J in *Re TMS (GB) Ltd*[52] accepted that the same general principles should apply in determining whether a disqualification order should be made because under both sections the issue is whether the director is 'unfit' to be concerned in the management of a company.

However, the court in considering whether or not a disqualification order should be made under s.8 (as distinct from the question of the period of disqualification once it is decided that an order is appropriate) will not derive assistance from the significant body of caselaw under s.6. In *Re Samuel Sherman plc* Judge Paul Baker QC took this view[53] both because s.6 cases arise in the context of insolvency and because the Court of Appeal in *Re Sevenoaks Stationers (Retail) Ltd* stressed the need to hold to the statutory words rather than statements in other cases. Various matters have been taken into account by the courts under s.8. **12.4.3**

(i) In *Re Samuel Sherman plc* the court considered that loss to individuals was more serious than loss to trading creditors. Judge Paul Baker QC pointed out[54] that a trade creditor has 'immediate remedies available to him' whereas a shareholder 'holding only a few shares in a public company is in a much more precarious position and has no practicable remedy'. In that case the company had embarked on a course of action that was ultra vires and involved a number of persistent and deliberate breaches of important statutory provisions. Judge Paul Baker QC

---

[51] Per Dillon LJ at p. 174.
[52] 26 November 1993, unrep.
[53] [1991] WLR 1070 at p. 1084C–D.
[54] At p. 1085H.

accepted[55] that there was no dishonesty on the part of the director; he had himself lost a substantial investment; there had been no concealment of relevant transactions; there were sufficient accounting records to produce the accounts; he had cooperated with the DTI examiners and with the liquidator; and he had given up a number of directorships in other companies. These matters did not, however, cause Judge Paul Baker QC to refrain from making a disqualification order. The order was for five years and it is unclear whether but for these factors in mitigation the term would have been any longer.

(ii) In *Re Minet Holdings plc*[56] Hoffman J considered an uncontested report that stated that a director had paid no regard to his fiduciary duties and was prompted only by a desire to achieve and maintain an extravagant lifestyle and which the report referred to as 'systematic dishonest plunder'. Possible arguments by the respondents who were not represented that they now lived in Florida and were 'probably at least over the age of 60' were not of 'any particular significance'. Hoffman J ordered a 10-year period of disqualification.

(iii) In *Re Looe Fish Ltd*[57] Jonathan Parker J found[58] that a director displayed a clear lack of commercial probity when abusing his power as a director in connection with an allotment of shares (which had the effect of preventing other shareholders from wresting control of the company) but also took into account that no question of insolvency arose in the case and that the director did not act out of motives of personal gain, nor did he receive any improper benefit. Jonathan Parker J made a disqualification order for two years and six months.

(iv) In *Re TMS (GB) Ltd*[59] Arden J noted that the purpose of a disqualification order was to protect the public. It was material that the directors' conduct in that case principally affected individual members of the public, who were neither trade creditors nor commercial lenders, and that the effects on them of mismanagement were, and should have been expected to be, severe. This made the directors' conduct more serious and the greater the seriousness, the longer the period of disqualification

55 At p. 1086A–C.
56 10 February 1992, unrep.
57 [1993] BCLC 1160.
58 At p. 1172.
59 26 November 1993, unrep.

required to protect the interests of the public. In relation to mitigation Arden J made an allowance for the directors' decision not to contest the application but not as great as had the decision been made at an earlier stage or if they had more clearly accepted some responsibility. The mitigation including the decision not to contest the proceedings caused Arden J to reduce what would otherwise have been a disqualification order for a period of six years to five and a half years.

Notwithstanding the difference in approach under s.6 and s.8 as to whether disqualification orders will be made, the courts will adopt the same approach as to whether the delay in bringing the proceedings under either section amounts to oppression and an abuse of process.[60] It has also been held that the Secretary of State is not obliged to stay disqualification proceedings under s.8 where a director offers undertakings including never to act as a director of a company in the future because undertakings do not have the same effect as Parliament has given to a disqualification order made under the statutory machinery.[61] **12.4.4**

12.5 CRIMINAL PROSECUTIONS

Matters that come to light in the course of an investigation into a company may lead to a criminal prosecution where the DTI is the prosecuting authority under, in particular, the Companies Act 1985 and the Financial Services Act 1986. The DTI's powers in this respect link in to those of other prosecuting authorities.[62] **12.5.1**

Investigations carried out under Financial Services Act 1986 s.177 may, in particular, lead to prosecutions for insider dealing pursuant to **12.5.2**

60 See *Secretary of State for Trade and Industry v Ashman* per Jacob J, 26 June 1997, NLP.

61 See *Re Blackspur Group plc and others; Re Atlantic Computer Systems plc and another* [1998] 1 WLR 423 where the Court of Appeal refused both an application for a stay and judicial review of the Secretary of State's decision not to accept undertakings and stay the proceedings. See also *Secretary of State for Trade and Industry v Rogers* [1996] 1 WLR 1569.

62 See 11.4 above. Note the convention between prosecuting authorities to provide arrangements for ensuring effective co-ordination of decision making and handling in related cases that are the responsibility of different authorities, signed in February 1998.

Criminal Justice Act 1993, Part V.[63] Briefly, an individual who has information as an insider[64] is guilty of insider dealing if in particular circumstances he deals in securities[65] that are price-affected securities in relation to the information.[66] The particular circumstances are that the acquisition or disposal in question occurs on a regulated market,[67] or that the person dealing relies on a professional intermediary[68] or is himself acting as a professional intermediary.[69] Encouraging another person to deal in price-affected securities or disclosing the information to another person will, in specified circumstances, also constitute an offence.[70] There are a number of defences.[71] In particular an individual who deals has a defence if he shows

- (i) that he did not at the time expect the dealing to result in a profit attributable to the fact that the information in question was price-sensitive information in relation to the securities,[72] or
- (ii) that at the time he believed on reasonable grounds that the information had been disclosed widely enough to ensure that none of those taking part in the dealing would be prejudiced by not having the information,[73] or
- (iii) that he would have done what he did even if he had not had the information.[74]

There are other different defences for those who encourage another to deal[75] or disclose information to another person.[76] An individual guilty of insider dealing is liable on summary conviction to a fine not exceeding the statutory maximum[77] or imprisonment for up to six months or both,[78] and on conviction on indictment to a fine or imprisonment for up to seven years or both.[79]

63 Generally see B. Hannigan *Insider Dealing* 2nd edn (1994); B. Rider & M. Ashe *Insider Crime: The New Law* (1993).
64 Insider is defined in Criminal Justice Act 1993 s.57 and see also s.56.
65 Dealing in securities is defined in s.55.
66 S.52(1).
67 Regulated market is defined in s.60(1).
68 Professional intermediary is defined in s.59.
69 S.52(3).
70 S.52(2).
71 S.53.
72 S.53(1)(a).
73 S.53(1)(b).
74 S.53(1)(c).
75 S.53(2).
76 S.53(3).
77 Currently £5,000.
78 S.61(1)(a).

12.6 SUBSEQUENT ACTION DECIDED UPON BY OFFICIALS

The above statutory regimes provide for the Secretary of State to take action but not in terms which indicate that it is for him alone to take the action. However, in *Re Golden Chemical Products Ltd*[80] the Secretary of State acting by the Inspectors of Companies in the Department of Trade authorised two officers of the Department pursuant to Companies Act 1967 s.109[81] to require a company to produce books and papers. Subsequently a petition for the winding up of the company was presented alleging that it appeared to the Secretary of State expedient in the public interest that the company should be wound up under Companies Act 1967 s.35. The Secretary of State had, however, never considered the matter and it was the Inspector of Companies who, by departmental practice rather than express delegation, had believed it expedient to present the petition. When this exercise of power was challenged Brightman J noted that[82] the power given by s.35 was 'of a most formidable nature, which may cause serious damage to the reputation and financial stability of the company'. However, Brightman J referred to the line of authority permitting Ministers to entrust Departmental officials with the exercise of powers conferred on the Minister by statute[83] and found that in the present case the Inspector of Companies exercised the powers conferred on the Secretary of State unless he decided to refer a particular matter to his superior. Brightman J rejected a suggested distinction that the initial decision-making process could be performed by someone other than the Minister if, but only if, it leads to no serious invasion of the freedom or property rights of the subject.[84] Thus the Secretary of State was entitled to act through the Inspector of Companies in presenting the petition for the winding up of the company. There is no reason why the other possible follow-up action to an 12.6.1

---

79 S.61(1)(b). Note that investigations under other provisions can result in criminal prosecutions. For example, an investigation under Financial Services Act 1986 s.105 could lead to a prosecution under s.4 for carrying on investment business without authorisation.

80 [1976] 1 Ch 300.

81 See now Companies Act 1985 s.447.

82 At p. 310A.

83 See *Carltona Ltd v Commissioners of Works* [1943] 2 All ER 560; *Lewisham Metropolitan Borough and Town Clerk v Roberts* [1949] 2 KB 608 and *R v Skinner* [1968] 2 QB 700.

84 At p. 310D–F.

investigation may not be taken by the Secretary of State also acting through a responsible official rather than him personally taking the action.

12.7 CHALLENGING A DECISION CONCERNING SUBSEQUENT ACTION

12.7.1 In the exercise of his discretion the Secretary of State may decide to take a particular course of action or no action against a company that has been the subject of an investigation or those involved with the company. In such circumstances, the Secretary of State's decision is susceptible to judicial review. In *R v Secretary of State for Trade and Industry ex p. Lonrho plc*,[85] Lonrho challenged the decision of the Secretary of State not to apply for a disqualification order against the Fayed brothers following the report of inspectors appointed under Companies Act 1985 s.432(2) to investigate the affairs of House of Fraser Holdings plc of which the Fayed brothers were directors. In view of the role played by Lonrho leading up to the publication of the report,[86] the Divisional Court found that Lonrho had sufficient interest to seek to ensure that the Secretary of State acted lawfully in any action that he took or did not take in the light of the inspectors' report. The Divisional Court, however, found the Secretary of State's decision to be lawful. Neill LJ quoted from the affidavit sworn by the head of the investigation division at the DTI, from which it was clear that the Secretary of State had received advice on the scope of the Company Directors Disqualification Act 1986 and, in particular, the scope of s.8. The Secretary of State had also taken a number of considerations into account including that the primary purpose of the 1986 Act was to protect the public rather than to punish individuals; there was no evidence of any financial loss to any creditor or member of House of Fraser Holdings plc as a result of the conduct complained of, the publication of the inspectors' report and ensuing publicity would enable all those who might have dealings with the Fayeds in their capacity as company directors to judge whether their interests were likely to be at risk; and there was no evidence that the Fayeds, who had been directors of House of Fraser since 1985, had abused the advantages and privileges deriving

[85] [1992] BCC 325.
[86] See 9.2.3 above.

from limited liability. Neill LJ could find no adequate grounds for saying that the Secretary of State took immaterial matters into account. Neill LJ turned to the suggestion that the Secretary of State's decision was Wednesday unreasonable[87] and used the test of irrationality in *Council of Civil Service Unions v Minister for the Civil Service*[88]:

> It applies to a decision which is so outrageous in its defiance of logic or of accepted moral standards that no sensible person who had applied his mind to the question to be decided could have arrived at it.

Applying that test Neill LJ found that the Secretary of State's decision was not perverse.[89] McCullough J[90] reached the same result.

The result in *ex p. Lonrho* and the earlier case of the same name concerning the Secretary of State's initial refusal to publish the Inspectors' report and to refer the matter to the Monopolies and Mergers Commission[91] show the latitude that the courts will afford the Secretary of State in the context of his follow-up action upon receipt of a report. This latitude is the result of the relevant legislation giving the Secretary of State a broad discretion and the reluctance of the courts to second-guess the exercise of such discretion. Thus, although judicial review is available as a means of challenging a decision either to take or not to take follow-up action, any challenge based, in particular, on allegations of an irrational exercise of discretion (such as failing to take account of relevant matters or Wednesbury unreasonableness) will need a strong case to succeed.[92] A further complication faces someone against whom it is decided to take action and who wishes to challenge that decision because the court may decline to give the relief sought in judicial review proceedings on the basis that the person or company aggrieved has an alternative remedy, e.g. defending the disqualification proceedings brought against the director or the winding up petition presented against the company. 12.7.2

87 See *Associated Provincial Picture Houses v Wednesbury Corporation* [1948] 1 KB 223.

88 [1985] AC 374 at p. 410G.

89 At p. 338B.

90 At p. 339.

91 [1989] 1 WLR 525 and see 9.2.3 above.

92 See also *Re Walter L Jacob & Co. Ltd* [1989] BCLC 345 at p. 353g–i and *Re Blackspur Group and others; Re Atlantic Computer Systems plc and another* [1998] 1 WLR 422.

Chapter 13

THE USE OF EVIDENCE AND REPORTS IN CIVIL AND CRIMINAL PROCEEDINGS

13.1 ADMISSIBILITY OF STATEMENTS TO INVESTIGATORS IN LEGAL PROCEEDINGS GENERALLY

The legislation provides that a statement made by a person in compliance with a requirement imposed by virtue of Companies Act 1985 ss.434, 442, 446 or 447, Financial Services Act 1986 ss.94, 105 or 177, Companies Act 1989 s.83, Insurance Companies Act s.44 or Insolvency Act 1986 s.218(5) may be used in evidence against him.[1] These statutory provisions are of a procedural nature and therefore apply to answers given by witnesses who were examined under the statutory investigation regimes before the particular provisions came into force.[2] These particular specific statutory provisions appear to reflect the general position that answers must be admissible if the statutory regime is to achieve its purpose.[3] **13.1.1**

In *Karak Rubber Co. Ltd v Burden*[4] Brightman J considered the effect of an equivalent earlier statutory provision[5] (Companies Act 1967 s.50) and concluded that the only answers that were admissible in evidence under the Act were those given by a person to questions put to him in **13.1.2**

---

1 Companies Act 1985 s.434(5), s.443(1), s.446(3), s.447(8), Financial Services Act 1986 s.94(3), s.105(5), s.177(6), Companies Act 1989 s.83(6), Insurance Companies Act 1982 s.44(5) and Insolvency Act 1986 s.219(2).

2 See *Selangor United Rubber Estates Ltd v Cradock (No. 2)* [1968] 1 WLR 319, *R v Harris* [1970] 1 WLR 1252.

3 See *R v Harz* [1967] 1 AC 760 and *R v Harris* [1970] 1 WLR 1252.

4 [1971] 1 WLR 1748.

5 The forerunner of Companies Act 1985 s.434(5).

exercise, so far as relevant, of the powers under the section of the statute concerned. The answers admissible included answers on oath, but Brightman J concluded[6] that unsworn answers given as a result of informal questioning were not admissible. However, in *London Securities Ltd v Nicholson*[7] Browne-Wilkinson J pointed out,[8] that in *R v Harris*[9] Mackenna J had held that quite apart from Companies Act 1967 s.50, sworn evidence given by a witness to inspectors was admissible in subsequent criminal proceedings and that MacKenna J had relied largely on *R v Scott*[10] where the Court of Criminal Appeal had held that unsworn evidence given by a bankrupt on his examination was admissible against him on a subsequent criminal charge. Browne-Wilkinson J held that these cases established that, even without s.50, both sworn and unsworn evidence given to inspectors is admissible against the witnesses in subsequent criminal proceedings. Browne-Wilkinson J noted[11] that *R v Harris* and *R v Scott* had not been cited in *Karak Rubber Co. Ltd v Burden* and that therefore Brightman J's decision did not impair these earlier decisions. Thus the position appears to be that the statutory sections, which provide that a statement made by a person in compliance with a requirement imposed by the relevant legislation may be used in evidence against him, will have the effect that sworn evidence given to investigators is admissible in subsequent proceedings against the person who provided the evidence, whereas the common law position has the effect that both sworn and unsworn evidence of any witness will be so admissible against him.[12] However, as appears from *R v Cheltenham Justices ex p. Secretary of State for Trade*[13] the transcripts of evidence of other witnesses will not be admissible evidence in criminal proceedings, but where a witness makes a statement that is contrary to a statement that he himself had previously made, he may have his attention drawn to the earlier statement and be asked to explain it.

6 At p.1751A–C.
7 [1980] 1 WLR 948.
8 At p. 953D–E.
9 [1970] WLR 1252.
10 (1856) Dears & B.47.
11 At p. 953G–H.
12 See also Civil Evidence Act 1995 concerning hearsay in civil proceedings.
13 [1977] 1 WLR 95.

13.2 INCRIMINATING STATEMENTS TO INVESTIGATORS AS EVIDENCE IN LEGAL PROCEEDINGS

The general principles at 13.1 would have the effect that answers given 13.2.1
to investigators may be used in legal proceedings against the person who gave the answers. However, it is necessary to consider the link between the statutory regimes concerning the investigation of companies and the Police and Criminal Evidence Act 1984[14] in criminal cases and the European Convention on Human Rights. In *R v Seelig, R v Spens*[15] the Court of Appeal considered the relationship between answers given to inspectors appointed under Companies Act 1985 s.432 and the provisions protecting the position of defendants in criminal proceedings under the Police and Criminal Evidence Act 1984. The answers concerned were given to inspectors appointed by the DTI and were given before the defendants were charged with criminal offences. Section 67(9) of Police and Criminal Evidence Act 1984 provides

> Persons other than police officers who are charged with the duty of investigating offences or charging offenders shall in the discharge of that duty have regard to any relevant provision of such a code.

At a hearing before Henry J, Mr Seelig had argued that inspectors appointed by the DTI were charged with the duty of investigating offences within the meaning of s.67(9) and that consequently a caution should be administered to a person to be questioned. At the earlier 'Guinness' trial, Henry J had ruled that[16] the inspectors did not have this duty:

> When one looks at the obligation on them under the Companies Act 1985 their obligation is to investigate the affairs of the company and to report. In the course of such investigation criminal offences will often emerge, but the fact that they do so does not alter the duty of the inspectors. Their duty is to investigate the affairs of the company and to ascertain the facts; they are not conducting a trial of those investigated. It is for others to investigate any criminal offences that may be uncovered by the inspectors. The inspectors may be required by the Secretary of State to provide under section 437(1A) material which might point to the commission of crime, but it is not for them to investigate whether that material

14 See 11.4 above.
15 [1992] 1 WLR 148.
16 Quoted at [1992] 1 WLR 148 at pp. 157H–8C.

> constitutes offences as such. Parliament, when setting out the duties of inspectors in the Act of 1985, which was after the Police and Criminal Evidence Act 1984, in my judgment chose their words carefully, and therefore the codes do not apply.

That ruling was maintained at a subsequent hearing before Henry J. Watkins LJ giving the judgment of the Court of Appeal stated that[17]

> whether a body or a person conducting some kind of inquiry is subject to section 67(9) is a question of fact in each case. It is, in our view, quite impossible to give a generalised answer to the question arising out of section 67(9). We take Henry J to have found as a fact that the inspectors in the present case were not investigating offences. Upon all the evidence before him it was a conclusion at which we think he could justifiably arrive.

It remains unclear whether, and if so, in what circumstances those investigating companies will be affected by s.67(9). Those carrying out an investigation into the affairs of a company as a fact-finding exercise will probably not normally be affected by s.67(9) but there is a greater doubt about, for example, inspectors appointed under Financial Services Act 1986 s.177 given the circumstances in which inspectors may be appointed under that section, although in *Styr v HM Advocate*[18] the Scots High Court held that such inspectors were not obliged to administer a caution.[19]

The Court of Appeal in *R v Seelig, R v Spens* was also required to consider the effect of Police and Criminal Evidence Act 1984 s.76(2). **13.2.2**
That subsection provides

> If, in any proceedings where the prosecution proposes to give in evidence a confession made by an accused person, it is represented to the court that the confession was or may have been obtained (a) by oppression of the person who made it, or (b) in consequence of anything said or done which was likely, in the circumstances existing at the time, to render unreliable any confession which might be made by him in consequence thereof, the court shall not allow the confession to be given in evidence against him except in so far as the prosecution proves to the court beyond reasonable doubt that the confession (notwithstanding that it may be true) was not obtained as aforesaid ... .

---

17 At p. 158G–H.
18 [1994] SLT 5.
19 Note also *R v Director of the Serious Fraud Office ex p. Smith* [1993] AC 1 and *R v Wallace Duncan Smith* (1994) 99 Cr App R 233.

Henry J at the first Guinness trial had found that a witness before the inspectors was under a duty to answer questions even though his answers may tend to incriminate him.[20] Henry J in the present case referred to the scheme envisaged by Companies Act 1985 Part XIV and stated[21] that it could not be oppressive for the inspectors to question 'someone as intelligent and sophisticated as an experienced merchant banker like Lord Spens, without explaining the full import of Part XIV'. Henry J added that[22] it is not for the inspectors to be concerned whether a truthful answer might incriminate a witness and if that were the case, 'their inquiries would be severely curtailed, and the statutory purpose for which they were appointed, to some extent, defeated'. Further, Henry J concluded[23] that he did not see 'how the failure to give [the witness] such a warning is likely to render answers freely given unreliable'. The Court of Appeal found that,[24] for the reason given by Henry J, he had been right to reject the case that evidence should be excluded under s.76(2). Thus the courts have effectively taken the view that so long as the inspectors carry out their questioning for the purposes for which they have been appointed (rather than, for example, instead to specifically assist a prosecutor) the evidence that is subsequently used in criminal proceedings will not normally have been obtained in such a way that it should be excluded under s.76(2).[25]

The final aspect of the Police and Criminal Evidence Act 1984, which the Court of Appeal was required to consider in *R v Seelig, R v Spens*, was the application of ss.78(1) and 82(3). These provide **13.2.3**

> 78(1) In any proceedings the court may refuse to allow evidence on which the prosecution proposes to rely to be given if it appears to the court that, having regard to all the circumstances, including the circumstances in which the evidence was obtained, the admission of the evidence would have such an adverse effect on the fairness of the proceedings that the court ought not to admit it ... .
>
> 82 ... (3) Nothing in this Part of this Act shall prejudice any power of the court to exclude evidence (whether by preventing questions from being put or otherwise) at its discretion.

---

20 See *Re London United Investments Limited* [1992] Ch 578 and generally 6.10.
21 See [1992] 1 WLR 148 at p. 159D.
22 See p. 159F–G.
23 See p. 159H.
24 At p. 160A.
25 It appears, however, that the Codes of Practice under the Police and Criminal Evidence Act 1984 may be of assistance when the court is considering the general discretion to exclude unfair evidence under s.78(1) — see *R v Wallace Duncan Smith* (1994) 99 Cr App R 233 at p. 241.

Henry J had noted[26] that whereas an individual can simply refuse to assist the police with their inquiries, Mr Seelig when questioned by inspectors appointed by the DTI could not have refused to assist the inspectors without running risks (that the inspectors could apply to the court which could punish as a contempt). Henry J had added, however, that this was not a conclusive answer for four reasons[27]:

> First, because of the public importance which Parliament attaches to the investigation and punishment of company fraud, and the importance that it attaches to getting the truth in such matters. Second, because those likely to be questioned under that statutory regime are those whose responsibilities under the Companies Act 1985 and at common law in relation to shareholders funds and the integrity of the market are reflected in the privileged position they have. It is not asking too much, in my judgment, to impose limits on their civil rights, as Parliament has done by an obligation to answer questions in circumstances where those answers may be used in criminal proceedings against them. Third, general protections designed to be wide enough to protect the weak, the inarticulate and the suggestible from having to answer in the strange and hostile environment of a police station are less obviously needed to protect those likely to be major witnesses in a section 432 investigation who will usually be intelligent, sophisticated, self-confident and articulate, usually accompanied by lawyers, giving evidence by prior appointment in an environment not so foreign to them. Fourthly, and fundamentally, the fact that they are treated less favourably than the average man accused of crime is because the legislature has decided that they should, and, as I have said, a review of the history of the legislation and the authorities concerning it show that that is no accident, no unintended legislative muddle.
>
> Bearing all those matters in mind, it seems to me that in these cases on these facts that the admission in the evidence of material obtained under the inquisitorial process before a defendant is charged does not have such adverse effect on the fairness of the proceedings that the court should exclude it. It will usually be different once the defendant is charged, for a charge usually marks the end of the investigative process and the beginning of the accusatorial process. Accordingly, I do not think it right to exclude the DTI interviews of these defendants.

The Court of Appeal found no flaw in this exercise of discretion.[28] The Court of Appeal reached this conclusion having noted that the case

---

26 See p. 161B–C.
27 See p. 161C–H.
28 P. 161H and p. 162B.

was concerned with 'extremely astute professional men' who had been advised at one time or another by very experienced City solicitors and that[29] there was 'sound reason for admitting the so-called confessions having regard to the relevant legislation that Parliament has deliberately enacted, albeit that that may appear to tend towards unfairness especially when set against the relevant proceedings in the Act of 1984'.[30] What remains unanswered, however, is the extent to which the answers to questions put in other contexts, e.g. to those who are not 'extremely astute professional men', may amount to unfairness.

13.2.4 The issue was further examined by the Court of Appeal in *R v Saunders and others*[31] concerning an appeal against conviction in 'the Guinness trial'. The appellants did not contest that Companies Act 1985 Part XIV had overridden the privilege against self-incrimination[32] and did not challenge that answers so obtained could be admitted in criminal proceedings. It was pointed out that there were three possible methods of questioning the appellants — the police, the Serious Fraud Office or by the DTI inspectors.[33] Only the third course permitted questioning without the safeguards of Police and Criminal Evidence Act 1984, and the admission of the answers at the criminal trial. Reference was made to *Hamilton v Naviede*[34] in which Lord Browne-Wilkinson had noted the unexplained anomaly in that Criminal Justice Act 1987 s.2(8) provided protection in respect of the use that could be made of a self-incriminatory statement, and that the unexplained anomaly could be taken into account when the trial judge was exercising powers under Police and Criminal Evidence Act 1984 s.78. Lord Taylor of Gosforth LCJ noted the view that there was a very different regime of interviews by DTI inspectors compared with interviews by the police or the Serious Fraud Office, and noted that the inspectors are investigators, not prosecutors or potential prosecutors, and they are bound to act fairly and to give anyone they propose to criticise a fair opportunity to answer what is alleged against them.[35] It had been argued that in applying s.78 the judge should have recourse to Article 6 of the European Convention on Human Rights but Lord Taylor LCJ said English Courts could only

---

29 At p. 162A.
30 The proceedings against Mr Seelig were on medical grounds not proceeded with and Lord Spens was acquitted.
31 [1996] 1 Cr App R 463.
32 See 6.10 above.
33 At. p. 476B–C.
34 [1995] 2 AC 75.
35 At p. 477A–C.

have recourse to the Convention when English law was ambiguous or unclear. Lord Taylor LCJ said that Parliament had made its intentions quite clear in Companies Act 1985 s.434(5). It would not be right for a judge to exercise his discretion to exclude evidence simply on the ground that Parliament ought not to have countenanced the possibility of self-incrimination or to bring s.434(5) in to line with Criminal Justice Act 1987 s.2(8), a step Parliament had not taken.[36] Lord Taylor LCJ agreed that in considering whether the particular application of the statutory regime in a given case created any unfairness, a judge could, as part of the background setting, have in mind that under that regime there was an obligation to answer the inspectors' questions on pain of sanctions.[37] In the present case, the Court of Appeal found that there was no abuse of process or improper collusion and nothing in the circumstances rendered the admission of the transcripts that the trial judge had admitted in evidence unfair. In particular, the Court of Appeal noted that the inspectors had been left to conduct their inquiries and interviews independently without introduction, briefing or prompting by the prosecuting authority, and that the interviews by the inspectors were conducted fairly and unobjectionably.[38]

The extent to which evidence given to inspectors appointed under Companies Act 1985 may be used in criminal proceedings has, however, been considered by the European Court of Human Rights in *Saunders v United Kingdom*.[39] The applicant argued that he had been denied a fair trial in breach of Article 6(1) of the European Convention on Human Rights. The relevant part of Article 6(1) provides **13.2.5**

> In the determination of ... any criminal charge against him, everyone is entitled to a fair ... hearing ... by an independent and impartial tribunal....

The applicant's argument was in relation to the use of statements obtained by the DTI inspectors during the criminal proceedings against him. The majority judgment pointed out that[40]

> the right to silence and the right not to incriminate oneself, are generally recognised international standards which lie at the heart of a fair procedure

---

[36] At p. 478B–C.
[37] At p. 478D.
[38] At p. 484D–G. *Cf. R v Wallace Duncan Smith* (1994) 99 Cr App R 233 where an interview with a supervisor on behalf of the Bank of England was excluded from subsequent criminal proceedings under Police and Criminal Evidence Act 1984 s.78(1).
[39] [1997] BCC 872.
[40] Majority judgment, para. 68.

> under art. 6. Their rationale lies, inter alia, in the protection of the accused against improper compulsion by the authorities thereby contributing to the avoidance of miscarriages of justice and to the fulfilment of the aims of art. 6.

The UK Government argued that nothing said by the applicant in the course of the interviews was self-incriminating and that he had merely given exculpatory answers or answers that, if true, would serve to confirm his defence. This was rejected in the majority judgment, which noted that some of the applicant's answers were of an incriminating nature in the sense that they contained admissions of knowledge of information that tended to incriminate him.[41] The majority concluded that the evidence supported the claim that the transcripts of the applicant's evidence, whether directly self-incriminating or not, were used in the course of the proceedings in a manner that sought to incriminate the applicant.[42] The Court did not find it necessary to decide whether the right not to incriminate oneself is absolute or whether infringements may be justified in particular circumstances.[43] The majority continued[44]:

> [The Court] does not accept the Government's argument that the complexity of corporate fraud and the vital public interest in the investigation of such fraud and the punishment of those responsible could justify such a marked departure as that which occurred in the present case from one of the basic principles of a fair procedure. Like the Commission, it considers that the general requirements of fairness contained in art. 6, including the right not to incriminate oneself, apply to criminal proceedings in respect of all types of criminal offences without distinction from the most simple to the most complex. The public interest cannot be invoked to justify the use of answers compulsorily obtained in a non-judicial investigation to incriminate the accused during the trial proceedings. It is noteworthy in this respect that under the relevant legislation statements obtained under compulsory powers by the Serious Fraud Office cannot, as a general rule, be adduced in evidence at the subsequent trial of the person concerned. Moreover the fact that statements were made by the applicant prior to his being charged does not prevent their later use in criminal proceedings from constituting an infringement of the right.

---

41 Majority judgment, para. 71.
42 Para. 72.
43 Para. 74.
44 Para. 74.

The majority concluded from its analysis and the fact that Companies Act 1985 s.434(5) authorises the subsequent use in criminal proceedings of statements obtained by the inspectors, the procedural safeguards including the inspectors being independent and subject to judicial supervision, that the person questioned was entitled to be legally represented before them and provided with a transcript of his responses which he could correct or expand and the provisions of Police and Criminal Evidence Act 1984 ss.76 and 78 could not provide the Government with a defence, since the safeguards did not operate to prevent the use of the statements in the criminal proceedings. The Court therefore held by 16 votes to 4 that there was a violation of Article 6(1).[45]

The majority decided that in view of its finding that there was a violation of article 6(1) there was no need to decide whether there had been any misuse of power by the prosecuting authorities.[46] When considering the applicant's claim for 'just satisfaction' under Article 50 the majority said they could not 'speculate as to the question whether the outcome of the trial would have been any different had use not been made of the transcripts by the prosecution'[47] but made an award of £75,000 in respect of costs. **13.2.6**

The approach in *Saunders v United Kingdom* has implications for the use that may be made of transcripts of evidence given to those investigating companies in criminal proceedings. The approach taken by the majority of the European Court of Human Rights contrasts markedly with the Court of Appeal in *R v Seelig, R v Spens* and *R v Saunders*. The Court of Appeal in *R v Saunders* had noted, however, that although domestic law was 'unambiguous', if Mr Saunders were to succeed in relation to the argument concerning Article 6(1) (as he subsequently did), the United Kingdom's treaty obligations would require consideration to be given to the effect of the decision in the United Kingdom. **13.2.7**

---

45 Note the contrasting approach in the dissenting judgment of Judge Martens — 'Assume that the "right to silence" and the "privilege against self-discrimination" are not absolute ... but — like other rights implied in art. 6 — allow for limitations; assume, further, that such limitations cannot be taken into account unless they are in accordance with the law, pursue a legitimate aim and are proportionate to that aim ... then the question becomes whether these requirements are fulfilled in the present case?' (para. 2) [1997] BCC 872 at p. 896.

46 Majority judgment, paras 77–80.

47 Para. 86.

The effect of the decision in *Saunders v United Kingdom* was considered in *R v Morrissey, R v Staines*.[48] The appellants challenged their convictions of counselling or procuring another to deal in securities while being a prohibited person. One ground of challenge was to the admission in evidence of answers obtained by inspectors appointed under Financial Services Act 1986 s.177 using coercive powers, which, it was said, affected the fairness of the proceedings so adversely that the Court of Appeal should have ruled that such answers should have been excluded. The Crown accepted that were an application to be made to the Convention institutions, the use of the answers obtained from the appellants would be likely to be held to constitute a violation of Article 6 of the Convention. Sir Thomas Bingham MR said the submission on behalf of the appellants essentially rested on Police and Criminal Evidence Act 1984 s. 78(1). He added[49] 13.2.8

> The difficulty, as it seems to us, which the appellants face is to show that the court should exercise its powers under section 78(1) to exclude, because of its adverse effect on the conduct of the proceedings, material which section 177(6) has expressly stipulated may be used in evidence against a defendant. No doubt the admission of evidence under section 177(6) is subject to the overriding direction of the court to exclude under section 78(1). But there is, so far as we can see, nothing which distinguishes this case from other similar cases. If the court were to rule here that this evidence should be excluded, it would be obliged to exclude such evidence in all such cases. That would amount to a repeal, or a substantial repeal, of an English statutory provision which remains in force in deference to a ruling which does not have direct effect and which, as a matter of strict law, is irrelevant.

Sir Thomas Bingham concluded[50]

> the present position is very unsatisfactory. It would appear that the appellants have or certainly may have grounds for complaining in Strasbourg and, if the penalty is enforced and they incur costs in seeking relief, they may have claims to compensation against Her Majesty's Government. That is not, however, something which the courts can remedy. Our domestic law remains as declared by this court in *R v Saunders*.

It is not clear whether the Human Rights Bill currently proceeding through Parliament will have an impact. The Act will allow courts to interpret legislation afresh with a view, wherever possible, to interpreting 13.2.9

[48] [1997] *The Times*, 1 May; transcript.
[49] Transcript p. 26.
[50] Transcript pp. 28–9.

it consistently with the European Convention. This opens up the possibility of interpreting the underlying legislation requiring witnesses to answer questions where there is silence as to the privilege against self-incrimination in such a way that the privilege is not impliedly excluded[51] or, alternatively, to read Police and Criminal Evidence Act 1984 s.78 in such a way as to exclude incriminating answers obtained under compulsion. In the light of *Saunders* the use that will in future be made of transcripts of evidence given to those investigating companies in subsequent criminal proceedings was the subject of an announcement by the Attorney General on 3rd February 1998 and it is inextricably linked to the relationship between statutory investigations into companies and investigations by prosecuting authorities such as the Serious Fraud Office.[52] The Attorney General announced that the Government 'proposes to bring forward legislation when a suitable opportunity arises' to ensure that domestic law is fully compatible with the United Kingdom's obligations under the European Convention. As an interim measure, he set out guidelines about the handling of cases where the evidence available to the prosecution included answers obtained by the exercise of compulsory powers. The note of guidelines stated

> 1. The purpose of this note is to provide guidance for prosecuting authorities in England and Wales and in Northern Ireland about the approach to be adopted towards evidence available to prosecutors in the form of answers obtained by the exercise of compulsory powers such as those available under Section 434 of the Companies Act 1985. It takes account of the judgment of the European Court of Human Rights in *Saunders v UK* (1997 23 EHRR 313).
>
> 2. For the purposes of these Guidelines the expression 'answers obtained under compulsory powers' is used to mean answers given under compulsion by a person who is or subsequently becomes a defendant, being answers which may be used in evidence against the defendant under:
>
> Section 43(5) or 44(5) of the Insurance Companies Act 1982;
> Section 434(5), 443, 446(3) or 447(8) of the Companies Act 1985;
> Section 433 of the Insolvency Act 1986;
> Section 94(3), 105(5) or 177(6) of the Financial Services Act 1986;
> Section 41(10) or 42(5) of the Banking Act 1987;
> Section 2(8) of the Criminal Justice Act 1987;
> Section 83(6) of the Companies Act 1989.

[51] See 6.10 above.
[52] See Ch 11.

These guidelines also apply to any such answers obtained through any other procedure in legislation concerned with the regulation of commercial or financial activities carried on by companies or individuals, or with the investigation of the financial affairs of companies or individuals which includes the power to compel answers.

3. In all cases the prosecution should not normally (i.e. subject to the discretionary exceptions mentioned in paragraph 4) use in evidence as part of its case or in cross-examination answers obtained under compulsory powers.

4. There is discretion for such answers to be used in evidence in the following circumstances:
(i) where the defendant who provided the answers himself introduces them in evidence;
(ii) where the defendant has been subject to a statutory duty to provide answers in the course of an administrative or regulatory procedure, or has been required to answer truthfully in the course of judicial proceedings, and the subsequent prosecution is based on
  (a) a failure or refusal to answer;
  (b) an omission to disclose a material fact which should have been disclosed; or
  (c) the giving of an untruthful answer.

Examples of such offences are section 1 of the Perjury Act 1911, section 451 of the Companies Act 1985, section 353 of the Insolvency Act 1986, section 94 of the Banking Act 1987 and section 2(14) of the Criminal Justice Act 1987.

The European Court of Human Rights in *Saunders v United Kingdom* **13.2.10**
found that the direct use of incriminating compelled testimony was an infringement of the guarantee of a fair trial in Article 6 of the European Convention on Human Rights, but did not deal with the issue of where such compelled evidence leads the prosecuting authorities to other already existing evidence that they may wish to use in the criminal proceedings, i.e. derivative evidence. However, guidance may be obtained from *Ferreira v Levin*[53] where the South African Constitutional Court considered analogous provisions to UK law but in the context of insolvency. The Court found that the correct balance between the public interest in investigating insolvent companies and protecting the constitutional guarantee of freedom and security of the person could be achieved by giving the trial judge a direction to exclude evidence to which the prosecution was led by the compelled testimony, but added that

[53] 1996 1 (SA) 984.

evidence that could not have been obtained or the significance of which would not have been appreciated without the compelled testimony should normally be excluded.[54]

The possible impact of *Saunders v United Kingdom* was tested in the context of company director disqualification proceedings arising from an investigation into a company in *Secretary of State for Trade and Industry v McCormick*.[55] Jacob J rejected the argument that transcripts and extracts of a report produced by inspectors pursuant to an appointment under Companies Act 1985 s.432 should be excluded. Notwithstanding *Saunders v United Kingdom* Jacob J referred to *R v Saunders* and *R v Morrissey, R v Staines*[56] and found domestic law to be clear. He explained that the reasoning in the criminal cases is that Parliament has made the compelled evidence admissible and it would be a wrong exercise of the power under Police and Criminal Evidence Act 1984 s.78 to rule out that which Parliament had ruled in. He said that in relation to disqualification proceedings the position as to the admissibility of the compelled evidence is 'even stronger' for there is no provision corresponding to s.78. Jacob J went on to reject an argument that where the compelled evidence was referred to in affidavits it could be excluded under the court's power in RSC Order 41 rule 6 to strike out any matter that is oppressive. He did not accept that it was inherently oppressive to use compelled evidence for an express purpose contemplated by Parliament. He also did not see how the court could say that the material could be inadmissible in the face of Companies Act 1985 s.441(1), which provides for the contents of an inspectors' report to be evidence. Finally, however, Jacob J concluded **13.2.11**

> [Counsel] for the Secretary of State made it plain that the Secretary of State was keeping under constant review the position of the United Kingdom's obligation under the treaty in relation to the use of compelled evidence in company director disqualification proceedings. It would of course be most unsatisfactory if at the end of the day it was held that such evidence should not have been used.

[54] See also *Thomson Newspapers Ltd v Canada (Director of Investigation and Research)* (1990) 67 DLR (4th) 161 at p. 204 and *RJS v The Queen* (1995) 121 DLR (4th) 589.

[55] 30 April 1997, unrep. See also *R v Secretary of State for Trade and Industry ex p. McCormick* Indep. 15 January 1998, Rimer J and [1998] COD 160 C.A.

[56] 13.2.4–13.2.8 above.

Jacob J made no comment as to whether or not the use would have been a breach of the European Convention on Human Rights.[57]

13.2.12 However, this point arose in *R v Secretary of State for Trade and Industry ex p. McCormick*[58] where the applicant sought to challenge the exercise of discretion by the Secretary of State to use transcripts of evidence in directors' disqualification proceedings on the basis that because the transcripts recorded evidence obtained from him under compulsion of the law in Companies Act 1985 s.434(5) it was unfair that the transcripts should be used in the proceedings. It was accepted that the transcripts were relevant to issues in the disqualification proceedings and that they were admissible under s.434(5). The applicant referred to the Secretary of State's policy in relation to not using transcripts in relevant criminal proceedings,[59] but Rimer J and the Court of Appeal held that disqualification proceedings were not criminal proceedings under domestic law[60] and nor were they for the purposes of Article 6 of the European Convention on Human Rights.[61] If disqualification proceedings were regarded as civil proceedings then questions concerning the privilege of self-incrimination did not arise. Rimer J held that the legislation under which an individual can be required to assist in an investigation of the company's affairs reflected the consideration that the right of an individual to trade through the medium of a limited company carried with it a duty to account for the stewardship when the venture goes wrong, and it is part of a regulatory process whose existence is in the public interest and is of high importance. He added

> There is ... much to be said for the view that it is in the public interest that the proper and effective operation of the regulatory process fairly justifies the use of material which is made expressly admissible by the legislation, whose admission will not involve the overriding of any legal privilege and whose use will be likely to be of material assistance to the

---

57 See the argument in the context of criminal proceedings at 13.2.9 above.

58 Indep, 15 January 1998, Rimer J and [1998] COD 160 C.A.

59 See now the statement set out at 13.2.9.

60 See *Secretary of State for Trade and Industry v Baker and others* [1998] 2 WLR 667 in which Sir Richard Scott V-C stated at p. 685D–F that disqualification proceedings, although properly classified as civil proceedings, do not involve litigation about private rights but involve public law. He added that the proceedings have, in many respects, much more in common with criminal proceedings than with civil litigation about private rights.

61 See also the Commission admissibility decision in *EDC v United Kingdom* [1998] BCC 370, which proceeded on the basis that disqualification proceedings were civil rather than criminal, although it is not clear whether the point was argued in that case.

court in arriving at its decision as to whether or not the allegations of unfitness have been established.

Morritt LJ in the Court of Appeal explained

> It would not be sensible to allow the evidence 'independent of the will' of the person in question in the form of the Report and any documents produced to the Inspectors by the witness but exclude the witness's explanation of the latter which justified an opinion or fact set out in the former. Given that the Secretary of State is not bound to exercise her powers on the footing that disqualification proceedings involve not a criminal charge but the determination of a civil right and obligation I see no reason why she should conclude that a fair hearing requires her to abstain from using the director's evidence to the inspectors.

Rimer J and the Court of Appeal found neither the Secretary of State's view that the use of the transcripts in the disqualification proceedings would not be unfair, nor the decision to continue to use them, to be irrational.[62]

13.3 ADMISSIBILITY OF FINDINGS OF INVESTIGATORS IN LEGAL PROCEEDINGS

Pursuant to statute, a copy of any report of inspectors appointed under Companies Act 1985 Part XIV, certified by the Secretary of State to be a true copy, is admissible in any legal proceedings as evidence of the opinion of the inspectors in relation to any matter contained in the report and in proceedings on an application under Company Directors Disqualification Act 1986 as evidence of any fact stated therein.[63] A **13.3.1**

[62] In *Secretary of State for Trade and Industry v Hinchcliffe* [1998] *The Times*, 2 February, Rattee J rejected an application for a stay of proceedings under Company Directors Disqualification Act 1986 s.6 where it had been argued that the procedure under the 1986 Act contravened several provisions of the European Convention and that the proceedings should be stayed pending incorporation of the European Convention.

[63] Companies Act 1985 s.441(1). In *Re Minet Holdings plc*, 10 February 1992, unrep. Hoffman J noted that the inspectors were appointed under Companies Act 1948, not Companies Act 1985 as required by s.441 but held that Companies Consolidation (Consequential Provisions) Act 1985 had the effect that on the repeal of the 1948 Act the appointment of inspectors under s.165(1)(b) of the Act did not lapse, but was thereafter to be treated as if it had been made under the 1985 Act, and it followed that the requirements for the admissibility of the inspectors' report were satisfied.

document purporting to be such a certificate will be received in evidence and be deemed to be such a certificate unless the contrary is proved.[64] The legislation only deals with the position of inspectors appointed under Companies Act 1985 Part XIV and does not, for example, deal with any reports that may be written by other persons appointed to investigate aspects of a company.

The historical common law position concerning the reports of inspectors is that they are not evidence of anything contained in them but are merely evidence of the opinion of the inspectors.[65] This position was reiterated in *Savings & Investment Bank Ltd v Gasco Investments (Netherlands) B.V.*[66] in which Peter Gibson J explained that the forerunner of the statutory provision at 13.3.1[67] dealt merely with the formality of how the inspectors' reports were to be proved in legal proceedings and was not a blanket provision allowing reports to be used in all cases as evidence.[68] He consequently struck out parts of an affidavit that had been sworn on behalf of a plaintiff for injunctive relief in civil proceedings. **13.3.2**

Notwithstanding the general historical position concerning inspectors' reports at 13.3.2, a line of authority created exceptions in the specific case of information obtained under statutory powers, which the Secretary of State is required to take into account in deciding whether certain proceedings should be commenced.[69] These exceptions are based on a line of authority in the context of where the Secretary of State decides to present a winding up petition following an investigation into a company.[70] In *Re ABC Coupler and Engineering Co. Ltd*[71] Buckley J considered a petition to wind up a company supported by affidavits exhibiting inspectors' reports. Buckley J noted that the reports were hearsay and took the view that where grave changes were levelled against individuals in a winding up or where the case was one of complexity **13.3.3**

[64] Companies Act 1985 s.441(2).
[65] See *Re Grosvenor and West End Railway Terminus Hotel Co. Ltd* (1897) 76 L.T. 337.
[66] [1984] 1 WLR 271.
[67] Companies Act 1948, s.171 as amended by Companies Act 1981 (and previously Companies Act 1862 s.61).
[68] [1984] 1 WLR 271 at p. 282C–D. Peter Gibson J also ruled that inspectors' reports were not records within Civil Evidence Act 1968 s.4.
[69] See Ch 12.
[70] See 12.2.
[71] [1962] 1 WLR 1236.

turning upon the conduct of persons who are more or less in the relationship of partners in a company, the court would not, in the exercise of its discretionary jurisdiction, be satisfied merely with prima facie evidence. In *Re Travel and Holiday Clubs Ltd*[72] Pennycuick J was faced with an application to wind up a company on the just and equitable ground with an affidavit in support filed by inspectors exhibiting their report. Pennycuick J explained that in the present case the report was made by persons acting in a statutory fact-finding capacity and, being unchallenged by the company, was admissible as material on which the court was entitled to act. He noted the decision in *Re ABC Coupler and Engineering Co. Ltd* but stated[73]

> It seems to me that it would not be in accordance with the apparent intention of the section that, where inspectors appointed under the Act have made a report, the court should not be entitled to look at that report and accept it not as hearsay evidence but as material of a different character altogether, and should have to be satisfied anew by evidence of the ordinary nature as to the facts found in the report.

This approach was maintained by Pennycuick J in *Re SBA Properties Ltd.*[74] When considering a winding up petition presented by the Board of Trade, Pennycuick J noted[75] that the question was whether the court could 'treat the inspector's report not as evidence in the ordinary sense, but as material upon which, if it is not challenged, the court can proceed to make a winding up order on the ground that it is just and equitable to do so'. In *Re Allied Produce Co. Ltd*[76] Buckley J explained that in *Re ABC Coupler and Engineering Co. Ltd* the company appeared and was supported by creditors to oppose the petition, whereas in neither of the two cases before Pennycuick J did the company appear and that was 'an important distinction'. In *Re Koskot Interplanetary (UK) Ltd*[77] Megarry J referred to all four of these earlier cases and explained that the statutory section concerning winding up petitions presented by the Board of Trade had the effect of making special categories of evidence or material including the inspectors' reports admissible, even though

72 [1967] 1 WLR 711.
73 At p. 715E–F.
74 [1967] 1 WLR 799.
75 At p. 806E.
76 [1967] 1 WLR 1469.
77 [1972] 3 All ER 829.

hearsay. In *Re Armvent Ltd*[78] the petition was opposed and after referring to dicta in *Re SBA Properties Ltd* Templeman J explained that[79] the reference to challenge means

> challenge by somebody with knowledge of the facts coming along and saying the inspectors' report is wrong and being willing to put forward an affidavit and to be cross-examined, and to be judged in the witness box on the evidence which he puts forward in contradiction of the inspectors' report.

Templeman J, however, went further and stated[80]

> It seems to me even if the report of the inspectors is challenged nevertheless it ought to be treated as prima facie evidence and that it ought to be left to a judge in any case having read the report and having seen the witnesses to make up his own mind whether it is just and equitable to wind up the company.

Thus, Templeman J in *Re Armvent Ltd* envisaged a role for inspectors' reports even where the contents are challenged, although once evidence was sworn to the contrary, then if the Secretary of State failed to support the report by direct evidence that removed doubt on the validity of the inspectors' conclusion, the court should not be slow to dismiss the petition.[81] Further, it would be open to a company, without filing any evidence to challenge the inspectors' findings and to submit that the findings, even if wholly correct, are not sufficient to show that it is just and equitable that the company should be wound up.[82] Finally, in *Re St Piran Ltd* Dillon J explained[83] the reasoning underlying the line of cases as a combination of two factors. First, the report was not ordinary hearsay evidence because the inspectors acted in a statutory fact-finding capacity. Secondly, it would be nonsensical if the court could not take the report into consideration in deciding whether it was just and equitable that the company should be wound up when by the very terms of the statutory provision concerning winding up petitions brought by the Secretary of State, he has concluded that it is expedient that the winding-up petition should be presented or that the company should be wound up. Dillon J also held that where a winding up petition was

---

78 [1975] 1 WLR 1679.
79 At p. 1685F–G.
80 At p. 1685H.
81 See p. 1686B–C.
82 See *Re St Piran Ltd* [1981] 3 All ER 270 at p. 276j.
83 At pp. 275j–6b.

presented by a minority shareholder rather than the Secretary of State, the shareholder could rely on the report.[84]

The line of authority concerning the use of reports of investigators in support of winding up petitions was considered by the Court of Appeal in *Re Rex Williams Leisure plc*[85] where an affidavit had been sworn in support of an application for a disqualification order under Company Directors Disqualification Act 1986 s.8 by a person who had been appointed by the DTI to investigate under Companies Act 1985 s.447 a payment by the company.[86] Hoffman LJ noted that in the case of public interest in winding up petitions, the material that the Secretary of State may take into consideration includes whatever is gathered under the inspection and investigation powers of Companies Act 1985 Part XIV[87] and that there was more or less the same phraseology in Company Directors Disqualification Act 1986 s.8.[88] Hoffman LJ noted that in public interest winding up petitions all the evidence had to show was that it was in the public interest that the company should be wound up to enable the official receiver to investigate its affairs, but that in a disqualification application the Secretary of State must prove facts which show that the director is unfit. He took the view that the distinction went to weight rather than admissibility since, in a disqualification application, hearsay evidence untested by cross-examination of the informant may be insufficient to satisfy the burden of proof against opposing evidence. Hoffman LJ continued that, once the Secretary of State knows from the opposing affidavits which material facts are seriously in dispute, he may be well advised to reinforce his case by affidavits from appropriate informants.[89] Staughton LJ and Russell LJ agreed with Hoffman LJ, although Staughton LJ said that[90] he would have hesitated to accept the doctrine that there was an implied statutory provision as to the use of hearsay as evidence (or provisional evidence until it is challenged) but the doctrine is now of 'respectable antiquity, having been established between 1967 and 1975'.[91] **13.3.4**

---

84 See p. 276b–j.
85 [1994] Ch 350 affirming the decision of Nicholls V-C at [1994] Ch 1.
86 Had the affidavit relied on an inspectors' report rather than an investigation under s.447 the report would have been admissible as evidence of fact — see Companies Act 1985 s.441(1) and 13.3.1.
87 See Insolvency Act 1986 s.124A and 12.2 above.
88 See 12.4 above.
89 Generally see [1994] Ch 350 at p. 367B.
90 At p. 369C.
91 See also *Secretary of State v Ashcroft* [1997] 3 WLR 319 concerning Company Directors Disqualification Act 1986 s.7.

The question of the admissibility of reports of investigators in civil proceedings has, however, been affected by Civil Evidence Act 1995.[92] The Act provides that in civil proceedings evidence shall not be excluded on the ground that it is hearsay.[93] The Act provides certain safeguards in relation to hearsay evidence in that parties need to tender a notice of proposal to adduce hearsay evidence[94] and there is a power to call a witness for cross-examination on a hearsay statement.[95] The Civil Evidence Act 1995 also sets out the considerations relevant to the weighing of hearsay evidence and regard may be had, in particular, to whether it would have been reasonable and practicable for the party by whom the evidence was adduced to have produced the maker of the original statement as a witness; whether the original statement was made contemporaneously with the occurrence or existence of the matters stated; whether the evidence involves multiple hearsay; whether any person involved had any motive to conceal or misrepresent matters; whether the original statement was an edited account, or was made in collaboration with another for a particular purpose; and whether the circumstances in which the evidence is adduced as hearsay are such as to suggest an attempt to prevent proper evaluation of its weight.[96] Importantly, however, nothing in the Act affects the admissibility of evidence otherwise admissible and the safeguards (including the considerations relevant to the weighing of hearsay evidence) do not apply in relation to hearsay evidence admissible apart from the Act, notwithstanding that the same evidence may also be admissible by virtue of the Act. Therefore, although the Civil Evidence Act 1995 widens the circumstances in which formal or informal reports of investigations may be admissible as evidence in civil proceedings, the line of authorities at 13.3.3 and 13.3.4 remains good law and the comments made in those authorities in relation to the weight to be attached to the reports as evidence continue to be influential. **13.3.5**

One particular issue concerning the use of the findings of investigators is that the person seeking to rely on them should do so with sufficient clearness. In *Re St Piran Ltd*[97] the whole of the inspectors' report **13.3.6**

---

92 See also Rules of the Supreme Court (Amendment) 1996-SI 1996/3219.

93 S.1(1). Hearsay is defined as 'a statement made otherwise than by a person while giving oral evidence in the proceedings which is tendered as evidence of the matters stated' and references to hearsay include hearsay of whatever degree — s.1(2).

94 S.2.

95 S.3 and Rules of the Supreme Court (Amendment) 1996 r.22.

96 S.4.

97 [1981] 3 All ER 270 at p. 277e–j.

had been incorporated into the petition and the company argued that it was embarrassing because it did not make sufficiently clear what case the petitioner thought it could make of the report, and did not identify the specific matters in the report on which the petitioner intended to rely. Dillon J said that what emerged from the report was a complex picture, and that with such a report it was for the petitioner's advisers to do the necessary work of selection and identify the matters discussed in the report on which the petition was really relying. Dillon J consequently found the petition to be embarrassing and adjourned the motion to give an opportunity for the petitioner to propose amendments to the petition to particularise the complaints.

Finally, it seems clear that, whatever the position in respect of transcripts of evidence and reports, the investigators' internal memoranda and drafts of the report will not be admissible as evidence.[98] 13.3.7

[98] See *Re Astra Holdings plc; Secretary of State for Trade and Industry v Anderson and others* [1998] *The Times*, 13 January and 8.7.1 above.

Chapter 14

PROPOSALS FOR REFORM

The system for investigating companies has been considered on various occasions over the years, resulting in amendments to the regime.[1] The approach and, most noticeably, the issue of what safeguards there should be for those who may be criticised and possibly face further action as a consequence of an investigation have been the subject of particular debate.[2]

14.1 COUNCIL FOR THE SECURITIES INDUSTRY—DEPARTMENT OF TRADE INSPECTIONS AND PROSECUTIONS (1979); LAW REFORM COMMITTEE OF THE INNS OF COURT OF ENGLAND AND WALES — COMPANY INVESTIGATIONS SYSTEM (1980); GOVERNMENT REVIEW (1980)

14.1.1 The companies investigation regime was considered in two reports in 1979 and 1980 and led to a statement by the Secretary of State for Trade. The Council for the Securities Industry produced a report on Department of Trade Inspections and Prosecutions in 1979.[3] The report made recommendations to accelerate investigations and prosecutions and to safeguard witnesses. It recommended that the Department should act quickly in deciding whether inspectors should be appointed; that the inspectors' terms of appointment should be more specific and not imply

---

1 See Ch 2.

2 See, e.g. L. Sealy *Companies — Inquisition, Twentieth-Century Style* [1974] CLJ 225; and T. Hadden *Company Law and Capitalism* 2nd edn (1977) at pp. 282–6 and pp. 352–63.

3 See D. Sugarman (1980) 1 Co Law 108 and 154.

a need to inquire into all the company's affairs and that the Secretary of State should set a period within which he would wish a report to be made (normally six months). The Council recommended the appointment of full-time legal inspectors and said that part-time inspectors should be appointed from a list of suitably experienced barristers, solicitors and accountants. In relation to fairness towards witnesses the Council accepted that the inquisitional form of investigation was necessary. It recommended that witnesses should be told in advance and in reasonable detail which matters and documents inspectors would examine them on, that inspectors should be specific in indicating the evidence they intended to use and the nature of the criticisms they intended to make on the basis of that evidence and that witnesses should be given an opportunity to comment. The Council also argued that reports should be strictly factual and avoid character studies of witnesses or criticisms of their conduct.

The Senate of the Inns of Court produced a report on the company investigations system in 1980.[4] It was critical of the system and recommended the creation of a Statutory Securities Commission to supervise companies with the power, not only of fact-finding, but also to bring civil proceedings to prevent or remedy abuses.[5] Additionally, the Report suggested a number of temporary measures: **14.1.2**

(i) when a minister appoints inspectors he should give them his reasons and the allegations that require investigation;
(ii) reports should not be published unless, in the opinion of the Department, the public interest or the interests of shareholders or creditors require publication;
(iii) inspectors should refrain from expressing opinions and judgments;
(iv) in the case of a liquidation the Department should be free, with the consent of the liquidator, to bring proceedings on behalf of a company without first requiring a Companies Acts investigation;
(v) in winding up proceedings and proceedings alleging that a company's affairs are being or have been conducted in an

4 See D. Sugarman (1980) 1 Co Law 302.
5 See also T. Hadden *Fraud in the City: Enforcing the Rules* (1980) 1 Co Law 9 setting out a proposal to establish a single company law enforcement commission with overall control over the processes for monitoring possible abuses, investigating suspected offences and prosecuting in appropriate cases.

unfairly prejudicial manner a preliminary statutory investigation would be necessary; and

(vi) witnesses should be informed of the subject matter on which they will be questioned and any documents to which it is intended to refer; they should be informed that they are entitled to be represented; and should be told if they are not compellable witnesses.

In May 1980, the then Secretary of State for Trade announced the outcome of his review, being concerned that the system should maintain public confidence.[6] The Secretary of State envisaged greater use of what is now Companies Act 1985 s.447 rather than full inspections. He announced that to treat witnesses more fairly the Department of Trade would publish a handbook and *Notes for Guidance of Inspectors Appointed under the Companies Act 1980*.[7] The Secretary of State set a 12-month time limit on inspections subject to extensions but where inspections could not be completed within 12 months inspectors would be required to provide interim reports. The Department would indicate to inspectors on appointment the particular matters on which a report was desired. Although he believed it desirable that a member of the legal profession be appointed as the inspector, he would not look so frequently among the most senior members of the bar whose commitments were heavy. The Council for the Securities Industry gave the Secretary of State's proposals a cautious welcome.[8] 14.1.3

14.2 *THE HOUSE OF COMMONS: TRADE AND INDUSTRY COMMITTEE'S THIRD REPORT: (1990) COMPANY INVESTIGATIONS* AND THE GOVERNMENT'S RESPONSE

The regime for the investigation of companies was considered again in the *House of Commons, Trade and Industry Committee's Third Report:* 14.2.1

6 Hansard 19 May 1990 at col. 15–8. See D. Sugarman (1981) 2 Co Law 79.

7 See now the *Investigations Handbook* and Ch 3 above.

8 But note the criticism by D. Sugarman at (1981) 2 Co Law 79 at pp. 80–1, in particular of the increased use of the forerunner of Companies Act 1985 s.447 instead of the relevant inspection procedure.

Company Investigations, which was produced in 1990.[9] The Government responded to the recommendations made by the Committee later the same year.[10]

14.2.2 As a general proposition, the Committee concluded that the interests of consumers, non-equity investors, creditors and employees do not attract the attention they deserve[11] and recommended that broader interests than just the duties of directors and the rights of shareholders should be reflected in company law and the way in which it is applied.[12] The Government in its response felt the purposes of company law and of investigations included the protection of creditors. Further, it added that the interests of consumers (who may also be creditors), employees and others are generally provided for outside the framework of company law but could be relevant to any investigation of misconduct. The Government also referred to regulatory provisions for companies in particular sectors and regulatory rules of the Securities and Investments Board (now the Financial Services Authority), the Stock Exchange and the Takeover Panel.[13]

14.2.3 When considering issues relating to starting an investigation the Committee recommended that the permission for auditors to disclose confidential information to the supervisory authorities should be raised to the level of a statutory obligation[14] and that obligations should be imposed in the UK on intermediaries to exercise reasonable care to ensure that they do not facilitate dishonest transactions.[15] In relation to the former recommendation, the Government was concerned that the imposition of a statutory obligation would undermine the traditional relationship of confidence between the auditor and his audit client and felt that if the accountancy profession was willing to undertake this task it was best done by professional guidance.[16] In response to the latter recommendation, the Government referred to the provisions aimed at preventing and detecting money laundering in certain circumstances, but was concerned about new and additional regulatory and compliance burdens that would result from the Committee's recommendation. The Government also referred to the international front and what at that

9 HC 36 1989–1990.
10 Cm 1149.
11 Report, para. 14.
12 Report, para. 15; Recommendation 1.
13 Response, p. 7.
14 Report, para. 33; Recommendation 2.
15 Report, para. 35; Recommendation 3.
16 Response pp. 7–8.

time was a draft EC Directive aimed at preventing the use of the financial system for the purpose of money laundering and would consider whether the proposal could lead to any useful action.[17]

A number of recommendations dealt with matters, such as personnel and the timing for carrying out investigations, and these were considered by the Government.[18] The Committee also considered the conduct of investigations and recommended that the then *Handbook of the Companies Inspection System* should be updated annually to give more information on the practical conduct of investigations.[19] The present *Investigations Handbook* was produced in 1990[20] and the then Government stated that guidance to inspectors would be amended as frequently as necessary[21] but none has been published. **14.2.4**

The Committee considered the nature of the inspectors' reports and, in particular, whether they should draw conclusions since there was a concern that drawing conclusions caused delay whilst witnesses responded to possible criticisms of them.[22] However, the Committee noted that if, for example, wrongdoing was the result of a meeting attended by five people and there were five different versions of the facts and the inspectors could do no more than report the five different accounts without comment, it would hardly be a basis for remedial action or disciplinary proceedings.[23] Further, they added, if a report does not identify those to blame for some misconduct, it will also fail to exonerate others involved whose actions were blameless.[24] The Committee recommended that inspectors should continue to draw conclusions from the evidence they take.[25] The Committee also recommended that inspectors should make recommendations about whether some action should be taken against individuals and any remedial steps to prevent similar events occurring,[26] with any recommendations for prosecution or disciplinary action by employers or regulatory bodies in respect of individuals to be contained in a separate appendix to their **14.2.5**

17 Response p. 8. See now the Money Laundering Regulations 1993 — SI 1993/1933 as amended.
18 Report, paras 36–53, 170–181; Recommendations 4–9, 30–32; Response, pp. 8–10.
19 Report, paras 54–62; Recommendation 10.
20 See Ch 3 above.
21 Response, p. 10.
22 Report, paras 63–77.
23 Report, para. 66.
24 Report, para. 67.
25 Report, para. 73; Recommendation 11.
26 Report, para. 74; Recommendation 12.

report.[27] The Committee also recommended that the then *Handbook of the Companies Inspection System* be amended to advise inspectors to serve on all those to be criticised in a report the substance of that criticism, with a deadline for response of 21 days, and that any response received that the inspectors do not accept should be published as an annex to their report.[28] Finally, in this section, the Committee recommended that witnesses should be provided with a copy of the transcript of their evidence.[29]

14.2.6 The Government agreed that inspectors should continue to draw conclusions.[30] The Government also agreed about inspectors making recommendations as to action against individuals and remedial steps. However, it did not agree that such recommendations should be in a separate appendix. The Government felt a preferable approach would be for inspectors to notify the Secretary of State (otherwise than in their report) of any matters that they believe to be relevant to further action against individuals, and when inspectors wish to comment on the current law or matters of procedure it may, in many circumstances, be appropriate in the public interest for that comment to be made in the report, which may be published.[31] The Government felt it would be undesirable to advise inspectors to follow a fixed procedure in respect of serving criticisms in all cases. It also did not accept the recommendation as to the publication of responses to criticisms that are not accepted by inspectors and noted that such a recommendation would encourage witnesses to make written responses containing embarrassing material in order to prejudice the possibility of publication.[32] The Government accepted that witnesses should be provided with a copy of the transcript of their evidence unless in a particular case the inspectors have compelling reasons, such as fears about confidentiality for withholding it.[33]

14.2.7 The Committee made various recommendations in relation to publication[34] to which the Government responded[35] (and which are discussed in Ch 9 above)[36].

---

27 Report, para. 75; Recommendation 13.
28 Report, para. 76; Recommendation 14.
29 Report, para. 77; Recommendation 15.
30 Response, p. 11.
31 Response, p. 11.
32 Response, p. 12.
33 Response, p. 12.
34 Report, paras 78–88 and Recommendations 16–18.
35 Response, pp. 12–3.
36 See 9.2.2 above.

The Committee, when considering the international nature of economic crime recommended that the Government take steps to establish through the Organisation for Economic Cooperation and Development (OECD) a database of commercial malefactors and designate a UK regulatory body (such as the DTI) as the leading agent in ensuring coordination.[37] The Government considered that the advantages of such a database would be minimal, the difficulties inherent in creating and maintaining it major, and its value to improve cooperation would be small. The Government believed that the more effective course would be to continue to improve the existing situation in which records are maintained domestically and to which the various UK regulators have access for the purposes of exercising their own responsibilities, and added that these regulators have effective links with their overseas counterparts and other authorities, who also maintain records.[38] 14.2.8

The Committee when considering the interrelationship between the UK regulatory authorities recommended that a central clearing house be established to track all cases dealt with by different regulatory bodies, to maintain a database of people convicted (or otherwise publicly censured) for commercial malpractice, fraud, insider dealing, disqualified as directors, etc. and to supply information to other authorities abroad. It also recommended that the DTI should monitor closely the performance of the SIB and self-regulating organisations.[39] The Government had reservations as to the principle of creating a central clearing house and the tasks proposed for it. The Government did agree, however, to consider whether further steps were necessary to improve information exchange between regulators in the area.[40] As regards the SIB, the Government believed that the continuing power of the Secretary of State to withdraw functions from the SIB under Financial Services Act 1986 s.114 and the requirements for reporting to Parliament in respect of functions carried out by the SIB under Financial Services Act 1986 s.117 met the Committee's recommendations.[41] 14.2.9

The Committee were concerned about the effectiveness of the sanctions where reports revealed wrongdoing, and felt that in addition to regulatory proceedings there is a case for companies and individuals undertaking a greater share of the burden of enforcement rather than 14.2.10

---

37 Report, paras 89–95 and Recommendation 19.
38 Response, pp. 13–4.
39 Report, paras 96–107; Recommendations 20 and 21.
40 Response pp. 14–5.
41 Response, p. 15.

relying on the DTI. The Committee recommended that regulatory bodies and employers should report to the DTI within a prescribed time the action they have taken as a result of inspectors' reports.[42] The Government responded by referring to its regular liaison meetings with regulators and also to the fact that employers report to the regulatory authority, of which they or their employees are members, the action taken against their employees for breaching in-house rules following investigations into insider dealing.[43]

The Committee considered the specific case of House of Fraser plc[44] and, in addition to views on that particular case, the Committee recommended that company law be amended to provide that if inspectors report that directors have given false information to them the Secretary of State should automatically apply to the court for their disqualification and that knowingly or recklessly misleading inspectors should be made a specific criminal offence.[45] The Government accepted neither recommendation. It did not accept that there should be automatic reference to the court and it believed that the existing criminal law, in particular the Perjury Act 1911, is adequate to deal with cases where false evidence is given to inspectors.[46] **14.2.11**

When considering the provisions governing insider dealing[47] the Committee made recommendations in relation to the substantive law, the mode of trial[48] and that steps be taken to introduce civil sanctions against insider dealing[49] to which the Government responded.[50] On the issue of investigations, the Committee noted that Companies Act 1989 gives the DTI powers to allow the Stock Exchange to prosecute cases directly[51] and recommended that the DTI should decide within 21 days of cases being referred to them by the Stock Exchange whether (1) to appoint inspectors or (2) to allow the Stock Exchange to prosecute.[52] **14.2.12**

---

42 Report, paras 108–17; Recommendation 22.
43 Response, pp. 15–6.
44 Report, paras 118–40.
45 Report, para. 139; Recommendation 23.
46 Response, p. 16.
47 Report, paras 141–69.
48 Recommendations 25 and 27.
49 Recommendation 29.
50 Response, pp. 17–8. Note also the debate in Standing Committee B considering the Criminal Justice Bill 1993 on 15 June 1993 (at col. 201–12) in which the then opposition proposed that a specialist body should take responsibility for the detection and prosecution of insider dealing.
51 Report, para. 155.
52 Report, para. 168; Recommendation 28.

The Government responded in relation to the timescales but noted that not all referrals could be treated as formal requests for the appointment of inspectors under Financial Services Act 1986 s.177, nor did the contents of such requests always make them suitable candidates for either of the two alternatives referred to by the Committee.[53]

The Committee considered the expense of investigations[54] and recommended that greater steps be taken to recover the costs of investigations from the companies and individuals involved unless the inspectors find no evidence of wrongdoing.[55] The Government responded by referring to the cost of the investigations system being largely met by the corporate sector through the fees charged by Companies House rather than the tax payer, and the Government was also against a more general power to recover costs.[56] **14.2.13**

14.3 PROCEDURES AT INQUIRIES AND THE 'SALMON CARDINAL PRINCIPLES'

The general material on the procedures that are appropriate for inquiries is of relevance to investigations into companies given their inquisitorial nature. This ranges from the Royal Commission on Tribunals of Inquiry in 1966[57] through to literature generated as a result of Sir Richard Scott's Inquiry into the Export of Defence Equipment and Dual-Use Goods to Iraq and Related Prosecutions published in 1996. **14.3.1**

The report of the Royal Commission on Tribunals under the Chairmanship of Lord Justice Salmon stated that the difficulty and injustice with which persons involved in an inquiry may be faced can largely be removed if six 'cardinal principles' are strictly observed. **14.3.2**

(i) Before any person becomes involved in an inquiry, the Tribunal must be satisfied that there are circumstances that affect him and which the Tribunal proposes to investigate.
(ii) Before any person who is involved in an inquiry is called as a witness he should be informed of any allegations that are made against him and the substance of the evidence in support of them.

[53] Response, pp. 17–8.
[54] Report, paras 182–7.
[55] Report, para. 187; Recommendation 33.
[56] Response, p. 18 and see also 10.3.1 above.
[57] Cmnd.3121/1966.

(iii) (a) He should be given an adequate opportunity of preparing his case and of being assisted by legal advisers.
(b) His legal expenses should normally be met out of public funds.
(iv) He should have the opportunity of being examined by his own solicitor or counsel and of stating his case in public at the inquiry.
(v) Any material witnesses he wishes called at the inquiry should, if reasonably practicable, be heard.
(vi) He should have the opportunity of testing by cross-examination conducted by his own solicitor or counsel any evidence that may affect him.[58]

The cardinal principles in the Salmon Report were accepted by the Government in a White Paper,[59] which also accepted the recommendation from the Salmon Report that there should be no statutory rules of procedure because of the need for flexibility and to avoid unnecessary delay by alleged breaches of statutory rules.[60] Although there is an obligation of fairness,[61] despite the contents of the Government's White Paper, no legislation has been introduced making the Salmon principles mandatory.[62] Indeed in *Crampton v Secretary of State*[63] (concerning an inquiry into the events at a hospital, which had culminated in the conviction of a nurse for counts including murder) Lord Bingham MR said that the Salmon Commission was established to review the workings of the Tribunals of Inquiry (Evidence) Act 1921 and the recommendations of the Commission were clearly directed to inquiries under that Act and 'while the rationale of the six cardinal principles is undoubtedly sound and anyone conducting an inquiry of this kind is well advised to have regard to them, the Royal Commission Report itself has not been embodied in legislation and numerous inquiries have been conducted, and satisfactorily conducted, since 1966 without observing the letter of those principles'.

---

58 See pp. 17–8 of the Report. The six principles are elaborated at pp. 22–8 of the Report. Note also the conclusions at pp. 44–7.

59 Cmnd.5313/1973, para. 17 although it considered that there would be circumstances in which certain of the principles were capable of being observed only in the spirit and not in the letter.

60 Para. 12.

61 See Ch 5 and Ch 7.

62 Note that the Report of the Committee of the JUSTICE — All Souls Review of Administrative Law in the United Kingdom (1986) recommended that at 'ad hoc inquiries' there should be a reference to the six cardinal principles (p. 329).

63 9 July 1993, unrep. C.A.

14.3.3 Prior to publication of his report, Sir Richard Scott considered the six Salmon principles.[64] He had reservations about a number of them in relation to his investigation and felt the language of the principles was coloured by familiarity with adversarial proceedings and was inapposite to inquisitorial proceedings. For example, in relation to principle (iii) he was of the view that persons who are asked to assist an inquisitorial inquiry by giving evidence on matters being investigated do not have a 'case'.[65] Sir Richard Scott regarded the judgments in the Court of Appeal in *Re Pergamon Press Ltd*[66] as a useful guide to the approach to be adopted to the requirements of fairness at an inquisitorial inquiry. Referring, in particular, to a passage from Sachs LJ, Sir Richard Scott argued that the 'inflexible and literal application of the six Salmon principles to each and every Inquiry would produce in many cases procedures unsuitable to the object in hand' and concluded that the procedures to be adopted in order to achieve fairness in an inquiry must be designed to fit the circumstances and requirements of the particular inquiry.[67]

14.3.4 Amongst the critics of Sir Richard Scott's approach was Lord Howe of Aberavon[68] who, in asking whether the inquiry was non-adversarial, rejected the suggestion that ministers and officials appearing before the Inquiry did not have to make 'a case'.[69] He noted Sir Richard Scott's reference to *Re Pergamon Press Ltd* but was of the view that such inquiries were 'a very special case' because they are designed to root out wrongdoing on the part of those suspected of abusing the 'great privilege ... of operating under the system of limited liability'.[70] He also noted that the procedures are conducted in private (unlike the Scott Inquiry), they have been the subject of criticism[71] and that the procedures had been modified since the time of *Re Pergamon Press Ltd* such that DTI inspectors were advised to give legal advisers the opportunity to question their clients if they wish to do so and to make representations.[72] Therefore, Sir Richard Scott referred to *Re Pergamon Press Ltd* and the procedures relating to investigations into companies to justify

---

64 *Procedures at Inquiries — The Duty to be Fair* (1995) 111 LQR 596.
65 At p. 604.
66 [1971] 1 Ch 388 and see 7.2 above.
67 (1995) 111 LQR 596 at p. 613.
68 See *Procedure at the Scott Inquiry* [1996] PL 445.
69 At p. 457.
70 Note the words used by the Lord Advocate (Lord Rodger of Earlsferry) reported at HL Deb, col 235 (16 February 1994).
71 E.g. by Lord Lester of Herne Hill reported at HL Deb, col 230 (16 February 1994).
72 [1996] PL 445 at pp. 452–3.

the procedures he had adopted, whereas Lord Howe's response was to differentiate between the two and note the criticisms of the procedures applied in relation to investigations into companies. Thus, no conclusion can be drawn from this debate as to whether greater reference should be had to the Salmon principles by those carrying out investigations into companies (even if the legislation could be amended to allow the witnesses, for example, to give evidence in public).

Finally, the Salmon principles have been referred to in Parliament on the subject of company investigations. In the House of Lords in 1994, Lord Boardman introduced a debate on inquisitorial tribunals and inquiries, which centred on inquiries under Companies Act 1985, by reference to the Salmon Commission and the 'cardinal principles'[73] and other speakers also referred to them favourably in the context of investigations into companies.[74] The inspection procedures were also criticised by Lord Lester of Herne Hill[75] because a report could be made and published on the basis of a process that had each of eight features present: **14.3.5**

(i) it need not respect the presumption of innocence;
(ii) the process is conducted in secret by the inspectors with no safeguard of open justice;
(iii) it does not require the inspectors to follow any prescribed procedures, but leaves them free to conduct their investigations in any way that they consider appropriate;
(iv) it does not require the inspectors to inform the individuals under investigation about the identity of witnesses against them;
(v) it does not entitle those under investigation to confront or cross-examine witnesses or even have access to the file containing the evidence against them;
(vi) it entitles inspectors to rely upon evidence that would be inadmissible in a court of law and to prepare a report on the basis of evidence of that kind;
(vii) it vests in the Secretary of State a sweeping broad discretion to publish the inspectors' findings to the whole world with massive publicity, even though the findings are likely or certain to destroy the reputation of those under investigation; and
(viii) despite the severe damage to personal and commercial reputation, the process does not allow the condemned individual any

73 HL Deb, col 208–12 (16 February 1994).
74 E.g. Lord Morris at col. 228–9.
75 At col. 230–1.

right of appeal or indeed any effective access to a court of law at all to challenge the findings or to attempt to recover his reputation.[76]

He agreed with the reforms proposed in 1980 by the Law Reform Committee of the Senate of the Inns of Court of England and Wales.[77] The Lord Advocate (Lord Rodger of Earlsferry), however, accepted that there must be occasions when individuals feel that they have been criticised unfairly but said that this has to be balanced against the important benefits that flow from the reports published.[78] He added that even though occasionally there may be criticisms that people feel are unjustified, nonetheless the public interest is served by the kind of system that we have at the moment.[79] He concluded, after referring to other types of investigation, including large disaster inquiries, that there is no single solution.[80]

14.4 FINANCIAL SERVICES AUTHORITY CONSULTATION PAPER 10 ON MARKET ABUSE (JUNE 1998)

It is proposed that the new Financial Services Reform Bill will include provisions conferring powers on the Financial Services Authority to impose civil sanctions on persons who engage in market abuse on certain designated markets. The statutory framework will be at a high level of generality and the Financial Services Authority will have the power to promulgate a code of conduct that will indicate in broad terms the types of conduct that are likely to fall foul of the statutory precepts and the types of conduct which are not. The Financial Services Authority therefore issued a consultation paper — 'Market Abuse Part 1: Consultation on a draft Code of Market Conduct'. The consultation paper identifies three categories of market manipulation — artificial transactions,[81] **14.4.1**

[76] Note in relation to (viii) the analysis of the European Court of Human Rights in *Fayed v United Kingdom* (1994) 18 EHRR 393 at 7.7.3 above.
[77] Col. 231.
[78] Col. 236.
[79] Col. 237.
[80] Col. 238. Note also the House of Commons debate on 4th June 1997 centring on the investigations into Guinness plc and House of Fraser plc.
[81] Consultation Paper paras 36–42.

price manipulation[82] and the dissemination of inaccurate or misleading information.[83] It is proposed that the Code will explain the principles that should be applied in relation to the use of information that is relevant to the price of protected investments.[84]

It is proposed that the Financial Services Authority will be able to exercise compulsory powers of investigation in circumstances where, in the opinion of the Financial Services Authority, there is reason to believe that a breach of the statutory precepts may have occurred.[85] Further, the Financial Services Authority will be able to bring criminal proceedings in respect of existing insider dealing offences under Criminal Justice Act 1993 and misleading statements and practices offences currently found in Financial Services Act 1986 s.47. The Financial Services Authority will agree guidelines with the Serious Fraud Office, Crown Prosecution Service and DTI, who will retain their existing powers, as to which agency will pursue a particular type of case.[86] **14.4.2**

The consultation paper notes that an investigation will not result in any determination of the issues that arise in a particular case. In particular, the exercise of investigation powers will not prejudge whether any proceedings should be commenced in a particular case. However, in view of the limitations on the admissibility of evidence in criminal proceedings, where it appears likely that the Financial Services Authority may wish to commence a criminal prosecution against a person, the Financial Services Authority will need to consider whether it is appropriate for that person to be subject to a statutory requirement to answer questions in order to establish the full facts or, rather, whether to interview that person under caution in accordance with the requirements of Police and Criminal Evidence Act 1984. The consultation papers adds that wherever a person is subject to a compulsory requirement to answer questions, he will have the assurance that any answers given will not be admissible in subsequent criminal proceedings.[87] **14.4.3**

It is intended that where it appears to the Financial Services Authority that a breach of the statutory precepts has taken place the Financial **14.4.4**

---

82 Paras 43–61.
83 Paras 62–70.
84 Paras 71–126.
85 Para. 12.
86 Para. 14.
87 Para. 129. See 11.2, 11.3 and 13.2 above. The consultation paper also deals with the issue of the relationship between 'civil fines' and criminal proceedings — paras 136–44.

Services Authority will have the power to order the person responsible to disgorge any profits made or loss avoided as a result of the breach, to make a restitutionary payment or pay compensation to victims of the misconduct, to pay a fine and to pay the costs of the investigation.[88] Decisions by the Financial Services Authority will be subject to an appeal on all issues of fact and law to the independent financial services appeal tribunal to be established under the Bill and from there, on points of law only, to the appropriate court.[89]

[88] Para. 6.
[89] Para. 7.

APPENDIX

RELEVANT STATUTORY PROVISIONS AS AT 1 JULY 1998

(1) Insurance Companies Act 1982 ss.37, 43A, 44, 44A, 46–8 and sch 2B
(2) Companies Act 1985 ss.431–57, 460, 721
(3) Company Directors Disqualification Act 1986 s.8
(4) Financial Services Act 1986 ss.94, 105–6, 177–82
(5) Insolvency Act 1986 ss.124A, 218–9
(6) Companies Act 1989 ss.82–91
(7) Open-ended Investment Companies (Investment Companies with Variable Capital) Regulations 1996 (SI 1996/2827)

INSURANCE COMPANIES ACT 1982

POWERS OF INTERVENTION

37. Grounds on which powers are exercisable

(1) The powers conferred on the Treasury by sections 38 to 45 below shall be exercisable in relation to any insurance company to which this Part of this Act applies and shall be exercisable in accordance with the following provisions of this section.

(2) The powers conferred by sections 38 and 41 to 45 below shall be exercisable on any of the following grounds–

(a) that the Treasury consider the exercise of the power to be desirable for protecting policy holders or potential policy holders of the company against the risk that the company may be unable to meet its liabilities or, in the case of long-term business, to fulfil the reasonable expectations of policy holders or potential policy holders;

(aa) that the company is a UK or non-EC company and it

appears to the Treasury that any of the criteria of sound and prudent management is not or has not been or may not be or may not have been fulfilled with respect to the company;

(b) that it appears to the Treasury:
   (i) that the company has failed to satisfy an obligation to which it is or was subject by virtue of this Act or any enactment repealed by this Act or by the Insurance Companies Act 1974;
   [(ia) ...]
   (ii) that a company of which it is a subsidiary has failed to satisfy an obligation to which it is or was subject by virtue of section 29(7) above or section 24(6) of the Insurance Companies Act 1974 or section 8(6) of the Insurance Companies Amendment Act 1973; or
   (iii) that a subordinate company within the meaning of section 31 above of the company has failed to satisfy an obligation to which it is or was subject by virtue of that section or section 26 above, or section 22 or 26 of the Insurance Companies Act 1974 or of section 6 or 10 of the said Act of 1973;

(c) that it appears to the Treasury that the company has furnished misleading or inaccurate information to the Treasury under or for the purposes of any provision of this Act or any enactment repealed by this Act or by the Insurance Companies Act 1974;

(d) that the Treasury are not satisfied that adequate arrangements are in force or will be made for the reinsurance of risks against which persons are insured by the company in the course of carrying on business, being risks of a class in the case of which the Treasury consider that such arrangements are required;

(e) that there exists a ground on which the Treasury would be prohibited, by section 5(1B) or (1C), 7, 8 or 9 above, from issuing an authorisation with respect to the company if it were applied for;

(f) that it appears to the Treasury that there has been a substantial departure from any proposal or forecast submitted to him by the company in accordance with section 5 above;

(g) that the company has ceased to be authorised to effect contracts of insurance, or contracts of a particular description, in an EFTA State where it has its head office or an

EEA State where it has in accordance with section 9(2) above made a deposit;

(h) that the company is a Swiss general insurance company which has ceased to be authorised to effect contracts of insurance, or contracts of a particular description, in Switzerland.

(3) The powers conferred on the Treasury by sections 39, 40 and 40A below shall not be exercisable in relation to an insurance company except–

(a) where the Treasury have given (and not revoked) a direction in respect of the company under section 11 or 12A above or section 11 of the Insurance Companies Act 1981; or

(b) on the ground that it appears to the Treasury that the company has failed to satisfy an obligation to which it is or was subject by virtue of section 33, 34 or 35 above or section 26B, 26C, or 26D of the Insurance Companies Act 1974; or

(c) on the ground that a submission by the company to the Treasury of an account or statement specifies, as the amount of any liabilities of the company, an amount appearing to the Treasury to have been determined otherwise than in accordance with valuation regulations or, where no such regulations are applicable, generally accepted accounting concepts, bases and policies or other generally accepted methods appropriate for insurance companies or

(d) on the grounds that the company is a UK or non-EC company and it appears to the Treasury that the company has failed to satisfy an obligation to which it is or was subject by virtue of section 32 or 35A above.

(4) The power conferred on the Treasury by subsections (2) to (4) of section 44 below shall also be exercisable on the ground that the Treasury consider the exercise of that power to be desirable in the general interests of persons who are or may become policy holders of insurance companies to which this Part of this Act applies, and references in those subsections to a company include references to any body (whether incorporated or not) which appears to the Treasury to be an insurance company to which this Part of this Act applies.

(4A) The powers conferred on the Treasury by sections 43A and 44 below shall be exercisable in respect of a UK or non-EC company to obtain information to enable the Treasury to perform their functions under this Act.

(5) Any power conferred on the Treasury by section 38, 41, 42, 44(1) or 45 below shall also be exercisable, whether or not any of the grounds specified in subsections (2) and (4) above exists, in relation to–

(a) any body in respect of which the Treasury have issued an authorisation;

(b) any insurance company to which this Part of this Act applies in the case of which a person has become a controller within the meaning of section 96C(1)(c), (d) or (e) below,

(c) any UK company in a case where a person has notified an intention to acquire a notifiable holding in accordance with section 61A(1) below,

if that power is exercised before the expiration of the period of five years beginning with the date on which the authorisation was issued or that person became such a controller or acquired such a holding, as the case may be; but no requirement imposed by virtue of this subsection shall continue in force after the expiration of the period of ten years beginning with that date.

(6) The power conferred on the Treasury by section 45 below shall not be exercisable except in a case in which they consider that the purpose mentioned in that section cannot be appropriately achieved by the exercise of the powers conferred by sections 38 to 44 below or by the exercise of those powers alone.

(7) The Treasury shall, when exercising any power conferred by sections 38 to 45 below, state the ground on which they are exercising it or, if they are exercising it by virtue of subsection (5) above, that they are so exercising it; but this subsection shall not apply where the Treasury have given notice under section 46 below of the proposed exercise of the power.

(8) The grounds specified in subsections 2(b) to (g) and (4) above are without prejudice to the ground specified in subsection (2)(a) above.

(9) This section shall apply in relation to the powers conferred on the Secretary of State below as it applies in relation to the powers conferred by that section on the Treasury, except that–

(a) in subsection (2)–

(i) the references in paragraphs (a), (aa) and (b) to the Treasury shall be construed as references to the Secretary of State;

(ii) in paragraph (c), the first reference to the Treasury

shall be construed as a reference to the Secretary of State; and
(iii) paragraphs (d) to (f) shall not apply;
(b) in subsections (4) and (4A), the references to the Treasury shall be construed as references to the Secretary of State;
(c) subsection (5) shall not apply; and
(d) in subsection (7) the references to the Treasury shall be construed as references to the Secretary of State; and the words from 'but this' to the end shall not apply.

43A. General investigations

(1) The Treasury may appoint one or more competent persons to make an investigation into and report to the Treasury on–
(a) whether the criteria of sound and prudent management are fulfilled with respect to any insurance company which is a UK or non-EC company; or
(b) where a person has notified the Treasury under section 60 or 61 below of his intention to become a controller of any such company, whether those criteria would be so fulfilled if that person became such a controller;
and the Treasury shall give written notice of any such appointment to the company.
(2) It shall be the duty of every person who is or was a director, manager, controller, agent, actuary, auditor or solicitor of a company that is under investigation–
(a) to produce to the persons appointed under subsection (1) above, within such time and at such place as they may require, all documents relating to the company which are in his custody or power;
(b) to attend before the persons so appointed at such time and place as they may require; and
(c) otherwise to give those persons all assistance in connection with the investigation which he is reasonably able to give;
and those persons may take copies of or extracts from any documents produced to them under paragraph (a) above.
(3) For the purpose of exercising his powers under this section a person appointed under subsection (1) above may enter any premises occupied by a company which is being investigated by him under this section; but he shall not do so without prior notice in writing unless he has reasonable cause to believe that if such

a notice were given any documents whose production could be required would be removed, tampered with or destroyed

(4) A person exercising powers by virtue of an appointment under this section shall, if so required, produce evidence of his authority.

(5) A statement made by a person in compliance with a requirement imposed by virtue of this section may be used in evidence against him.

44. Power to obtain information and require production of documents

(1) The Treasury may require a company to furnish them, at specified times or intervals, with information about specified matters being, if the Treasury so require, information verified in a specified manner.

(2) The Treasury may –

(a) require a company to produce, at such time and place as the Treasury may specify, such documents as the Treasury may specify; or

(b) authorise any person, on producing (if required so to do) evidence of his authority, to require a company to produce to them forthwith any documents which that person may specify.

(2A) Subsections (1) and (2) above shall have effect as if any reference to a company included a reference to any person who is or has been a controller, officer, agent or employee of a UK or non-EC company and to any body corporate which is or has been –

(a) a parent undertaking or subsidiary undertaking of such a company;

(b) a subsidiary undertaking of a parent undertaking of such a company;

(c) a parent undertaking of a subsidiary undertaking of such a company.

(2B) The Treasury may require a UK or non-EC company to furnish them, at a specified time, with a report by a specified person, being an actuary or accountant or other person with relevant professional skills, on any matter about which the Treasury have required, or could require, the company to provide information under subsection (1) above.

(3) Where by virtue of subsection (2) above the Treasury have or a person authorised by them has power to require the production of any documents from any company, the Treasury or that person shall have the like power to require production of those documents from any person who appears to them or, as the case may be, him to be in possession of them; but where any person from whom such production is required claims a lien on documents produced by him, the production shall be without prejudice to the lien.

(4) Any power conferred by or by virtue of subsections (2), (2A) and (3) above to require a company or other person to produce documents shall include power –

(a) if the documents are produced –

(i) to take copies of them or extracts from them; and

(ii) to require that person, or any other person who is a present or past director, controller or auditor of, or is or was at any time employed by, the company in question, to provide an explanation of any of them;

(b) if the documents are not produced, to require the person who was required to produce them to state, to the best of his knowledge and belief, where they are.

(4A) Any person authorised by the Treasury may, on producing if required evidence of his authority, enter any premises occupied by–

(a) a UK or non-EC company on which a requirement under subsection (1) or (2) above has been imposed; or

(b) a person on whom or a body on which such a requirement has been imposed by virtue of subsection (2A) above,

for the purpose of obtaining the information or documents required to be furnished or produced and exercising the powers conferred by subsection (4) above.

(5) A statement made by a person in compliance with a requirement imposed by virtue of this section may be used in evidence against him.

(6) In this section 'document' includes information recorded in any form; and, in relation to information recorded otherwise than in legible form, the power to require its production includes power to require the production of a copy of the information in legible form.

(7) This section shall apply to the Secretary of State and persons authorised by him as it applies to the Treasury and persons authorised by them; and for this purpose references in this section

to the Treasury shall be construed as references to the Secretary of State.

44A. Entry and Search of Premises

(1) A justice of the peace may issue a warrant under this section if satisfied on information on oath given by or on behalf of the Treasury, or by a person authorised to exercise powers under section 44 above, that there are reasonable grounds for believing that there are on any premises documents whose production has been required under section 44(2) to (4) above and which have not been produced in compliance with the requirement.

(2) A justice of the peace may also issue a warrant under this section if satisfied on information on oath given by or on behalf of the Treasury, or by a person authorised to exercise powers under section 44 above –

(a) that there are reasonable grounds for believing that an offence has been committed for which the penalty on conviction on indictment is imprisonment for a term of not less than two years and that there are on any premises documents relating to whether the offence has been committed,

(b) that the Treasury or, as the case may be, the authorised person have power to require the production of the documents under section 44(2) to (4) above, and

(c) that there are reasonable grounds for believing that if production was so required the documents would not be produced but would be removed from the premises, hidden, tampered with or destroyed.

(3) A warrant under this section shall authorise a constable, together with any other person named in it and any other constables–

(a) to enter the premises specified in the information, using such force as is reasonably necessary for the purpose;

(b) to search the premises and take possession of any documents appearing to be such documents as are mentioned in subsection (1) or (2), as the case may be, or to take, in relation to any such documents, any other steps which may appear to be necessary for preserving them or preventing interference with them;

(c) to take copies of any such documents; and

(d) to require any person named in the warrant to provide an explanation of them or to state where they may be found.

(4) If in the case of a warrant under subsection (2) the justice of the peace is satisfied on information on oath that there are reasonable grounds for believing that there are also on the premises other documents relevant to the investigation, the warrant shall also authorise the actions mentioned in subsection (3) to be taken in relation to such documents.

(5) A warrant under this section shall continue in force until the end of the period of one month beginning with the day on which it is issued.

(6) Any documents of which possession is taken under this section may be retained–
  (a) for a period of three months; or
  (b) if within that period proceedings to which the documents are relevant are commenced against any person for any criminal offence, until the conclusion of those proceedings.

(7) In the application of this section to Scotland for the references to a justice of the peace substitute references to a justice of the peace or a sheriff, and for the references to information on oath substitute references to evidence on oath.

(8) In this section 'document' includes information recorded in any form.

(9) The powers conferred by this section shall be exercisable in relation to information on oath given by or on behalf of the Secretary of State as they are exercisable in relation to information on oath given by or on behalf of the Treasury; and for this purpose the reference in subsection (2)(b) to the Treasury shall be construed as a reference to the Secretary of State.

46. Notice of Proposed Exercise of Powers on Ground of Unfitness of Certain Persons

(1) Before exercising with respect to a company any power or powers conferred by sections 38 to 45 above on the ground that they would be prohibited from issuing an authorisation to the company because of the unfitness of a person for the position held by him (not being that of a controller of the company), the Treasury shall serve on that person a written notice stating–
  (a) that the Treasury are considering exercising a power or

powers conferred by those sections and the ground on which they are considering the exercise of the power or powers; and

(b) that the person on whom the notice is served may, within the period of one month from the date of service of the notice, make written representations to the Treasury and, if that person so requests, oral representations to an officer of the Treasury appointed for the purpose by the Treasury.

(2) Unless the Treasury, after considering any representations made in accordance with subsection (1) above by the person served with a notice under that subsection, decide not to exercise the power or powers in relation to which the notice was served, they shall before exercising the power or powers serve on the company a written notice–

(a) containing the matters mentioned in paragraphs (a) and (b) of that subsection, taking references to the person there mentioned as references to the company; and

(b) specifying the power or powers that they propose to exercise and, if the power or one of them is that conferred by section 45 above, specifying the manner of its proposed exercise.

(3) A notice under this section shall give particulars of the ground on which the Treasury are considering the exercise of the power or powers in question.

(4) Where representations are made in accordance with this section the Treasury shall take them into consideration before exercising the power or powers in question.

(5) A requirement imposed on a company in the exercise of any power or powers to which this section applies may be framed so as to come into effect after the expiration of a specified period (or such longer period as the Treasury may allow) unless before the expiration of that period the person whose fitness is in question has ceased to hold the position concerned.

47. Rescission, Variation and Publication or Requirements

(1) The Treasury may rescind a requirement imposed under sections 38 to 45 above if it appears to them that it is no longer necessary for the requirement to continue in force, and may from time to time vary any such requirement.

(1A) The Secretary of State may rescind a requirement imposed by him under section 44 above if it appears to him that it is no longer necessary for the requirement to continue in force, and may from time to time vary any such requirement.

(2) No requirement imposed by virtue of subsection (5) of section 37 above shall be varied after the expiration of the period of five years mentioned in that subsection except in a manner which relaxes that requirement.

(3) Where a requirement is imposed under section 40 above or any such requirement is rescinded or varied the Treasury shall forthwith serve–

(a) except where paragraph (b) below applies, on the registrar of companies or on the registrar of companies in Northern Ireland or on both;

(b) if the requirement is imposed on a registered society, on the appropriate registrar as defined by section 73(1) of the Industrial and Provident Societies Act 1965 in the case of a society registered in Great Britain or on the registrar as defined by section 101(1) of the Industrial and Provident Societies Act (Northern Ireland) 1969 in the case of a society registered in Northern Ireland;

a written notice stating that fact and, in the case of a notice of the imposition of a requirement, setting out the terms of the requirement, in the case of a notice of the rescission of a requirement, identifying the requirement and, in the case of a notice of a variation of a requirement, identifying the requirement and setting out the terms of the variation.

(4) A notice served in pursuance of subsection (3) above on the registrar of companies or the registrar of companies in Northern Ireland shall be open to inspection, and a copy thereof may be procured by any person on payment of such fee as the Secretary of State or, in the case of a notice served on the registrar of companies in Northern Ireland, the Department of Commerce for Northern Ireland may direct; and every document purporting to be certified by the registrar of companies or the registrar of companies in Northern Ireland to be a copy of such a notice shall be deemed to be a copy of that notice, and shall be received in evidence as if it were the original notice unless some variation between it and the original is proved.

(5) Section 71(1) of the said Act of 1965 (which empowers the Treasury to make regulations respecting, among other things, the inspection of documents kept by the appropriate registrar under that Act) and section 97(1) of the said Act of 1969 (which

confers corresponding powers on the Department of Commerce for Northern Ireland) shall have effect as if the reference to documents so kept included a reference to notices served in pursuance of subsection (3) above on the appropriate registrar or, as the case may be, on the registrar.

47A. Restriction on Disclosure of Information

Schedule 2B to this Act (which, subject to certain exceptions, restricts the disclosure of information obtained under or by virtue of this Act) shall have effect.

47B. Privilege from Disclosure

(1) A requirement imposed under section 43A or 44(2) to (4) above shall not compel the production by any person of a document which he would in an action in the High Court or, in Scotland, in the Court of Session be entitled to refuse to produce on grounds of legal professional privilege or authorise the taking of possession of any such document which is in his possession.

[(2) ...]

48. Power of Secretary of State to Bring Civil Proceedings on Behalf of Insurance Company

(1) Section 438(1) of the Companies Act (power of Secretary of State to bring civil proceedings on behalf of body corporate) shall have effect in relation to an insurance company to which this Part of this Act applies (whether or not a body corporate) as if the reference to any information or document obtained under the provisions there mentioned included a reference to any information or document obtained under this Act or any enactment repealed by this Act or by the Insurance Companies Act 1974.

(2) The Secretary of State may bring civil proceedings in the name and on behalf of an insurance company to which this Part of this Act applies (whether or not a body corporate) under Article

431(1) of the Companies (Northern Ireland) Order 1986 and that subsection shall have effect in relation to such an insurance company as if the reference to any information or document obtained under the provisions there mentioned included a reference to any information or document obtained under this Act or any enactment repealed by this Act or by the Insurance Companies Act 1980 and any reference to the Department of Commerce for Northern Ireland were a reference to the Secretary of State.

(2A) The Treasury may exercise the powers conferred on the Secretary of State by virtue of subsections (1) and (2) above; and sections 451A(2) and 452(1) of the Companies Act 1985 shall apply in relation to the Treasury as they apply in relation to the Secretary of State.

(3) Where under a judgment given or decree pronounced in proceedings brought by virtue of section 438(1) of the Companies Act or Article 431(1) of the said Order of 1986 on behalf of an insurance company a sum is recovered in respect of a loss of assets representing a fund or funds maintained by the company in respect of its longterm business, the court shall direct that the sum shall be treated for the purposes of this Act as assets of that fund or those funds and this Act shall have effect accordingly.

SCHEDULE 2B: RESTRICTION ON DISCLOSURE OF INFORMATION

PART I: INFORMATION RELATING TO UK, EC AND NON-EC COMPANIES

1. Restriction on Disclosure

(1) Subject to the following provisions of this Part of this Schedule, information which–

(a) is restricted information for the purposes of this paragraph; and

(b) relates to the business or other affairs of a relevant person,

shall not be disclosed without the consent of the person from whom the information was obtained and, if different, the person to whom it relates.

(2) Subject to sub-paragraph (3) below, information is restricted

information for the purposes of this paragraph if it was obtained by the Treasury or the Secretary of State for the purposes of, or in the discharge of, functions under this Act or any rules or regulations made under this Act (whether or not by virtue of any requirement to supply it made under those provisions).

(3) Information is not restricted information for the purposes of this paragraph if–

(a) it has been made available to the public from other sources, or

(b) it is information in the form of a summary or is information so framed as not to enable information relating to any particular person to be ascertained from it.

(4) The following are relevant persons for the purposes of this paragraph, namely–

(a) any UK, EC or non-EC company or any member of Lloyd's; and

(b) any controller, manager, chief executive, general representative, agent or employee of such a company.

(5) Any person who discloses information in contravention of this paragraph shall be guilty of an offence and liable–

(a) on conviction or indictment, to imprisonment for a term not exceeding two years or to a fine, or to both;

(b) on summary conviction, to imprisonment for a term not exceeding three months or to a fine not exceeding the statutory maximum, or to both.

2. Disclosure for Facilitating Discharge of Functions by Secretary of State

(1) Paragraph 1 above does not preclude the disclosure of information in any case in which disclosure is for the purpose of enabling or assisting the Treasury or the Secretary of State to discharge functions under this Act or any rules or regulations made under this Act (whether or not by virtue of any requirement to supply it made under those provisions).

3. Disclosure for Facilitating Discharge of Functions by Other Regulatory Authorities

(1) Paragraph 1 above does not preclude the disclosure by the Treasury or the Secretary of State to any person specified in the first column of the following table if the Treasury or, as the case may be, the Secretary of State considers that the disclosure would enable or assist that person to discharge the functions specified in relation to him in the second column of that Table.

	Person	*Functions*
1.	The Secretary of State	Functions under the Companies Act, the Company Securities (Insider Dealing) Act 1985, the Insolvency Act 1986, the Company Directors Disqualification Act 1986, the Financial Services Act 1986, or Part II, III or VII of the Companies Act 1989.
1A.	The Financial Services Authority	Functions under the Financial Services Act 1986 (other than as a designated agency within the meaning of that Act), the Banking Act 1987 or section 171 of the Companies Act 1989.
2.	The Treasury	Functions under the Financial Services Act 1986 or under Part III or VII of the Companies Act 1989.
3.	An inspector appointed under Part XIV of the Companies Act or section 94 or 177 of the Financial Services Act 1986.	Functions under that Part or that section.
4.	A person authorised to exercise power under section 43A or 44 above, section 447 of the Companies Act, section 106 of the Financial Services Act 1986 or section 84 of the Companies Act 1989.	Functions under that section.

5.	The Friendly Societies Commission, the Registrar of Friendly Societies for Northern Ireland and the Assistant Registrar of Friendly Societies for Scotland.	Functions under the enactments relating to friendly societies or under the Financial Services Act 1986.
6.	The Industrial Assurance Commissioner or the Industrial Assurance Commissioner for Northern Ireland.	Functions under the enactments relating to industrial assurance.
7.	The Building Societies Commission	Functions under the Building Societies Act 1986 and protecting the interests of the shareholders and depositors of building societies.
	The Occupational Pensions Regulatory Authority	Functions under the Pension Schemes Act 1993 or the Pensions Act 1995, or any enactment in force in Northern Ireland corresponding to either of them.
8.	The Director General of Fair Trading	Functions under the Fair Trading Act 1973 except Part II, the Consumer Credit Act 1974, the Restrictive Trade Practices Act 1976, the Estate Agents Act 1979, the Competition Act 1980 or the Control of Misleading Advertisements Regulations 1988.
9.	A designated agency (within the meaning of the Financial Services Act 1986)	Functions under that Act or Part VII of the Companies Act 1989.
10.	A transferee body (within the meaning of the Financial Services Act 1986) or the competent authority (within the meaning of that Act).	Functions under that Act.

11.	Any of the following (within the meaning of the Financial Services Act 1986), namely, a recognised self-regulating organisation, a recognised investment exchange, a recognised professional body and a recognised clearing house.	Functions in its capacity as a recognised self-regulating organisation, recognised investment exchange, recognised professional body or a recognised clearing house.
12.	The Department of Economic Development in Northern Ireland	Functions under enactments relating to companies or insolvency.
13.	An inspector appointed by the Department of Economic Development in Northern Ireland under enactments relating to companies or insolvency.	Functions under those enactments.
14.	A person authorised to exercise powers under Article 440 of the Companies (Northern Ireland) Order 1986.	Function under that Article.
15.	An official receiver	Functions under enactments relating to insolvency.
16.	The Panel on Take-overs and Mergers	All functions
17.	The Bank of England	All functions.
18.	A body administering a scheme under section 54 of the Financial Services Act 1986.	Functions under the scheme.
19.	A body established by order under section 46 of the Companies Act 1989.	Functions under Part II of that Act.
20.	A supervisory body (as defined in section 30 of the Companies Act 1989) or a qualifying body (as defined in section 32 of that Act).	Functions under that Act.
21.	[ ]	
22.	The Council of Lloyd's, the Committee of Lloyd's or the Disciplinary Committee or Appeal Tribunal established under the Lloyd's Act 1982.	Functions under the Lloyd's Acts 1871 to 1982 and functions under bye-laws made under those Acts.

23.	The Tribunal under the Prevention of Fraud (Investments) Act 1958.	Functions under that Act.
24.	The Monopolies and Mergers Commission.	Functions under the Fair Trading Act 1973 and the Competition Act 1980.
25.	An auditor appointed under section 21 above, section 384 of the Companies Act 1985 or section 107 of the Financial Services Act 1986 or a person approved under section 108 of the Financial Services Act 1986.	All functions.
26.	A recognised supervisory body (within the meaning of Part II of the Companies Act 1989 or Part III of the Companies (Northern Ireland) Order 1990).	Functions in its capacity as such a body under that Part, or functions in relation to disciplinary proceedings against auditors.
27.	A recognised professional body (within the meaning of section 391 of the Insolvency Act 1986 or Article 350 of the Insolvency (Northern Ireland) Order 1989).	Functions in its capacity as such a body under that Act or that Order, or functions in relation to disciplinary proceedings against insolvency practitioners (within the meaning of that Act or that Order).
28.	An actuary exercising functions under this Act.	Those functions.
29.	The Institute of Actuaries or the Faculty of Actuaries.	Supervisory functions in relation to an actuary exercising functions under this Act.

(2) Paragraph 1 above does not preclude the disclosure by any person specified in the first column of the table in sub-paragraph (1) above of information obtained by him by virtue of that sub-paragraph if he makes the disclosure–

(a) with the consent of the Treasury or the Secretary of State; and

(b) for the purpose of enabling or assisting him to discharge any functions specified in relation to him in the second column of that Table;

and before deciding whether to give consent to such a disclosure by any person the Treasury or, as the case may be, the Secretary of State shall take account of any representations made by that person as to the desirability of or the necessity for the disclosure.

(3) Paragraph 1 above does not preclude–
 (a) the disclosure of information to the Treasury; or
 (b) the disclosure of information to the Secretary of State for purposes other than those specified in relation to him in sub-paragraph (1) above,

if (in either case) disclosure is in accordance with Article 16(6) of the third general insurance Directive, or Article 15(6) of the third long term insurance Directive.

(4) Paragraph 1 above does not preclude the disclosure of information for the purpose of enabling or assisting any public or other authority not specified in the first column of the table in sub-paragraph (1) above to discharge any functions if disclosure is in accordance with Article 16 of the third general insurance Directive, or Article 15 of the third long term insurance Directive.

(5) Paragraph 1 above does not preclude the disclosure of information for the purpose of enabling or assisting an authority in a country or territory outside the United Kingdom to exercise functions corresponding to those of–
 (a) the Bank of England;
 (b) the Secretary of State under this Act or the Financial Services Act 1986;
 (ba) the Treasury under this Act or, by virtue of article 2 of the Transfer of Functions (Insurance) Order 1997, under the Financial Services Act 1986;
 (c) the designated agency under that Act or rules or regulations made under that Act; or
 (d) the competent authority under Part IV of that Act; or
 (e) the Financial Services Authority under that Act (other than in its capacity as a designated agency) or the Banking Act 1987.

(6) Sub-paragraph (5) above does not apply in relation to disclosure to an authority that is not an authority in another member State unless the Treasury are or the Secretary of State is satisfied that the authority is subject to restrictions on further disclosures at least equivalent to those imposed by this Part of this Schedule.

(7) Information that is disclosed to a person in pursuance of sub-paragraph (1) or (2) above shall not be used otherwise than for the purpose mentioned in that sub-paragraph.

(8) Any person who uses information in contravention of sub-paragraph (7) above shall be liable on summary conviction to imprisonment for a term not exceeding three months or to a fine not exceeding level 5 on the standard scale or to both.

(9) Subject to sub-paragraph (10) below any reference in this paragraph to enabling or assisting any person to discharge or exercise any functions is a reference to enabling or assisting that person to discharge or exercise those functions in relation to–
   (a) a financial market;
   (b) persons carrying on the business of banking or insurance, Consumer Credit Act businesses or the business of providing other financial services; or
   (c) persons involved in the operation of occupational pension schemes (within the meaning of the Pension Schemes Act 1993 or, in Northern Ireland, the Pension Schemes (Northern Ireland) Act 1993)

   and in this sub-paragraph 'Consumer Credit Act business' has the same meaning as in the Banking Coordination (Second Council Directive) Regulations 1992.

(10) Sub-paragraph (9) above shall not apply in relation to references to enabling or assisting the discharge or exercise of the following functions, namely–
   (a) functions of the Secretary of State under Part XIV of the Companies Act 1985, Part XIII of the Insolvency Act 1986 or Part II of the Companies Act 1989 or, so far as relating to the breach of any law relating to companies, under section 83 of the Companies Act 1989;
   (b) functions of an inspector under Part XIV of the Companies Act 1985 or, so far as relating to offences involving securities of a company, under section 177 of the Financial Services Act 1986;
   (c) functions of a person authorised to exercise powers under section 84 of the Companies Act 1989, so far as relating to the breach of any law relating to companies;
   (d) functions of the Department of Economic Development in Northern Ireland under Part XV of the Companies (Northern Ireland) Order 1986, Part XII of the Insolvency (Northern Ireland) Order 1989 or Part III of the Companies (Northern Ireland) Order 1990;
   (e) functions of an inspector under Part XV of the Companies (Northern Ireland) Order 1986;
   (f) functions of a recognised professional body (within the

meaning of section 391 of the Insolvency Act 1986 or Article 350 of the Insolvency (Northern Ireland) Order 1989);

(g) functions of a recognised supervisory body (within the meaning of Part II of the Companies Act 1989 or Part III of the Companies (Northern Ireland) Order 1990).

4. OTHER PERMITTED DISCLOSURES

(1) Paragraph 1 above does not preclude the disclosure of information

(a) for the purpose of enabling or assisting the Deposit Protection Board to discharge its functions under the Banking Act 1987;

(b) with a view to the institution of, or otherwise for the purposes of, any criminal proceedings, whether under this Act or otherwise;

(c) for the purpose of enabling or assisting the Council of the Stock Exchange to discharge its functions in relation to insurance companies;

(d) with a view to the institution of, or otherwise for the purposes of, proceedings under section 6, 7 or 8 of the Company Directors Disqualification Act 1986 in respect of a director or former director of an insurance company;

(e) with a view to the institution of, or otherwise for the purposes of, any civil proceedings arising under or by virtue of the Financial Services Act 1986 or proceedings before the Financial Services Tribunal, if those proceedings relate to an insurance company;

(f) with a view to the institution of, or otherwise for the purposes of, any disciplinary proceedings relating to the exercise by an auditor or actuary of his professional duties;

(g) in pursuance of a Community obligation.

(2) Paragraph 1 above does not preclude the disclosure by the Treasury or the Secretary of State to the Director of Public Prosecutions, the Director of Public Prosecutions for Northern Ireland, the Lord Advocate, a procurator fiscal or a constable of–

(a) information obtained by virtue of section 43A, 44 or 44A above; or

(b) information in the possession of the Treasury or the

Secretary of State as to any suspected contravention in relation to which the powers conferred by those sections are exercisable.

5. INFORMATION SUPPLIED BY A SUPERVISORY AUTHORITY

(1) Paragraph 1 above applies also to information, which–
  (a) has been supplied to the Treasury or the Secretary of State for the purposes of any relevant functions by a supervisory authority in a member State other than the United Kingdom; or
  (b) has been obtained for those purposes by the Treasury or the Secretary of State, or by a person acting on their behalf, in another member State.

(2) Subject to sub-paragraphs (3) and (4) below, information supplied or obtained as mentioned in sub-paragraph (1)(a) or (b) above shall not be disclosed except as provided by paragraph 1 above or–
  (a) for the purpose of enabling or assisting the Treasury or the Secretary of State to discharge any relevant functions; or
  (b) with a view to the institution of, or otherwise for the purposes of, criminal proceedings, whether under this Act or otherwise.

(3) Information supplied as mentioned in sub-paragraph (1)(a) above may be disclosed–
  (a) to a relevant recipient, if the supervisory authority that supplied the information consents to its disclosure and the case is one in which information to which paragraph 1 above applies could be so disclosed by virtue of paragraph 3(1) above; or
  (b) to the Treasury or the Secretary of State, if that authority consents to its disclosure and the case is one in which information to which paragraph 1 above applies could be so disclosed by virtue of paragraph 3(3) above.

(4) Information obtained as mentioned in sub-paragraph (1)(b) above may be disclosed–
  (a) to a relevant recipient, if the supervisory authority in the member State concerned consents to its disclosure and the case is one in which information to which paragraph 1

above applies could be so disclosed by virtue of paragraph 3(1) above; or

(b) to the Treasury or the Secretary of State, if that authority consents to its disclosure and the case is one in which information to which paragraph 1 above applies could be so disclosed by virtue of paragraph 3(3) above.

(4A) Before the Treasury or the Secretary of State discloses information to any person under sub-paragraph (3) above, they shall notify the supervisory authority which supplied the information of the name and responsibilities of that person.

(5) In this paragraph–

'relevant information' (a) in relation to the Treasury means their functions under this Act, and (b) in relation to the Secretary of State, means his functions under this Act;

'relevant recipient' means a person specified in any of entries 1 to 7, 12, 13 and 17 in the Table in paragraph 3(1) above.

PART II: INFORMATION RELATING TO OTHER PERSONS

6. Restriction on Disclosure

(1) Subject to paragraph 7 below, no information which–

(a) has been obtained under section 44(2) to (4) or 44A above; and

(b) relates to the business or other affairs of a person who is not a relevant person for the purposes of paragraph 1 above,

shall be disclosed without the consent of the person from whom the information was obtained and, if different, the person to whom it relates.

(2) A person who discloses any information in contravention of this paragraph shall be guilty of an offence under section 449 of the Companies Act or Article 442 of the Companies (Northern Ireland) Order 1986 and liable accordingly.

7. Permitted Disclosures

(1) Paragraph 6 above does not preclude the disclosure of information to any person who is a competent authority for the purposes

of section 449 of the Companies Act or Article 442(1)(a) to (e) of the Companies (Northern Ireland) Order 1986.

(2) Paragraph 6 above does not preclude the disclosure of information as mentioned in any of the paragraphs except (m) of subsection (1) of section 180 of the Financial Services Act 1986 or in subsection (3) or (4) of that section, or as mentioned in section 449(1) of the Companies Act or Article 442 of that Order.

(3) Paragraph 6 above does not preclude the disclosure of any such information as is mentioned in section 180(5) of the Financial Services Act 1986 by any person who by virtue of that section is not precluded by section 179 of that Act from disclosing it.

COMPANIES ACT 1985

PART XIV: INVESTIGATION OF COMPANIES AND THEIR AFFAIRS; REQUISITION OF DOCUMENTS

APPOINTMENT AND FUNCTIONS OF INSPECTORS

431. INVESTIGATION OF A COMPANY ON ITS OWN APPLICATION OR THAT OF ITS MEMBERS

(1) The Secretary of State may appoint one or more competent inspectors to investigate the affairs of a company and to report on them in such manner as he may direct.

(2) The appointment may be made –
   - (a) in the case of a company having a share capital, on the application either of not less than 200 members or of members holding not less than one tenth of the shares issued,
   - (b) in the case of a company not having a share capital, on the application of not less than one fifth in number of the persons on the company's register of members, and

(c) in any case, on application of the company;

(3) The application shall be supported by such evidence as the Secretary of State may require for the purpose of showing that the applicant or applicants have good reason for requiring the investigation.

(4) The Secretary of State may, before appointing inspectors, require the applicant or applicants to give security, to an amount not exceeding £5,000, or such other sum as he may by order specify, for payment of the costs of the investigation.

An order under this subsection shall be made by statutory instrument subject to annulment in pursuance of a resolution of either House of Parliament.

432. OTHER COMPANY INVESTIGATIONS

(1) The Secretary of State shall appoint one or more competent inspectors to investigate the affairs of a company and report on them in such manner as he directs, if the court by order declares that its affairs ought to be so investigated.

(2) The Secretary of State may make such an appointment if it appears to him that there are circumstances suggesting–

(a) that the company's affairs are being or have been conducted with intent to defraud its creditors or the creditors of any other person, or otherwise for a fraudulent or unlawful purpose, or in a manner which is unfairly prejudicial to some part of its members, or

(b) that any actual or proposed act or omission of the company (including an act or omission on its behalf) is or would be so prejudicial, or that the company was formed for any fraudulent or unlawful purpose, or

(c) that persons concerned with the company's formation or the management of its affairs have in connection therewith been guilty of fraud, misfeasance or other misconduct towards it or towards its members, or

(d) that the company's members have not been given all the information with respect to its affairs which they might reasonably expect.

(2A) Inspectors may be appointed under subsection (2) on terms that any report they may make is not for publication; and in such a case, the provisions of section 437(3) (availabilityand publication of inspectors' reports) do not apply.

(3) Subsections (1) and (2) are without prejudice to the powers of

the Secretary of State under section 431; and the power conferred by subsection (2) is exercisable with respect to a body corporate notwithstanding that it is in course of being voluntarily wound up.

(4) The reference in subsection (2)(a) to a company's members includes any person who is not a member but to whom shares in the company have been transferred or transmitted by operation of law.

433. Inspectors' powers during investigation

(1) If Inspectors appointed under section 431 or 432 to investigate the affairs of a company think it necessary for the purposes of their investigation to investigate also the affairs of another body corporate, which is or at any relevant time has been the company's subsidiary or holding company, or a subsidiary of its holding company or a holding company of its subsidiary, they have power to do so; and they shall report on the affairs of the other body corporate so far as they think that the result of their investigation of its affairs are relevant to the investigation of the affairs of the company first mentioned above.

[(2) ...]

434. Production of documents and evidence to inspectors

(1) When inspectors are appointed under section 431 or 432, it is the duty of all officers and agents of the company, and of all officers and agents of any other body corporate whose affairs are investigated under section 433(1)–
   - (a) to produce to the inspectors all documents of or relating to the company or, as the case may be, the other body corporate which are in their custody or power,
   - (b) to attend before the inspectors when required to do so, and
   - (c) otherwise to give the inspectors all assistance in connection with the investigation which they are reasonably able to give.

(2) If the inspectors consider that an officer or agent of the company or other body corporate, or any other person, is or may be in possession of information relating to a matter which they believe to be relevant to the investigation, they may require him–
- (a) to produce to them any documents in his custody or power relating to that matter,
- (b) to attend before them, and
- (c) otherwise to give them all assistance in connection with the investigation which he is reasonably able to give;

and it is that person's duty to comply with the requirement.

(3) An inspector may for the purposes of the investigation examine any person on oath, and may administer an oath accordingly.

(4) In this section a reference to officers or to agents includes past, as well as present, officers or agents (as the case may be); and 'agents', in relation to a company or other body corporate, includes its bankers and solicitors and persons employed by it as auditors, whether these persons are or are not officers of the company or other body corporate.

(5) An answer given by a person to a question put to him in exercise of powers conferred by this section (whether as it has effect in relation to an investigation under any of sections 431 to 433, or as applied by any other section in this Part) may be used in evidence against him.

(6) In this section 'documents' includes information recorded in any form; and, in relation to information recorded otherwise than in legible form, the power to require its production includes power to require the production of a copy of the information in legible form.

[435. ...]

436. Obstruction of inspectors treated as contempt of court

(1) If any person–
- (a) fails to comply with section 434(1)(a) or (c),
- (b) refuses to comply with a requirement under section 434(1)(b) or (2), or
- (c) refuses to answer any question put to him by the inspectors for the purposes of the investigation,

the inspectors may certify that fact in writing to the court.

(2) The court may thereupon enquire into the case; and, after hearing any witnesses who may be produced against or on behalf of the alleged offender and after hearing any statement that may be offered in defence, the court may punish the offender in like manner as if he had been guilty of contempt of the court.

437. Inspectors' reports

(1) The inspectors may, and if so directed by the Secretary of State shall, make interim reports to the Secretary of State, and on the conclusion of their investigation shall make a final report to him. Any such report shall be written or printed, as the Secretary of State directs.

(1A) Any persons who have been appointed under section 431 or 432 may at any time and, if the Secretary of State directs them to do so, shall inform him of any matters coming to their knowledge as a result of their investigations.

(1B) If it appears to the Secretary of State that matters have come to light in the course of the inspectors' investigation which suggest that a criminal offence has been committed, and those matters have been referred to the appropriate prosecuting authority, he may direct the inspectors to take no further steps in the investigation or to take only such further steps as are specified in the direction.

(1C) Where any investigation is the subject of a direction under subsection (1B), the inspectors shall make a final report to the Secretary of State only where–

(a) they were appointed under section 432(1) (appointment in pursuance of an order of the court), or

(b) the Secretary of State directs them to do so.

(2) If the inspectors were appointed under section 432 in pursuance of an order of the court, the Secretary of State shall furnish a copy of any report of theirs to the court.

(3) In any case the Secretary of State may, if he thinks fit–

(a) forward a copy of any report made by the inspectors to the company's registered office,

(b) furnish a copy on request and on payment of the prescribed fee to–

(i) any member of the company or other body corporate which is the subject of the report,

(ii) any person whose conduct is referred to in the report,

(iii) the auditors of that company or body corporate,
(iv) the applicants for the investigation,
(v) any other person whose financial interests appear to the Secretary of State to be affected by the matters dealt with in the report, whether as a creditor of the company or body corporate, or otherwise, and

(c) cause any such report to be printed and published.

438. POWER TO BRING CIVIL PROCEEDINGS ON A COMPANY'S BEHALF

(1) If from any report made or information obtained under this Part it appears to the Secretary of State that any civil proceedings ought in the public interest to be brought by any body corporate, he may himself bring such proceedings in the name and on behalf of the body corporate.

(2) The Secretary of State shall indemnify the body corporate against any costs or expenses incurred by it in or in connection with proceedings brought under this section.

439. EXPENSES OF INVESTIGATING A COMPANY'S AFFAIRS

(1) The expenses of an investigation under any of the powers conferred by this Part shall be defrayed in the first instance by the Secretary of State, but he may recover those expenses from the persons liable in accordance with this section.
There shall be treated as expenses of the investigation, in particular, such reasonable sums as the Secretary of State may determine in respect of general staff costs and overheads.

(2) A person who is convicted on a prosecution instituted as a result of the investigation, or is ordered to pay the whole or any part of the costs of proceedings brought under section 438, may in the same proceedings be ordered to pay those expenses to such extent as may be specified in the order.

(3) A body corporate in whose name proceedings are brought under that section is liable to the amount or value of any sums or property recovered by it as a result of those proceedings; and any amount for which a body corporate is liable under this subsection is a first charge on the sums or property recovered.

(4) A body corporate dealt with by an inspectors' report, where the inspectors were appointed otherwise than of the Secretary of State's own motion, is liable except where it was the applicant for the investigation, and except so far as the Secretary of State otherwise directs.

(5) Where inspectors were appointed–
  (a) under section 431, or
  (b) on an application under section 442(3),
the applicant or applicants for the investigation is or are liable to such extent (if any) as the Secretary of State may direct.

(6) The report of inspectors appointed otherwise than of the Secretary of State's own motion may, if they think fit, and shall if the Secretary of State so directs, include a recommendation as to the directions (if any) which they think appropriate, in the light of their investigation, to be given under subsection (4) or (5) of this section.

(7) For purposes of this section, any costs or expenses incurred by the Secretary of State in or in connection with proceedings brought under section 438 (including expenses incurred under subsection (2) of it) are to be treated as expenses of the investigation giving rise to the proceedings.

(8) Any liability to repay the Secretary of State imposed by subsections (2) and (3) above is (subject to satisfaction of his right to repayment) a liability also to indemnify all persons against liability under subsections (4) and (5); and any such liability imposed by subsection (2) is (subject as mentioned above) a liability also to indemnify all persons against liability under subsection (3).

(9) A person liable under any one of those subsections is entitled to contribution from any other person liable under the same subsection, according to the amount of their respective liabilities under it.

(10) Expenses to be defrayed by the Secretary of State under this section shall, so far as not recovered under it, be paid out of money provided by Parliament.

[440. ...]

441. Inspectors' report to be evidence

(1) A copy of any report of inspectors appointed under this Part, certified by the Secretary of State to be a true copy, is admissible in any legal proceedings as evidence of the opinion of the inspectors in relation to any matter contained in the report and, in proceedings on an application under section 8 of the Company Directors Disqualification Act 1986, as evidence of any fact stated therein.

(2) A document purporting to be such a certificate as is mentioned above shall be received in evidence and be deemed to be such a certificate, unless the contrary is proved.

OTHER POWERS OF INVESTIGATION AVAILABLE TO THE SECRETARY OF STATE

442. Power to investigate company ownership

(1) Where it appears to the Secretary of State that there is good reason to do so, he may appoint one or more competent inspectors to investigate and report on the membership of any company, and otherwise with respect to the company, for the purpose of determining the true persons who are or have been financially interested in the success or failure (real or apparent) of the company or able to control or materially to influence its policy.

(2) The appointment of inspectors under this section may define the scope of their investigation (whether as respects the matter or the period to which it is to extend or otherwise) and in particular may limit the investigation to matters connected with particular shares or debentures.

(3) If an application for investigation under this section with respect to particular shares or debentures of a company is made to the Secretary of State by members of the company, and the number

of applicants or the amount of shares held by them is not less than that required for an application for the appointment of inspectors under section 431(2)(a) or (b), then, subject to the following provisions, the Secretary of State shall appoint inspectors to conduct the investigation applied for.

(3A) The Secretary of State shall not appoint inspectors if he is satisfied that the application is vexatious; and where inspectors are appointed their terms of appointment shall exclude any matter in so far as the Secretary of State is satisfied that it is unreasonable for it to be investigated.

(3B) The Secretary of State may, before appointing inspectors, require the applicant or applicants to give security, to an amount not exceeding £5,000, or such other sums as he may by order specify, for payment of the costs of the investigation.
An order under this subsection shall be made by statutory instrument which shall be subject to annulment in pursuance of a resolution of either House of Parliament.

(3C) If on an application under subsection (3) it appears to the Secretary of State that the powers conferred by section 444 are sufficient for the purposes of investigating the matters which inspectors would be appointed to investigate, he may instead conduct the investigation under that section.

(4) Subject to the terms of their appointment, the inspectors' powers extend to the investigation of any circumstances suggesting the existence of an arrangement or understanding which, though not legally binding, is or was observed or likely to be observed in practice and which is relevant to the purposes of the investigation.

443. Provisions applicable on investigation under s.442

(1) For purposes of an investigation under section 442, sections 433(1), 434, 436 and 437 apply with the necessary modifications of references to the affairs of the company or to those of any other body corporate, subject, however, to the following subsections.

(2) Those sections apply to –

(a) all persons who are or have been, or whom the inspector has reasonable cause to believe to be or have been, financially interested in the success or failure or the apparent success or failure of the company or any other body corporate whose membership is investigated with that of the company, or able to control or materially influence its policy (including persons concerned only on behalf of others), and

(b) any other person whom the inspector has reasonable cause to believe possesses information relevant to the investigation,

as they apply in relation to officers and agents of the company or the other body corporate (as the case may be).

(3) If the Secretary of State is of opinion that there is good reason for not divulging any part of a report made by virtue of section 442 and this section, he may under section 437 disclose the report with the omission of that part; and he may cause to be kept by the registrar of companies a copy of the report with that part omitted or, in the case of any other such report, a copy of the whole report.

[(4) ...]

444. Power to obtain information as to those interested in shares, etc.

(1) If it appears to the Secretary of State that there is good reason to investigate the ownership of any shares in or debentures of a company and that it is unnecessary to appoint inspectors for the purpose, he may require any person whom he has reasonable cause to believe to have or to be able to obtain any information as to the present and past interests in those shares or debentures and the names and addresses of the persons interested and of any persons who act or have acted on their behalf in relation to the shares or debentures to give any such information to the Secretary of State.

(2) For this purpose a person is deemed to have an interest in shares or debentures if he has any right to acquire or dispose of them or of any interest in them, or to vote in respect of them, or if his consent is necessary for the exercise of any of the rights of other persons interested in them, or if other persons interested in them can be required, or are accustomed, to exercise their rights in accordance with his instructions.

(3) A person who fails to give information required of him under this section, or who is giving such information makes any statement that he knows to be false in a material particular, or recklessly makes any statement which is false in a material particular, is liable to imprisonment or a fine, or both.

445. Power to impose restrictions on shares and debentures

(1) If in connection with an investigation under either section 442 or 444 it appears to the Secretary of State that there is difficulty in finding out the relevant facts about any shares (whether issued or to be issued), he may by order direct that the shares shall until further order be subject to the restrictions of Part XV of this Act.

(1A) If the Secretary of State is satisfied that an order under subsection (1) may unfairly affect the rights of third parties in respect of shares then the Secretary of State, for the purpose of protecting such rights and subject to such terms as he thinks fit, may direct that such acts by such persons or descriptions of persons and for such purposes as may be set out in the order, shall not constitute a breach of the restrictions of Part XV of this Act.

(2) This section, and Part XV in its application to orders under it, apply in relation to debentures as in relation to shares save that subsection (1A) shall not so apply.

446. Investigation of share dealings

(1) If it appears to the Secretary of State that there are circumstances suggesting that contraventions may have occurred, in relation to a company's shares or debentures, of section 323 or 324 (taken with Schedule 13), or of subsections (3) to (5) of section 328 (restrictions on share dealings by directors and their families; obligation of director to disclose shareholding in his own company), he may appoint one or more competent inspectors to carry out such investigations as are requisite to establish whether or not such contraventions have occurred and to report the result of their investigations to him.

(2) The appointment of inspectors under this section may limit the

period to which their investigation is to extend or confine it to shares or debentures of a particular class, or both.

(3) For purposes of an investigation under this section, sections 434 [to 437] apply–
  (a) with the substitution, for references to any other body corporate whose affairs are investigated under section 433(1), of a reference to any other body corporate which is, or has at any relevant time been, the company's subsidiary or holding company, or a subsidiary of its holding company, ...
  [(b)...]

(4) Sections 434 to 436 apply under the preceding subsection–
  (a) to any individual who is an authorised person within the meaning of the Financial Services Act 1986;
  (b) to any individual who holds a permission granted under paragraph 23 of Schedule 1 to that Act;
  (c) to any officer (whether past or present) of a body corporate which is such an authorised person or holds such a permission;
  (d) to any partner (whether past or present) in a partnership which is such an authorised person or holds such a permission;
  (e) to any member of the governing body or officer (in either case whether past or present) of an unincorporated association which is such an authorised person or holds such a permission,

  as they apply to officers of the company or of the other body corporate.

[(5)–(7) ...]

REQUISITION AND SEIZURE OF BOOKS AND PAPERS

447. SECRETARY OF STATE'S POWER TO REQUIRE PRODUCTION OF DOCUMENTS

[(1) ...]

(2) The Secretary of State may at any time, if he thinks there is good reasons to do so, give directions to a company requiring it, at

such time and place as may be specified in the directions, to produce such documents as may be so specified.

(3) The Secretary of State may at any time, if he thinks there is good reason to do so, authorise an officer of his or any other competent person, on producing (if so required) evidence of his authority, to require a company to produce to him (the officer or other person) forthwith any documents which he (the officer or other person) may specify.

(4) Where by virtue of subsection (2) or (3) the Secretary of State or an officer of his or other person has power to require the production of documents from a company, he or the officer or other person has the like power to require production of those documents from any person who appears to him or the officer or other person to be in possession of them; but where any such person claims a lien on documents produced by him, the production is without prejudice to the lien.

(5) The power under this section to require a company or other person to produce documents includes power–

- (a) if the documents are produced –
  - (i) to take copies of them or extracts from them, and
  - (ii) to require that person, or any other person who is a present or past officer of, or is or was at any time employed by, the company in question, to provide an explanation of any of them;
- (b) if the documents are not produced, to require the person who was required to produce them to state, to the best of his knowledge and belief, where they are.

(6) If the requirement to produce documents or provide an explanation or make a statement is not complied with, the company or other person on whom the requirement was so imposed is guilty of an offence and liable to a fine.

Sections 732 (restriction on prosecutions), 733 (liability of individuals for corporate default) and 734 (criminal proceedings against unincorporated bodies) apply to this offence.

(7) However, where a person is charged with an offence under subsection (6) in respect of a requirement to produce any documents, it is a defence to prove that they were not in his possession or under his control and that it was not reasonably practicable for him to comply with the requirement.

(8) A statement made by a person in compliance with such a requirement may be used in evidence against him.

(9) In this section 'documents' includes information recorded in any

form; and, in relation to information recorded otherwise than in legible form, the power to require its production includes power to require the production of a copy of it in legible form.

448. ENTRY AND SEARCH OF PREMISES

(1) A justice of the peace may issue a warrant under this section if satisfied on information on oath given by or on behalf of the Secretary of State, or by a person appointed or authorised to exercise powers under this Part, that there are reasonable grounds for believing that there are on any premises documents whose production has been required under this Part and which have not been produced in compliance with the requirement.

(2) A justice of the peace may also issue a warrant under this section if satisfied on information on oath given by or on behalf of the Secretary of State, or by a person appointed or authorised to exercise powers under this Part–

(a) that there are reasonable grounds for believing that an offence has been committed for which the penalty on conviction on indictment is imprisonment for a term of not less than two years and that there are on any premises documents relating to whether the offence has been committed,

(b) that the Secretary of State, or the person so appointed or authorised, has power to require the production of the documents under this Part, and

(c) that there are reasonable grounds for believing that if production was so required the documents would not be produced but would be removed from the premises, hidden, tampered with or destroyed.

(3) A warrant under this section shall authorise a constable, together with any other person named in it and any other constables–

(a) to enter the premises specified in the information, using such force as is reasonably necessary for the purpose;

(b) to search the premises and take possession of any documents appearing to be such documents as are mentioned in subsection (1) or (2), as the case may be, or to take, in relation to any such documents, any other steps which may appear to be necessary for preserving them or preventing interference with them;

(c) to take copies of any such documents; and

(d) to require any person named in the warrant to provide an explanation of them or to state where they may be found.

(4) If in the case of a warrant under subsection (2) the justice of the peace is satisfied on information on oath that there are reasonable grounds for believing that there are also on the premises other documents relevant to the investigation, the warrant shall also authorise the actions mentioned in subsection (3) to be taken in relation to such documents.

(5) A warrant under this section shall continue in force until the end of the period of one month beginning with the day on which it is issued.

(6) Any documents of which possession is taken under this section may be retained–
- (a) for a period of three months; or
- (b) if within that period proceedings to which the documents are relevant are commenced against any person for any criminal offence, until the conclusion of those proceedings.

(7) Any person who intentionally obstructs the exercise of any rights conferred by a warrant issued under this section or fails without reasonable excuse to comply with any requirement imposed in accordance with subsection (3)(d) is guilty of an offence and liable to a fine.
Sections 732 (restriction on prosecutions), 733 (liability of individuals for corporate default) and 734 (criminal proceedings against unincorporated bodies) apply to this offence.

(8) For the purposes of sections 449 and 451A (provisions for security of information) documents obtained under this section shall be treated as if they had been obtained under the provision of this Part under which their production was or, as the case may be, could have been required.

(9) In the application of this section to Scotland for the references to a justice of the peace substitute references to a justice of the peace or a sheriff, and for the references to information on oath substitute references to evidence on oath.

(10) In this section 'document' includes information recorded in any form.

449. Provision for Security of Information Obtained

(1) No information or document relating to a company which has been obtained under section 447 ... shall, without the previous

consent in writing of that company, be published or disclosed, except to a competent authority, unless the publication or disclosure is required –

(a) with a view to the institution of or otherwise for the purposes of criminal proceedings;

(ba) with a view to the institution of, or otherwise for the purposes of, any proceedings on an application under section 6, 7 or 8 of the Company Directors Disqualification Act 1986;

(c) for the purposes of enabling or assisting any inspector appointed under this Part, or under section 94 or 177 of the Financial Services Act 1986, to discharge his functions;

(cc) for the purpose of enabling or assisting any person authorised to exercise powers or appointed under section 43A or 44 of the Insurance Companies Act 1982, section 447 of this Act, section 106 of the Financial Services Act 1986 or section 84 of the Companies Act 1989 to discharge his functions;

(d) for the purpose of enabling or assisting the Secretary of State or the Treasury to exercise any of their functions under this Act, the insider dealing legislation, *the Prevention of Fraud (Investments) Act 1958*, the Insurance Companies Act 1982, the Insolvency Act 1986, the Company Directors Disqualification Act 1986, the Financial Services Act 1986 or Part II, III or VII of the Companies Act 1989,

(dd) for the purpose of enabling or assisting the Department of Economic Development for Northern Ireland to exercise any powers conferred on it by the enactments relating to companies or insolvency or for the purposes of enabling or assisting any inspector appointed by it under the enactments relating to companies to discharge his functions

(de) for the purpose of enabling or assisting the Chief Registrar of friendly societies or the Assistant Registrar of friendly societies for Scotland to discharge the functions under the enactments relating to friendly societies;

(df) for the purpose of enabling or assisting the Friendly Societies Commission to discharge its functions under the Financial Services Act 1986;

(dg) for the purpose of enabling or assisting the Occupational Pensions Regulatory Authority to discharge their functions under the Pension Schemes Act 1993 or the Pensions Act 1995 or any enactment in force in Northern Ireland corresponding to either of them;

[(e)...]

(f) for the purpose of enabling or assisting the Bank of England to discharge its functions;

(fa) for the purpose of enabling or assisting the Financial Services Authority to discharge:

(i) any functions under the Financial Services Act 1986, other than as a designated agency within the meaning of that Act;

(ii) its functions under the Banking Act 1987; or

(iii) its functions under section 171 of the Companies Act 1989.

(g) for the purpose of enabling or assisting the Deposit Protection Board to discharge its functions under that Act,

(h) for any purpose mentioned in section 180(1)*(b)*, *(e)*, *(h)*, or *(n)* of the Financial Services Act 1986,

(hh) for the purpose of enabling or assisting a body established by order under section 46 of the Companies Act 1989 to discharge its functions under Part II of that Act, or of enabling or assisting a recognised supervisory or qualifying body within the meaning of that Part to discharge its functions as such;

(i) for the purpose of enabling or assisting the Industrial Assurance Commissioner or the Industrial Assurance Commissioner for Northern Ireland to discharge his functions under the enactments relating to industrial assurance,

(j) for the purpose of enabling or assisting the Insurance Brokers Registration Council to discharge its functions under the Insurance Brokers (Registration) Act 1977,

(k) for the purpose of enabling or assisting an official receiver to discharge his functions under the enactments relating to insolvency or for the purpose of enabling or assisting a body which is for the time being a recognised professional body for the purposes of section 391 of the Insolvency Act 1986 to discharge its functions as such,

(l) with a view to the institution of, or otherwise for the purposes of, any disciplinary proceedings relating to the exercise by a solicitor, auditor, accountant, valuer or actuary of his professional duties,

(ll) with a view to the institution of, or otherwise for the purposes of, any disciplinary proceedings relating to the discharge by a public servant of his duties;

(m) for the purpose of enabling or assisting an overseas regulatory authority to exercise its regulatory functions.

(1A) In subsection (1)–

(a) in paragraph (ll) 'public servant' means an officer or servant of the Crown or of any public or other authority for the time being designated for the purposes of that paragraph by the Secretary of State by order made by statutory instrument; and

(b) in paragraph (m) 'overseas regulatory authority' and 'regulatory functions' have the same meaning as in section 82 of the Companies Act 1989.

(1B) Subject to subsection (1C), subsection (1) shall not preclude publication or disclosure for the purpose of enabling or assisting any public or other authority for the time being designated for the purposes of this subsection by the Secretary of State by an order in a statutory instrument to discharge any functions which are specified in the order.

(1C) An order under subsection (1B) designating an authority for the purpose of that subsection may–

(a) impose conditions subject to which the publications or disclosure of any information or document is permitted by that subsection; and

(b) otherwise restrict the circumstances in which that subsection permits publication or disclosure.

(1D) Subsection (1) shall not preclude the publication or disclosure of any such information as is mentioned in section 180(5) of the Financial Services Act 1986 by any person who by virtue of that section is not precluded by section 179 of that Act from disclosing it.

(2) A person who publishes or discloses any information or document in contravention of this section is guilty of an offence and liable to imprisonment or a fine, or both.

Sections 732 (restriction on prosecutions), 733 (liability of individuals for corporate default) and 734 (criminal proceedings against unincorporated bodies) apply to this offence.

(3) For the purposes of this section each of the following is a competent authority–

(a) the Secretary of State,

(b) an inspector appointed under this Part or under section 94 or 177 of the Financial Services Act 1986,

(c) any person authorised to exercise powers under section 44 of the Insurance Companies Act 1982, section 447 of this

Act, section 106 of the Financial Services Act 1986 or section 84 of the Companies Act 1989,

(d) the Department of Economic Development in Northern Ireland,

(e) the Treasury,

(f) the Bank of England,

(g) the Lord Advocate,

(h) the Director of Public Prosecutions, and the Director of Public Prosecutions for Northern Ireland,

(ha) the Financial Services Authority, other than in its capacity as a designated agency within the meaning of the Financial Services Act 1986,

(i) any designated agency or transferee body within the meaning of the Financial Services Act 1986, and any body administering a scheme under section 54 of or paragraph 18 of Schedule 11 to that Act (schemes for compensation of investors),

(j) the Chief Registrar of friendly societies,

(jj) the Friendly Societies Commission,

(k) the Industrial Assurance Commissioner,

(l) any constable,

(m) any procurator fiscal.

(3A) Any information which, may by virtue of this section, be disclosed to a competent authority may be disclosed to any officer or servant of the authority.

(4) A statutory instrument containing an order under subsection (1A)(a) or (1B) is subject to annulment in pursuance of a resolution of either House of Parliament.

450. PUNISHMENT FOR DESTROYING, MUTILATING, ETC. COMPANY DOCUMENTS

(1) An officer of a company, or of an insurance company to which Part II of the Insurance Companies Act 1982 applies, who–

(a) destroys, mutilates or falsifies, or is privy to the destruction, mutilation or falsification of a document affecting or relating to the company's property or affairs, or

(b) makes, or is privy to the making of, a false entry in such a document, is guilty of an offence, unless he proves that he had no intention to conceal the state of affairs of the company or to defeat the law.

(2) Such a person as above mentioned who fraudulently either parts with, alters or makes an omission in any such document or is privy to fraudulent parting with, fraudulent altering or fraudulent making of an omission in, any such document, is guilty of an offence.

(3) A person guilty of an offence under this section is liable to imprisonment or a fine, or both.

(4) Sections 732 (restriction on prosecutions), 733 (liability of individuals for corporate default) and 734 (criminal proceedings against unincorporated bodies) apply to an offence under this section.

(5) In this section 'document' includes information recorded in any form.

451. Punishment for Furnishing False Information

A person who, in purported compliance with a requirement imposed under section 447 to provide an explanation or make a statement, provides or makes an explanation or statement which he knows to be false in a material particular or recklessly provides or makes an explanation or statement which is so false, is guilty of an offence and liable to imprisonment or a fine, or both.

Sections 732 (restriction on prosecutions), 733 (liability of individuals for corporate default) and 734 (criminal proceedings against unincorporated bodies) apply to this offence.

451A. Disclosure of Information by Secretary of State or Inspector

(1) This section applies to information obtained under sections 434 to 446.

(2) The Secretary of State may, if he thinks fit–

(a) disclose any information to which this section applies to any person to whom, or for any purpose for which, disclosure is permitted under section 449, or

(b) authorise or require an inspector appointed under this Part to disclose such information to any such person or for any such purpose.

(3) Information to which this section applies may also be disclosed by an inspector appointed under this Part to–
(a) another inspector appointed under this Part or an inspector appointed under section 94 or 177 of the Financial Services Act 1986, or
(b) a person authorised to exercise powers or appointed under section 43A or 44 of the Insurance Companies Act 1982, section 447 of this Act, section 106 of the Financial Services Act 1986 or section 84 of the Companies Act 1989.

(4) Any information which may by virtue of subsection (3) be disclosed to any person may be disclosed to any officer or servant of that person.

(5) The Secretary of State may, if he thinks fit, disclose any information obtained under section 444 to–
(a) the company whose ownership was the subject of the investigation,
(b) any member of the company,
(c) any person whose conduct was investigated in the course of the investigation,
(d) the auditors of the company, or
(e) any person whose financial interests appear to the Secretary of State to be affected by matters covered by the investigation.

SUPPLEMENTARY

452. Privileged Information

(1) Nothing in sections 431 to 446 requires the disclosure to the Secretary of State or to an inspector appointed by him –
(a) by any person of information which he would in an action in the High Court or the Court of Session be entitled to refuse to disclose on grounds of legal professional privilege except, if he is a lawyer, the name and address of his client,
[(b)...]

(1A) Nothing in section 434, 443 or 446 requires a person (except as mentioned in subsection (1B) below) to disclose information or produce documents in respect of which he owes an obligation of confidence by virtue of carrying on the business of banking unless–

(a) the person to whom the obligation of confidence is owed is the company or other body corporate under investigation,

(b) the person to whom the obligation of confidence is owed consents to the disclosure or production, or

(c) the making of the requirement is authorised by the Secretary of State.

(1B) Subsection (1A) does not apply where the person owing the obligation of confidence is the company or other body corporate under investigation under section 431, 432 or 433.

(2) Nothing in sections 447 to 451 compels the production by any person of a document which he would in an action in the High Court or the Court of Session be entitled to refuse to produce on grounds of legal professional privilege, or authorises the taking of possession of any such document which is in the person's possession.

(3) The Secretary of State shall not under section 447 require, or authorise an officer of his or other person to require, the production by a person carrying on the business of banking of a document relating to the affairs of a customer of his unless either it appears to the Secretary of State that it is necessary to do so for the purpose of investigating the affairs of the first-mentioned person, or the customer is a person on whom a requirement has been imposed under that section, or under section 43A or 44(2) to (6) of the Insurance Companies Act 1982 (provision corresponding to section 447).

453. Investigation of Overseas Companies

(1) The provisions of this Part apply to bodies corporate incorporated outside Great Britain which are carrying on business in Great Britain, or have at any time carried on business there, as they apply to companies under this Act; but subject to the following exceptions, adaptations and modifications.

(1A) The following provisions do not apply to such bodies

(a) section 431 (investigation on application of company or its members),

(b) section 438 (power to bring civil proceedings on the

company's behalf),

(c) sections 442 to 445 (investigation of company ownership and power to obtain information as to those interested in shares, &c), and

(d) section 446 (investigation of share dealings).

(1B) The other provisions of this Part apply to such bodies subject to such adaptations and modifications as may be specified by regulations made by the Secretary of State.

(2) Regulations under this section shall be made by statutory instrument subject to annulment in pursuance of a resolution of either House of Parliament.

PART XV: ORDERS IMPOSING RESTRICTIONS ON SHARES (SECTIONS 210, 216, 445)

454. Consequence of Order Imposing Restrictions

(1) So long as any shares are directed to be subject to the restrictions of this Part then, subject to any directions made in relation to an order pursuant to sections 210(5A), 216(1B), 445(1A) or 456(1A) or subject in the case of an interim order pursuant to section 216(1A) to the terms of that order –

(a) any transfer of those shares or, in the case of unissued shares, any transfer of the right to be issued with them, and any issue of them, is void;

(b) no voting rights are exercisable in respect of the shares;

(c) no further shares shall be issued in right of them or in pursuance of any offer made to their holder; and

(d) except in a liquidation, no payment shall be made of any sums due from the company on the shares, whether in respect of capital or otherwise.

(2) Where shares are subject to the restrictions of subsection (1)(a), any agreement to transfer the shares or, in the case of unissued shares, the right to be issued with them is void (except such agreement or right as may be made or exercised under the terms of directions made by the Secretary of State or the court under sections 210(5A), 216(1B), 445(1A), 456(1A) or of an interim order made

under section 216(1A) or an agreement to transfer the shares on the making of an order under section 456(3)(b) below).

(3) Where shares are subject to the restrictions of subsection (1)(c) or (d), an agreement to transfer any right to be issued with other shares in right of those shares, or to receive any payment on them (otherwise than in a liquidation) is void (except such agreement or right as may be made or exercised under the terms of directions made by the Secretary of State or the court under sections 210(5A), 216(1B), 445(1A), 456(1A) or of an interim order made under section 216(1A) or an agreement to transfer any such right on the transfer of the shares on the making of an order under section 456(3)(b) below).

455. Punishment for attempted evasion of restrictions

(1) Subject to the terms of any directions made under sections 210(5A), 216(1B), 445(1A) or 456 or of an interim order made under section 216(1A) a person is liable to a fine if he –
   (a) exercises or purports to exercise any right to dispose of any shares which, to his knowledge, are for the time being subject to the restrictions of this Part or of any right to be issued with any such shares, or
   (b) votes in respect of any such shares (whether as holder or proxy), or appoints a proxy to vote in respect of them, or
   (c) being the holder of any such shares, fails to notify of their being subject to those restrictions any person whom he does not know to be aware of that fact but does know to be entitled (apart from the restrictions) to vote in respect of those shares whether as holder or as proxy, or
   (d) being the holder of any such shares, or being entitled to any right to be issued with other shares in right of them, or to receive any payment on them (otherwise than in a liquidation), enters into any agreement which is void under section 454(2) or (3).

(2) Subject to the terms of any directions made under sections 210(5A), 216(1B), 445(1A) or 456 or of an interim order made under section 216(1A) if shares in a company are issued in contravention of the restrictions, the company and every officer of it who is in default is liable to a fine.

(3) Section 732 (restriction on prosecutions) applies to an offence under this section.

456. Relaxation and Removal of Restrictions

(1) Where shares in a company are by order made subject to the restrictions of this Part, application may be made to the court for an order directing that the shares be no longer so subject.

(1A) Where the court is satisfied that an order subjecting the shares to the restrictions of this Part unfairly affects the rights of third parties in respect of shares then the court, for the purpose of protecting such rights and subject to such terms as it thinks fit and in addition to any order it may make under subsection (1), may direct on an application made under that subsection that such acts by such persons or descriptions of persons and for such purposes, as may be set out in the order, shall not constitute a breach of the restrictions of Part XV of this Act. Subsection 3 does not apply to an order made under this subsection.

(2) If the order applying the restrictions was made by the Secretary of State, or he has refused to make an order disapplying them, the application may be made by any person aggrieved; and if the order was made by the court under section 216 (non-disclosure of share holding), it may be made by any such person or by the company.

(3) Subject as follows, an order of the court or the Secretary of State directing that shares shall cease to be subject to the restrictions may be made only if–

(a) the court or (as the case may be) the Secretary of State is satisfied that the relevant facts about the shares have been disclosed to the company and no unfair advantage has accrued to any person as a result of the earlier failure to make that disclosure, or

(b) the shares are to be transferred for valuable consideration and the court (in any case) or the Secretary of State (if the order was made under section 210 or 445) approves the transfer.

(4) Without prejudice to the power of the court to give directions under subsection (1A), where shares in a company are subject to the restrictions, the court may on application order the shares to be sold, subject to the court's approval as to the sale, and may also direct that the shares shall cease to be subject to the restrictions.

An application to the court under this subsection may be made by the Secretary of State (unless the restrictions were imposed by court order under section 216), or by the company.

(5) Where an order has been made under subsection (4), the court may on application make such further order relating to the sale or transfer of the shares as it thinks fit.

An application to the court under this subsection may be made–

(a) by the Secretary of State (unless the restrictions on the shares were imposed by court order under section 216), or

(b) by the company, or

(c) by the person appointed by or in pursuance of the order to effect the sale, or

(d) by any person interested in the shares.

(6) An order (whether of the Secretary of State or the court) directing that shares shall cease to be subject to the restrictions of this Part, if it is–

(a) expressed to be made with a view to permitting a transfer of the shares, or

(b) made under subsection (4) of this section,

may continue the restrictions mentioned in paragraphs (c) and (d) of section 454(1), either in whole or in part, so far as they relate to any right acquired or offer made before the transfer.

(7) Subsection (3) does not apply to an order directing that shares shall cease to be subject to any restrictions which have been continued in force in relation to those shares under subsection (6).

457. Further provisions on sale by court order of restricted shares

(1) Where shares are sold in pursuance of an order of the court under section 456(4) the proceeds of sale, less the costs of the sale, shall be paid into court for the benefit of the persons who are beneficially interested in the shares; and any such person may apply to the court for the whole or part of those proceeds to be paid to him.

(2) On application under subsection (1) the court shall (subject as provided below) order the payment to the applicant of the whole

of the proceeds of sale together with any interest thereon or, if any other person had a beneficial interest in the shares at the time of their sale, such proportion of those proceeds and interest as is equal to the proportion which the value of the applicant's interest in the shares bears to the total value of the shares.

(3) On granting an application for an order under section 456(4) or (5) the court may order that the applicant's costs be paid out of the proceeds of sale; and if that order is made, the applicant is entitled to payment of his costs out of those proceeds before any person interested in the shares in question receives any part of those proceeds.

PART XVII: PROTECTION OF COMPANY'S MEMBERS AGAINST UNFAIR PREJUDICE

....

460. ORDER ON APPLICATION OF SECRETARY OF STATE

(1) If in the case of any company–

(a) the Secretary of State has received a report under section 437, or exercised his powers under section 447 or 448 of this Act or section 43A or 44(2) to (6) of the Insurance Companies Act 1982 ..., and

(b) it appears to him that the company's affairs are being or have been conducted in a manner which is unfairly prejudicial to the interests of its members generally or of some part of its members, or that any actual or proposed act or omission of the company (including an act or omission on its behalf) is or would be so prejudicial.

he may himself (in addition to or instead of presenting a petition ... for the winding up of the company) apply to the court by petition for an order under this Part.

(2) In this section (and, so far as applicable for its purposes, in the section next following) 'company' means any body corporate that is liable to be wound up under this Act.

....

721. Production and Inspection of Books where Offence Suspected

(1) The following applies if on an application made–
(a) in England and Wales, to a judge of the High Court by the Director of Public Prosecutions, the Secretary of Sate or a chief officer of police, or
(b) in Scotland, to one of the Lords Commissioners of Justiciary by the Lord Advocate,
there is shown to be reasonable cause to believe that any person has, while an officer of a company, committed an offence in connection with the management of the company's affairs and that evidence of the commission of the offence is to be found in any books or papers of or under the control of the company.

(2) An order may be made–
(a) authorising any person named in it to inspect the books or papers in question, or any of them, for the purpose of investigating and obtaining evidence of the offence, or
(b) requiring the secretary of the company or such other officer of it as may be named in the order to produce the books or papers (or any of them) to a person named in the order at a place so named.

(3) The above applies also in relation to any books or papers of a person carrying on the business of banking so far as they relate to the company's affairs, as it applies to any books or papers of or under the control of the company, except that no such order as is referred to in subsection (2)(b) shall be made by virtue of this subsection.

(4) The decision of a judge of the High Court or of any of the Lords Commissioners of Justiciary on an application under this section is not appealable.

COMPANY DIRECTORS DISQUALIFICATION ACT 1986

8. Disqualification after Investigation of Company

(1) If it appears to the Secretary of State from a report by inspectors

under section 437 of the Companies Act or section 94 or 177 of the Financial Services Act 1986, or from information or documents obtained under section 447 or 448 of the Companies Act, or section 105 of the Financial Services Act 1986 or section 2 of the Criminal Justice Act 1987 or section 28 of the Criminal Law (Consolidation) (Scotland) Act 1995 or section 83 of the Companies Act 1989, that it is expedient in the public interest that a disqualification order should be made against any person who is or has been a director or shadow director of any company, he may apply to the court for such an order to be made against that person.

(2) The court may make a disqualification order against a person where, on an application under this section, it is satisfied that his conduct in relation to the company makes him unfit to be concerned in the management of a company.

(3) In this section 'the court' means the High Court or, in Scotland, the Court of Session.

(4) The maximum period of disqualification under this section is 15 years.

FINANCIAL SERVICES ACT 1986

94. INVESTIGATIONS

(1) The Secretary of State may appoint one or more competent inspectors to investigate and report on–

(a) the affairs of, or of the manager or trustee of, any authorised unit trust scheme;

(b) the affairs of, or of the operator or trustee of, any recognised scheme so far as relating to activities carried on in the United Kingdom; or

(c) the affairs of, or of the operator or trustee of, any other collective investment scheme,

if it appears to the Secretary of State that it is in the interests of the participants to do so or that the matter is of public concern.

(2) An inspector appointed under subsection (1) above to investigate the affairs of, or of the manager, trustee or operator of, any scheme may also, if he thinks it necessary for the purposes of that investigation, investigate the affairs of, or of the manager, trustee or operator of, any other such scheme as is mentioned in

that subsection whose manager, trustee or operator is the same person as the manager, trustee or operator of the first-mentioned scheme.

(3) Sections 434 to 436 of the Companies Act 1985 (production of documents and evidence to inspectors), ..., shall apply in relation to an inspector appointed under this section as they apply to an inspector appointed under section 431 of that Act but with the modifications specified in subsection (4) below.

(4) In the provisions applied by subsection (3) above for any reference to a company ... there shall be substituted a reference to the scheme under investigation by virtue of this section...and any reference to an officer...of the company shall include a reference to any director of the manager, trustee or operator of the scheme.

(5) A person shall not under this section be required to disclose any information or produce any document that he would be entitled to refuse to disclose or produce on grounds of legal professional privilege in proceedings in the High Court or on grounds of confidentiality as between client and professional legal adviser in proceedings in the Court of Session except that a lawyer may be required to furnish the name and address of his client.

(6) Where a person claims a lien on a document its production under this section shall be without prejudice to the lien.

(7) Nothing in this section requires a person (except as mentioned in subsection (7A) below) to disclose any information or produce any document in respect of which he owes an obligation of confidence by virtue of carrying on the business of banking unless–

(a) the person to whom the obligation of confidence is owed consents to the disclosure or production, or

(b) the making of the requirement was authorised by the Secretary of State.

(7A) Subsection (7) does not apply where the person owing the obligation of confidence or the person to whom it is owed is–

(a) the manager, operator or trustee of the scheme under investigation, or

(b) a manager, operator or trustee whose own affairs are under investigation.

(8) An inspector appointed under this section may, and if so directed by the Secretary of State shall, make interim reports to the Secretary of State and on the conclusion of his investigation shall make a final report to him.

(8A) If it appears to the Secretary of State that matters have come to light in the course of the inspectors' investigation which suggest that a criminal offence has been committed, and those matters have been referred to the appropriate prosecuting authority, he may direct the inspectors to take no further steps in the investigation or to take only such further steps as are specified in the direction.

(8B) Where an investigation is the subject of a direction under subsection (8A), the inspectors shall make a final report to the Secretary of State only where the Secretary of State directs them to do so.

(9) Any such report shall be written or printed as the Secretary of State may direct and the Secretary of State may, if he thinks fit–

(a) furnish a copy, on request and on payment of the prescribed fee, to the manager, trustee or operator or any participant in a scheme under investigation or any other person whose conduct is referred to in the report; and

(b) cause the report to be published.

(10) A person who is convicted on a prosecution instituted as a result of an investigation under this section may in the same proceedings be ordered to pay the expenses of the investigation to such extent as may be specified in the order.

There shall be treated as expenses of the investigation, in particular, such reasonable sums as the Secretary of State may determine in respect of general staff costs and overheads.

105. Investigation Powers

(1) The powers of the Secretary of State under this section shall be exercisable in any case in which it appears to him that there is good reason to do so for the purpose of investigating the affairs, or any aspect of the affairs, of any person so far as relevant to any investment business that he is or was carrying on or appears to the Secretary of State to be or to have been carrying on.

(2) Those powers shall not be exercisable for the purpose of investigating the affairs of any exempted person unless he is an appointed representative or the investigating is in respect of investment business in respect of which he is not an exempted person and shall not be exercisable for the purpose of investigating the affairs of a member of a recognised self-regulating organisation or a person certified by a recognised professional body in respect of investment business in the carrying on of which he is subject to its rules unless–

(a) that organisation or body has requested the Secretary of State to investigate those affairs; or
(b) it appears to him that the organisation or body is unable or unwilling to investigate them in a satisfactory manner.

(3) The Secretary of State may require the person whose affairs are to be investigated ('the person under investigation') or any connected person to attend before the Secretary of State at a specified time and place and answer questions or otherwise furnish information with respect to any matter relevant to the investigation.

(4) The Secretary of State may require the person under investigation or any other person to produce at a specified time and place any specified documents which appear to the Secretary of State to relate to any matter relevant to the investigation; and–
(a) if any such documents are produced, the Secretary of State may take copies or extracts from them or require the person producing them or any connected person to provide an explanation of any of them;
(b) if any such documents are not produced, the Secretary of State may require the person who was required to produce them to state, to the best of his knowledge and belief, where they are.

(5) A statement by a person in compliance with a requirement imposed by virtue of this section may be used in evidence against him.

(6) A person shall not under this section be required to disclose any information or produce any document which he would be entitled to refuse to disclose or produce on grounds of legal professional privilege in proceedings in the High Court or on grounds of confidentiality as between client and professional legal adviser in proceedings in the Court of Session except that a lawyer may be required to furnish the name and address of his client.

[(7) ...]

(8) Where a person claims a lien on a document its production under this section shall be without prejudice to the lien.

(9) In this section –
'connected person', in relation to any other person means–
(a) any person who is or was that other person's partner,

employee, agent, appointed representative, banker, auditor or solicitor; and

(b) where the other person is a body corporate, any person who is or was a director, secretary or controller of that body corporate or of another body corporate of which it is or was a subsidiary; and

(c) where the other person is an unincorporated association, any person who is or was a member of the governing body or an officer or controller of the association; and

(d) where the other person is an appointed representative, any person who is or was his principal; and

(e) where the other person is the person under investigation (being a body corporate), any related company of that body corporate and any person who is a connected person in relation to that company;

'documents' includes information recorded in any form and, in relation to information recorded otherwise than in legible form, the power to require its production includes power to require the production of a copy of the information in legible form;

'related company', in relation to a person under investigation (being a body corporate), means any other body corporate which is or at any material time was–

(a) a holding company or subsidiary of the person under investigation;

(b) a subsidiary of a holding company of that person; or

(c) a holding company of a subsidiary of that person,

and whose affairs it is in the Secretary of State's opinion necessary to investigate for the purpose of investigating the affairs of that person.

(10) Any person who without reasonable excuse fails to comply with a requirement imposed on him under this section shall be guilty of an offence and liable on summary conviction to imprisonment for a term not exceeding six months or to a fine not exceeding the fifth level on the standard scale, or to both.

(11) A person who is convicted on a prosecution instituted as a result of an investigation under this section may in the same proceedings be ordered to pay the expenses of the investigation to such extent as may be specified in the order.

There shall be treated as expenses of the investigation, in particular, such reasonable sums as the Secretary of State may determine in respect of general staff costs and overheads.

106. Exercise of Investigation Powers by Officer, etc.

(1) The Secretary of State may authorise any officer of his or any other competent person to exercise on his behalf all or any of the powers conferred by section 105 above but no such authority shall be granted except for the purpose of investigating the affairs, or any aspects of the affairs, of a person specified in the authority.

(2) No person shall be bound to comply with any requirement imposed by a person exercising powers by virtue of an authority granted under this section unless he has, if required to do so, produced evidence of his authority.

(2A) A person shall not by virtue of an authority under this section be required to disclose any information or produce any documents in respect of which he owes an obligation of confidence by virtue of carrying on the business of banking unless–

(a) he is the person under investigation or a related company,

(b) the person to whom the obligation of confidence is owed is the person under investigation or a related company,

(c) the person to whom the obligation of confidence is owed consents to the disclosure or production, or

(d) the imposing on him of a requirement with respect to such information or documents has been specifically authorised by the Secretary of State.

In this subsection 'documents', 'person under investigation' and 'related company' have the same meaning as in section 105.

(3) Where the Secretary of State authorises a person other than one of his officers to exercise any powers by virtue of this section that person shall make a report to the Secretary of State in such manner as he may require on the exercise of those powers and the results of exercising them.

PART VII: INSIDER DEALING

177. Investigations into Insider Dealing

(1) If it appears to the Secretary of State that there are circumstances suggesting that there may have been a contravention of section

1, 2, 4 or 5 of the Company Securities (Insider Dealing) Act 1985, he may appoint one or more competent inspectors to carry out such investigations as are requisite to establish whether or not any such contravention has occurred and to report the results of their investigations to him.

(2) The appointment under this section of an inspector may limit the period during which he is to continue his investigation or confine it to particular matters.

(2A) At any time during the investigation the Secretary of State may vary the appointment by limiting or extending the period during which the inspector is to continue his investigation or by confining the investigation to particular matters.

(3) If the inspectors consider that any person is or may be able to give information concerning any such contravention they may require that person–

(a) to produce to them any documents in his possession or under his control relating to the company in relation to whose securities the contravention is suspected to have occurred or to its securities;

(b) to attend before them; and

(c) otherwise to give them all assistance in connection with the investigation which he is reasonably able to give;

and it shall be the duty of that person to comply with that requirement.

(4) An inspector may examine on oath any person who he considers is or may be able to give information concerning any such contravention, and may administer an oath accordingly.

(5) The inspectors shall make such interim reports to the Secretary of State as they think fit or he may direct and on the conclusion of the investigation they shall make a final report to him.

(5A) If the Secretary of State thinks fit, he may direct the inspector to take no further steps in the investigation or to take only such further steps as are specified in the direction; and where an investigation is the subject of such a direction, the inspectors shall make a final report to the Secretary of State only where the Secretary of State directs them to do so.

(6) A statement made by a person in compliance with a requirement imposed by virtue of this section may be used in evidence against him.

(7) A person shall not under this section be required to disclose any information or produce any document which he would be entitled to refuse to disclose or produce on grounds of legal

professional privilege in proceedings in the High Court or on grounds of confidentiality as between client and professional legal adviser in proceedings in the Court of Session.

(8) A person shall not under this section be required to disclose any information or produce any document in respect of which he owes an obligation of confidence by virtue of carrying on the business of banking unless–
  (a) the person to whom the obligation of confidence is owed consents to the disclosure or production, or
  (b) the making of the requirement was authorised by the Secretary of State.

(9) Where a person claims a lien on a document its production under this section shall be without prejudice to his lien.

(10) In this section 'document' includes information recorded in any form; and in relation to information recorded otherwise than in legible form the power to require its production includes power to require the production of a copy of the information in legible form.

(11) A person who is convicted on a prosecution instituted as a result of an investigation under this section may in the same proceedings be ordered to pay the expenses of the investigation to such extent as may be specified in the order.

There shall be treated as expenses of the investigation, in particular, such reasonable sums as the Secretary of State may determine in respect of general staff costs and overheads.

178. Penalties for failure to cooperate with s.177 investigations

(1) If any person–
  (a) refuses to comply with any request under subsection (3) of section 177 above; or
  (b) refuses to answer any question put to him by the inspectors appointed under that section with respect to any matter relevant for establishing whether or not any suspected contravention has occurred;

the inspectors may certify that fact in writing to the court and the court may inquire into the case.

(2) If, after hearing any witness who may be produced against or on behalf of the alleged offender and any statement that may be

offered in defence, the court is satisfied that he did without reasonable excuse refuse to comply with such a request or answer any such question, the court may–

(a) punish him in like manner as if he had been guilty of contempt of the court; or
(b) direct that the Secretary of State may exercise his powers under this section in respect of him;

and the court may give a direction under paragraph (b) above notwithstanding that the offender is not within the jurisdiction of the court if the court is satisfied that he was notified of his right to appear before the court and of the powers available under this section.

(3) Where the court gives a direction under subsection (2)(b) above in respect of an authorised person the Secretary of State may serve a notice on him –

(a) cancelling any authorisation of his to carry on investment business after the expiry of a specified period after the service of the notice;
(b) disqualifying him from becoming authorised to carry on investment business after the expiry of a specified period;
(c) restricting any authorisation of his in respect of investment business during a specified period to the performance of contracts entered into before the notice comes into force;
(d) prohibiting him from entering into transactions of a specified kind or entering into them except in specified circumstances or to a specified extent;
(e) prohibiting him from soliciting business from persons of a specified kind or otherwise than from such persons; or
(f) prohibiting him from carrying on business in a specified manner or otherwise than in a specified manner.

(4) The period mentioned in paragraphs (a) and (c) of subsection (3) above shall be such period as appears to the Secretary of State reasonable to enable the person on whom the notice is served to complete the performance of any contracts entered into before the notice comes into force and to terminate such of them as are of a continuing nature.

(5) Where the court gives a direction under subsection (2)(b) above in the case of an unauthorised person the Secretary of State may direct that any authorised person who knowingly transacts investment business of a specified kind, or in specified circumstances or to a specified extent, with or on behalf of that unauthorised person shall be treated as having contravened rules

made under Chapter V of Part I of this Act or, in the case of a person who is an authorised person by virtue of his membership of a recognised self-regulating organisation or certification by a recognised professional body, the rules of that organisation or body.

(6) A person shall not be treated for the purposes of subsection (2) above as having a reasonable excuse for refusing to comply with a request or answer a question in a case where the contravention or suspected contravention being investigated relates to dealing by him on the instructions or for the account of another person, by reason that at the time of the refusal–
  (a) he did not know the identity of that other person; or
  (b) he was subject to the law of a country or territory outside the United Kingdom which prohibited him from disclosing information relating to the dealing without the consent of that other person, if he might have obtained that consent or obtained exemption from that law.

(7) A notice served on a person under subsection (3) above may be revoked at any time by the Secretary of State by serving a revocation notice on him; and the Secretary of State shall revoke such a notice if it appears to him that he has agreed to comply with the relevant request or answer the relevant question.

(8) The revocation of such a notice as is mentioned in subsection (3)(a) above shall not have the effect of reviving the authorisation cancelled by the notice, except where the person would (apart from the notice) at the time of the revocation be an authorised person by virtue of his membership of a recognised self-regulating organisation or certification by a recognised professional body; but nothing in this subsection shall be construed as preventing any person who has been subject to such a notice from again becoming authorised after the revocation of the notice

(9) If it appears to the Secretary of State–
  (a) that a person on whom he serves a notice under subsection (3) above is an authorised person by virtue of an authorisation granted by a designated agency or by virtue of membership of a recognised self-regulating organisation or certification by a recognised professional body; or
  (b) that a person on whom he serves a revocation notice under subsection (7) above was such an authorised person at the time that the notice which is being revoked was served,

he shall serve a copy of the notice on that agency, organisation or body.

(10) The functions to which section 114 above applies shall include the functions of the Secretary of State under this section but any transfer of those functions shall be subject to a reservation that they are to be exercisable by him concurrently with the designated agency and so as to be exercisable by the agency subject to such conditions or restrictions as the Secretary of State may from time to time impose.

PART VIII: RESTRICTIONS ON DISCLOSURE OF INFORMATION

179. Restrictions on Disclosure of Information

(1) Subject to section 180 below, information which is restricted information for the purposes of this section and relates to the business or other affairs of any person shall not be disclosed by a person mentioned in subsection (3) below ('the primary recipient') or any person obtaining the information directly or indirectly from him without the consent of the person from whom the primary recipient obtained the information and if different, the person to whom it relates.

(2) Subject to subsection (4) below, information is restricted information for the purposes of this section if it was obtained by the primary recipient for the purposes of, or in the discharge of his functions under, this Act or any rules or regulations made under this Act (whether or not by virtue of any requirement to supply it made under those provisions).

(3) The persons mentioned in subsection (1) above are–
- (a) the Secretary of State
- (aa) the Treasury
- (b) any designated agency, transferee body or body administering a scheme under section 54 above;
- (ba) the Financial Services Authority, other than in its capacity as a designated agency;
- (c) the Director General of Fair Trading;
- (d) the Chief Registrar of friendly societies;
- (e) the Friendly Societies Commission;
- [(f)...]
- (g) any member of the Tribunal;

(h) any person appointed or authorised to exercise any powers under section 94, 106 or 177 above ; … .

(i) any officer or servant of any such person as is mentioned in paragraphs (a) to (h) above;

(j) any constable or other person named in a warrant issued under this Act.

(4) Information shall not be treated as restricted information for the purposes of this section if it has been made available to the public by virtue of being disclosed in any circumstances in which or for any purpose for which disclosure is not precluded by this section.

(5) Subject to section 180 below, information obtained by the competent authority in the exercise of its functions under Part IV of this Act or received by it pursuant to a Community obligation from any authority exercising corresponding functions in another member State shall not be disclosed without the consent of the person from whom the competent authority obtained the information and, if different, the person to whom it relates.

(6) Any person who contravenes this section shall be guilty of an offence and liable–

(a) on conviction on indictment, to imprisonment for a term not exceeding two years or to a fine, or to both;

(b) on summary conviction, to imprisonment for a term not exceeding three months or to a fine not exceeding the statutory maximum, or to both.

180. EXCEPTIONS FROM RESTRICTIONS ON DISCLOSURE

(1) Section 179 above shall not preclude the disclosure of information–

(a) with a view to the institution of or otherwise for the purposes of criminal proceedings;

(b) with a view to the instruction of or otherwise for the purposes of any civil proceedings arising under or by virtue of this Act or proceedings before the Tribunal;

(bb) for the purpose of enabling or assisting the Treasury to exercise any of their powers under the enactments relating to insurance companies, under this Act or under Part III or VII of the Companies Act 1989;

(c) for the purpose of enabling or assisting the Secretary of State to exercise any powers conferred on him by this Act or by the enactments relating to companies, insurance companies or insolvency or by Part II, III or VII of the Companies Act 1989, or for the purpose of enabling or assisting any inspector appointed by him under the enactments relating to companies to discharge his functions;

(d) for the purpose of enabling or assisting the Department of Economic Development for Northern Ireland to exercise any powers conferred on it by the enactments relating to companies or insolvency or for the purpose of enabling or assisting any inspector appointed by it under the enactments relating to companies to discharge his functions;

(e) for the purpose–

  (i) of enabling or assisting a designated agency to discharge its functions under this Act or Part VII of the Companies Act 1989,

  (ii) of enabling or assisting a transferee body or the competent authority to discharge its functions under this Act, or

  (iii) of enabling or assisting the body administering a scheme under section 54 above to discharge its functions under the scheme;

(f) for the purpose of enabling or assisting the Bank of England to discharge its functions under the Banking Act 1987 or any other functions;

(g) for the purpose of enabling or assisting the Deposit Protection Board to discharge its functions under that Act;

(h) for the purpose of enabling or assisting the Friendly Societies Commission to discharge its functions under this Act, the enactments relating to friendly societies or the enactments relating to industrial assurance;

(hh) for the purpose of enabling or assisting a body established by order under section 46 of the Companies Act 1989 to discharge its functions under Part II of that Act, or of enabling or assisting a recognised supervisory or qualifying body within the meaning of that Part to discharge its functions as such;

(i) for the purpose of enabling or assisting the Industrial Assurance Commissioner or the Industrial Assurance Commissioner for Northern Ireland to discharge his functions under the enactments relating to industrial assurance;

(j) for the purpose of enabling or assisting the Insurance

Brokers Registration Council to discharge its functions under the Insurance Brokers (Registration) Act 1977;

(k) for the purpose of enabling or assisting an official receiver to discharge his functions under the enactments relating to insolvency or for the purpose of enabling or assisting a body, which is for the time being a recognised professional body for the purposes of section 391 of the Insolvency Act 1986, to discharge its functions as such;

(l) for the purpose of enabling or assisting the Building Societies Commission to discharge its functions under the Building Societies Act 1986;

(m) for the purpose of enabling or assisting the Director General of Fair Trading to discharge his functions under this Act;

(mm) for the purpose of enabling or assisting the Occupational Pensions Regulatory Authority or the Pensions Compensation Board to discharge their functions under the Pension Schemes Act 1993 or the Pensions Act 1995 or any enactment in force in Northern Ireland corresponding to either of them;

(n) for the purpose of enabling or assisting a recognised self-regulating organisation, recognised investment exchange, recognised professional body, or recognised clearing house to discharge its functions as such;

(nn) to an Operator approved under the Uncertificated Securities Regulations 1995 if the information is necessary to ensure the proper functioning of a relevant system within the meaning of those Regulations in relation to defaults and potential defaults by market-participants;

(o) with a view to the institution of, or otherwise for the purposes of, any disciplinary proceedings relating to the exercise by a solicitor, auditor, accountant, valuer or actuary of his professional duties;

(oo) with a view to the institution of, or otherwise for the purposes of, any disciplinary proceedings relating to the discharge by a public servant of his duties;

(p) for the purpose of enabling or assisting any person appointed or authorised to exercise any powers under section 43A or 44 of the Insurance Companies Act 1982, section 447 of the Companies Act 1985, section 94, 106 or 177 above or section 84 of the Companies Act 1989 to discharge his functions;

(q) for the purpose of enabling or assisting an auditor of an authorised person or a person approved under section 108 above to discharge his functions;

(qq) for the purpose of enabling or assisting an overseas regulatory authority to exercise its regulatory functions;

(r) if the information is or has been available to the public from other sources;

(s) in a summary or collection of information framed in such a way as not to enable the identity of any person to whom the information relates to be ascertained; or

(t) in pursuance of any Community obligation.

(1A) In subsection (1) –

(a) in paragraph (oo) 'public servant' means an officer or servant of the Crown or of any public or other authority for the time being designated for the purposes of that paragraph by order of the Secretary of State; and

(b) in paragraph (qq) 'overseas regulatory authority' and 'regulatory functions' have the same meaning as in section 82 of the Companies Act 1989.

(2) Section 179 above shall not preclude the disclosure of information to the Secretary of State or to the Treasury if the disclosure is made in the interests of investors or in the public interest.

(3) Subject to subsection (4) below, section 179 above shall not preclude the disclosure of information for the purpose of enabling or assisting any public or other authority for the time being designated for the purposes of this subsection by an order made by the Secretary of State to discharge any functions which are specified in the order.

(4) An order under subsection (3) above designating an authority for the purposes of that subsection may –

(a) impose conditions subject to which the disclosure of information is permitted by that subsection; and

(b) otherwise restrict the circumstances in which that subsection permits disclosure.

(5) Section 179 above shall not preclude the disclosure–

(a) of any information contained in an unpublished report of the Tribunal which has been made available to any person under this Act, by the person to whom it was made available or by any person obtaining the information directly or indirectly from him;

(b) of any information contained in any notice or copy of a notice served under this Act, notice of the contents of which has not been given to the public, by the person on whom it was served or any person obtaining the information directly or indirectly from him;

(c) of any information contained in the register kept under section 102 above by virtue of subsection (1)(e) of that section, by a person who has inspected the register under section 103(2) or (3) above or any person obtaining the information directly or indirectly from him.

[(6) ... .]

(7) Section 179 above shall not preclude the disclosure of information by the Director General of Fair Trading or any officer or servant of his or any person obtaining the information directly or indirectly from the Director or any such officer or servant if the information was obtained by the Director or any such officer or servant for the purposes of or in the discharge of his functions under this Act (whether or not he was the primary recipient of the information within the meaning of section 179 above) and the disclosure is made–

(a) for the purpose of enabling or assisting the Director, the Secretary of State or any other Minister, the Monopolies and Mergers Commission or any Northern Ireland department to discharge any function conferred on him or them by the Fair Trading Act 1973 (other than Part II or III of that Act), the Restrictive Trade Practices Act 1976 or the Competition Act 1980; or

(b) for the purposes of any civil proceedings under any of those provisions;

and information shall not be treated as restricted information for the purposes of section 179 above if it has been made available to the public by virtue of this subsection.

(8) The Secretary of State may by order modify the application of any provision of this section so as–

(a) to prevent the disclosure by virtue of that provision; or

(b) to restrict the extent to which disclosure is permitted by virtue of that provision,

of information received by a person specified in the order pursuant to a Community obligation from a person exercising functions in relation to a collective investment scheme who is also so specified.

(9) An order under subsection (1A)(a), (3) or (8) above shall be subject to annulment in pursuance of a resolution of either House of Parliament.

181. DIRECTIONS RESTRICTING DISCLOSURE OF INFORMATION OVERSEAS

(1) If it appears to the Secretary of State to be in the public interest to do so, he may give a direction prohibiting the disclosure to any person in a country or territory outside the United Kingdom, which is specified in the direction, or to such persons in such a country or territory as may be so specified, of such information to which this section applies as may be so specified.

(2) A direction under subsection (1) above–

(a) may prohibit disclosure of the information to which it applies by all persons or only by such persons or classes of person as may be specified in it; and

(b) may prohibit such disclosure absolutely or in such cases or subject to such conditions as to consent or otherwise as may be specified in it;

and a direction prohibiting disclosure by all persons shall be published by the Secretary of State in such manner as appears to him to be appropriate.

(3) This section applies to any information relating to the business or other affairs of any person, which was obtained (whether or not by virtue of any requirement to supply it) directly or indirectly–

(a) by a designated agency, a transferee body, the competent authority or any person appointed or authorised to exercise any powers under section 94, 106 or 177 above (or any officer or servant of any such body or person) for the purposes or in the discharge of any functions of that body or person under this Act or any rules or regulations made under this Act or of any monitoring agency functions; or

(b) by a recognised self-regulating organisation, a recognised professional body, a recognised investment exchange or a recognised clearing house other than an overseas investment exchange or clearing house (or any officer or servant of such an organisation, body, investment exchange or clearing house) for the purposes or in the discharge of any of its functions as such or of any monitoring agency functions.

(4) In subsection (3) above 'monitoring agency functions' means any functions exercisable on behalf of another body by virtue of arrangements made pursuant to paragraph 4(2) of Schedule 2,

paragraph 4(6) of Schedule 3, paragraph 3(2) of Schedule 4 or paragraph 3(2) of Schedule 7 to this Act or of such arrangements as are mentioned in section 39(4)(b) above.

(5) A direction under this section shall not prohibit the disclosure by any person other than a person mentioned in subsection (3) above of–
- (a) information relating only to the affairs of that person; or
- (b) information obtained by that person otherwise than directly or indirectly from a person mentioned in subsection (3) above.

(6) A direction under this section shall not prohibit the disclosure of information in pursuance of any Community obligation.

(7) A person who knowingly discloses information in contravention of a direction under this section shall be guilty of an offence and liable
- (a) on conviction on indictment, to imprisonment for a term not exceeding two years or to a fine, or to both;
- (b) on summary conviction, to imprisonment for a term not exceeding three months or to a fine not exceeding the statutory maximum, or to both.

(8) A person shall not be guilty of an offence under this section by virtue of anything done or omitted to be done by him outside the United Kingdom unless he is a British citizen, a British Dependent Territories citizen, a British Overseas citizen or a body corporate incorporated in the United Kingdom.

182. Disclosure of Information under Enactments Relating to Fair Trading, Banking, Insurance and Companies

The enactments mentioned in Schedule 13 to this Act shall have effect with the amendments there specified (which relate to the circumstances in which information obtained under those enactments may be disclosed).

INSOLVENCY ACT 1986

124A. Petition for Winding up on Grounds of Public Interest

(1) Where it appears to the Secretary of State from:–

(a) any report made or information obtained under Part XIV of the Companies Act 1985 (company investigations, &c),
(b) any report made under section 94 or 177 of the Financial Services Act 1986 or any information obtained under section 105 of that Act,
(c) any information obtained under section 2 of the Criminal Justice Act 1987 or section 52 of the Criminal Justice (Scotland) Act 1987 (fraud investigations), or
(d) any information obtained under section 83 of the Companies Act 1989 (powers exercisable for purpose of assisting overseas regulatory authorities),

that it is expedient in the public interest that a company should be wound up, he may present a petition for it to be wound up if the court thinks it just and equitable for it to be so.

This section does not apply if the company is already being wound up by the court.

INVESTIGATION AND PROSECUTION OF MALPRACTICE

218. Prosecution of delinquent officers and members of company

(1) If it appears to the court in the course of a winding up by the court that any past or present officer, or any member, of the company has been guilty of any offence in relation to the company for which he is criminally liable, the court may (either on the application of a person interested in the winding up or of its own motion) direct the liquidator to refer the matter to the prosecuting authority.

(2) 'The prosecuting authority' means –
(a) in the case of a winding up in England and Wales, the Director of Public Prosecutions, and
(b) in the case of a winding up in Scotland, the Lord Advocate.

(3) If in the case of a winding up by the court in England and Wales it appears to the liquidator, not being the official receiver, that any past or present officer of the company, or any member of it, has been guilty of an offence in relation to the company for which he is criminally liable, the liquidator shall report the matter to the official receiver.

(4) If it appears to the liquidator in the course of a voluntary winding up that any past or present officer of the company, or any member of it, has been guilty of an offence in relation to the company for which he is criminally liable, he shall–
(a) forthwith report the matter to the prosecuting authority, and
(b) furnish to that authority such information and give to him such access to and facilities for inspecting and taking copies of documents (being information or documents in the possession or under the control of the liquidator and relating to the matter in question) as the authority requires.

(5) Where a report is made to him under subsection (4), the prosecuting authority may, if he thinks fit, refer the matter to the Secretary of State for further enquiry; and the Secretary of State–
(a) shall thereupon investigate the matter reported to him and such other matters relating to the affairs of the company as appear to him to require investigation, and
(b) for the purpose of his investigation may exercise any of the powers which are exercisable by inspectors appointed under section 431 or 432 of the Companies Act to investigate a company's affairs.

(6) If it appears to the court in the course of a voluntary winding up that–
(a) any past or present officer of the company, or any member of it, has been guilty as above-mentioned, and
(b) no report with respect to the matter has been made by the liquidator to the prosecuting authority under subsection (4),

the court may (on the application of any person interested in the winding up or of its own motion) direct the liquidator to make such a report.

On a report being made accordingly, this section has effect as though the report had been made in pursuance of subsection (4).

219. COMMENCEMENT OF WINDING UP BY THE COURT

(1) For the purpose of an investigation by the Secretary of State under section 218(5), any obligation imposed on a person by any provision of the Companies Act to produce documents or give information to, or otherwise to assist, inspectors appointed

as mentioned in that subsection is to be regarded as an obligation similarly to assist the Secretary of State in his investigation.

(2) An answer given by a person to a question put to him in exercise of the powers conferred by section 218(5) may be used in evidence against him.

(3) Where criminal proceedings are instituted by the prosecuting authority or the Secretary of State following any report or reference under section 218, it is the duty of the liquidator and every officer and agent of the company past and present (other than the defendant or defender) to give to that authority or the Secretary of State (as the case may be) all assistance in connection with the prosecution which he is reasonably able to give. For this purpose 'agent' includes any banker or solicitor of the company and any person employed by the company as auditor, whether that person is or is not an officer of the company.

(4) If a person fails or neglects to give assistance in the manner required by subsection (3), the court may, on the application of the prosecuting authority or the Secretary of State (as the case may be) direct the person to comply with that subsection; and if the application is made with respect to a liquidator, the court may (unless it appears that the failure or neglect to comply was due to the liquidator not having in his hands sufficient assets of the company to enable him to do so) direct that the costs shall be borne by the liquidator personally.

COMPANIES ACT 1989

POWERS EXERCISABLE TO ASSIST OVERSEAS REGULATORY AUTHORITIES

82. Request for Assistance by Overseas Regulatory Authority

(1) The powers conferred by section 83 are exercisable by the Secretary of State for the purpose of assisting an overseas regulatory authority that has requested his assistance in connection with inquiries being carried out by it or on its behalf.

(2) An 'overseas regulatory authority' means an authority which in a country or territory outside the United Kingdom exercises –
(a) any function corresponding to–
(i) a function under the Financial Services Act 1986 of a designated agency, transferee body or competent authority (within the meaning of that Act),
(ii) a function of the Secretary of State under the Insurance Companies Act 1982, the Companies Act 1985 or the Financial Services Act 1986, or
(iii) a function of the Financial Services Authority under the Banking Act 1987, or
(b) any function in connection with the investigation of, or the enforcement of rules (whether or not having the force of law) relating to, conduct of the kind prohibited by Part V of the Criminal Justice Act 1993 (insider dealing), or
(c) any function prescribed for the purposes of this subsection by order of the Secretary of State, being a function that in the opinion of the Secretary of State relates to companies or financial services.

An order under paragraph (c) shall be made by statutory instrument which shall be subject to annulment in pursuance of a resolution of either House of Parliament.

(3) The Secretary of State shall not exercise the powers conferred by section 83 unless he is satisfied that the assistance requested by the overseas regulatory authority is for the purposes of its regulatory functions.

An authority's 'regulatory functions' means any functions falling within subsection (2) and any other functions relating to companies or financial services.

(4) In deciding whether to exercise those powers the Secretary of State may take into account, in particular–
(a) whether corresponding assistance would be given in that country or territory to an authority exercising regulatory functions in the United Kingdom;
(b) whether the inquiries relate to the possible breach of a law, or other requirement, which has no close parallel in the United Kingdom or involves the assertion of a jurisdiction not recognised by the United Kingdom;
(c) the seriousness of the matter to which the inquiries relate, the importance to the inquiries of the information sought in the United Kingdom and whether the assistance could be obtained by other means;

(d) whether it is otherwise appropriate in the public interest to give the assistance sought.

(5) Before deciding whether to exercise those powers in a case where the overseas regulatory authority is a banking supervisor, the Secretary of State shall consult the Financial Services Authority. A 'banking supervisor' means an overseas regulatory authority with respect to which the Financial Services Authority has notified the Secretary of State, for the purposes of this subsection, that it exercises functions corresponding to those of the Authority under the Banking Act 1987.

(6) The Secretary of State may decline to exercise those powers unless the overseas regulatory authority undertakes to make such contribution towards the costs of their exercise as the Secretary of State considers appropriate.

(7) References in this section to financial services include, in particular, investment business, insurance and banking.

83. Power to Require Information, Documents or Other Assistance

(1) The following powers may be exercised in accordance with section 82, if the Secretary of State considers there is good reason for their exercise.

(2) The Secretary of State may require any person–

(a) to attend before him at a specified time and place and answer questions or otherwise furnish information with respect to any matter relevant to the inquiries,

(b) to produce at a specified time and place any specified documents which appear to the Secretary of State to relate to any matter relevant to the inquiries, and

(c) otherwise to give him such assistance in connection with the inquiries as he is reasonably able to give.

(3) The Secretary of State may examine a person on oath and may administer an oath accordingly.

(4) Where documents are produced the Secretary of State may take copies or extracts from them.

(5) A person shall not under this section be required to disclose information or produce a document which he would be entitled to refuse to disclose or produce on grounds of legal professional privilege in proceedings in the High Court or on grounds of confidentiality as between client and professional legal adviser

in proceedings in the Court of Session, except that a lawyer may be required to furnish the name and address of his client.

(6) A statement by a person in compliance with a requirement imposed under this section may be used in evidence against him.

(7) Where a person claims a lien on a document, its production under this section is without prejudice to his lien.

(8) In this section 'documents' includes information recorded in any form; and, in relation to information recorded otherwise than in legible form, the power to require its production includes power to require the production of a copy of it in legible form.

84. EXERCISE OF POWERS BY OFFICER, &C

(1) The Secretary of State may authorise an officer of his or any other competent person to exercise on his behalf all or any of the powers conferred by section 83.

(2) No such authority shall be granted except for the purpose of investigating–

(a) the affairs, or any aspects of the affairs, of a person specified in the authority, or

(b) a subject-matter so specified,

being a person who, or subject-matter which, is the subject of the inquiries being carried out by or on behalf of the overseas regulatory authority.

(3) No person shall be bound to comply with a requirement imposed by a person exercising powers by virtue of an authority granted under this section unless he has, if required, produced evidence of his authority.

(4) A person shall not by virtue of an authority under this section be required to disclose any information or produce any documents in respect of which he owes an obligation of confidence by virtue of carrying on the business of banking unless–

(a) the imposing on him of a requirement with respect to such information or documents has been specifically authorised by the Secretary of State, or

(b) the person to whom the obligation of confidence is owed consents to the disclosure or production.

In this subsection 'documents' has the same meaning as in section 83.

(5) Where the Secretary of State authorises a person other than one of his officers to exercise any powers by virtue of this section,

that person shall make a report to the Secretary of State in such manner as he may require on the exercise of those powers and the results of exercising them.

85. Penalty for failure to comply with requirements, &c

(1) A person who without reasonable excuse fails to comply with a requirement imposed on him under section 83 commits an offence and is liable on summary conviction to imprisonment for a term not exceeding six months or to a fine not exceeding level 5 on the standard scale, or both.

(2) A person who in purported compliance with any such requirement furnishes information which he knows to be false or misleading in a material particular, or recklessly furnishes information which is false or misleading in a material particular, or commits an offence and is liable –

(a) on conviction on indictment, to imprisonment for a term not exceeding two years or to a fine, or both;

(b) on summary conviction, to imprisonment for a term not exceeding six months or to a fine not exceeding the statutory maximum, or both.

86. Restrictions on disclosure of information

(1) This section applies to information relating to the business or other affairs of a person which–

(a) is supplied by an overseas regulatory authority in connection with a request for assistance, or

(b) is obtained by virtue of the powers conferred by section 83, whether or not any requirement to supply it is made under that section.

(2) Except as permitted by section 87 below, such information shall not be disclosed for any purpose –

(a) by the primary recipient, or

(b) by any person obtaining the information directly or indirectly from him,

without the consent of the person from whom the primary

recipient obtained the information and, if different, the person to whom its relates.

(3) The 'primary recipient' means, as the case may be –
   (a) the Secretary of State,
   (b) any person authorised under section 84 to exercise powers on his behalf, and
   (c) any officer or servant of any such person.

(4) Information shall not be treated as information to which this section applies if it has been made available to the public by virtue of being disclosed in any circumstances in which, or for any purpose for which, disclosure is not precluded by this section.

(5) A person who contravenes this section commits an offence and is liable–
   (a) on conviction on indictment, to imprisonment for a term not exceeding two years or to a fine, or both;
   (b) on summary conviction, to imprisonment for a term not exceeding three months or to a fine not exceeding the statutory maximum, or both.

87. EXCEPTIONS FROM RESTRICTIONS ON DISCLOSURE

(1) Information to which section 86 applies may be disclosed–
   (a) to any person with a view to the institution of, or otherwise for the purposes of, relevant proceedings,
   (b) for the purpose of enabling or assisting a relevant authority to discharge any relevant function (including functions in relation to proceedings),
   (c) to the Treasury, if the disclosure is made in the interests of investors or in the public interest,
   (d) if the information is or has been available to the public from other sources,
   (e) in a summary or collection of information framed in such a way as not to enable the identity of any person to whom the information relates to be ascertained, or
   (f) in pursuance of any Community obligation.

(2) The relevant proceedings referred to in subsection (1)(a) are–
   (a) any criminal proceedings,
   (b) civil proceedings arising under or by virtue of the Financial Services Act 1986 and proceedings before the Financial Services Tribunal, and

(c) disciplinary proceedings relating to–
  (i) the exercise by a solicitor, auditor, accountant, valuer or actuary of his professional duties, or
  (ii) the discharge by a public servant of his duties.

(3) In subsection (2)(c)(ii) 'public servant' means an officer or servant of the Crown or of any public or other authority for the time being designated for the purposes of that provision by order of the Secretary of State.

(4) The relevant authorities referred to in subsection (1)(b), and the relevant functions in relation to each such authority, are as follows:

Authority	*Functions*
The Secretary of State.	Functions under the enactments relating to companies, insurance companies or insolvency, or under the Financial Services Act 1986 or Part II, this Part or Part VII of this Act.
The Treasury.	Functions under the enactments relating to insurance companies, under the Financial Services Act 1986 or under this Part or Part VII of this Act.
An inspector appointed under Part XIV of the Companies Act 1985 or section 94 or 177 of the Financial Services Act 1986.	Functions under that Part of that section.
A person authorised to exercise powers or appointed under section 43A or 44 of the Insurance Companies Act 1982, section 447 of the Companies Act 1985, section 106 of the Financial Services Act 1986 or section 84 of this Act.	Functions under that section.
An overseas regulatory authority.	Its regulatory functions (within the meaning of section 82 of this Act).
The Department of Economic Development in Northern Ireland or a person appointed or authorised by that Department.	Functions conferred on it or him by the enactments relating to companies or insolvency.

A designated agency within the meaning of the Financial Services Act 1986.	Functions under that Act or Part VII of this Act.
A transferee body or the competent authority within the meaning of the Financial Services Act 1986.	Functions under that Act.
The body administering a scheme under section 54 of the Financial Services Act 1986.	Functions under the scheme.
A recognised self-regulating organisation, recognised professional body, recognised investment exchange, recognised clearing house or recognised self-regulating organisation for friendly societies (within the meaning of the Financial Services Act 1986).	Functions in its capacity as an organisation, body, exchange or clearing house recognised under that Act.
The Chief Registrar of Friendly Societies...and the Assistant Registrar of Friendly Societies for Scotland.	Functions under ... the enactments relating to friendly societies or building societies.
The Friendly Societies Commission.	Functions under the enactments relating to Friendly Societies or under the Financial Services Act 1986.
The Bank of England.	Any of its functions.
The Financial Services Authority.	Functions under the Financial Services Act 1986 (other then as a designated agency within the meaning of that Act), the Banking Act 1987 or section 171 of the Companies Act 1989.
The Deposit Protection Board.	Functions under the Banking Act 1987.
A body established by order under section 46 of this Act.	Functions under Part II of this Act.
A recognised supervisory or qualifying body within the meaning of Part II of this Act.	Functions as such a body.

The Industrial Assurance Commissioner and the Industrial Assurance Commissioner for Northern Ireland.	Functions under the enactments relating to industrial assurance.
The Insurance Brokers Registration Council.	Functions under the Insurance Brokers (Registration) Act 1977.
The Official Receiver or, in Northern Ireland, the Official Assignee for company liquidations or for bankruptcy.	Functions under the enactments relating to insolvency.
A recognised professional body (within the meaning of section 391 of the Insolvency Act 1986).	Functions in its capacity as such a body under the Insolvency Act 1986.
The Building Societies Commission.	Functions under the Building Societies Act 1986.
The Occupational Pensions Regulatory Authority.	Functions under the Pension Schemes Act 1993 or the Pensions Act 1995 or any enactment in force in Northern Ireland corresponding to either of them.
The Director General of Fair Trading.	Functions under the Financial Services Act 1986.
A person authorised by the Secretary of State under sections 245C of the Companies Act 1985.	Functions relating to the securing of compliance by companies with the accounting requirements of that Act.
The Director General of the National Lottery.	Functions under sections 5 to 10 inclusive and section 15 of the National Lottery etc. Act 1993.

(5) The Secretary of State may by order amend the Table in subsection (4) so as to–
- (a) add any public or other authority to the Table and specify the relevant functions of that authority,
- (b) remove any authority from the Table, or
- (c) add functions to, or remove functions from, those which are relevant functions in relation to an authority specified in the Table; and the order may impose conditions subject to which, or otherwise restrict the circumstances in which, disclosure is permitted.

(6) An order under this section shall be made by statutory instrument which shall be subject to annulment in pursuance of a resolution of either House of Parliament.

88. Exercise of powers in relation to Northern Ireland

(1) The following provisions apply where it appears to the Secretary of State that a request for assistance by an overseas regulatory authority may involve the powers conferred by section 83 being exercised in Northern Ireland in relation to matters which are transferred matters within the meaning of the Northern Ireland Constitution Act 1973.

(2) The Secretary of State shall before deciding whether to accede to the request consult the Department of Economic Development in Northern Ireland, and if he decides to accede to the request and it appears to him–

(a) that the powers should be exercised in Northern Ireland, and

(b) that the purposes for which they should be so exercised relate wholly or primarily to transferred matters,

he shall by instrument in writing authorise the Department to exercise in Northern Ireland his powers under section 83.

(3) The following provisions have effect in relation to the exercise of powers by virtue of such an authority with the substitution for references to the Secretary of State of references to the Department of Economic Development in Northern Ireland–

(a) section 84 (exercise of powers by officer, &c),

(b) section 449 of the Companies Act 1985, section 53 or 54 of the Building Societies Act 1986, sections 179 and 180 of the Financial Services Act 1986, section 84 of the Banking Act 1987 and sections 86 and 87 above (restrictions on disclosure of information), and

(c) section 89 (authority for institution of criminal proceedings); and references to the Secretary of State in other enactments, which proceed by reference to those provisions, shall be construed accordingly as being or including references to the Department.

(4) The Secretary of State may after consultation with the Department of Economic Development in Northern Ireland revoke an authority given to the Department under this section.

(5) In that case nothing in the provisions referred to in subsection (3)(b) shall apply so as to prevent the Department from giving the Secretary of State any information obtained by virtue of the

authority; and (without prejudice to their application in relation to disclosure by the Department) those provisions shall apply to the disclosure of such information by the Secretary of State as if it had been obtained by him in the first place.

(6) Nothing in this section affects the exercise by the Secretary of State of any powers in Northern Ireland–

(a) in a case where at the time of acceding to the request it did not appear to him that the circumstances were such as to require him to authorise the Department of Economic Development in Northern Ireland to exercise those powers, or

(b) after the revocation by him of any such authority;

and no objection shall be taken to anything done by or in relation to the Secretary of State or the Department on the ground that it should have done by or in relation to the other.

89. PROSECUTIONS

Proceedings for an offence under section 85 or 86 shall not be instituted—

(a) in England and Wales, except by or with the consent of the Secretary of State or the Director of Public Prosecutions;

(b) in Northern Ireland, except by or with the consent of the Secretary of State or the Director of Public Prosecutions for Northern Ireland.

90. OFFENCES BY BODIES CORPORATE, PARTNERSHIPS AND UNINCORPORATED ASSOCIATIONS

(1) Where an offence under section 85 or 86 committed by a body corporate is proved to have been committed with the consent or connivance of, or to be attributable to any neglect on the part of, a director, manager, secretary or other similar officer of the body, or a person purporting to act in any such capacity, he as well as the body corporate is guilty of the offence and liable to be proceeded against and punished accordingly.

(2) Where the affairs of a body corporate are managed by its members, subsection (1) applies in relation to the acts and

defaults of a member in connection with his functions of management as to a director of a body corporate.

(3) Where an offence under section 85 or 86 committed by a partnership is proved to have been committed with the consent or connivance of, or to be attributable to any neglect on the part of, a partner, he as well as the partnership is guilty of the offence and liable to be proceeded against and punished accordingly.

(4) Where an offence under section 85 or 86 committed by an unincorporated association (other than a partnership) is proved to have been committed with the consent or connivance of, or to be attributable to any neglect on the part of, any officer of the association or any member of its governing body, he as well as the association is guilty of the offence and liable to be proceeded against and punished accordingly.

91. JURISDICTION AND PROCEDURE IN RESPECT OF OFFENCES

(1) Summary proceedings for an offence under section 85 may, without prejudice to any jurisdiction exercisable apart from this section, be taken against a body corporate or unincorporated association at any place at which it has a place of business and against an individual at any place where he is for the time being.

(2) Proceedings for an offence alleged to have been committed under section 85 or 86 by an unincorporated association shall be brought in the name of the association (and not in that of any of its members), and for the purposes of any such proceedings any rules of court relating to the service of documents apply as in relation to a body corporate.

(3) Section 33 of the Criminal Justice Act 1925 and Schedule 3 to the Magistrates' Courts Act 1980 (procedure on charge of offence against a corporation) apply in a case in which an unincorporated association is charged in England and Wales with an offence under section 85 or 86 as they apply in the case of a corporation.

(4) In relation to proceedings on indictment in Scotland for an offence alleged to have been committed under section 85 or 86 by an unincorporated association, section 74 of the Criminal Procedure (Scotland) Act 1975 (proceedings on indictment against bodies corporate) applies as if the association were a body corporate.

(5) Section 18 of the Criminal Justice Act (Northern Ireland) 1945 and Schedule 4 to the Magistrates' Courts (Northern Ireland) Order 1981 (procedure on charge of offence against a corporation) apply in a case in which an unincorporated association is charged in Northern Ireland with an offence under section 85 or 86 as they apply in the case of a corporation.

(6) A fine imposed on an unincorporated association on its conviction of such an offence shall be paid out of the funds of the association.

OPEN-ENDED INVESTMENT COMPANIES (INVESTMENT COMPANIES WITH VARIABLE CAPITAL) REGULATIONS 1996 SI 1996/2827

21. INVESTIGATIONS: FUNCTIONS OF SECRETARY OF STATE AND SIB

In regulations 22 to 24 below, 'relevant authority' means the Secretary of State or SIB and, in relation to any investigation carried out by an inspector, means the person who appointed the inspector in question.

22. INVESTIGATIONS: POWERS AND DUTIES OF INSPECTORS

(1) A relevant authority may appoint one or more competent inspectors to investigate and report on the affairs of, or of any director or depositary of, an investment company with variable capital if it appears to the authority that it is in the interests of shareholders of the company to do so or the matter is of public concern.

(2) An inspector appointed under paragraph (1) above to investigate the affairs of, or of any director or depositary of, a company may also, if he thinks it necessary for the purposes of that investigation, investigate the affairs of, or (as the case may be) of the directors, depositary, trustee or operator of,

(a) an investment company with variable capital the directors of which include any of the directors of the company whose affairs are being investigated by virtue of that paragraph;

(b) an investment company with variable capital, the directors of which include any of the directors of the depositary whose affairs are being investigated by virtue of that paragraph;

(c) an investment company with variable capital, the depositary of which is–

(i) the same as the depositary of the company whose affairs are being investigated by virtue of that paragraph; or

(ii) the depositary whose affairs are being investigated by virtue of that paragraph;

(d) an investment company with variable capital the directors of which include–

(i) the director whose affairs are being investigated by virtue of that paragraph; or

(ii) any director of a body corporate which is the director whose affairs are being investigated by virtue of that paragraph;

(e) a collective investment scheme the manager or operator of which is a director of the company whose affairs are being investigated by virtue of that paragraph;

(f) a collective investment scheme the trustee of which is–

(i) the same as the depositary of the company whose affairs are being investigated by virtue of that paragraph; or

(ii) the depositary whose affairs are being investigated by virtue of that paragraph; or

(g) a collective investment scheme the manager or operator of which is–

(i) the director whose affairs are being investigated by virtue of that paragraph; or

(ii) a director of a body corporate which is the director whose affairs are being investigated by virtue of that paragraph.

(3) Sections 434 and 436 of the 1985 Act (production of documents and evidence to inspectors) shall apply in relation to an inspector appointed under this regulation as they apply to an inspector appointed under section 431 of that Act but with the modifications specified in paragraph (4) below.

(4) In the provisions applied by paragraph (3) above–
(a) for any reference to a company there shall be substituted a reference to the company, director or depositary under investigation by virtue of paragraph (1) above;
(b) any reference to an officer of the company shall include a reference to–
(i) any director of the company or depositary under investigation by virtue of paragraph (1) above; or
(ii) where the director under investigation by virtue of that paragraph is a body corporate, any director of that body:
(c) for any reference to any other body corporate whose affairs are investigated under section 433(1) of the 1985 Act there shall be substituted a reference to any other investment company with variable capital or collective investment scheme under investigation by virtue of paragraph (2) above; and
(d) any reference to an officer of such a body corporate shall include a reference to the depositary and directors of an investment company with variable capital or the trustee and operator of a collective investment scheme.

(5) This regulation and regulations 23 and 24 below confer the same powers in relation to a shadow director of an investment company with variable capital as they confer in relation to a director of such a company.

23. INVESTIGATIONS: DISCLOSURE

(1) A person shall not under regulation 22 above be required to disclose any information or produce any document which he would be entitled to refuse to disclose or produce on grounds of legal professional privilege in proceedings in the High Court or on grounds of confidentiality as between client and professional legal adviser in proceedings in the Court of Session except that a lawyer may be required to furnish the name and address of his client.

(2) Nothing in regulation 22 above requires a person (except as mentioned in paragraph (3) below) to disclose any information or produce any document in respect of which he owes an obligation of confidence by virtue of carrying on the business of banking unless–
(a) the person to whom the obligation of confidence is owed

consents to the disclosure or production; or
(b) the making of the requirement was authorised by the relevant authority.
(3) Paragraph (2) above does not apply where the person owing the obligation of confidence or to whom it is owed is–
(a) an investment company with variable capital, director or depositary under investigation by virtue of paragraph (1) of regulation 22 above; or
(b) an investment company with variable capital, or any other person, under investigation by virtue of paragraph (2) of that regulation.

24. INVESTIGATIONS: SUPPLEMENTARY

(1) Where a person claims a lien on a document, its production under regulation 22 above shall be without prejudice to the lien.
(2) An inspector appointed under regulation 22 above may, and if directed by the relevant authority shall, make interim reports to the authority and on the conclusion of his investigation shall make a final report to the authority.
(3) If it appears to the relevant authority that matters have come to light in the course of an inspector's investigation which suggest that a criminal offence has been committed, and those matters have been referred to the appropriate prosecuting authority, the relevant authority may direct the inspector to take no further steps in the investigation or to take only such steps as are specified in the direction.
(4) Where an investigation is the subject of a direction under paragraph (3) above, the inspector shall make a final report to the relevant authority only where it directs him to do so.
(5) Each final report shall be written or printed as the relevant authority may direct and the authority may, if it thinks fit–
(a) furnish a copy, on request and on payment of the prescribed fee–
(i) to any director or shareholder, or to the depositary, of a company under investigation by virtue of paragraph (1) of regulation 22 above;
(ii) where a director under investigation by virtue of that paragraph is a body corporate, to any director of that body;
(iii) to any director of a depositary under investigation by

virtue of that paragraph; or

(iv) to any other person whose conduct is referred to in the report; and

(b) cause the report to be published.

(6) A person who is convicted on a prosecution instituted as a result of an investigation under regulation 22 above may, in the same proceedings, be ordered to pay the expenses of the investigation to such extent as may be specified in the order.

(7) For the purposes of paragraph (6) above, there shall be treated as expenses of the investigation, in particular, such reasonable sums as the relevant authority may determine in respect of general staff costs and overheads.

(8) The powers in section 205 of the 1986 Act (general power to make regulations), as they apply in relation to fees to be prescribed for the purposes of section 94(9) of that Act (investigations in respect of authorised unit trusts etc.), shall be exercisable in relation to fees to be prescribed for the purposes of paragraph (5)(a) above–

(a) for like purposes; and

(b) subject to the same conditions.

APPENDIX 2

DRAFT FINANCIAL SERVICES AND MARKETS BILL — SUMMARY

At the end of July 1998, the Government produced the draft Financial Services and Markets Bill. Part IX of the Bill sets out the Financial Services Authority's (FSA) proposed investigation powers. It is proposed that the FSA will have the power to require information or documents from an authorised person, a formerly authorised person, a person connected with an authorised person, or a recognised investment exchange or clearing house. The FSA can set a reasonable timescale for the production of the information or documents and can require an authorised person to take reasonable steps to verify the information provided.[1] The FSA may require an authorised person, a formerly authorised person, or a body connected with them, to supply a report by an accountant or other person nominated or approved by the FSA.[2] **1**

The draft bill provides specific powers for the FSA to investigate the business of an authorised person or an appointed representative (or the ownership or control of an authorised person).[3] There are powers for the FSA to investigate suspected contraventions of certain provisions of the Financial Services and Markets Bill and related offences[4] and to investigate suspected market abuse,[5] the criminal offence of insider dealing (Criminal Justice Act 1993 Part V) and the offence of false or misleading statements and practices.[6] **2**

The FSA will have powers to enter premises with or without a warrant from a Justice of the Peace (or a Sheriff in Scotland).[7] The FSA will be obliged to inform a person who is under investigation of the appointment of an investigator.[8] This does not apply where the investigator is appointed to investigate suspected market abuse, insider dealing or the **3**

1 Clause 95.
2 Clause 96.
3 Clause 97.
4 Clause 98.
5 As defined in clause 56.
6 As defined in clause 212. See clause 99.
7 Clauses 100 and 101.
8 Clause 103.

offences of false or misleading statements and practices. The FSA have explained that this is because in that case the investigator will be looking into circumstances at the outset rather than investigating a particular person.[9] The draft Bill also permits employees of the FSA or the Secretary of State to act as investigators and permits the FSA to control the scope, timetable and conduct of the investigation.[10] It is proposed that investigators may require a person under investigation or any other connected person to attend before them and answer questions and/or provide information or specified documents which are relevant to the investigation.[11] The investigator may administer an oath.[12]

A statement made by a person in compliance with the compulsory 4
powers is admissible in proceedings. However, such a statement is admissible in criminal proceedings only where it is produced in evidence in those proceedings by the person who made it or the proceedings are for perjury or for providing false or misleading information to the FSA or Secretary of State.[13] There are supplemental provisions in relation to information and documents.[14] The investigator may obtain documents from third parties. The person requiring the production of documents may make copies of them and/or require the person producing them, or a director, controller, an employee or an auditor of that person to explain the nature or content of the documents. In the event of a failure to provide a required document, the person who had been required to produce it can be required to state, to the best of their knowledge, where it is. Documents subject to legal professional privilege may be withheld although a lawyer can be compelled to disclose the name of his client.

---

9 Draft explanatory notes on the draft bill, July 1998, p. 43.

10 Clause 103.

11 Clause 104.

12 The specific provision in clause 104(1)(a) allowing an investigator to require a person to 'answer questions on oath' avoids the debate under provisions such as Companies Act section 434(2) where inspectors can require witnesses 'to attend before them' and 'otherwise give them all assistance ...' and where the power to require answers to questions must be implied.

13 This is the direct consequence of the decision in *Saunders v United Kingdom* [1997] BCC 872 — see 13.2 above. Notwithstanding that the consultation document contains a statement that the Government takes the view that the Financial Services and Markets Appeals Tribunal, which is the forum for an appeal for a finding of market abuse, complies with the requirements of Article 6 of the European Convention on Human Rights (consultation document page 37), it is arguable that the concept of a fine for market abuse is a criminal sanction (notwithstanding the domestic civil label) and that the use of answers under compulsory powers should not be admissible in market abuse cases.

14 Clause 105.

Documents subject to banking confidentiality may also be withheld unless the person holding them is the person under investigation or a related company; or the person to whom the duty of confidence is owed, is the person under investigation or a related company; or the person to whom the duty is owed, consents to its disclosure; or the disclosure has been specifically authorised by the FSA. If a person claims a lien on a document, its production does not affect the lien.

The Bill sets out the offences for a person who fails to comply with requirements imposed by the investigators.[15] The cost of an investigation may be recovered, at the court's discretion, from a person who is convicted of an offence where the prosecution is instituted as a result of an investigation under this part of the Bill.[16] 5

FINANCIAL SERVICES AND MARKETS BILL — DRAFT SECTIONS

PART IX: INFORMATION GATHERING AND INVESTIGATIONS

95. AUTHORITY'S POWER TO REQUIRE INFORMATION

(1) The Authority may, by notice in writing given to an authorised person, require him –
  (a) to provide specified information or information of a specified description; or
  (b) to produce specified documents or documents of a specified description.

(2) The information or documents must be provided or produced–
  (a) before the end of such reasonable period as may be specified; and
  (b) at such place as may be specified.

(3) An officer who has written authorisation from the Authority to

[15] Clause 106.
[16] Clause 107.

do so may require an authorised person without delay–

(a) to provide the officer with specified information or information of a specified description; or

(b) to produce to him specified documents or documents of a specified description.

(4) This section applies only to information and documents reasonably required in connection with the exercise by the Authority of functions which it has under, or as a result of, this Act.

(5) The Authority may require any information provided under this section to be verified in such manner as it may reasonably require.

(6) The powers conferred by subsections (1) and (3) may also be exercised to impose requirements on–

(a) a person who is connected with an authorised person;

(b) a recognised investment exchange or recognised clearing house.

(7) In this section–

'authorised person' includes a person who was at any time an authorised person but who has ceased to be an authorised person;

'officer' means an officer of the Authority and includes a member of the Authority's staff or an agent of the Authority; and

'specified' means specified in the notice (in subsections (1) and (2)) or specified in the authorisation (in subsection (3)).

(8) For the purposes of this section, the question whether a person is connected with an authorised person, or a person who is the subject of an investigation under this Part, is to be determined in accordance with the provisions of Schedule 7.

96. Accountants' Reports

(1) The Authority may, by notice in writing given to a person to whom subsection (2) applies, requires him to provide the Authority with a report by an accountant or other person with relevant professional skill, on any matter about which the Authority has required or could require an authorised person to provide information under section 95.

(2) This subsection applies to–

(a) an authorised person ('A');

(b) a holding company, subsidiary or related company of A;

(c) a subsidiary or related company of a holding company of A;

(d) a holding company of a subsidiary of A;
(e) a body corporate in the case of which a shareholder controller of A, either alone or with any associate or associates, is entitled to exercise, or control the exercise of, more than 20 per cent of the voting power at a general meeting of A; or
(f) a partnership of which A is, or has at any relevant time been, a member.

(3) The Authority may require the report to be in such form as may be specified in the notice.

(4) The accountant or other person appointed to make a report required by subsection (1) must be a person nominated or approved by the Authority.

(5) 'Authorised person' includes a person who was at any time an authorised person but who has ceased to be an authorised person.

97. GENERAL POWER TO INVESTIGATE

(1) If it appears to the Authority or the Secretary of State ('the investigating authority') that there are good reasons for doing so, the investigating authority may appoint one or more competent persons to conduct an investigation on its behalf into–
(a) the nature, conduct or state of the business of an authorised person or of an appointed representative;
(b) a particular aspect of that business; or
(c) the ownership or control of an authorised person.

(2) If a person appointed under subsection (1) thinks it necessary for the purposes of his investigation, he may also investigate the business of any body corporate which is or has at any relevant time been–
(a) a holding company, subsidiary or related company of the person under investigation ('A');
(b) a subsidiary or related company of a holding company of A;
(c) a holding company of a subsidiary of A; or
(d) a body corporate in the case of which a shareholder controller of A, either alone or with any associate or associates, is entitled to exercise, or control the exercise of, more than 20 per cent. of the voting power at a general meeting of A;

or the business of any partnership of which A is or has at any relevant time been a member.

(3) If a person appointed under subsection (1) decides to investigate the business of any body under subsection (2) he must give that body written notice of his decision.

(4) The power conferred by this section may be exercised in relation to a former authorised person (or appointed representative) but only in relation to–

(a) business carried on at any time when he was an authorised person (or appointed representative); or

(b) the ownership or control of a former authorised person at any time when he was an authorised person.

(5) 'Business' includes any part of the business of an authorised person, including a part which does not consist of carrying out regulated activities.

98. INVESTIGATIONS OF SUSPECTED CONTRAVENTIONS

(1) If the Authority has reasonable grounds for suspecting that a person–

(a) has contravened section 7 or 40(6),

(b) has contravened any regulation made under section 73,

(c) is guilty of an offence under section 12(1), 13(1), 17(4), 40(5), 106, 120, 201, 213(1) or 214, or Schedule 4, or

(d) is guilty of a related offence,

it may appoint one or more competent persons to conduct an investigation on its behalf.

(2) If the Secretary of State has reasonable grounds for such a suspicion he may appoint one or more competent persons to conduct an investigation on his behalf.

(3) 'Related offence' means an offence under any enactment other than this Act–

(a) which the Authority has power to prosecute under this Act; but

(b) which it would not otherwise have power to investigate.

99. INVESTIGATION IN CASES OF SUSPECTED MARKET ABUSE, ETC.

(1) If it appears to the Authority or the Secretary of State ('the

investigating authority') that there are circumstances suggesting that one or more of the following events have occurred–

(a) a person is or has engaged in market abuse,

(b) an offence under section 212 has been committed by any person, and

(c) an offence under Part V of the Criminal Justice Act 1993 (insider dealing) has been committed by any person,

the investigating authority may appoint one or more competent persons to conduct an investigation on its behalf.

(2) If the person or persons appointed to conduct an investigation under this section consider that any person is or may be able to give information which is relevant to the investigation they may require that person–

(a) to produce to them any documents in his possession or under his control which appear to them to be relevant to the investigation,

(b) to attend before them, and

(c) otherwise to give them all assistance in connection with the investigation that he is reasonably able to give,

and it shall be the duty of that person to comply with that requirement.

(3) A person appointed to conduct an investigation under this section may examine on oath any person who he considers is or may be able to give information which is relevant to the investigation, and may administer an oath accordingly.

100. INVESTIGATION OF INDIVIDUALS

(1) The Authority may appoint one or more competent persons to conduct an investigation on its behalf if it has reasonable grounds for suspecting–

(a) that an individual is not a fit and proper person to be employed in connection with any kind of regulated activity, or a particular kind of regulated activity;

(b) that an individual has failed to comply with a statement or principle issued under section 48; or

(c) that an individual has, when employed in connection with a regulated activity carried on by an authorised person, been concerned in a contravention by the authorised person of a relevant requirement.

(2) For the purposes of subsection (1)(c), the following are relevant requirements–
   (a) a requirement imposed by or under this Act; and
   (b) a requirement which is imposed by or under any other Act and whose contravention constitutes an offence which the Authority has power to prosecute under this Act.

(3) In this section, references to employment include references to employment otherwise than under a contract of service.

101. POWER TO ENTER PREMISES WITHOUT A WARRANT

(1) In this section and section 102 'a request for information' means a notice given under this Part, which requires a person to provide information or to produce documents.

(2) A person who has written authorisation from the investigating authority to do so may enter any premises occupied by–
   (a) an authorised person, or
   (b) an appointed representative,

   to whom a request for information has been given (the 'occupier').

(3) That power may be exercised only for the purpose of–
   (a) obtaining any of the required information which the occupier has failed to provide;
   (b) obtaining any required document which the occupier has failed to produce; or
   (c) checking the accuracy of information which the occupier has provided in response to the notice.

(4) Subsection (5) applies if the investigating authority has reasonable cause to believe that, if a request for information were to be duly given to an authorised person or an appointed representative ('A') under this Part–
   (a) the notice would not be complied with; or
   (b) documents to which the notice would relate would be removed, tampered with or destroyed.

(5) A person who has written authorisation from the investigating authority to do so may, for the purpose of obtaining such information or documents as are specified in the authorisation, enter any premises occupied by A.

(6) Only information or documents that could be specified in a request for information may be specified in the authorisation referred to in subsection (5).

(7) If asked to do so by the occupier, the person authorised under subsection (1) or (5) must produce evidence of his authorisation before exercising the power given by that subsection.
(8) A person entering premises under this section ('the investigator') may–
   (a) take with him such equipment as appears to him to be necessary;
   (b) require any person on the premises to produce any relevant document and, if the document is produced, to provide an explanation of it;
   (c) require any person on the premises to state, to the best of his knowledge and belief, where any relevant document is to be found;
   (d) take copies of, or extracts from, any document that is produced;
   (e) require any information that is held in a computer and is accessible from the premises and which the investigator considers relates to any relevant matter, to be produced in a form–
      (i) in which it can be taken away; and
      (ii) in which it is visible and legible.
(9) 'Investigating authority' means the Authority or the Secretary of State or, if a person has been appointed to conduct an investigation on behalf of one of them, that person.
(10) 'Premises' does not include domestic premises.

102. ENTRY OF PREMISES UNDER WARRANT

(1) A justice of the peace may issue a warrant under this section if satisfied on information on oath given by or on behalf of the investigating authority that there are reasonable grounds for believing–
   (a) that a person to whom a request for information has been given under this Part has failed (wholly or in part) to comply with that request; and
   (b) that there are on the premises specified in the warrant documents or information that have been requested in a request for information.
(2) A justice of the peace may also issue a warrant under this section if satisfied on information on oath given by or on behalf of the investigating authority that there are reasonable grounds for

believing

(a) that an offence for which the maximum sentence on conviction on indictment is two years or more has been (or is being) committed by any person;

(b) that there are on the premises specified in the warrant documents relevant to whether that offence has been (or is being) committed;

(c) that the investigating authority has power to require the production of the documents; and

(d) that if production of the documents was so required, they would not be produced but would be removed from the premises, hidden, tampered with or destroyed.

(3) A warrant under this section shall authorise a constable, together with any other person named in it and any other constables–

(a) to enter the premises specified in the warrant, using such force as is reasonably necessary for the purpose;

(b) to search the premises and take possession of any documents appearing to be documents of a kind in respect of which a warrant under subsection (1) or (2) was issued ('the relevant kind') or to take, in relation to any such documents, any other steps that may appear to be necessary for preserving them or preventing interference with them;

(c) to take copies of any documents appearing to be of the relevant kind; and

(d) to require any person named in the warrant to provide an explanation of any document appearing to be of the relevant kind or to state where it may be found.

(4) A warrant under this section continues in force until the end of the period of one month beginning with the day on which it is issued.

(5) Any documents of which possession is taken under this section may be retained–

(a) for a period of three months; or

(b) if within that period proceedings to which the documents are relevant are commenced against any person for any criminal offence, until the conclusion of those proceedings.

(6) In the application of this section to Scotland–

(a) for the references to a justice of the peace substitute references to a justice of the peace or a sheriff; and

(b) for the references to information on oath substitute references to evidence on oath.

(7) 'Investigating authority' means the Authority or the Secretary of State or, if a person has been appointed to conduct an investigation on behalf of one of them, that person.

103. Investigations: General

(1) This section applies if–
  (a) the Authority appoints one or more competent persons ('investigators') under section 97, 98, 99 or 100 to conduct an investigation on its behalf;
  (b) the Secretary of State appoints one or more competent persons ('investigators') under sections 97, 98 or 99 to conduct an investigation on his behalf.

(2) Except in the case of an investigation under section 99, the Authority or (as the case may be) the Secretary of State must give written notice to the person who is the subject of the investigation ('the person under investigation') of the appointment of an investigator.

(3) Nothing prevents–
  (a) the Authority from appointing a person who is a member of its staff as an investigator;
  (b) the Secretary of State from appointing a person who is a member of the staff of his department as an investigator.

(4) An investigator must make a report of his investigation to the Authority (or the Secretary of State) unless otherwise directed by the Authority (or the Secretary of State).

(5) The Authority (or the Secretary of State) may, by a direction to an investigator, control–
  (a) the scope of the investigation;
  (b) the period during which the investigation is to be conducted;
  (c) the conduct of the investigation; and
  (d) the reporting of the investigation.

(6) The direction may, in particular–
  (a) confine the investigation to particular matters;
  (b) extend the investigation to additional matters;
  (c) require the investigator to discontinue the investigation or to take only such steps as are specified in the directions;
  (d) require the investigator to make such interim reports of the investigation as may be so specified;
  (e) require the investigator not to make a report of the investigation.

104. POWERS OF INVESTIGATORS

(1) A person conducting an investigation under section 97, 98 or 100 ('the investigator') may require the person who is the subject of the investigation ('the person under investigation') or any person connected with the person under investigation–
  (a) to attend before the investigator at a specified time and place and answer questions on oath; or
  (b) otherwise provide such information as the investigator may reasonably require for purposes of the investigation.

(2) The investigator may also require the person under investigation or any other person to produce at a specified time and place any specified documents or documents of a specified description–
  (a) which appear to the investigator to relate to any matter relevant to the investigation; and
  (b) the production of which it is reasonable for the investigator to require.

(3) For the purposes of any such investigation as is referred to in subsection (1), an investigator may administer an oath.

(4) A statement made by a person in compliance with a requirement imposed under–
  (a) any of the provisions mentioned in subsection (1), or
  (b) section 99,

is admissible in evidence in any proceedings.

(5) But a statement made by a person in compliance with such a requirement is not admissible in evidence in criminal proceedings unless–
  (a) he himself produces that statement in evidence in those proceedings; or
  (b) those proceedings are proceedings for an offence of perjury or for an offence under section 106(4).

(6) In the case of an investigation under section 100, a person is connected with the person under investigation if he is or was–
  (a) the partner, employer, employee or agent of the person under investigation;
  (b) a director, secretary or controller of–
    (i) a body corporate of which the person under investigation is or was a director or secretary; or
    (ii) a body corporate in the same group as a body corporate within subparagraph (i);
  (c) a member of the governing body, or an officer or controller, of an unincorporated association of which the person under

investigation is or was a member of the governing body or an officer or controller; or
(d) the banker, solicitor, accountant or actuary of
(i) the person under investigation; or
(ii) a person falling within paragraph (b) or (c).
(7) In any other case, the question whether a person is connected with the person under investigation is to be determined in accordance with Schedule 7.
(8) 'Specified' means specified in a notice in writing.

105. INFORMATION AND DOCUMENTS: SUPPLEMENTAL PROVISIONS

(1) If the investigating authority has power under this Part to require a person to produce a document but it appears to the authority that the document is in the possession of a third person, the authority may exercise that power in relation to the third person.
(2) If a document is produced in response to a requirement imposed under this Part, the person to whom it is produced may
(a) take copies or extracts from the document; or
(b) require the person producing the document, or any relevant person, to provide an explanation of the document.
(3) If a person ('A') who is required under this Part to produce a document fails to do so, the person requiring its production may require A to state, to the best of his knowledge and belief, where the document is.
(4) No person may be required under this Part to produce or disclose a privileged communication.
(5) But a lawyer may be required to furnish the name and address of his client.
(6) No person may be required under this Part to disclose information or produce a document in respect of which he owes an obligation of confidence by virtue of carrying on the business of banking unless
(a) he is the person under investigation or a related company;
(b) the person to whom the obligation of confidence is owed is the person under investigation or a related company;
(c) the person to whom the obligation of confidence is owed consents to the disclosure or production; or
(d) the imposing on him of a requirement with respect to such

information or document has been specifically authorised by the Authority.

(7) If a person claims a lien on a document its production under this Part does not affect the lien.

(8) 'Relevant person', in relation to a person who is required to produce a document, means a person who–
  (a) has been or is proposed to be a director or controller of that person;
  (b) has been or is an auditor of that person; or
  (c) has been or is an employee of that person.

(9) 'Investigating authority' means the Authority or the Secretary of State or, if a person has been appointed to conduct an investigation on behalf of one of them, that person.

106. OFFENCES

(1) A person who fails, without reasonable excuse, to comply with a requirement imposed on him under this Part is guilty of an offence.

(2) A person guilty of an offence under subsection (1) is liable on summary conviction to imprisonment for a term not exceeding six months or to a fine not exceeding level 5 on the standard scale, or to both.

(3) A person who knows or suspects that an investigation is being or is likely to be conducted under this Part is guilty of an offence if–
  (a) he falsifies, conceals, destroys or otherwise disposes of a document which he knows or suspects is or would be relevant to such an investigation, or
  (b) he causes or permits the falsification, concealment, destruction or disposal of such a document,

unless he proves that he had no intention of concealing facts disclosed by the documents from the investigator.

(4) A person who, in purported compliance with a requirement imposed on him under this Part–
  (a) provides information which he knows to be false or misleading in a material particular, or
  (b) recklessly provides information which is false or misleading in a material particular,

is guilty of an offence.

(5) A person guilty of an offence under subsection (3) or (4) is liable

(a) on summary conviction, to imprisonment for a term not exceeding six months or to a fine not exceeding the statutory maximum, or to both,

(b) on conviction on indictment, to imprisonment for a term not exceeding two years or to a fine, or to both.

(6) Any person who intentionally obstructs the exercise of any rights conferred by a warrant under section 102 is guilty of an offence and liable on summary conviction to imprisonment for a term not exceeding three months or to a fine not exceeding level five on the standard scale, or to both.

107. Costs of investigations

(1) A person who is convicted of a prosecution instituted as a result of an investigation under this Part may, in the same proceedings, be ordered to pay the expenses of the investigation to such extent as may be specified in the order.

(2) If the investigator is a member of the Authority's staff, there are to be treated as expenses of the investigation, in particular, such reasonable sums as the Authority may determine in respect of general staff costs and overheads.

(3) If the investigator is a member of the staff of a government department, there are to be treated as expenses of the investigation, in particular, such reasonable sums as the Minister in charge of the department may determine in respect of general staff costs and overheads.

SUBJECT INDEX